Heroes by Force

A list directory of African-Americans
who served the Civil War Confederacy
and past life regression artwork and stories.

"Inclusion is the only
way to eradicate
racism and divide"

Compiled, Illustrated and Edited by
Gregory G. Newson

Table of contents

I pay homage to my forced DNA that left the shores of Africa. I with no inheritance or reparation am humble to embrace a legacy of forgotten soldiers.

I know there sweat, blood was the reason that forced the creation of the Emancipation Proclamation
and the Cannon Fodder Massachusetts 54.

Published By; Newson Publishing
P.O. Box 88
2570 Main Street
Conway, SC 29526-9998
Web site: www.NewsonPublishing.com
E-mail: gregorynewson15@gmail.com

Heroes by Force

The primary aim of this book is to celebrate the service of all African Americans who served in the Confederacy, whether they enlisted, were drafted or were ordered to serve by their masters. Many are baffled as to why African Americans would fight for the Old South.

As an African American born and raised in Harlem, New York with a Black Panther-influenced background, I would venture to respond as would my predecessors of that time period: **"It was better to fight for the devil you do know then go fight for the devil you don't."**

Slave narratives and testimonies from black soldiers of the era reveal that they fought for the South because their land was being invaded by a nation attempting to impose its will on them. Some whites regarded slaves as though they were members of their extended family.

Many of the bodyguards had grown up as servants and played as companion to their masters. Together, they participated in all the major wars of the country's history, including the Mexican-American War. Whole towns and families shared cultures in a manner unfamiliar to modern Americans.

Despite the vigorous, organized efforts of today's politically-motivated historians and Black Confederate deniers, these soldiers were real fighting men whose combat performances and sacrifices should not be silenced. This is contrary to today's Confederacy deniers on social media and their active cronies who faithfully follow the liberal party line of political correctness.

Simply put, these African-American fighting men, both slave and free, were not the stuff of fiction or romance, as those with vested interests in denial of the truth have long claimed.

As a result, this book was published with the sole intention of illuminating a basic and incontrovertible reality about the black Southern experience by presenting long-obscured realities of black fighting men. Denying that these brave, African-American Rebels, sacrificed their lives on the battlefield has been a huge injustice rooted in personal goals that have nothing to do with history.

As a result of the historical record's obvious exclusion of African American Confederates, this book will attempt to correct this fundamental injustice and you the viewer of this list may be tempted to fine a hidden ancestry. Because of the purposeful silence of this remarkable chapter and unique strand of American history, today's well-organized attempts to reject the heroics and sacrifices of African-American Confederates are little more than a sophisticated and stealthy form of racism which can only be extinguish with inclusion

The African-American Confederates who fought on the battlefield have become the most forgotten troops of the Civil War for a variety of reasons, including today's arbitrary political and popular cultural requirements. Furthermore, because of politics, African-American Confederates have become today's most contentious historical issue in a nation ripped apart by racial differences and simmering economic resentments.

Ironically, although Confederate statues and tributes to great Southern military commanders are being demolished around the country today, especially in the South, the historical legacy of African-Americans has remained unaffected: a classic contradiction. After all, no statues or memorials have ever been erected to honor the sacrifice of African-American Confederates.

To be sure, while the vast majority of African Americans, particularly slaves, served in Confederate armies in menial and supportive roles, this fact has resulted in the automatic dismissal of the far smaller number, but African-Americans Confederates did fight on both sides of the Potomac River for the south.

What should not be overlooked is that, in certain circumstances, African-American Confederates smoothly blended the two duties of bodyguard and enlisted servants, much like the ancient heroes during the brutal battle of Thermopylae: a situation that has now boosted the estimated number of African-American fighting men to 14,000+.

Soldier Status Denied- Many have claimed that the majority of African Americans were slaves who were compelled to fight against their will or forced by their owners.

As a result, they contend that free or enslaved blacks were not actual soldiers since they worked merely as assistant surgeons, blacksmiths, brakemen, bodyguards, chefs, hospital assistants, laborers, musicians, teamsters, maids and hospital stewards. How can anybody argue that the African American Confederates were not soldiers? Perhaps it's because these skeptics have never served in the military?

Some slaves followed their owners to battle and, after their masters were slain, many remained with the military unit until the end of the war. Others accompanied their dead master's body home to be buried and then returned to the battlefront to rejoin the unit in which the master had served.

Despite the fact that most African Americans were assigned to jobs as cooks, singers, maids, and workers, many were permitted to take up arms and participate in battle. Mankind has an implanted desire to always want to prove their worthiness to other men, and with danger surrounding you, an easy decision is made, pick up a weapon to defend your life or companion.

Freedom In Battle- On the battlefield, many African Americans enjoyed greater freedom than they did at home or on the plantations. Because of the brotherhood that developed as a result of serving together in combat, many of them were even treated with respect by other troops. As a result, a large number of African Americans, including blacksmiths and teamsters from the Goochland Light Artillery, left their traditional jobs to work the cannons of the Virginia artillery unit at Chaffin's Bluff in Henrico County, Virginia, in order to defend Richmond before the national government's official use of African-American troops in early 1865.

The north side of the James River below the city of Richmond, whose economic existence had long depended on the canal, was observed and defended from this crucial military high ground. An African American Confederate named Frederick was legally identified as an artillerist and operated the earthen defense network artillery southeast of Richmond. As a result, Frederick was paid the same as white artillerymen—$12 per month—to defend Richmond.

Four companies of black and white troops, recruited from workers at the Tredegar Iron Works' war production complex, rehearsed and readied for the possibility of facing the invaders of the state of Virginia on the battlefield. During the conflict, vast numbers of black sailors fought aboard Confederate warships and commercial boats, including manning cannons during land engagements and sailing the high seas.

After all, in the history of nations all across the world, especially during the days of piracy, employment at sea had long been a racial equalizer. Captain Bartholomew Roberts' pirate ship had roughly 180 white men and over 50 black men from the French West Indies islands on board during the Golden Age of Piracy.

Members of the crew of the C.S.S. ironclads and the most renowned sea raider of the Civil War, the C.S.S. Alabama, were black sailors who worked guns with lightning speed in combat. Black seamen from the legendary maritime raider C.S.S. Shenandoah were among the final Confederates to surrender in the war.

One of these slaves was Edward Weeks, whose war ended in November 1865. In February 1865, Confederate Secretary of the Navy Stephen R. Mallory, who had served as a Florida senator from 1851 to 1861 before requiring additional African American seamen for its naval vessels, estimating that 1,150 were needed due to attrition.

As a result, many enslaved African Americans were pro-Confederate fighting men in the belief that the Rebel government, state or national, or masters would ultimately confer freedom on them and their families, which was their ultimate desire.

There was also the possibility of a brighter future: something well worth fighting for and risking one's life for a slave, whose motivations differed from those of free African Americans in this context. Heroes do not ask for permission to be heroes.

Heroism Among African-American Soldiers As the author of this work, I've been exploring the nature and roots of heroism, studying exemplary cases of heroism and people's choices to act—or not act—heroically. In that time, I've come to define heroism as an activity with several components. Firstly, it's performed to serve others in need—whether that's a person, group or community—or in defense of certain ideals.

Secondly, it's engaged in voluntarily, even in military contexts, as heroism remains an act that goes beyond military duty. Historians have not gained or fully studied the participation of African Americans in the American Revolution and the Civil War. These historians neglected to consider the lives and presence of African Americans during the colonial period, the meaning of the American Revolution to them and how military service by black soldiers changed the attitude of whites towards throughout the original 13 colonies.

To a person in the 19th and 20th century, it would seem incredible that African Americans, the majority of whom were then slaves, should have been allowed to join the Continental Army to fight the Revolutionary War. The layman may forget that, during the 18th century, slavery was a patriarchal institution rather than the economic plantation system that it morphed into with the invention and proliferation of mechanical appliances, which launched the worldwide Industrial Revolution.

During the 18th century, a number of slaves, who interacted closely with their masters, were gradually enlightened and later emancipated. As a result of these interactions, African Americans served not only in the American Revolution but in every war of consequence after the colonial period.

Some masters sent their slaves to the frontlines of war to perform menial labor and to fight in the places of their owners. Other slaves received more consideration in the heat of war and, thus the system of slavery then lost almost all of its rigor. In some cases, the slave code fell into disuse as many Afican Americans served as privateers or documented pirates. This is in large part because many slaves preferred to take occasional chances dodging bullets than to bear the lash and ran away from their masters.

At the start of the Civil War, free men of color and slaves volunteered to fight for the Confederacy, and while they were not legally authorized to fight, many did so unofficially.

Confederate Pensions

The most common misunderstanding is that African Americans were invisible throughout the American Revolution and did not take direct action to gain freedom for the country. These misinterpretations of history derive mostly from 19th-century attempts to airbrush history as slavery became a significantly more controversial topic. The Lost Cause narrative consigned African American contributions for the nation's history to secondary footnotes when appropriate for debate and such deceptive efforts persisted into the 20th century. It wasn't until the 1960s that a new generation of researchers, historians and scholars peeled back the layers of neglect and recognized the significance of early African Americans in key events of the American Revolution. Both the Continental and British armies would enroll African Americans in their ranks. Fighting for liberation or liberty was not the motivation for enlisting civilians into duty, especially in the case of the American Cause. At the start of the conflict, free black citizens were able to join the Continental army and did so. This was while the army corps was still being assembled; there was no formal order or etiquette in place regarding who may join. We must also recognize that white and black troops were not separated.

To understand how the British forced/influence African Americans into service, we must first look at Lord Dunmore's proclamation of 1775, which stated that all enslaved people in Virginia who fled and joined the British/Loyalist army would be lawfully emancipated. As much as some of us would like to believe it was done as a pure act of abolitionism, it was actually a method of creating havoc in the Virginian and other Southern plantation ecosystems. John Murray, Earl of Dunmore, as Virginia's royal governor, was attempting to dissuade white Southern Rebels from forming in order to keep them occupied. The notion of black slaves rising up and toppling their masters with murderous force frightened the dominant white

perpetrators of slavery more than anything else. "The end justifies the means" capitulation: Act No. 63, 1923 S.C. Acts 107 allowed African Americans who had served at least six months as cooks, servants or attendants to apply for a pension.

South Carolina permitted pensions for African Americans who had served, but owing to a flood of applications, the state chose to limit them to African Americans who had served as slaves or laborers. Thus, anybody who presented themselves as a soldier may have had their application dismissed unless they reapplied as a soldier. Only those who lived to pension age and were aware of the benefit were eligible for a pension and there were further limits. Affidavits signed by a white soldier who knew about their service were required for African Americans. Most states that awarded African Americans pensions stipulated that they must have served from the beginning to the conclusion of the war.

The states that issued Confederate pensions to African-Americans who worked as body servants, cooks, laborers, musicians, guards, teamsters, holsters, hospital stewards are; Alabama, Arkansas, Florida, Georgia, Louisiana, Kansas, Kentucky Louisiana, Maryland, Mississippi, Missouri, North Carolina, Oklahoma, South Carolina, Tennessee, Texas and Virginia.

Bio: Gregory G. Newson is a graphic designer, painter and publisher and a participant in a 2015 research study in a past-life regression therapy experiment tailored for the Civil War.

Also known as PLR, this form of therapy was developed by psychologists and psychiatrists to rely on hypnosis to resurrect memories from previous lives or reincarnations to treat mental illness. The session was directed and supervised by Dr. Joseph Mancini Jr., a certified clinical hypnotherapist.

Mr Newson works out of Conway, South Carolina. Originally from Harlem, New York and himself a descendant of slaves from Jacksonville, Florida, Newson discovered his talent and interest in art in middle school. Entered into art shows by his school teacher, he took first prize in one as a member of the Hamilton Teen Artist Group and earned a scholarship from famed American painter/illustrator Norman Rockwell to Par-

ticipate in the Connecticut Famous Artist School Home Cor-home respondent Art School.

At the same time gaining local publicity, Newson conducted radio talk show interviews and was touted in New York Amsterdam newspapers as a "Promising Harlem Art Genius". But in the Civil Rights era, Newson stopped painting to join the Black Panther Party and engage in social justice movements.

Upon maturing from his emotions years later, Newson applied for and became an interior book designer for Viking Press publishing company in New York City.

But later he moved to his ancestral native home in Jacksonville, Florida, and traveled throughout the Deep South and resumed his graphic development But after accidentally finding the home of Confederate General Thomas "Stonewall" Jackson in Lexington, Virginia. He was inspired to return to art after learning that Jackson began the first black Sunday school to teach blacks to read the Bible despite Virginia law forbidding the practice. After this discovery, Newson decided that he would devote his artwork to studying the Civil War, the history and lives of African-American slaves and black Confederate officers.

He founded his own publishing company, Newson Publishing, under which he painted and published his first graphic novel titled Stonewall Jackson and the Uppity Spy. And the start of a series of books entitled "CSA Buried Treasures."

Confederate Rank Structure and Abbreviations

Cons	-	Conscript	2CF	-	2nd Class Fireman
Rot	-	Recruit	2CNS		2nd Class Naval Storekeeper
Pvt	-	Private	3CB	-	3rd Class Boy
2CP	-	2nd Class Private	AE	-	Assistant Engineer
Cpl	-	Corporal	APM	-	Assistant Paymaster
CQM	-	Corporal Quarter Master	IAQM	-	Assistant Quarter Master
1 Cpl	-	First Corporal	Art	-	Artificer
2 Cpl	-	Second Corporal	ASur	-	Assistant Surgeon
3 Cpl	-	Third Corporal	BB	-	Brigade Band
Sgt	-	Sergeant	BM	-	Band Master
CSgt	-	Commissary Sergeant	BS		Black Smith
1 Sgt	-	First Sergeant	Bug	-	Bugler
2 Sgt	-	Second Sergeant	Can	-	Cannoneer
3 Sgt	-	Third Sergeant	CBug	-	Chief Bugler
4 Sgt	-	Fourth Sergeant	CC	-	Commander's Clerk
SgtMaj	-	Sergeant Major	CCOP	-	Chief Clerk Office of Pay
132Lt		Brevet Second Lieutenant	CH	-	Coal Heaver
J2Lt	-	Junior Second Lieutenant	CP	-	Chief Pilot
2nd Lt	-	Second Lieutenant	Drum	-	Drummer
1st Lt	-	First Lieutenant	Far	-	Farrier
S1Lt	-	Senior First Lieutenant	GS	-	Gunsmith
Capt	-	Captain	HS		Hospital Steward
COO	-	Captain Ordinance Officer	LM	-	Landsman
Maj		Major	MAA	-	Master at Arms
AMaj	-	Adjutant Major	Mid	-	Midshipman
LtCol	-	Lieutenant Colonel	MLC	-	Marechal Logistics Chief
Col.	-	Colonel	MM	-	Masters Mate
Gen.	-	General	Mus	-	Musician
CSMC	-	Confederate States Marines Corps	OrdO	-	Ordinance Officer
CSN	-	Confederate States Navy	FMC	-	Free Men of Color
CSS	-	Confederate States Ship	PMC	-	Paymaster Clerk
FMC	-	Free Men of Color	QG	-	Quarter Gunner
KIA	-	Killed in Action	QMS	-	Quarter Master Sergeant
P.O.W.	-	Prisoner of War	RQM	-	Regiment Quarter Master
UCV	-	United Confederate Veterans	SM	-	Seaman
WIA.		Wounded in Action	Surg	-	Surgeon

seeking African-American relatives who may have fought for the Confederacy during the American Civil War. I hope that anyone looking for information about their ancestors will find this book useful. I've also included contact information for each state that granted pensions to African-Americans who served in the Confederacy and whose records are available online for free. The contact information is usually taken directly from the state's website. In addition, there are other sources indicated in the bibliography that may be relevant. Each regiment kept

Blacks may not have a service record, it's a good idea to look up that person's master if one is available.

Free Men of Color (FMC) and even slaves leased themselves out as servants to white soldiers. Also keep in mind that some slaves took their masters' last name after freedom, while others did not, and still others altered their names. On each page, there are five columns. I've put together a list of the information that each of you will need.

Column contains, See example below:
Column One - Person's full name along with other names used
Column Two - The Company the person served in
Column Three - The Unit or ship the person served in
Column Four - The Rank achieved by the person in the unit of record or job title
Column Five - Whether the person was a Slave or a Free Man of Color (FMC) and other miscellaneous information found

NAME	CO.	UNIT	RANK	SLAVE / FREE MISC
Alfred		36th Regiment Alabama Infantry		
Appleton	K	33rd Regiment Alabama Infantry	Drumme Servant	
Bob		4th Alabama		
Dow	C	15' Regiment Alabama Infantry	Servant	
Griffin	A	6th Regiment Alabama Cavalry Served as a Servant to his master Bat Smith	Servant	Slave of Bat Smith, when Bat Smith was shot and left on the battlefield, Griffin risked his life ignoring pleas for him to not go. Griffin retrieved Smith's body then accompanied him home
Henry		Alabama Eutaw Rifles	Servant	Slave of 1st Lieutenant H. Y. Webb
Isham		34th Alabama Capt. Charles L. Lumsdens Battery (Light Artillery) CSA	Body Servant Free Negro	Servant to Sgt. John A. Caldwell
James	C	13th Regiment Alabama Infantry	Laundress	
Jerry	D	21th Regiment Alabama infantry	Private	

This book is compiled with national archives, state archives, Confederate pension records, service records, Confederate land grants, slave narratives, books, old newspaper listings, muster rolls, and prisoner of war documents are all used to compile this collection of records.

The Confederate monument at Arlington National Cemetery is the first military monument in the United States Capitol to commemorate an African-American soldier. Moses Ezekiel, a Sephardic Jewish Confederate, sculpted the monument in 1914, maybe to accurately depict the racial makeup of the Confederate Army. A black Confederate soldier walking in step with white Confederate troops is pictured. A " and a white soldier handing his infant to a black woman for safety" is also seen.

In Canton, Mississippi, a monument was made to commemorate an unnamed Black Confederate soldier who served as a Servant and was slain in action.

Another memorial can be seen at Walker Top Church on Burkemont Mountain in North Carolina's South Mountains State Park. Henry Brown, a drummer of Company E, 1st Regiment South Carolina, has a memorial in Darlington, South Carolina (Darlington Guards).

Another Black Confederate memorial, dedicated to the Confederate slaves who helped protect and defend the women and children left alone during the war, was constructed in 1895 in Fort Mill, South Carolina.

The Confederate army was not all white; it was made up of people from all across the **South.**

The Confederate army was not all white; it was made up of servicemen from across the South. The army and navy of the South represented the region's population, who were of every race, creed and nationality.

However, the brutal Northern army tradition of burning down Southern courthouses and the deliberate deletion of innumerable Confederate papers on the subject of Southern blacks from the official national archives were both carried out.

This made chronicling and storing documentation on the lives and military services of diverse members of the Confederate Army supremely difficult.

As a result of such destruction, Southern archivists, librarians and scholars appreciated and sought to preserve the remainder of their postbellum material as much as possible.

Southern historians have established the following statistics on diversity in the Confederate Army, despite the fact that this directory presents minor military percentages.

The Confederate army and fleet consisted of around one million whites, 300,000 to one million African Americans, 70,000 Native Americans, 60,000 Hispanic Americans, 50,000 foreigners, 12,000 Jewish Americans and 10,000 Asian Americans, all in declining numerical order.

True Southerners of all races are proud of our region's diverse past and the numerous contributions given to Dixie by members of other races, faiths and cultures.

The "great majority" of the South's 3.5 million black slaves stayed in the region during the Civil War with 93 percent being faithful to Dixie.

They swore their devotion to their home states, the South and their families instead of Lincoln's phony proclamation of independence.

While their owners left for the battlefield, the slaves operated their fields, farmed, generated supplies for the Confederate forces and safeguarded their master's family and property.

C.S. Marine Corp and C.S. Navy

NAME	UNIT	RANK	SLAVE / FREE MISC NOTES
Berryman, William	Blockade Runner	Pilot	From Westmoreland, VA. Captured at Coff Neck, Maryland. P.O.W.
Brown, Eli	CSS Patrick Henry	Private	Slave
Bugg, William	CSS Isondiga, CSS	Pilot	
Butcher, John	James River Gun Boat	Private	FMC
Cleaper, Charles	CSS Chicora	Sailor	FMC, Surrendered at Appomattox
Cole, Robert	CSS Patrick Henry		Slave
Dallas, Moses	Savannah Squadron	Pilot	
Deveaux, John	Savannah Squadron	Private	
Gray, Benjamin H.	CSS Albermarle	Powder Boy	
Green, David	James River Squadron, CSS Virginia II	Landsman	
Hicks, James (Heck)	CSS Chicora	Sailor	FMC, Surrendered at Appomattox
Johnson, Joseph	CSS Chicora	Sailor	FMC, Surrendered at Appomattox
Leonard, Henry	James River Squadron, CSS Virginia II	Landsman	
Lewis, W. S.	C.S.S. Alabama served as a Servant to James Thurston In The Marine Corps	Servant	Charleston County, South Carolina Conf Pensioner App # 1854
Moore, James	CSS Georgia	Private	
Name not known	CSS Shenandoah	Private	
Polk, Randall	CSS Georgia	Landsman	
Price, James	James River Squadron	Private	
Robinson, Johnny	CSS Chicora	Pilot	Runaway Slave
Snowden, George	CSS Macon	Cabin Boy	
Stiles, Charles B.	CSS Macon	Landsman	
Tate, Hampton	Blockade Runner	Private	FMC, POW at Point Lookout, MD.
Terry, C. P.	Commodore Tucker's Brigade	Private	Surrendered at Appomattox
Walden, Edward W.	CSS Savannah	Landsman	
Weeks, Edward	CSS Shenandoah	Private	
White, David H.	CSS Alabama	Wardroom Mess Steward	He had been a U.S. Slave from Delaware but was captured and volunteered for the C.S. Navy. During the final battle with the USS Kearsarge off Cherbourg, France, in 1864, he was KIA, and went down with the Alabama and drowned.
Williamson, Ely	Steamer at Battle of Roanoke Island, NC	Pilot	Resident of Roanoke NC. WIA Had his arm shattered from elbow to wrist

ALABAMA

In 1867 Alabama began granting pensions to Confederate veterans who had lost arms or legs. In 1886 the State began granting pensions to veterans' widows. In 1891 the law was amended to grant pensions to indigent veterans or their

Directory of African American Confederates in the U.S. Civil War

widows. Alabama imposed the tax to fund pensions for Confederate soldiers and their widows, and still collects it today.

1 percent goes to preserve and operate the state's Confederate Memorial Park in rural Mountain Creek.

NAME	CO.	UNIT	RANK	SLAVE / FREE MISC
Alfred		36th Regiment Alabama Infantry		
Appleton	K	33rd Regiment Alabama Infantry	Drumme Servant	
Bob		4th Alabama		
Dow	C	15' Regiment Alabama Infantry	Servant	
Griffin	A	6th Regiment Alabama Cavalry Served as a Servant to his master Bat Smith	Servant	Slave of Bat Smith, when Bat Smith was shot and left on the battlefield, Griffin risked his life ignoring pleas for him to not go. Griffin retrieved Smith's body then accompanied him home
Henry		Alabama Eutaw Rifles	Servant	Slave of 1st Lieutenant H. Y. Webb
Isham		34th Alabama Capt. Charles L. Lumsdens Battery (Light Artillery) CSA	Body Servant Free Negro	Servant to Sgt. John A. Caldwell
James	C	13th Regiment Alabama Infantry	Laundress	
Jerry	D	21th Regiment Alabama infantry	Private	
Jerry	F&S	57th Regiment Alabama Infantry	Drummer	Slave
Jim	A	15th Regiment Alabama Infantry	Servant	
Jim			Private	Served as a servant to Abel Crawford.
Jim		34th Alabama Capt. Charles L. Lumsdens Battery (Light Artillery) CSA	Cook	Served as a servant to Potts, the Cook Boss.
John		36t Regiment Alabama Infantry	Private	
Nury	B	15th Regiment Alabama Infantry	Servant	
Pomp		Unknown Alabama Unit	Cook	Was at the Battle of Seven Pines, or Fair Oaks, near Richmond (May 31 and June 1, 1862.
Reuben		34th Alabama Capt. Charles L. Lumsdens Battery (Light Artillery) CSA	Cook	
Reuben		1st Regiment Alabama	Private	P.O.W. at Camp Butler, Illinois sent to Vicksburg for prisoner exchange on Sept
Russell		Alabama Eutaw Rifles	Servant	Slave of 3rd Lt. J. J. Winston
Saul	C	13th Regiment Alabama Infantry	Laundress	
Sirus		15th Regiment Alabama Infantry	Servant	
Tyler		1st Artillery, Army of Alabama	Servant	Slave of 1st Sgt Witham Wellborn

It's lonely at the top

Southern general Robert E. Lee's image is everywhere. His silhouette is so easily recognizable that it is one of the most powerful symbols of the Confederacy.

Tales are spun and legends told portraying the level of respect and awe enlisted men under his watch held for him—how they would stare at him in silence as he rode by them while mounted on his beautiful, well-bred horse Traveler and how they would spontaneously cheer and rush toward him for any modicum of recognition.

And yet, he seems utterly unlovable when his persona is recreated from historic sources.

Imagine how surprised you would be to learn that the fabled Confederate General, also nicknamed "Marble Man" because of his stature and personal comportment even at age 18, kept a chicken as a pet named Nellie for two years.

She was a little black hen who came in Lee's camp with a consignment of chickens given to the army of northern Virginia for sustenance, perhaps in early 1865.

Nellie fled, finding safety in a tent with an open flap and knowing that staying with the flock would bring her no good.

She stayed since the tent was warm and free of fowl killers or natural predators. Nellie lay an egg beneath the cot in the tent, as chickens are inclined to do, and settled herself down on it to watch what would happen.

Luckily, the following transpired: the tent belonged to Lee and he had a fresh egg for breakfast.

The small black hen's life was saved, thanks to these two strokes of unbelievable luck. Depending on the source relating the story, Lee called her "Nellie" or "Hen."

Directory of African American Confederates in the U.S. Civil War

Name		Unit	Role	Notes
Ward	B	23rd Regiment Alabama Infantry Served as a Body Servant to Milton Butterfield	Body Servant	Milton Butterfield was killed at Stone Mountain, GA near Atlanta. He was buried near Stone Mountain by Ward, who then delivered the letter to Milton's wife Martha along with a letter from Milton's Commanding Officer.
Wash		34th Alabama Capt. Charles L. Lumsdens Battery (Light Artillery) CSA	Servant	Served as a servant to Dr. Jarrett, Wash died at Knoxville.
William		Alabama Eutaw Rifles	Servant	Slave 2nd Lieutenant R. E. Watkins
Abney, John	C	56th Regiment, Alabama Partisan Rangers (1st Alabama Partisan Rangers) Served as a servant to J. M. Abney	Servant	Lauderdale County, MS Conf Pensioner, He enlisted at Choctow County, Alabama.
Abney, John		56' Alabama Regiment Cavalry	Private	Lauderdale County, MS Conf Pensioner
Adair, Sam		Unknown Alabama Unit	Private	Father may have been white.
Amarine, Dave	F	57th Regiment Alabama Infantry	Fifer	Slave
Anderson, Charley		21st Alabama Infantry	Private	Holmes County, MS Conf Pensioner
Ball, Harry		58" Alabama Infantry	Private	Yazoo-Tallahatchie County, MS Conf Pensioner
Barbor, Benjamin A.	E	2nd Battalion Hilliard's Legion, Alabama	Servant	
Bibb, William	G	12th Alabama Infantry	Shoe Maker	Slave of Capt. Algenon S. Bibb. Rutherford County, TN Conf Pensioner Rcd #C136
Birdsong, William		Unknown Alabama Unit	Private	Captured at Madison, Alabama P.O.W. and Political Prisioner at Camp Morton, Indiana, Died there and now buried at Greenfield Park, Indianapolis
Bishop, Prymus		11th Alabama Infantry	Servant	Hinds County, MS Conf Pensioner, battle injury.
Bobbett, Jim		34" Alabama Capt. Charles L. Lumsdens Battery (Light Artillery) CSA	Body Servant	Served as a servant to his master Pvt. James R. Maxwell.
Boldy, Henry		Unknown Alabama Unit	Private	From Chase, AL. Attended the UCV Reunion in Arkansas 1928
Boyd, Jesse		7" Alabama Cavalry	Private	Forrest County, MS Conf Pensioner
Boykin, William		10th Alabama Cavalry (Barbiere's Battalion),(Capt. Thomas J. Goldsby's Company) Served as a body servant to Dr. Thomas Boykin	Body Servant	Slave of Dr. Tom Boykin Kershaw County, South Carolina Conf Pensioner App # 6572
Brewer, Gray		5th Alabama Infantry	Private	Lee County, MS Conf Pensioner
Broach, Sam		56th Alabama Cavalry	Servant	Kemper County, MS Conf Pensioner
Brock, Tobias H.		30th Alabama Infantry	Private	Wayne County, MS
Brooks, George		22rd Alabama Infantry	Private	Washington County, MS Conf Pensioner

Name		Unit	Role	Notes
Brown, Dave		8th Alabama Infantry	Servant	Yazoo County, MS Conf Pensioner
Buck, Billy		34th Alabama Capt. Charles L. Lumsdens Battery (Light Artillery)	Cook	
Buckingham, Jim		Unknown Alabama Unit	Private	From Florence County, AL Attended the UCV Reunion Barbeque in Florence, Alabama 1908
Bush, Charley		General and Staff Officers, Corps, Division and Brigade Staffs, Non-com. Staffs and Bands, Enlisted Men, Staff Departments, C.S.A. Served as a body servant to LtCol. John Pelham	Body Servant	Slave
Cagle, Adam		Unknown Alabama Unit	Private	Captured at Madison, Alabama P.O.W. and Political Prisioner at Camp Morton, Indiana, Died there and now buried at Greenfield Park, Indianapolis
Cagle, William		Unknown Alabama Unit	Private	P.O.W. and Political Prisioner, Captured at Madison, Alabama
Cash, Charley		5th Alabama Infantry	Private	Leflore County, MS Conf Pensioner
Clemens, George (Clements)	F H	41th Regiment, Alabama Infantry 5th Regiment, Alabama Infantry Served as servant to his master Capt. Luther Morgan Clements	Servant	Slave of Morgan Clemens of Tuscaloosa, Alabama. According to his daughter Joanna (Anna) Baker in Mississippi Slave Narratives.
Coleman, David E.	I	6th Alabama Infantry Slave of Lt. Coleman	Private	Slave, TN Conf Pensioner # C100. Buried at Good Springs Cemetery in Pulaski, TN.
Coleman, Jacob	A	11th Alabama Infantry		TN Conf Pensioner #C2. Buried at Nicely Cemetery, Pulaski, TN.
Cross, Samuel H.	D	35th Regiment Alabama Volunteer Infantry	Cook Private	Slave of Scip Cross
Doss, Abe		5th Alabama Infantry		Clay County, MS Conf Pensioner
Dubose, Ned		Jeff Davis Artillery, Alabama	Private	
Dunwoody, Charles		Unknown Alabama Unit	Private	Served and was KIA, when the Federals attacked South Carolina, according to William L. Dunwoody his son in Arkansas Slave Narratives.
Eddings, Bennett	D	5th Regiment Alabama Infantry 5th (Monroe Guards) Served as a servant to Capt. J. W. Williams who was killed, he then served under Capt. Chew the Assistant Brigade Surgeon	Servant	Lauderdale County, MS Conf Pensioner, Slave of Capt. J. W. Williams.
Emerson, Flinn	F K	4" Regiment, Alabama Volunteer Militia 40th Regiment Alabama Infantry Served as a servant to his master 1st Lt William B. Bingham	Cook Servant	Lauderdale County, MS Conf Pensioner, Slave of W. B. Bingham.
Fielder, Moses		24th Alabama Infantry	Private	Yazoo County, MS Conf Pensioner
Freeman, Alfred		2nd Alabama Cavalry	Servant	Jones County, MS Conf Pensioner

During the first year of the war, a huge number of people were drafted into Confederate working groups.

In January, a message from Mr. Riordan in Charleston to Hon. Percy Walker in Mobile indicated that considerable numbers of Negroes from Alabama's plantations were working on the re-doubts, which were characterized as "quite substantially made, strengthened by sandbags and sheet iron" when completed.

In the South, enslaved people were used in the army to build fortifications.

Fuller, Lee		5" Alabama Calvary	Private	Fayette County, TN Conf Pensioner, application rejected.
Glover, Charley		11th Alabama Infantry	Servant	Decatur, Newton County, MS Conf Pensioner
Goodgame, Abe	B	12th Regiment Alabama Served as a servant to LtCol. John C. Goodgame	Servant	Mulatto Slave, POW at Fort McHenry
Gray, Mat		Served as a body servant to Capt. John Lewis	Body Servant	Member of the Egbert Jones Camp, U.C.V., Attended the UCV Reunion in Arkansas 1928
Gwynne, R. A.		Unknown Alabama Unit	Servant	He attended the "Last Confederate Reunion," held at Montgomery, Alabama in September 1944.
Hamilton, Henry	L	3'd Alabama Cavalry	Private	Huntsville, Alabama
Hamilton, Henry		28-h Alabama Infantry	Private	Oktibbeha County, MS Conf Pensioner
Harris, Charley		17th Alabama Infantry	Servant	Tallahatchie County, MS Conf Pensioner, battle injury.
Harris, Richard	I	15th Regiment Alabama Infantry	Colored Orderly	Born in England, Enlisted in Greeneville, E. Tennessee
Harris, Thomas A.		Unknown Alabama Unit	Body Servant	
Harrison, Joe		42nd Alabama Infantry	Servant	Clarke County, MS Conf Pensioner
Harrison, William H.	G	59th Alabama Infantry Served as a body servant to his master Gummal L. Harrison	Body Servant	Slave of Gummal L. Harrison. According to his statement in the Arkansas Slave Narratives, he was captured at Bulls Gap and forced to fight for the Union.
Harrison, William H.	H	61st Alabama Infantry	Private	Arkansas, Monroe County Conf Pensioner, application #7808. Application was denied in 1907, for no proof of service.
Howard, Henry	G	6th Alabama Volunteer Infantry Regiment (The Autauga Rifles)	Servant	
Hudson, David		4th Alabama Infantry	Private	Noxubee County, MS Conf Pensioner, battle injury.
Hudson, Morris		4th Alabama Infantry	Servant	Yazoo County, MS Conf Pensioner
Hughes, Richard		10th Alabama Infantry	Servant	Webster County, MS Conf Pensioner
Jarmon, Major		56th Alabama Cavalry Partisans	Private	Monroe County, MS Conf Pensioner
Jimerson, Robert		43rd Alabama Infantry	Servant	Harrison County, MS Conf Pensioner
Johnson, Alex		4th Alabama Infantry	Servant	Bolivar County, MS Conf Pensioner
Jones, Aleck		Unknown Alabama Unit	Private	From Florence County, AL 1908. at UCV Barbeque
Jones, Rufus (Rube)		34th Alabama Capt. Charles L. Lumsdens Battery (Light Artillery) CSA	Body Servant	Servant to T. Alex Dearing
Kelley, John	D	10th Regiment Alabama Infantry	Private	Slave on the Mullen Flat Wm. Lanier Plantation

This image is from the Alabama Department of Archives and History, showing participants at what was billed as the "Last Confederate Reunion," held at Montgomery, Alabama in September 1944.

The African American man at center is identified, from the archives' catalog description, as Dr. R. A. Gwynne of Birmingham, Alabama a fomer Black Confederate.

Name		Unit / Service	Rank/Role	Notes
King, Unknown		Served with his master Capt. King who was KIA	Private	Slave
Kirkland, John		7th Alabama Cavalry	Private	Hinds County, MS Conf Pensioner
Lacy, Bat		7th Alabama Cavalry	Regt Teamster	Holmes County, MS Conf Pensioner
Lamar, Floyd	C C	6th Alabama Infantry Home Guard 5th Alabama Infantry 56th Alabama Infantry Served under his Master 4Th Cpl M. B. Lamar, carried him home when he was wounded, and was offered his freedom which he refused.	Servant	Slave of 4th Cpl. M.B. Lamar. Wise County, VA Conf Pensioner
Lavender, William		6th Alabama Infantry	Private	Panola County, MS Conf Pensioner
Lewis, Essex		Served as a Servant to Capt. Cam Patterson	Servant	Slave of Col. Nick Lewis of Morgan County, AL. Member of the Egbert Jones Camp, U.C.V.,
Light, Joseph		Unknown Alabama Unit	Private	P.O.W. and Political Prisioner at Camp Morton, Indiana, Died there and now buried at Greenfield Park, Indianapolis
Lindsey, John		4th Alabama Infantry Mahone's Brigade Served as a servant to his master Rufus Chestnut who was later killed at Gettysburg.	Servant	Lauderdale County, MS Conf Pensioner, Slave of Rufus Chestnut of Dallas County, Alabama.
Lucas, George		5th Alabama Cavalry	Regt Teamster	Bolivar County, MS Conf Pensioner
Matthews, Andrew (Andy)	G	2nd Alabama Infantry	Servant	Prentiss County, MS Conf Pensioner
McGlaun, Cash		57th Alabama Infantry	Servant	Pontotoc County, MS Conf Pensioner
McNeil, William		47th Alabama Infantry	Private	Madison County, MS Conf Pensioner
Miller, Jack		Moreland's Alabama Cavalry Battalion	Private	Tunica County, MS Conf Pensioner
Moore, Russell		54th Alabama Infantry		Chickasaw County, MS Conf Pensioner
Morgan, T. M.		26th Alabama Infantry	Regt Teamster	Monroe County, MS Conf Pensioner, non-battle injury.
Name not known		15th Regiment Alabama Infantry Served as a servant to his master Col. James Cantey	Servant	Slave of James Cantey of Alabama
Norman, Burt	G	2nd Alabama	Servant	Prentiss County, MS Conf Pensioner
Norris, Bill		Unknown Alabama Infantry (Capt 3. M. Johnson)	Private	Fayette County, TN Conf Pension Rcd # C276, application rejected.
Norwood, James		4th Regiment Alabama Cavalry Served as a servant to Jesse Norwood	Servant	Lauderdale County, MS Conf Pension filed in 1906 and denied for lack of proof
O'Bannon, Henry		20th Alabama Infantry	Private	Yazoo County, MS Conf Pensioner
Patterson, Jesse		6th Alabama Infantry	Bugler	Warren County, MS Conf Pensioner

Directory of African American Confederates in the U.S. Civil War

Patterson, Reuben		5th Alabama Cavalry Served as a Servant to Col. Josiah Patterson	Servant	Attended the UCV Reunion in Florence, Alabama 1921
Patterson, Thomas C.	H	61St Regiment Alabama Infantry	Servant	
Perry, Wade Hampton		40th Alabama Infantry	Private	Forrest-Perry County, MS Conf Pensioner
Phillips, Simon		Served as a servant to his master	Servant	Birmingham, AL. Attended the UCV Reunion in Arkansas 1928 Became the President of Alabama's Ex-Slave Association
Pickett, Ben		15th Alabama Battalion Cavalry Partisans	Private	Wayne County, MS Conf Pensioner
Powe, John		54' Alabama Infantry	Private	Wayne County, MS Conf Pensioner
Real, Dock		1" Alabama Infantry	Servant	Monroe County, MS Conf Pensioner
Reed (Reid) (Ellis), Jake		36th Alabama Infantry	Cook	Claiborne County, MS Conf Pensioner
Rivers, Quincy		9th Alabama Cavalry	Regt Teamster	Forrest County, MS Conf Pensioner
Russell, John	B	17TH Alabama Infantry	Private	
Scruggs, Calvin	E	44th Alabama Infantry Regiment	Servant	Slave of Walter (Wetly) Scruggs of Madison County, AL
Seawright, George Washington		7th Regiment Alabama Infantry		Attended the UCV Reunion in Florence, Alabama 1921
Sledge, Ned		4th Alabama Cavalry	Servant	Bolivar County, MS Conf Pensioner
Stallsworth, Gus		15th Alabama Battalion Cavalry Partisans	Servant	Wayne County, MS Conf Pensioner
Stewart, Peter		4th Alabama Cavalry	Private	Attended UCV Meeting 1919 according to the Rogersville News.
Stone, William		40th Alabama Infantry	Private	Monroe County, MS Conf Pensioner, non-bathe injury.
Taylor, Spencer		Was sent as a laborer to work on boats in Mobile, Alabama.	Laborer	Slave
Thomas, Ben	A	31st Alabama Infantry	Private	TN Conf Pension #49, application rejected.
Thompson, Joe		3rd Alabama Cavalry	Private	Forrest County, MS Conf Pensioner
Watkins, Samuel Crawford	E	42nd Alabama Infantry	Private	
Weatherford, Henry W.		16th Alabama Infantry	Cook	Arkansas, Yell County Conf Pensioner, application #25236. Application approved in 1921.
White, Unknown		Served building breastworks and hauling salt	Laborer	Slave of Ad White From Huntsville, Alabama. After the war he moved to Pine Bluff, Arkansas. According to his daughter Ada Moorehead in Arkansas Slave Narratives.
Williams, Bennett	D	5th Regiment Alabama Infantry Served as a servant to his master Capt. J. W. Williams	Servant	Lauderdale County, MS Conf Pensioner, battle injury. Slave of Capt. J. W. Williams,
Williams, Levi	E	12th Regiment Alabama	Private	Sumter County, Alabama

Williams, Zackary T.	6th Alabama Cavalry	Private	Bolivar County, MS Conf Pensioner
Willis, John	Unknown Alabama Unit	Private	Captured at Madison, Alabama P.O.W. and Political Prisioner at Camp Morton, Indiana, Died there and now buried at Greenfield Park, Indianapolis
Womack, Jack	Served as a Laborer working on fortifications (Breastworks) at Mobile, Alabama	Laborer Servant	Lauderdale County, MS Conf Pensioner,Slave of Mrs. Hattie Wire who, later stated in an affidavit that he was sent to government service during the war. He was wounded in service at Spanish Fort.
Yates, Fred	23rd Alabama Infantry	Private	Forrest County, MS Conf Pensioner
Young, Dave	11th Alabama Infantry	Private	Wayne County, MS Conf Pensioner
Young, James	K	29th Alabama Infantry	Private	

Alabama Depatment of Archives and History
Address: 36130, 624 Washington Ave, Montgomery, AL 36104
Phone: (334) 242-4435,
Web site: www.archives.alabama.gov

ARKANSAS

Arkansas became one of the first Southern states to give annual pensions to its resident exConfederate troops and their widows on April 2, 1891, when Act 91, "An act for the relief of certain soldiers of the late War Between the States," was passed.

Arkansas and the other former Confederate states agreed that C.S.A. pensions would be provided by the state in which the veteran or his widow lived at the time of application, not by the state from which he served.

Act 91 established the State Board of Pensions, which is made up of the governor, attorney general, and state auditor. At the same time, 75 local pension boards were established, one in each county.

Each was made up of the county judge, sheriff, and clerk of the county. Pensions were granted under the supervision of these boards. Pensions were once exclusively available to poor, indigent, or crippled soldiers who had been honorably discharged, as well as unmarried needy or indigent widows of veterans.

Needy widows whohad not remarried and were born before 1878, as well as widowed mothers of veterans, were added

to those who could claim for assistance starting in 1915.

Few veterans' moms, on the other hand, were still alive to apply. The law was amended that year to include a definition of indigence as someone with less than $500 in real estate or an annual income of less than $250.

Widows who married veterans prior to 1927 become eligible in 1937. However, in 1939, a requirement that applicants be born before 1870 was added. When a soldier dies, his widow is automatically entitled to his pension. The Arkansas General Assembly often added individual soldiers or widows

to the pension lists without regard to their eligibility during the 1920s and 1930s. From 1891 until 1915, the annual pension amount was $25.00. After that date, the annual fee was increased to $100.00. Most retirees were unable to get their entire annual stipend due to a lack of funding.

Payments in the form of State Treasury Warrants were mailed out once a year after the state board reviewed and approved them. Individual pensioners, on the other hand, did not receive any warrants.

Directory of African American Confederates in the U.S. Civil War

The county board received them and dispersed them. Several dozen African Americans who served in various capacities during the Civil War, as well as many citizens who worked for the Confederate Army or government, have applications in the collection. T

he majority of the inmates in the Arkansas Confederate Home were on the pension lists at the time of their admission.

When they entered that institution, however, they were

obliged to give up their pensions. Black History Commission of Arkansas. BHCA continues to collect materials on Arkansas's black history and history-makers for the Arkansas State Archives.

The commission works to raise awareness of the contributions and impact black Arkansans have had on the state's history.

NAME	CO.	UNIT	RANK	SLAVE / FREE MISC NOTES
, Abraham	B	33rd Arkansas Infantry	Cook	
, Albert	G	33rd Arkansas Infantry	Cook	
, Andrew	B	Hardy's Regiment Arkansas Infantry	Assistat Cook	
, Charley		Unknown Confederate Unit	Servant	P.O.W., Died and Buried at Oakwoods Cemetery in Chicago, IL. Possibly from Clay County, Arkansas
, Henry	E	24th Arkansas Infantry	Asst Cook	
, Jack		18th Arkansas Regiment Served as a Servant of Lt. Shelton	Servant	Slave, KIA, Fought along side his master at the battle of Belmont (1861) and refused to be evacuated when wounded, he later died of his wounds in the Overton Hospital.
, Nelson	B	33rd Arkansas Infantry	Cook	Slave
, Nick	K	33rd Arkansas Infantry	Cook	
, Oscar	C	15th Regiment, Arkansas Infantry (Josey's)	Servant	Slave of BGen. Lucius F. Polk of Columbia, TN.
, Robert	B	Hardy's Regiment Arkansas Infantry	Assistant Cook	
, William		1st Arkansas Infantry	Teamster	
, Zachary		Served four years as a soldier in the Confederate Army.	Private	He was a member of Bethel Church in Little Rock, AR. According to Mrs. Eliza Washington of Little Rock, Arkansas, in Arkansas Slave Narratives.
Baltimore, William		Unknown Arkansas Unit	Servant	Slave of Dr. Waters, U.S. Veteran Pensioner. Served as a servant in the Confederate Army, then was captured and conscripted into the USCT
Bartie, Chaplin B.		4th Arkansas Infantry	Private	
Berden, Humphrey P.	B	11th And 17th (Consolidated) Arkansas Infantry	Cook	
Berry, Dick		1st Arkansas Volunteers Under Col. Patrick R. Cleburne	Body Servant	Killed at the Battle of Franklin

Because their extremely visible participation in defending southern soil was so stunning to Northerners, military service men and civilians alike took the alarming news of these lethal black Confederate sharpshooters to heart. Soon this group of Confederate blacks became well-known throughout the Northern army.

After all, many Northerners felt that the war was primarily about the abolition of slavery so why should black Confederates resist the army's march and delight in murdering Yankees?

As a result of this disturbing paradox, Union troops' letters frequently reported the shocking incidence of encountering black Confederate soldiers on the front lines of Yorktown.

Hermon Clark, an enlisted man of the 117th New York Infantry Regiment, was among many who wrote similar letters at the time. Even two years later, in June 1865, an 89th New York Infantry Regiment soldier named George Hupman stationed with his unit outside Washington, D.C., was killed. His letters, when found, recounted the same type of discoveries.

A Union soldier had an opportunity to note the skill of determined "darkies" with their well-armed rifles.

Confederate black soldiers boldly stood out in plain view and coolly drew on targets of opportunity because they were good shots at long range. The soldiers became pretty well-known among the scouts and pickets and had established solid reputations for marksmanship. But a Union marksman shot down two black Confederate snipers, killing one and wounding the other, according to Alfred Bellard, a soldier of the 5th New Jersey Infantry Regiment from the Potomac.

Another federal trooper recounted the firing from still another black marksman at Yorktown, Virginia who caused so many problems in shooting down Union Army blue coats that an entire regiment was aligned to fire a concentrated volley at the sniper.

The black Confederate was wounded in the head and fell from a treetop where he had been cutting down Yankees for a long time. This reporter Yankee was astounded by what he saw at Yorktown where the twisting course of American history had come full circle and wrote about "a rebel Negro rifleman, who through his skill as a marksman, had done more injury to our men than any dozen of his white peers ... His habit was to perch himself in a big tree to annoy the Union men by firing upon them."

Private Truman Head, a veteran soldier of Colonel Hiram Berdan's 1st U.S. Sharpshooter Regiment in New York, was the Union soldier who eventually killed the deadly black Confederate.

Black, W. M.		Unknown Arkansas Unit	Private	Marrianna, AR. Attended the UCV Reunion in Arkansas 1928
Bragg, Alexander Hamilton George Washington (Alex Bragg)		Served as a Body Servant to Anton V. Bragg	Body Servant	Slave
Brandon, Rodger	I	3rd Arkansas Served as a Body Servant to Pvt. Bill Nat Smith	Body Servant Cook	
Burnett, C. L.	I	11th Arkansas Infantry	Private	
Butler, Unknown		Unknown Arkansas Unit	Private	Slave, Jefferson County AR Conf Pensioner. According to his wife Jennie Butler (Crittenden) in Arkansas Slave Narratives.
Chambers, Professor		Unknown Arkansas Unit	Private	Winston, AR. Attended the UCV Reunion in Arkansas 1928
Charleston, Sr., Willie Buck		Unknown Arkansas Unit	Private	His son Willie Buck Charleston Jr. made a statement in Slave Narratives.
Cummings, Albert		Unknown Arkansas Unit	Private	Slave, Served with his master Mr. Autrey who was KIA at the Battle of Poison Springs, Arkansas.
Dillahunty, Sam		19th Arkansas Infantry	Private	Arkansas, Sevier County Conf Pensioner, application #12040. His application was disallowed in 1907. Ex-slave.
Eberhardt, Steve	A	4th Arkansas Infantry Served Capt. George Eberhart	Cook Servant	Rome, GA. Attended the UCV Reunion in Arkansas 1928
Evans, R.M.		Unknown Arkansas Unit	Cook	P.O.W. at Camp Morton, Indiana, Died there and now buried at Greenfield Park, Indianapolis
Fitzhugh, Unknown		Unknown Arkansas Unit	Private	Served and was KIA, according to Henry Fitzhugh his son in Aransas Slave Narratives.
Ford, Gideon		9th Arkansas Infantry		Noxubee County, MS Goff Pensioner
Griffin, Dan	E	3rd Arkansas State Infantry (Griffith's) Served as a Body Servant to Capt. John Griffith and Pvt. Benjamin H. Griffin	Body Servant Cook	
Herren, Sam	A	Arkansas Mounted Rifles	Servant	Grenada County, MS Conf Pensioner
Herrod, Wesley		3rd Arkansas Cavalry	Private	Lafayette County, MS Conf Pensioner
Hogins, Frank	A	7th Arkansas Cavalry (Hill's Regiment)	Private	Servant of Pvt. Reece B. Hogins, AR Conf Pensioner Application #21163.
Horton, Unknown		Unknown Arkansas Unit	Private	Slave of Joe and Mary Horton from Horton's Island, Arkansas. According to his daughter Emma Moore in Arkansas Slave Narratives.
Lide, Amos	C	33rd Regiment, Arkansas Infantry	Cook	
Linsey, Sam	E	2nd Regiment, Arkansas Infantry	Servant	

Name		Unit/Service	Role	Notes
Mansfield, Ruben		Fulton and Camden Regiment, Arkansas, built breastworks and trenches.	Laborer	Arkansas, Nevada County Conf Pensioner, application #27285.
Martin, Samuel		Served in Arkansas	Servant Body Guard	Arkansas, Scott County Conf Pensioner, application #29202. His widow Delilah received his pension.
May, John		2nd Arkansa Cavalry	Servant	Copiah County, MS Conf Pensioner
McCallum, Edward	C	33rd Regiment, Arkansas Infantry	Cook	Arkansas, Scott County Conf Pensioner, application #29202.
McCollum,	C	33rd Regiment, Arkansas Infantry	Cook	
Muke, B.M.	G	19th Regiment, Arkansas Infantry (Dockery's)	Servant	
Name not known		Gratiot's 3rd Arkansas State Infantry Served as a body servant of Captain John Griffith	Body Servant	Capt. John Griffth's body servant was responsible for the death of General Nathaniel Lyon at the battle of Wilson's Creek.
Name not known		18th Arkansas Regiment Son of Jack who served as a Servant of Lt. Shelton	Servant	Slave, helped in the battle of Belmont (1861) by repeatedly reloading his father's (Jack) rifle. Jack was the Servant of Lt. Shelton
Name not known		Served as a servant to his master Joe Potts	Servant	Slave of Joe Potts, of Little River County, Arkansas. He was KIA, according to his daughter Judy Parker in Arkansas Slave Narratives.
Name not known		Unknown Arkansas Unit	Private	Slave of Sam and Phoebe Carson of Jefferson County. Served after he was sent by his master Sam Carson in place of Andrew Carson his master's son. According Mrs. Laura Hart a slave of Sam Carson, in Arkansas Slave Narratives.
Perry, Eli		Monroe's Arkansas Cavalry	Cook	Arkansas, Yell County Conf Pensioner, application #26585. ex-slave.
Pool, Henry		Unknown Arkansas Unit	Private	Slave of Mr. Pool. of Wattensaw, Arkansas. According to his grandson Lula Taylor in Arkansas Slave Narratives.
Randall, William		Arkansas (Gen. Price) Served as a cook under his master Sgt. Henry Wilkinson	Cook	Slave of P. H. Wilkinson. Chesterfield County, VA Conf Pensioner
Reed, J. C.			Private	Arkansas Conf Pensioner
Richardson, Charles		Morgan's Arkansas Cavalry	Servant	Washington County AR Conf Pensioner #21717 approved in 1917.
Shaw, Jim		11th Arkansas Cavalry	Private	Franklin County, MS Conf Pensioner
Taylor, Ned	I	3rd Arkansas Infantry	Servant	Arkansas, Hot Spring County Conf Pensioner, application #18754. Application approved in 1910.
Turner, Bart		1st Arkansas Volunteers Under Col. Patrick R. Cleburne	Body Servant	

Turner, Nat		1st Arkansas Volunteers Under Col. Patrick R. Cleburne	Body Servant	
Walker, Solomon		Unknown Arkansas County	Servant	Arkansas, Phillips County Conf Pensioner, application #27336. Application approved in 1926.
Weatherford, W. H.		Unknown Arkansas Unit	Private	Resident of Arkansas. Attended the UCV Reunion in Arkansas 1928
Wells, Joe Jones	F	8th Battalion, Arkansas Infantry Served under his master Captain R. Campbell Jones	Servant	Slave of Captain R. Campbell Jones According to his son John Wells, in Arkansas Slave Narratives.
Winfull, Dan		Unknown Arkansas Unit	Private	Resident of Sweet Home, AR. Attended the UCV Reunion in Arkansas 1928
Wiseman, Milt		1st Arkansas Volunteers Under Col. Patrick R. Cleburne	Body Servant	Killed at the Battle of Franklin
Wood, Henry	D	17th (Griffith's) Arkansas Infantry	Private	
Wright, Henry		15th Arkansas Infantry	Servant	Arkansas, Quachita County Conf Pensioner, application #29069. Application approved in 1925.

ARKANSAS STATE ARCHIVES /HISTORY COMMISSION
1 Capitol Mall, Little Rock, AR 72201, PHONE 501-682-6900, Web Site: www.arkansasheritage.com/

FLORIDA

As enslaved residents in the Confederate states, most African Americans had little choice but to support the Confederate war effort. Some went to war as servants to white southern officers. Others toiled in hard labor when the Confederate military impressed enslaved blacks for labor projects, such as building fortifications and transportation systems.

In 1885, Florida began granting Confederate soldiers pensions. The widows of veterans were granted eligibility in 1889. It indicates that African-American Soldiers and Servants were not eligible for pensions.

The Florida Confederate Pension Files, one of the most popular collections at the Florida State Archives, is now being digitized (Series 587). Over 7,300 Pensions Images are currently available online, out of a total of approximately 12,000 files. At the moment, you can search the files by surname (soldier's or widow's maiden name) or pension application number.

From 1885 through 1954, this series contains files on accepted and denied pension claims. Both veterans' and widows' pension applications (interfiled) are included in the pension files, however, accepted and denied claims are filed separately. The original application, any supplemental applications, proof of service and residency, and any correspondence between the applicant and the Board are all kept in most files. Name, date, and place of birth, dates, and places of enlistment and discharge, a brief account of duty, wounds sustained, sworn declarations on proof of service by comrades, War Department service abstracts, and place and length of Florida residency are all required on veterans' applications.

Her full name, date, and location of marriage, date, and place of her husband's death, place and length of residency in Florida, and proof of her husband's service are all included in the widow's application. The date and location of birth of the widows are also included in some early applications. Residents of Florida were eligible for Confederate pensions regardless of where they served during the war.

State Archives of Florida
R.A. Gray Building
500 South Bronough Street
Tallahassee, FL 32399-0250
Phone: (850) 245-6600
Web Site https://dos.myflorida.com/library-archives/

Behind the fighting ranks among the Confederate forces, whose daily needs for the war effort were as crucial as those on the front lines of conflict. Was the Blacksmith, he played a critical part in keeping the army running.

The need for physical resources expanded considerably as the war advanced into a more industrialized battle over the course of four years. Since the start of the war in 1861, the armies have grown in size and power, necessitating the addition of more troops, horses, and artillery. Railroads and carts were important modes of transportation for supplying the soldiers. The demand for iron and steel, which would be used to create railways, ironclads, artillery, and other military gear, skyrocketed. The blacksmith's role was to properly forge the metal and construct or maintain these devices for his country's army.

It was the smith's responsibility to create new engine components for supplies trains, as well as gear for the troops and especially the artillery. With both armies depending extensively on pack animals like mules and horses for mounted operations or hauling supplies, blacksmiths were called upon to make the thousands of shoes required for the animals. Farrier services were provided by a large number of military smiths.

NAME	CO.	UNIT	RANK	SLAVE / FREE MISC NOTES
Glasgow	C	1st Infantry Regiment, Florida	Musician	
Henry	H	4th Florida Infantry	Private	
Darns, Alex		Served as an orderly to Confederate Gen. E. Kirby	Orderly	Gen. Smith paid for Alex Darns medical school after the war.
Jackson, Junius		Unknown Florida Unit	Private	Slave of Mr. Henry of Monticello Jefferson County, FL
Jackson, Rufus	B	10th Florida Infantry	Private	
Milton, Randolph		Capt. J. Dunham's Company, Milton Light Artillery, Florida		Freed Slave
Osborne, Emanuel	B	3rd Infantry Regiment, Florida (St. Augustine Blues) Served under Capt. John Lott Phillips	Musician	FMC, St. Johns' County, Florida Conf Pensioner #A10008
Papino, Isaac	B	3rd Infantry Regiment, Florida (St. Augustine Blues) Served under Capt. John Lott Phillips	Musician	
Taylor, Washington		Kilcrease Light Artillery (Capt. Patrick Houstoun's), Florida Artillery	Cook	
Thomas, Acie		He served after he was impressed by the Confederate army for hauling food and ammunition to different points between Tallahassee and a city in Virginia	Laborer	Slave of Tom and Bryant Folsom of Jefferson County, Florida. According to his statements in Florida Slave Narratives.
Welters, Anthony T. (Fontane, Tony) (Huertas, Antonio)	B	3rd Infantry Regiment, Florida (St. Augustine Blues) Served under Capt. John Lott Phillips	Fifer	Former Slave, Member of E. Kirby Smith Camp, UCV.

GEORGIA

In 1870, Georgia began providing annuities to veterans who had lost a limb in battle. In 1879, the coverage was expanded to include other handicapped Confederate veterans and their widows living in Georgia. In 1894, the list of qualifying disabilities was broadened to include old age and poverty.

It indicates that African-American Soldiers and Servants were not eligible for pensions. The Georgia State Archives can provide information about Georgia records.

The foremost source for the names of Confederate soldiers in Georgia is Miss Lillian Henderson's ROSTER OF THE CONFEDERATE SOLDIERS OF GEORGIA published in 6 volumes from 1959-1964.

Unfortunately, this set includes only the names of those who served in regular infantry units; it does not include the names of soldiers who served in Confederate artillery, cavalry, or state militia units and legions.

Most Black Confederate would not be included since they were not regularly enrolled; but, some who served in infantry units (to include black women) are found in Miss Henderson's ROSTER. Apparently, some army cooks, musicians, and nurses were carried on muster rolls as shown in these above excerpts.

NAME	CO.	UNIT	RANK	SLAVE / FREE MISC
Aabram	c	11th Battalion Georgia Artillery (Sumter Artillery Battalion, 3rd Corps) Served as a Teamster hauling wood Under Major. John Lane	Teamster	Slave

Just be quiet.

Whether free or enslaved, African Americans were so deeply embedded in the fabric of Southern society over the centuries that some of them were socially conditioned to see the Deep South as their land as opposed to the Northern states above the Mason-Dixie line.

In other words, some black enclaves in different states grew to house Southern sympathizers. The degree of choice varied among freedmen and slaves though not by much.

As a result, Confederate blacks came to see the North as a common enemy of their beloved South—a white "foreigner" "invader from the north coming to wreak havoc on their homeland. This sentiment reflected only one of the main reasons so many black soldiers wore gray uniforms at the start of the war but it was a significant one.

As a result, many white Confederates, primarily from small family farms believed these black Confederates to be the closest of friends and true companions, and, to a degree, vice versa. This is because they had grown up together and knew each other well.

Thus, when the moment came in the tumultuous spring of 1861, it was only natural for many blacks to fight with white Southerners for regional and national reasons rather than political ones. The Forgotten Ties that Bind the Civil War Generation's Black and White Men. This intimate family and kindred spirit that many Southern blacks and whites shared was not an exception or stereotype as many scholars and his-

torians have come to believe.

In fact, white Confederate soldiers, from lowly privates to high-ranking officers, often demonstrated a genuine familial-like sentiment toward blacks more than what was seen in a more truly intolerant era in overall relative terms after the Civil War. Such views have been fully revealed in their personal letters dated 1861 to 1865.

For example, the wartime correspondence of a member of the 24th South Carolina Infantry, like so many other Confederate soldiers' letters, have shown as much. In particular, James Adams Tillman, a native of the "red clay hills" of a plantation called Chester, run by his family and located south of Edgefield, South Carolina, became exceptionally close to his slave, Peter.

Peter's family lived in a rural community of "comfortable and well-kept slaves" in South Carolina. The plantation house was roughly a half-mile away from huts occupied by slaves. Peter fared better than James, who saw Northerners who developed and imposed Reconstruction in his state as taking advantage of its economic weakness after the war.

Aside from being stricken with malaise from the realities of Reconstruction, James died in 1866 as a result of complications from his combat wounds. Surely, this rarely-mentioned, familial-like closeness between some Southern blacks and whites weighed heavily into the outcomes of the war and Reconstruction.

Directory of African American Confederates in the U.S. Civil War

Name	Co.	Unit	Role	Notes
Aaron	A	36th Georgia Infantry	Private	P.O.W. At Fort McHenry Prison Camp, captured on 9 May, 1864 at Resin, GA.
Aaron	C	3rd Battalion Georgia	Musician	
Abraham	C	1st (Olmstead's) Georgia Infantry	Cook	
Abraham	B	63rd Regiment Georgia Infantry	Cook	
Alick	K	4th Regiment Georgia (Sumter Light Guards) Served as a Body Servant to LtCol. David Read Evans Winn	Body Servant	
August	C	1st (Olmstead's) Georgia Infantry	Cook	
Ben	A,B	1st Georgia Regiment		Slave of Walter Norton
Brahm		4th Regiment Georgia Cavalry (Clinch's)	Cook	Slave
Carolina (Female)	D	1st Battalion Georgia Sharp Shooters	Cook	
Charles	C	12th Battalion Georgia Light Artillery	Musician	
Charles		22nd Georgia Infantry	Private	
Charles	I	54th Regiment Georgia Infantry	Chief Cook	
Charles		8th Georgia Cavalry		
Edmund	C	11th Battalion Georgia Artillery (Sumter Artillery Battalion, 3' Corps) Served as a Teamster hauling wood Under Major. John Lane	Teamster	Slave
Ellen (Female)		5th Regiment Georgia Cavalry	Laundress	
Frank	B	18th Georgia Battalion (Savannah Guards Battalion) Served as a servant to his lifelong master and friend Capt. George W. Stiles	Musician Servant	Slave of Capt. George Washington Stiles
Frank	E	50th Georgia Infantry	Private	
George	F	4th Regiment Georgia Cavalry (Clinch's)	Cook	Slave
Georgia (Female)		5th Regiment Georgia Cavalry	Slave	Slave
Hattie (Female)		5th Regiment Georgia Cavalry	Slave	Slave
Henry	E	61st Georgia Infantry	Musician	
Henry (Harry)		Nelson's Independent Company Georgia Cavalry Served with Col. Thomas Page Nelson	Servant	
Isaiah	F	1st (Olmstead's) Georgia Infantry	Musician	
Jack	C	18th Battalion Georgia Infantry	Musician	
James	C	10th Georgia Infantry	Private	
James	A	12th Battalion Georgia Light Artillery	Musician	
James	C	18th Battalion Georgia Infantry	Cook	
James	I	45th Georgia Infantry	Private	
Jeff		Served as a laborer building trenches. He was one of between twenty and thirty slaves sent by his master to help the Confederacy.	Laborer	Slave of Mark Childress, Panola County, MS.
Jim	C	18th Battalion Georgia Infantry	Cook	

Directory of African American Confederates in the U.S. Civil War

Jim	C	1st Battalion Georgia Sharpshooter	Private & Musician	
Jim		1st Georgia Infantry (Olmstead's) (Gallie's Co.)	Private & Musician	
Jim		5th Georgia Cavalry	Private	
Jim	A	Phillips' Legion, Georgia	Drummer	
John	A	1st Battalion Georgia Sharp Shooters	Chief Cook	
John	E	44th Georgia Volunteer Infantry Served Under Capt. Connally	Body Servant	Slave of Capt. Connally
John	B	63rd Georgia Infantry	Drummer	
John		Cobb's Legion, Georgia Cavalry Served as a body servant to Maj. William G. Deloney	Body Servant	
Louis	C	1st Battalion Georgia Infantry	Musician	
Luke	B	63rd Georgia Infantry	Cook	
Marlborough	S	40th Regiment Georgia Infantry Served as a servant to Maj. Raleigh S. Camp. Also served the State of	Servant	
Morris	G	12th Regiment Georgia Infantry Served as a Body Servant to Henry W. Thomas	Body Servant	
Murphy		19th Regiment Georgia Infantry (Mabry's Company)	Servant	
Nathan		1st (Olmstead's) Georgia Infantry	Servant	Captured near Richmond and returned with two horses taken from the Union camp.
Peter	G	19th Georgia Infantry	Private	
Randall		Served as a laborer building trenches. He was one of between twenty and thirty slaves sent by his master to help the Confederacy.	Laborer	Slave of Mark Childress, Panola County, MS.
Ruben	D	1st Battalion Georgia Sharp Shooters	Cook	
Sandy	C	1st (Olmstead's) Georgia Infantry	Cook	
Scott		57th Regiment Georgia	Servant	Slave
Teeny (Female)		Empire Hotel Hospital, Atlanta, Georgia	Laundress	Slave of L. B. Davis
Tom		Col. Cummings Georgia Unit	Servant	
Wesley		9th Georgia Regiment	Private	His commander made a speech of Wesley volunteering to take up the arms of a white soldier, which the soldier had thrown away and ran. He stated "Such a deed is worthy of remembrance, and should inspire our soldiery with tenfold energy and courage, if possible, for if servants will do this, what may not be accomplished by the master?"
William	A	1st Battalion Georgia Sharp Shooters	Musician	
William		Empire Hotel Hospital, Atlanta, Georgia	Cook	Slave of R. Rogers

Directory of African American Confederates in the U.S. Civil War

Name		Unit	Role	Notes
Africanus, Scipio	B	18th Georgia Battalion (Dubose Brigade)	Cook	Surrendered at Appomattox
Atkinson, Tom		Unknown Georgia Unit Served as a Body Servant to his Master Mr. Atkinson	Body Servant	Slave of Mr. Atkinson of Butts County, GA. According to his son Jack Atkinson, in Georgia Slave Narratives.
Bailor, Ned (Baylor)		4th Georgia Regiment (Brunswick Riflemen)	Drummer	
Baldwin, James E.		Unknown Georgia Unit	Servant	P.O.W. at Camp Morton, Indiana, Died there and now buried at Greenfield Park, Indianapolis
Benger, Charles		2nd Battalion Georgia (Macon Volunteers) Served under Capt. George S. Jones	Musician Fifer	
Bennett, David H.	E	26th Regiment Georgia Infantry	Private	
Bennett, T.	D	1st Battalion Georgia Infantry	2nt Lt.	
Bentley, Moses		7th Regiment Georgia	Private	Slave
Billingsley, Saul		51st Georgia Infantry	Private	Lee County, MS Conf Pensioner
Black, Josephus		Served as a Musician and Servant to Gen. John B.	Musician Servant	
Black, Solomon		13th Battalion Georgia	Musician	
Boynton, George		64th Regiment Georgia infantry Served as a servant to Lt.	Servant	Slave, Attended the Dallas, Texas UCV Reunion 1906
Brahm, Stave		4th (Clinch's) Georgia Cavalry	Cook	Slave
Brice, George		Read's Independent Company	Musician	
Brook, John	A	1st Battalion, Georgia Sharpshooters	Chief Cook	
Brown, Alfred		Served as a Surgeon's Assistant	Surgeon's Assistat	Was wounded twice at the Battle of Chickamauga
Brown, John	A	1st Battalion Georgia Sharp Shooters	Chief Cook	
Burden, Augustus		First Division of Georgia Volunteers Served as a body servant to his master Gen. William H. T. Walker who was KIA at Chickamauga.	Body Servant	Slave of General William H. T. Walker, of Windsor Springs, GA. According to Arkansas Slave Narratives
Burroughs, Luke	B	63rd Georgia Infantry	Chief Cook	
Burroughs, Lydia (Female)	D	63rd Georgia Infantry	Cook	
Burroughs, Sam		13th Battalion Georgia	Cook	
Burroughs, Sanyan	K	63rd Georgia Infantry	Cook	
Burroughs, Sydney	D	63rd Georgia Infantry	Cook	
Calhoun, Isaac	A	12th Georgia Battalion Light Artillery (Newnan Guards) Served as a cook accompanying his master Col. J. D. Calhoun	Captain of Cooking Dept	Slave of Col. J. D. Calhoun of Coweta County, GA
Carter, Gilbert		Unknown Georgia Unit	Fifer	Covington, Georgia
Clark, James	K	28th Regiment Georgia Infantry	Fifer	FMC, Denied Confederate Pension, Emanuel County, GA.
Clay, Willis		27th Georgia Infantry	Private	Yazoo County, MS Conf Pensioner
Cobb, Jesse		Cobb's Legion Served as a servant to his master Brig Gen. Thomas R. R. Cobb who was KIA at Fredericksburg, VA.	Servant	Slave of BGen. Thomas R. R. Cobb, of Athens, GA. According to a fellow plantation slave, Susan Castle, in Georgia Slave Narratives.

Directory of African American Confederates in the U.S. Civil War

Collar, Unknown		Served as a servant to his master Frank Collar	Servant	Slave of Frank Collar, according to his nephew Marshal Butler, in Georgia Slave Narratives.
Davidson, William	C	1st (Olmstead's) Georgia Infantry	Drummer	
Davis, Bacchus		Read's Independent Company	Musician	
Davis, Ben	K	50th Georgia Volunteer Infantry Regiment (Brooks County Volunteers) Served as a body servant to Capt. Pliny Sheffield	Body Servant	Slave
Davis, John		Served as a carriage driver for President Jefferson	Carriage Driver	Slave
Dawson, Catherine (Female)	H	63rd Georgia Infantry	Cook	
Dawson, Hannah (Female)	H	63rd Georgia Infantry	Cook	
De Lyon, Charles Henry	A D	1st (Olmstead's) Georgia Infantry 63rd Regiment	Musician	
De Votie, Peter	G	2nd Battalion Georgia Regiment, (Columbus Guards)	Musician	
Dix, Albert		Served as a cook and servant to Tom Dix.	Cook	Slave of Tom Dix, according to Easter Jackson in Georgia Slave Narratives.
Dix, Scott		Served as a cook and servant to John Dix.	Cook	Slave of Torn Dix, according to Easter Jackson in Georgia Slave Narratives.
Doings, Bill	H	14th Georgia Infantry Regiment	Cook	
Downs, Auss		Served as a servant to his master's son, Pvt. William Downs	Servant	Slave of Sam Downs He had one of his fingers shot off. According to his daughter Dosia Harris, in the Georgia Slave Narratives.
Drake, Henry Clay		32nd Georgia Infantry	Private	Panda County, MS Conf Pensioner
Dwelle, George		1st (Olmstead's) Georgia Infantry	Drummer	
Elder, Richmond		Georgia Served as a Servant to Joe Elder	Servant	Slave
Ely, Mary (Female)	H	54th Regiment Georgia Infantry	Slave	Slave of 1st Lt M. B. Ely
Fox, Joe	A	63rd Regiment Georgia Volunteer Infantry	Musician Nurse	
Gardeen, Louis	A	18th Georgia Battalion (Dubose Brigade)	Musician	Surrendered at Appomattox
Gelzer, George W.		4th (Clinch's) Georgia Cavalry	Slave	
Gray, Austin		57th Georgia Infantry		Hinds County, MS Conf Pensioner
Green, Charles	M	26th Regiment Georgia Volunteer Infantry	Musician	
Griffin, Allen		Georgia, Served as a Body Servant to W. T. Harbaum	Body Servant	
Griffin, Butler		26th Georgia Infantry	Private	Shelby County, TN Conf Pension #C150
Griffin, Lucius		54th Regiment Georgia Infantry	Musician	
Harris, Alexander	C	1st (Olmstead's) Georgia Infantry	Drummer	

Name		Unit	Role	Notes
Harris, Ned		Unknown Georgia Unit		Slave of Mr. Harris. Fought at the Battle of Corinth, Mississippi, According to his grand-daughter Mary Gaines, in Arkansas Slave Narratives.
Harris, Peter	A	2nd Battalion Georgia Regiment, (Columbus Guards)	Drummer	
Harvey, Simeon T.		1st (Olmstead's) Georgia Infantry	Musician	
Hastin, J. G.		42nd Georgia Calvary		Monroe County, TN Conf Pension # C84
Hayne, Charles Doughterty	B	32nd Regiment Georgia Infantry	Pvt	FMC
Heard, Chris		Served as a servant to his master's son Tom Heard who was KIA.	Body Servant	Slave of General Heard, According to his nephew Robert Heard, in Georgia Slave Narratives.
Hicks, Charles (Charles Page)	F C	14th Regiment Georgia Served as a servant to his master's son, Lt. James H. Hicks Jr. **ALSO SERVED THE UNION** 110th U.S. Colored Volunteer Infantry	Servant Cook	Slave of James Hicks of Emanuel County, GA. He served the Confederacy then according to his statement he was drafted into the Union Army, he later received a Federal Veteran's pension and attended Veterans Reunions as both a Federal soldier and as an honorary Confederate Soldier.
Hicks, Thomas C.	D	2nd Battalion Georgia Regiment, (Columbus Guards)	Musician, Fifer	
Howell, Jesse		2nd Battalion Georgia Regiment, (Columbus	Musician	
James, Alfred		8th Georgia Cavalry		Leflore County, MS Conf Pensioner
Johnson, Benjamin		Served as a servant	Servant	Slave of Judge Luke Johnson, he was WIA as was his master.
Johnson, Gus		Cobb's Georgia Cavalry Legion	Cook	Yazoo County, MS Conf Pensioner, battle
Jones, Clairborne		Served as a servant and cook to his master Capt. John	Cook Servan	Slave of Captain John Wilson
Jones, Lymus		2nd Battalion Georgia Regiment, (Columbus Guards)	Musician	
Jones, Nelson	A	63rd Georgia Infantry	Nurse	
Laurence, John		Served as a butcher in Savannah Georgia for the	Butcher	
Lee, Ab	G	12th Regiment Georgia Infantry Served as a Body Servant to Capt Alexander S. Reid	Body Servant	
Lee, Clark		1st Regiment Georgia	Private	Hamilton County, TN Conf Pensioner Rcd # C107
Lee, Robert	D	22nd Battalion Georgia Heavy Artillery	Musician Cook	
Lery, John	A	18th Georgia Battalion (Dubose Brigade)	Cook	Surrendered at Appomattox
Massey, Anthony		22nd Georgia Artillery (Siege) Battalion		Tunica County, MS Conf Pensioner
Matthewson, George	E	12th Georgia Regiment Served as a Servant to Dr. W. P. Smallwood	Body Servant	Henry County, TN Conf Pension # C37 * Cross of Honor for Bravery in Action

Name	Co.	Unit	Role	Notes
May, Jerry M.		7th Georgia	Private	Slave of William Wynn of Monroe County, GA. Jerry May attended fourteen Veterans reunions, he later assisted Mrs. Wynn the widow of his old master to obtain a widow's pension.
McCleskey, Henry		1st (Olmstead's) Georgia Infantry	Musician	
McCord, Henry	F	30th Regiment Georgia Infantry	Servant	
Middleton, Maurice	E	1st (Olmstead's) Georgia Infantry	Musician	
Miller, Joseph	C	1st (Olmstead's) Georgia Infantry	Drummer	
Mitchell, Richmond	E	29th Regiment Georgia Infantry Served as a Body Servant to Capt. Robert G. Mitchell	Body Servant	
Moody, Frank		1st Battalion Georgia Cavalry (Hughes	Musician	
Morgan, Elisha	A	63rd Georgia Infantry	Nurse Laundress	
Morgan, Ellen	A	63rd Georgia Infantry	Nurse Laundres	
Morris, Ellen	A	63rd Georgia Infantry	Musician Laundres	
Moss, Henry Cato Smith, Henry		Unknown Georgia Unit Served as a servant to Lt. Moss	Servant	Slave of Lt. Moss of Washington, Wilkes County, GA. Lafayette County, MS Conf Denied Pension due too was not in service at the end of the war as he was sent home to his mistress when his master Lt. Moss was KIA.
Name not known		Served as a Confederate Hospital Attendant	Hospital Attendant	Buried in small cemetery near Madison, Georgia. His grave has a Confederate Veteran Headstone and listed as unknown veteran
Name Not known		Served as a body servant to Capt. Thomas E. King	Body Servant	Slave of Thomas E. King of Cobb County, GA.
Page, Alfred		32nd Regiment Georgia Infantry Served Under Capt. Sparks, served on Sullivan's Island, Charleston	Cook	Marion County, South Carolina Conf Pensioner App # 8052
Parkman, Joe	A	18th Georgia Battalion (Dubose Brigade)	Musician	Surrendered at Appomattox
Patillo, Jack		Carried Mail from West Point, Georgia to Whitesville, Georgia and offices in between.	Mail Carrier Teamster	Amherst County, Virginia Conf Pensioner
Patrick, Cornelius		19th Georgia Infantry		Chickasaw County, MS Conf Pensioner, wounded in battle.
Phillips, John		Phillips Legion Served as a Body Servant to Col. Phillips	Body Servant	
Pinks, Emanuel		Unknown Georgia Unit Served as a Body Servant to W. T. Harbaum	Body Servant	
Polk, James	B	18th Georgia Battalion (Dubose Brigade)	Cook	Surrendered at Appomattox
Presley, F. C.	E	23rd Regiment Georgia Infantry	Private	Admitted to Chimborazo Hospital 1862
Preston, Nat		11th Georgia Infantry	Servant	Leflore County, MS Conf Pensioner

Quarterman, Stepney		46th Georgia Infantry	Private	Leflore County, MS Conf Pensioner
Ragan, Gus		Capt. Van Den Corput's Company, Georgia Light Artillery Served as a servant to his master Mose Wright and died in the war.	Servant	Slave of Mr. Mose Wright of Oglethorpe County, GA. According to Mrs. Adeline Willis his sister in Arkansas Slave Narratives
Ranger, Abram	B	63rd Georgia Infantry	Assistant Cook	
Read, William	C	18th Georgia Battalion (Dubose Brigade)	Cook	Surrendered at Appomattox
Reynolds, Sam		Georgia Military Institute Served as a Body Servant to Cadet Homer V. Reynolds.	Body Servant	Cobb County, GA. At the Battle of Atlanta, Sam Reynolds returned to Powder Springs several times during the conflict to take supplies to Cadet Reynolds.
Rhodes, Thomas		2nd Battalion Georgia Regiment, (Columbus Guards)	Fifer	
Richards, Meshak		Served as a Laborer, helped lay railroad tracks from Atlanta to Macon so the Confederate soldiers and ammunition could move faster	Laborer	Slave of Jimpson Neals, of Pike County, GA. According to his brother, Shadrack Richards' statement in Georgia Slave Narratives
Richards, Shadrack (Shade)		Served as a Body Servant to his masters son, Jimmy Neals, and tending to his horses. They were at the battle of Appomattox and at the Surrender.	Body Servant	Slave of Jimpson Neals, of Pike County, GA. According to his statement in Georgia Slave Narratives
Riley, David	D	30th Regiment Georgia Infantry	Musician	
Ross, John	A	29th Regiment Georgia Infantry	Drummer	FMC, Deserted Nov 13, 1862.
Rucker, Amos		33rd Regiment Georgia Served as a servant to Col. Alexander Sandy" Rucker Staff of Gen. Patrick Cleburne Served as a servant to the first cousin D.C.J. Cleburne	Cook	Slave, Was WIA being left permanently crippled. Member of W.H.T Walker Camp U.C.V in Atlanta
Salter, Cason		61st Georgia Infantry	Servant	Newton County, MS Conf Pensioner
Sanders, William		3rd Georgia Hospital, Augusta, Georgia Servant Of Dr. J. B. Baxley	Body Servant	Barnwell County, South Carolina Conf Pensioner App # 1470
Savally, Henry	M	26th Regiment Georgia Volunteer Infantry	Musician	
Schley, Wesley	A	2nd Battalion Georgia Infantry	Musician	
Searcy, Shadrick	I	46th Georgia Infantry		Hamilton County, TN Conf Pensioner Rcd # C235
Shackelford, Elijah		10th Georgia Infantry	Private	Maury County, TN Conf Pension
Sheftall, Jackson B.		Served as a butcher in Savannah Georgia and at Fort Pulaksi for the Confederate Army	Butcher	
Sheftall, William	7	The German Volunteers, Georgia Artillery	Drummer	Possible POW?
Small, Neptune		Served as a body servant to his childhood friend Capt. Henry Lord King who was killed in action at the Battle of Fredericksburg.	Body Servant	Slave of Capt. Henry Lord King
Small, Sandy		Served as a butcher in Savannah Georgia for the Confederate Army	Butcher	

Name		Unit	Role	Notes
Stinson, Fred		3rd Georgia Infantry	Private	Grenada County, MS Conf Pensioner, battle injury.
Styles, W. H.		Unknown Georgia Unit	Private	Member of the Fulton County, Georgia Confederate Veterans Association
Summerlin, S.A.R.		Empire Hotel Hospital, Atlanta Georgia	Matron	
Thompson, Dick	H	1st Regiment Georgia Cavalry (Newnan Guards) Served as a Servant to Lavender R. Ray	Servant	
Thompson, Robert		12th Georgia Infantry	Wash And	Yalobusha County, MS Conf Pensioner
Todd, Elbert		4th Georgia Infantry	Regt Teamster	Panola County, MS Conf Pensioner
Towns, Phil		Served as a servant to John Towns, his master's son.	Servant	Slave of George Washington Bonaparte Towns (Gov.) of Talbot County, GA. According to his wife Jennie Butler (Crittenden) in Arkansas Slave Narratives.
Vinson, Solomon		Served as a servant to his master Capt. Ike Vinson who was KIA. Solomon then accompanied the body home.	Cook Servant	Slave of Captain Ike Vinson of Oconee County, GA. According to Mrs. Addie Vinson in Arkansas Slave Narratives, she lived on the same plantation.
Waddell, George	A	18th Georgia Battalior (Dubose Brigade;	Musician	Surrendered at Appomattox
Wallace, George	G	12th Regiment Georgia Infantry Served as a Body Servant to Capt Howard Tinsley	Body Servant	Surrendered with General Lee at Appomattox, later served in the Georgia Senate. After the war he served on the Georgia Senate
Walton, Pat		Served as a servant to his master's son Rosalius Walton.	Servant	Slave of Major John Walton of Talbot County, GA. According to Mrs. Dink Walton Young in Arkansas Slave Narratives, she was also a slave on the same plantation.
Waters, William	C	1st (Olmstead's) Georgia	Fifer	
Whittle, John	B	2nd Battalion Georgia Infantry	Musician	
Wiggins, William		47th Regiment Georgia Infantry	Private	
Wiley, Joe		7th Georgia Infantry		Lee County, MS Conf Pensioner
Williams, Edward		Unknown Georgia Unit	Body Servant	Slave from Rosville, Georgia. His master was KIA, Edward then served the Union and later served in the Spanish American War in Cuba.
Williams, Henry	B	18th Georgia Battalion (Dubose Brigade)	Musician	Surrendered at Appomattox
Woods, Henry		46th Georgia Infantry	Private	Yazoo County, MS Conf Pensioner
Yancey, George Washington	E	4th Georgia Infantry		Obion County, TN Conf Pension
Yopp, Bill (Ten Cent Bill)	H	14th Georgia Volunteer Infantry (Laurens County's Blackshear Guards) a Bo Servant to Capt. Thomas McCall Yopp	Body Servant Drummer	Slave, Member of Atlanta U.C.V. Camp
Young, William	C	1st (Olmstead's) Georgia Infantry	Drummer	

Georgia Department of Archives and History

5800 Jonesboro Road, Morrow, GA 30260 Telephone: (678) 364-3700
Web Site: www.georgiaarchives.org/

KANSAS

It appears that neither White nor African-American soldiers received pensions. What's left out of the facts was black confederate soldiers was engaged at the Island Mound skirmish despite the fact that it was not a big fight, proved to be a frightening foreshadowing for the Confederacy: Black troops had been blooded on the battlefield for the Union and Southern cause, and they proven to be up to the task.

Although the Emancipation Proclamation, initially issued by President Abraham Lincoln on September 22, 1862, did not go into force until January 1, 1863, the Island Mound Skirmish put to rest any doubts regarding African Americans' ability or willingness to fight.

Over 186,000 African Americans finally fought for the Union to eliminate slavery, proving that they could and did. When the 1st Kansas entered federal service on January 13, 1863, it was renamed the 1st Regiment Kansas Volunteer Infantry (Colored), and it was one of the first African American regiments in federal service.

Unfortunately, the 1st Kansas' two black commissioning confederate officers, Captain William Matthews and Lieutenant Patrick Minor, were obliged to relinquish their commissions when they entered federal service.

NAME	CO.	UNIT	RANK	SLAVE / FREE MISC
Level!, Samuel		Unknown Kansas Unit Served as a servant to an officer	Servant	Scott, Kansas., P.O.W.
				at Alton Military Prison, in Alton, Illinois transferred to St. Louis, Missouri on Mar 3 1865.
Sargeant, William J.	C	7th Kansas Cavalry	Private	
Shook, Edward	A	8th Kansas Infantry	Under Cook	
Shook, Isaac	A	8th Kansas Infantry	Under Cook	

Kansas Historical Society

6425 SW 6th Avenue, Topeka KS 66615-1099
(Telephone) 785-272-8681, www.kshs.org/p/genealogy-indexes/18943

KENTUCKY

Combative black confederate soldiers die in prison

BLACK CONFEDERATES APPEARS ON THE LIST OF DEAD AT CAMP DOUGLAS, ILLINOIS

Appearing in the Memphis (Tennessee) Appeal of October 8, 1863 is a list of those who died as Confederate P.O.W's at Camp Douglas, Illinois.

Among the dead are a young Black Confederate, Hardin Blackwell of Ward's Company, 3rd Kentucky, who died of gunshot wounds. Although this article mentions the "excellent sanitary arrangements" at Camp Douglas, it is now documented that black prisoners in this camp died in great numbers.

The Confederate Pension Act, passed by the Kentucky General Assembly on March 4, 1912, gave financial assistance to destitute and handicapped Confederate veterans and their widows.

Each application typically includes the veteran's date and place of birth, as well as his unit designation and service period.

Our father sent me to get you.

Prior to the American Civil War, some Southerners attempted to Christianize black slaves.

Southern preachers responded to abolitionists' calls for an end to slavery by declaring that the "peculiar institution" was a sacred trust imposed on the South by traffickers from Britain and the Northern states. Slavery, some claimed, was imposed by God as a punishment for African idolatry.

In their view, if the South had been commissioned by God to establish a Christian republic, it was only natural that its victory in the war would be contingent on God's blessing. Slave children intially came to the Lexington Presbyterian Church to attend Sunday school in the autumn of 1855. The administrator of this ministry was Thomas J. "Stonewall" Jackson, a professor at the Virginia Military Institute.

Even though it was against Virginia law to teach blacks to read and write, Jackson thought that all, regardless of race, should learn to do both.

Professor Jackson was a leader and mentor to these children. He provided money to his students for Bibles and hymnals. Many of Jackson's Sunday-school students moved on to higher education because of his guidance. Some also became ministers of the Gospel.

Dave	A	8th Kentucky Cavalry Served as a Body Servant to Capt. Thomas W. McCann	Body Servant	Slave
George	B	7th Kentucky Mounted Infantry	Cook	
Henry	F	12th Kentucky Cavalry	Cook	
Henry	B	7th Kentucky Mounted Infantry	Cook	
Jacob	E	12th Kentucky Cavalry	Cook	
Jim		2nd Kentucky Regiment Served as a Servant to Col. Roger Hanson	Servant	Both were P.O.W.'s at Camp Chase, Ohio and Camp Morton, Indianapolias.
Jim	M	3rd Regiment, Kentucky Mounted Infantry	Cook	
Jim		8th Kentucky Cavalry Served as a Body Servant to Col. Roy S. Cluke	Body Servant	Slave
Jimmie	K	1st Kentucky Cavalry Regiment	Private	Princeton, KY
Jo		8th Kentucky Cavalry Served as a Body Servant to Maj. Robert S. Bullock	Body Servant	Slave
John		8th Kentucky Cavalry Served as a Body Servant to Pvt. Sam Downing	Body Servant	Slave
John	Q	8th Kentucky Cavalry Served as a Body Servant to Capt William E. Currey	Body Servant	Slave
, Lewis		8th Kentucky Cavalry Served as a Body Servant to Pvt's John and James W.	Body Servant	Slave
, Old Box		Morgan's Raiders Served as a servant to Gen. John Hunt Morgan	Servant	
, Richard III		8th Kentucky Cavalry Served as a Body Servant to, Adj. Thomas E. Eastin	Body Servant	Slave
, Sam	U	3rd Kentucky Mounted Infantry	Cook	
, Sam	A,C	3rd Kentucky Mounted Infantry	Cook	
, Sanford		8 Kentucky Cavalry Served as a Body Servant to, Pvt. Albert Dudley	Body Servant	Slave
, Sol	A	8th Kentucky Cavalry Served as a Body Servant to, Lt. Richard A. Spurr	Body Servant	Slave
, Thomas	B	7th Kentucky Mounted Infantry	Cook	
, William	C	4th Kentucky Cavalry Served under Lt. Thomas C. Blackwell	Body Servant	Slave
Allen, Marcus	Q	8th Kentucky Cavalry		FMC
Anderson, Ike	A	1st Kentucky Calvary		Stewart County, TN Conf Pension # C96, application rejected.
Battle, Hardin	G	7th Kentucky Cavalry	Private	
Bell, Zack Taylor	Q	8th Kentucky Cavalry		FMC
Boyd, George Washington		2nd Kentucky Cavalry		McMinn County, TN Conf Pension Rcd # C281

Brooks, George St.Pierre	I	7th Kentucky Cavalry Served as a Servant to Capt. Scofield his master's son-in-law. **ALSO SERVED 3rd Regiment United States Colored Cavalry**	Servant	Was captured by the 7th Ohio Cavalry and became a Soldier for the Union.
Childers, John		General Lyon's, 8th Kentucky Regiment	Servant	Grenada County, MS Conf Pensioner
Chin, Otello	Q	8th Kentucky Cavalry		FMC
Christian, 1	D	2nd Kentucky Cavalry (Morgan's)	Servant	P.O.W. at Camp Morton, Indiana, Died there and now buried at Greenfield Park, Indianapolis
Christian, Mason	Q	8th Kentucky Cavalry		FMC
Clarke, Unknown (Four Brothers)		Unknown Kentucky Unit		Slaves of Judge Toll of Henderson Kentucky. According to Anna Smith their sister in Ohio Slave Narratives. Her oldest brother was 50 when he joined the confederate army. Three other brothers were sent to the front. One was an ambulance attendant, one belonged to the cavalry, one an orderly sergeant and the other joined the infantry. All were killed in action.
Copeland, Ike		Served as a servant to Gen. Hiram B. Lyon	Servant	From Western Kentucky, Died in June 1904. He liked attending the Veteran Reunions. A home was provided to him by Gen. Lyon.
Crystal, Jim	Q	8th Kentucky Cavalry		FMC
Dortch, Charles	C	2nd Kentucky Calvary		Montgomery County, TN Conf Pension # C152, application rejected.
Gess, Milton	Q	8th Kentucky Cavalry Served as a servant to John Gess	Servant	Freed Slave
Gross, Labbs		Unknown Kentucky Unit		Louisa County, KY. P.O.W at the U.S. P.O.W. General Field Hospital, Department of the Cumberland
Jones, George	G	3rd Kentucky Mounted Infantry Served as a servant to Capt. Tipford Edwards	Servant	Lafayette County, MS Conf Pension not approved
Leavell, Rafe		Served as a servant to his master Marshall Leavell	Servant	Slave, From Christian County, KY
Marshall, Henry	B	14th Kentucky Cavalry	Servant	P.O.W. in Camp Chase, Ohio and Camp Douglas, Illinois. Was 14 yrs old KIA upon arriving at Camp Chase.
Martin, John		9th Kentucky Cavalry Served as a Body Servant and cook to his master Vince Browning	Body Servant Cook	Slave of Vince Browning, Tazewell County, VA Conf Pensioner
Pig, Joe	Q	8th Kentucky Cavalry		FMC
Prewet, John	Q	8th Kentucky Cavalry		FMC
Rowe, Will		2nd Kentucky Calvary		Henry County, TN Conf Pension Rcd # c249
Scott, Eli	Q	8th Kentucky Cavalry		FMC

Peter Vertrees, a Confederate black soldier- Kenneth C. Thomson of Bowling Green, Kentucky, has written many articles about This African American Rev. Peter Vertrees. "Years have gone since his death, but Peter Vertrees, a Baptist pastor and Confederate soldier [of the Seventh Kentucky Cavalry], lives on in the lives of those he touched," This well-known guy was a member of the fabled "Orphan Brigade" and wrote an autobiography for his wife Diora. He talks about his adventures as a sergeant and bodyguard in the Army of Tennessee's various campaigns, as well as his sixty-year ministry to the people of his adoptive state of Tennessee. "Black Soldier of the Confederacy: The Life and Legacy of Peter Vertrees, a Kentucky Orphan," by Scott E. Sallee, published in the June 1990 edition of Blue & Gray Magazine (Vol. VIII, No. 5). Identification of a Missouri Black Confederate. A 1993 publication entitled Branded as Rebels by Joanne Chiles Eakin and Donald R. Hale. Black Soldier of the Confederacy -- Peter Vertrees Rev. Peter Vertrees is the subject of several articles by Kenneth C. Thomson of Bowling Green, Kentucky. Mr. Thomson writes, "Years have passed since his death but the enduring legacy of Peter Vertrees, a Baptist minister and Confederate soldier [of the Seventh Kentucky Cavalry] lives in the lives of those he touched. This prominent gentleman served with the famed "Orphan Brigade," and dedicated an autobiography to his wife Diora.

Directory of African American Confederates in the U.S. Civil War

He mentions his experiences as a servant and bodyguard in the many campaigns of the Army of Tennessee and his ministry of over sixty years to the people of his adopted state of Tennessee. Scott E. Sallee's article entitled "Black Soldier of the Confederacy: The Life and Legacy of Peter Vertrees, a Kentucky Orphan" appeared in the June 1990 (Vol. VIII, No. 5) issue of the Blue & Gray Magazine. The following excerpt is courtesy of Mr. Sallee. In summing up his four years of service in the Confederate army, Peter wrote: Those days of conflict made a very great change in me at first but proved helpful to

me in the end... The many, many things which I learned in the service helped me in after years to know how to deport myself and bring credit to myself and those with whom I am cast .... [They] gave me a vision of the future which I could not have gotten otherwise.

My heart was touched with divine love and my life was inspired for nobler things. Those days of bitter conflict made lasting impressions on my mind. Never can I forget Shiloh and Vicksburg.

Smith, Unknown		Unknown Kentucky Unit	Private	He was KIA, according to his wife Anna Smith in Ohio Slave Anna Smith's husband later joined the war and was reported killed.
Spurr, Cleet	Q	8th Kentucky Cavalry	Private	FMC
Spurr, Juno	Q	8th Kentucky Cavalry	Private	FMC
Tyson, Alfred	B	12th Kentucky Calvary		Madison County, TN Conf Pension Rcd # C119
Vance, J. W.		CSA Mail Carrier, Kentucky	Mail Carrier	P.O.W. at Camp Morton, Indiana, Died there and now buried at Greenfield Park, Indianapolis
Veel, Jim	Q	8th Kentucky Cavalry	Private	FMC
Vertrees, Peter		6th Kentucky Calvary "Orphan Brigade" Dr. John Luther Vertrees	Cook Bodyguard Surgeon's Assistant	Sumner County, TN Conf Pension # C36. Peter was of mixed race, and accompanied his uncle Dr. John Luther Vertrees to war.
Webber, Lee	F	2nd Kentucky Calvary	Private	Shelby County, TN Conf Pension # C85
Wilson, Pempy	Q	8th Kentucky Cavalry	Private	

Kentucky Department for Libraries and Archives Research Room
300 Coffee Tree Road Frankfort, KY 40601 Telephone: 502-564-8704

LOUISIANA

The 1st Louisiana Native Guard (also known as the Corps d'Afrique) was one of the first all-black regiments in the Union Army. Based in New Orleans, Louisiana, it played a prominent role in the Siege of Port Hudson. Its members included a minority of free men of color from New Orleans; most were African-American former slaves who had escaped to join the Union cause and gain freedom. A Confederate regiment by the same name served in the Louisiana militia made up entirely of free men of color.Louisiana began paying destitute Confederate veterans or their widows' annuities in 1898. The Louisiana Division of Archives in Baton Rouge has microfilm of the applications and an index. This set of 152 microfilm rolls is owned by the Historical Genealogy Department. On their website, the Louisiana State Archives offers an index of these pension applications.

Although it appears that no pensions were awarded to African-Americans, I have included the information from the State Library and Archives below since some Mulatto males may have served as white men and obtained a pension? You must, however, know the name of the person you're looking for.

An alphabetical list of applicant names may be found online, and copies can be obtained through the Louisiana State Archives.

A user can also go to the LOUISIANA STATE ARCHIVES — GENEALOGY & HISTORY SECTION, Confederate Pension Applications Index Database, via the link below. Name Search by Alphabetical Order

NAME	CO.	UNIT	RANK	SLAVE I FREE MISC
Adam		Capt. Greenleaf's Company, (Orleans Light Horse), Louisiana Cavalry	Trumpeter	
Bernard	H	Orleans Fire Regiment, Louisiana Militia	A Surg	

The chickens have come home to roost

A copy is Available at newsoff...

This particular Confederate regiment contained members who could switch sides to join the all-black units of the Union Army: poor treatment by white soldiers and difficult field conditions resulted in many black officers and enlisted soldiers resigning from and deserting the 1st Louisiana Native Guard Corps.

In April 1864, the 1st Louisiana Native Guard was dissolved and its members joined the newly organized 73rd and 74th regiments of the U.S. Colored Troops of the Union Army.

It was based in New Orleans, Louisiana, and played a prominent role in the siege of Port Hudson. Its members included some free men of color from New Orleans; most were black former slaves who had escaped to join the Union cause and gain freedom.

After New Orleans fell to Admiral Farragut in April 1862, Union Major Benjamin F. Butler headquartered his 12,000-man Army of the Gulf in New Orleans.

On Sept. 17, 1862, Butler organized the Union Army's 1st Louisiana Native Guard regiment, some of whose members had served in the previous Confederate Native Guard regiment.

26B

Bill		3rd Louisiana Battalion,	Servant	Slave of Pvt William E. Towles, Pvt Towels was killed in a train wreck at Chunky Creek in 1863 Bill carried his body to be buried at Bayou Sara, Louisiana.
Dandy	E	7th Louisiana Infantry Served as a Servant of Cpl. James Stubb.	Cook Servant	Slave of Cpl. James Stubb
Dater	A	Fire Battalion Louisiana Militia		
Felix		Capt. Fenner's Battery, Louisiana Light Artillery	Cook Private	
George		Capt. Fenner's Battery, Louisiana Light Artillery	Cook Private	
Jake		Capt. Fenner's Battery, Louisiana Light Artillery	Cook Private	
Joe		Capt. Fenner's Battery, Louisiana Light Artillery	Cook Private	
John	B	22nd and 23rd Louisiana Infantry	Cook	
Jordan		Bridge's Battery, Louisiana Light Artillery	Private	P.O.W. Paroled at Greensboro, N. C.
Octave		Capt. Fenners Battery, Louisiana Light Artillery	Cook Private	
Oll Bruce	D	11th Louisiana Infantry	Laundress	
Sam	E	7th Louisiana Infantry Holster Served as a Servant of Cpl. James Stubb.	Servant	Slave of Cpl. James Stubb
Sam	G	1st Louisiana Heavy Artillery	Cook	
Stephen		Capt. Fenners Battery, Louisiana Light Artillery	Cook Priv	
Stewart		16th Louisiana Infantry Regiment Served as a servant to his master Capt. E. John Ellis	Servant	Slave of Captain E. John Ellis
Will	I	Orleans Guards Regiment, Louisiana	Private	
Adams, John	H	6th Regiment Louisiana Cavalry (Capt. Robert B. Love's	Private	FMC
Adams, Sam		17th Louisiana Infantry	Servant	Issacuena County, MS Conf Pensioner
Battise (Battest), Lawrence		4th Louisiana Cavalry	Cock	Washington County, MS Conf Pensioner
Baucum, Sam	G	1st Regiment, Louisiana Heavy Artillery (Regulars)	Cook Wagoner	Slave of Pvt. William Baucum, Co. G, 6th La. Arty P.O.W. Paroled Meridian, Miss
Blum, Henry	B	Donaldson Artillery	Cook	Surrendered at Appomattox
Butler, Jerry		2nd Louisiana Cavalry	Servant	Tate County, MS Conf Pensioner
Carnine, Levy		2nd Louisiana Infantry (De Soto Pelican Rifles) Served as a servant to Dr. Hogan	Cook Servant	Slave, also a Veteran of the Florida Indian War.
Carr, Tom		1st Louisiana Cavalry	Private	Wilkinson County, MS Conf Pensioner
Clapp, Willis		Unknown Louisiana Unit	Private	Slave of Warren Offord of Mer Rouge, Louisiana. He was KIA. According to his daughter Annie Parker in Arkansas Slave Narratives.

Directory of African American Confederates in the U.S. Civil War

Dowty, Lewis	G	Crescent Regiment, Louisiana Infantry	Servant Laundres	
Dudley, Monroe		1st Louisiana Light Artillery		Hinds County, MS Conf Pensioner
Fleming, Peter	G	Crescent Regiment, Louisiana Infantry	Servant Laundres	
Gardner, Jesse	H	6th Regiment Louisiana Cavalry (Capt. Robert B. Love's Company)	Private	FMC
Gardner, William	H	6th Regiment Louisiana Cavalry (Capt. Robert B. Love's Company)	Private	FMC
Garrett, Louis		15th Louisiana Infantry	Servant	Hinds County, MS Conf
Gaskins, George		1st Louisiana Light Artillery		Jefferson County, MS Conf Pensioner
Grappe, Gabriel	H	Capt. Thomas W. Fuller's Bossier Cavalry Company 6th Regiment Louisiana Cavalry (Capt. Robert B. Love's Company)	Private Teamster	FMC
Grappe, McGhee (Margil)	H	6th Regiment Louisiana Cavalry (Capt. Robert B.	Private	FMC
Guillory Jr., Evariste	I	2nd Louisiana Reserve Corps (Capt. M. McDavitt)	Private	FMC
Guillory Sr., Evariste	I	2nd Louisiana Reserve Corps (Capt. M.	Private	FMC
Harris, G. D.		3rd Louisiana Cavalry	Servant	Warren County, MS Conf Pensioner
Hawkins, Albert		4th Louisiana Cavalry		Adams County, MS Conf Pensioner, he was wounded in battle.
Herndon, Joseph		Louisiana Infantry Servant and son of Capt. John David	Servant	
Hill, W. H.	A	17th Louisiana Infantry		Arkansas, Columbia County Conf Pension, application #26059 his application was denied
Jackson, Andrew		16th Louisiana Infantry		Pike County, MS Conf Pensioner
Jackson, Sam		4th Louisiana Infantry	Servant	Claiborne County, MS Conf Pensioner
Jones, George		1st Louisiana Cavalry		Lincoln County, MS Conf Pensioner
Lathrop, H. S.		Captain Hutton's Co., (Crescent Arty. Co., A,)	Servant	
Lattier, Clark	E	1st Louisiana Heavy Artillery (Regulars)	Cook	Slave of Pvt. F. C. Lattier
Leport, L.	B	Donaldson Artillery	Servant	Surrendered at Appomattox
Lutz, Charles F.	F	8th Louisiana Infantry (Capt. James C. Pratt's Opelousas Guards)	Private	FMC, wounded in left arm and became a P.O.W., St Landry Parish, LA Conf pensioner, he passed as a white man he was a mulatto. Received his pension in 1900.
Mamply, John (Jonathan	B	Donaldson Artillery	Servant	Surrendered at Appomattox
Monroe, J.	G	7th Regiment, Louisiana Infantry	Servant	
Nance, George		4th Louisiana Infantry	Regt Teamster	Holmes County, MS Conf Pensioner
Noble, Jordan B.		Capt. Noble's Company, (Planche Guards), Louisiana Militia	Captain	FMC

Name		Unit	Rank	Notes
Perez, Sylvester	H	6th Regiment Louisiana Cavalry (Capt. Robert **B.** Love's	Private	FMC of Spanish and African Ancestry.
Perot, Alphonse	H	6th Regiment Louisiana Cavalry (Capt. Robert B. Love's Company)	Private	FMC
Perot, Joseph G.	**H**	**6**th Regiment Louisiana Cavalry (Capt. Robert B. Love's	Private	FMC
Perry, John		10th Louisiana Infantry	Servant	Hinds County, MS Conf Pensioner
Phelps, Thomas A.	D	5th RegimentLouisiana Infantry (De Soto Rifles) Served as a servant to Capt. Kountz	Servant	Slave, He wrote a letter home stating "I will leave...today for a scout about the woods for the Yankees...Give my love to mistress and master...P.S. Good by to the white folks until I kill a Yankee." "Published in the New Orleans Crescent"
Pierre-Auguste, Jean Baptiste	I	29th Louisiana Volunteer Infantr (Capt. James W. Bryan's Company)	Cook Private	FMC, St Landry Parish, LA Conf pensioner, he received his pension in 1915.
Pierre-Auguste, Lufoy	K	16th Louisiana Infantry Regiment (Captain Daniel Gober's Big Cane Rifles)	Private	FMC, from St. Landry Parish
Price, Henry		12th Louisiana Infantry	Private	Hinds County, MS Conf Pensioner
Robinson, Benson		4th Louisiana Cavalry	Private	Warren County, MS Conf Pensioner
Robinson, Marshall		16th Louisiana Infantry	Servant	Issaquena County, MS Conf Pensioner
Semple, John (Jonathan)	B	Donaldson Artillery	Servant	Surrendered at Appomattox
Slocum, Richard		3rd Louisiana Cavalry	Private	Washington County, MS Conf Pensioner
Spots, Thomas	A	21st Regiment, Louisiana Infantry (Patton's)	Cook	
Spotts, John	A	21st Regiment, Louisiana Infantry (Patton's)	Cook	
Strother, Tom		9th Louisiana infantry Served as a servant to Col. Richard Taylor	Body Servant	Slave of Col. Richard Taylor
Vernon, Samuel		16th Louisiana Infantry	Private	Marion County, MS Conf Pensioner
Webb, Steve		7th Louisiana Infantry	Servant	Bolivar County, MS Conf Pensioner
Webre, Theophile	E	18th Louisiana Infantry	Private	
Williams, George (1) Sr.		Watson Louisiana Light Artillery		Sunflower County, MS Conf Pensioner, non-battle injury
Williams, George (2)		Watson Louisiana Light Artillery	Servant	Sunflower County, MS Conf Pensioner
Wingfield, Miles		3rd Louisiana Cavalry	Private	Bolivar County, MS Conf Pensioner
Witt, Rube		Unknown Louisiana Unit	Private	Slave of Jess Witt of Harrison County, Texas. Enlisted in the Conf Army but the *war* ended before he could fight. According to his statements in Texas Slave Narratives.
Woods, Edward W.D.	G	Crescent Regiment, Louisiana Infantry	Servant Laundres	

The 1st Louisiana Native Guard was the Confederate Army's first designated black unit. When Louisiana Governor Thomas Overton Moore accepted a regiment of around 1,100 free African American men into the state military, the Guard was founded. When Governor Moore called for soldiers to defend Louisiana on April 17, 1861, a group of 10 prominent New Orleans free blacks convened a conference on April 22 at the city's Catholic Institute to declare their support for the Confederate cause. The assembly drew over 2,000 individuals, including 1,500 free blacks who signed a militia muster roll.

The Promotion

For black Confederate Civil War soldiers, "seeing the elephant" meant experiencing combat for the first time and all cooks were promoted at battle as soldiers when time and resources were short and the army needed surge capacity.

The Confederate soldiers of the Civil War were often hungry. They mostly ate hard crackers made from flour, water and salt called hardtack. Sometimes, they would also get salt pork or corn meal to eat. To supplement their meals, soldiers would also forage from the land around them. They would hunt game and gather fruit, berries and nuts whenever they could.

By the end of the war, many soldiers in the Confederate army were on the verge of starvation. Food shortages and military privation contributed in part to the Confederate mystique.

Directory of African American Confederates in the U.S. Civil War

On May 2, 1861, Governor Moore accepted their services and established the 1st Louisiana Native Guard Regiment. The Native Guard's first members were all Creoles who spoke French. Successful architects, brick masons, dentists, physicians, and carpenters were among those who joined the militia.

Regimental commanders were selected by the Governor, but company commanders were picked from the ranks of the unit by Creoles. Lieutenant Andre Cailloux was one of these Creole commanders, and he would subsequently join the Louisiana Native Guard Union unit, where he would die in a charge against Confederate soldiers at Port Hudson in 1863.

Lieutenant Morris W. Morris, who had previously served in the 1st Louisiana Native Guard (USA) Regiment, was also among the officers. Lt. Morris held the distinction of being the Confederate Army's only black Jewish officer and afterwards the Union Army's sole black Jewish officer.

Despite the early excitement for the Confederate cause among New Orleans' free men of color, both local and national Confederate authorities were wary of having black troops in their ranks. Because the 1st Louisiana Native Guard was never furnished with uniforms or guns, most of the soldiers had to rely on their own resources for clothes and weaponry.

The Louisiana State Legislature approved a statute requiring militia members to be white in January 1862. The 1st Louisiana Native Guard was dissolved on February 16, 1862.

The US Army and Navy commanders accepted the surrender of New Orleans two months later, on April 26, 1862. Major General Benjamin Franklin Butler addressed several members of the Guard about fighting the Confederates. About ten percent of them accepted his offer, and the 1st Louisiana Native Guard, USA was formed in September 1862.

NAME	CO	UNIT	RANK	ALL ARE FREE MEN OF COLOR MISC NOTES
Armant		1st Louisiana Native Guards, LA Militia	Private	Free Men of Color (FMC)
Boutte		1st Louisiana Native Guards, LA Militia	Private	Free Men of Color (FMC)
Popo		1st Louisiana Native Guards, LA Militia	Private	Free Men of Color (FMC)
Abelard, Joseph		1st Louisiana Native Guards, LA Militia	Sergean	Free Men of Color (FMC)
Achille, Joseph		1st Louisiana Native Guards, LA Militia	Private	Free Men of Color (FMC)
Adam, Antonio		1st Louisiana Native Guards, LA Militia	Private	Free Men of Color (FMC)
Adam, Manuel	A	1st Louisiana Native Guards, LA Militia	Private	Free Men of Color (FMC)
Adams, Emele		1st Louisiana Native Guards, LA Militia	Private	Free Men of Color (FMC)
Adolph, George		1st Louisiana Native Guards, LA Militia	Private	Free Men of Color (FMC)
Aibrier, Jean		1st Louisiana Native Guards, LA Militia	Private	Free Men of Color (FMC)
Alcide, Joseph		1st Louisiana Native Guards, LA Militia	Private	Free Men of Color (FMC)
Aldine, Louis		1st Louisiana Native Guards, LA Militia	Private	Free Men of Color (FMC)
Allian, Jesse		1st Louisiana Native Guards, LA Militia	Private	Free Men of Color (FMC)
Alugas, Geronne		1st Louisiana Native Guards, LA Militia	Private	Free Men of Color (FMC)
Alvez, Louis		1st Louisiana Native Guards, LA Militia	Private	Free Men of Color (FMC)
Ambuster, Achille		1st Louisiana Native Guards, LA Militia	Private	Free Men of Color (FMC)
Amont, J.		1st Louisiana Native Guards, LA Militia	Private	Free Men of Color (FMC)
Andre, Oscar		1st Louisiana Native Guards, LA Militia	Private	Free Men of Color (FMC)
Angelain, G.		1st Louisiana Native Guards, LA Militia	Private	Free Men of Color (FMC)
Angelain, L.		1st Louisiana Native Guards, LA Militia	Corporal	Free Men of Color (FMC)
Anson, Fanshu		1st Louisiana Native Guards, LA Militia	Private	Free Men of Color (FMC)
Antoine, Anthony		1st Louisiana Native Guards, LA Militia	Corporal	Free Men of Color (FMC)
Antoine, Engea		1st Louisiana Native Guards, LA Militia	Private	Free Men of Color (FMC)
Antoine, Joseph		1st Louisiana Native Guards, LA Militia	Private	Free Men of Color (FMC)
Armand, Adolph		1st Louisiana Native Guards, LA Militia	Private	Free Men of Color (FMC)
Armand, J.		1st Louisiana Native Guards, LA Militia	Private	Free Men of Color (FMC)
Armand, Joseph		1' Louisiana Native Guards, LA Militia	Private	Free Men of Color (FMC)
Armand, They		1st Louisiana Native Guards, LA Militia	Private	Free Men of Color (FMC)
Armstrong, Joseph		1st Louisiana Native Guards, LA Militia	Private	Free Men of Color (FMC)
Arnot, H. Z.		1st Louisiana Native Guards, LA Militia	Private	Free Men of Color (FMC)

Directory of African American Confederates in the U.S. Civil War

Arrit, Prasrer		1st Louisiana Native Guards, LAMilitia	Corporal	Free Men of Color (FMC)
Aubert, Charles		1st Louisiana Native Guards, LAMilitia	Sergeant	Free Men of Color (FMC)
August, Adolph		1st Louisiana Native Guards, LA	Private	Free Men of Color (FMC)
Auguste, Joseph		1st Louisiana Native Guards, LA	Private	Free Men of Color (FMC)
Auguste, Mertile		1st Louisiana Native Guards, LA	Private	Free Men of Color (FMC)
Auguste, Pierre		1st Louisiana Native Guards, LA	Private	Free Men of Color (FMC)
Auguste, T.		1st Louisiana Native Guards, LA	Private	Free Men of Color (FMC)
Augustin, Felix		1st Louisiana Native Guards, LAMilitia	Private	Free Men of Color (FMC)
Augustin, James		1st Louisiana Native Guards, LAMilitia	Corporal	Free Men of Color (FMC)
Augustin, Omer		1st Louisiana Native Guards, LAMilitia	Sgt Maj	Free Men of Color (FMC)
Auld, J.		1st Louisiana Native Guards, LAMilitia	Private	Free Men of Color FMC)
Avril, Estave		1st Louisiana Native Guards, LAMilitia	Private	Free Men of Color FMC)
Avril, Gabriel		1st Louisiana Native Guards, LAMilitia	Private	Free Men of Color FMC)
Avril, Ogeraald		1st Louisiana Native Guards, LAMilitia	Private	Free Men of Color (FMC)
Avril, P.		1st Louisiana Native Guards, LAMilitia	Private	Free Men of Color (FMC)
Aycart, J.		1st Louisiana Native Guards, LAMilitia	Private	Free Men of Color FMC)
Azemar, Joseph		1st Louisiana Native Guards, LAMilitia	Private	Free Men of Color (FMC
Balon, Benjamin		1st Louisiana Native Guards, LAMilitia	Private	Free Men of Color (FMC)
Bandur, S.		1st Louisiana Native Guards, LAMilitia	Private	Free Men of Color (FMC)
Barja, Dutreinl		1st Louisiana Native Guards, LAMilitia	Private	Free Men of Color (FMC)
Bartchy, James		1st Louisiana Native Guards, LAMilitia	Private	Free Men of Color (FMC)
Bartchy, Oscar		1st Louisiana Native Guards, LAMilitia	Private	Free Men of Color (FMC)
Barthaut, A.		1st Louisiana Native Guards, LA	Private	Free Men of Color (FMC)
Barthe, John		1st Louisiana Native Guards, LAMilitia	1st Lt	Free Men of Color (FMC)
Bazanac, Alphonse		1st Louisiana Native Guards, LAMilitia	Private	Free Men of Color (FMC)
Beaulien, J. B.		1st Louisiana Native Guards, LAMilitia	Corporal	Free Men of Color (FMC)
Bebelle, Joseph		1st Louisiana Native Guards, LAMilitia	Private	Free Men of Color (FMC)
Bedont, G.		1st Louisiana Native Guards. LAMilitia	Corporal	Free Men of Color (FMC)
Belain, Lowis		1st Louisiana Native Guards, LAMilitia	Private	Free Men of Color (FMC)
Bell, James		1st Louisiana Native Guards, LAMilitia	Private	Free Men of Color (FMC)
Belot, A.		1st Louisiana Native Guards, LAMilitia	Private	Free Men of Color (FMC)
Belot, Oelave		1st Louisiana Native Guards, LAMilitia	Private	Free Men of Color (FMC)
Belot, V.	C	1st Louisiana Native Guards, LAMilitia	Private	Free Men of Color (FMC)
Benjamin, A.		1st Louisiana Native Guards, LAMilitia	Private	Free Men of Color (FMC)
Benjamin, Antoine		1st Louisiana Native Guards, LAMilitia	Private	Free Men of Color (FMC)
Benot, Joseph		1st Louisiana Native Guards, LAMilitia	Private	Free Men of Color (FMC)
Bercier, Manuel		1st Louisiana Native Guards, LAMilitia	Private	Free Men of Color (FMC)
Bercy, Donald		1st Louisiana Native Guards, LAMilitia	Private	Free Men of Color (FMC)
Bernard, Euctide		1st Louisiana Native Guards, LAMilitia	Private	Free Men of Color (FMC)
Bernard, J.		1st Louisiana Native Guards, LAMilitia	Private	Free Men of Color (FMC)
Bernard, Joseph		1st Louisiana Native Guards, LAMilitia	Private	Free Men of Color (FMC)
Bernard, Jule		1st Louisiana Native Guards, LAMilitia	Private	Free Men of Color (FMC)
Bernard, L. M.		1st Louisiana Native Guards, LAMilitia	Private	Free Men of Color (FMC)
Bernard, W.		1st Louisiana Native Guards, LAMilitia	Private	Free Men of Color FMC)
Bertrand, Augustin		1st Louisiana Native Guards, LAMilitia	Private	Free Men of Color (FMC)
Bertrand, Louis		1st Louisiana Native Guards, LAMilitia	Private	Free Men of Color
Bertrand, Pierre		1st Louisiana Native Guards, LAMilitia	Private	Free Men of Color (FMC)
Bezon, Henry		1st Louisiana Native Guards, LAMilitia	Major	Free Men of Color (FMC)

Directory of African American Confederates in the U.S. Civil War

Bibi, John		1st Louisiana Native Guards, LA Militia	Private	Free Men of Color (FMC)
Bienvenu, Em		1st Louisiana Native Guards, LA Militia	Private	Free Men of Color (FMC)
Bijon, A.		1st Louisiana Native Guards, LA Militia	Private	Free Men of Color (FMC)
Bijon, B. M.		1st Louisiana Native Guards, LA Militia	Private	Free Men of Color (FMC)
Bijon, J.		1st Louisiana Native Guards, LA Militia	Private	Free Men of Color (FMC)
Bijon, P.		1st Louisiana Native Guards, LA Militia	Private	Free Men of Color (FMC)
Bijoux, Leander		1st Louisiana Native Guards, LA Militia	Private	Free Men of Color (FMC)
Birot, J.		1st Louisiana Native Guards, LA Militia	Private	Free Men of Color (FMC)
Blache, Ernest		1st Louisiana Native Guards, LA Militia	Sergeant	Free Men of Color (FMC)
Blaire, Francis		1st Louisiana Native Guards, LA Militia	Private	Free Men of Color (FMC)
Blancan, Buname		1st Louisiana Native Guards, LA Militia	Private	Free Men of Color (FMC)
Blanchard, Arthur		1st Louisiana Native Guards, LA Militia	Private	Free Men of Color (FMC)
Blanchard, Nicholas		1st Louisiana Native Guards, LA Militia	1st Sgt	Free Men of Color (FMC)
Blane, Henry		1st Louisiana Native Guards, LA Militia	Private	Free Men of Color (FMC)
Blasco, Aenetre		1st Louisiana Native Guards, LA Militia	Private	Free Men of Color (FMC)
Blondin, Charles		1st Louisiana Native Guards, LA Militia	Private	Free Men of Color (FMC)
Bodon, Francis		1st Louisiana Native Guards, LA Militia	Private	Free Men of Color (FMC)
Boguille, Orther		1st Louisiana Native Guards, LA Militia	Private	Free Men of Color (FMC)
Bonne, L.		1st Louisiana Native Guards, LA Militia	Sergeant	Free Men of Color (FMC)
Bonne, Valsin		1st Louisiana Native Guards, LA Militia	1st Lt	Free Men of Color (FMC)
Bono, Vincent		1st Louisiana Native Guards, LA Militia	Private	Free Men of Color (FMC)
Boree, Louis		1st Louisiana Native Guards, LA Militia	Private	Free Men of Color (FMC)
Botler, Robert		1st Louisiana Native Guards, LA Militia	Private	Free Men of Color (FMC)
Boutin, A.		1st Louisiana Native Guards, LA Militia	Private	Free Men of Color (FMC)
Boutt, Edonard	C	1st Louisiana Native Guards, LA Militia	Private	Free Men of Color (FMC)
Boutte, E.		1st Louisiana Native Guards, LA Militia	Private	Free Men of Color (FMC)
Boutte, L.		1st Louisiana Native Guards, LA Militia	Private	Free Men of Color (FMC)
Bra, Pirra		1st Louisiana Native Guards, LA Militia	Private	Free Men of Color (FMC)
Brad, N.		1st Louisiana Native Guards, LA Militia	Private	Free Men of Color (FMC)
Brana, Lucien		1st Louisiana Native Guards, LA Militia	1st Sgt	Free Men of Color (FMC)
Brayard, Henry		1st Louisiana Native Guards, LA Militia	Corporal	Free Men of Color (FMC)
Bresson, W.		1st Louisiana Native Guards, LA Militia	Private	Free Men of Color (FMC)
Brion, Bazele		1st Louisiana Native Guards, LA Militia	Serg.	Free Men of Color (FMC)
Broca, John		1st Louisiana Native Guards, LA Militia	Private	Free Men of Color (FMC)
Butler, C.		1st Louisiana Native Guards, LA Militia	Private	Free Men of Color (FMC)
Cabal, A.		1st Louisiana Native Guards, LA Militia	1st Lt	Free Men of Color (FMC)
Cadichon, Joseph		1st Louisiana Native Guards, LA Militia	Private	Free Men of Color (FMC)
Caillole, Jean		1st Louisiana Native Guards, LA Militia	Private	Free Men of Color (FMC)
Cailloux, Andre		1st Louisiana Native Guards, LA Militia	1st Lt	Free Men of Color (FMC)
Caliste, Joseph		1st Louisiana Native Guards, LA Militia	Private	Free Men of Color (FMC)
Camille, John		1st Louisiana Native Guards, LA Militia	Private	Free Men of Color (FMC)
Camps, J.		1st Louisiana Native Guards, LA Militia	Private	Free Men of Color (FMC)
Camps, Manuel		1st Louisiana Native Guards, LA Militia	Private	Free Men of Color (FMC)
Candi, Joseph		1st Louisiana Native Guards, LA Militia	Private	Free Men of Color (FMC)
Candiff, Daniel		1st Louisiana Native Guards, LA Militia	Private	Free Men of Color (FMC)
Canelle, Pierre		1st Louisiana Native Guards, LA Militia	1st Sgt	Free Men of Color (FMC)
Canonge, Zephire		1st Louisiana Native Guards, LA Militia	2nd Lt	Free Men of Color (FMC)
Capla, R. V.		1st Louisiana Native Guards, LA Militia	Corporal	Free Men of Color (FMC)

Carlon, L. J.		1st Louisiana Native Guards, LA Militia	Private	Free Men of Color FMC)
Carlon, N.		1st Louisiana Native Guards, LA Militia	Private	Free Men of Color FMC)
Carmouche, Louis		1st Louisiana Native Guards, LA Militia	Private	Free Men of Color (FMC)
Carrere, Etienne		1st Louisiana Native Guards, LA Militia	Private	Free Men of Color (FMC)
Carrere, Joseph		1st Louisiana Native Guards, LA Militia	Private	Free Men of Color (FMC)
Carrere, Nereston		1st Louisiana Native Guards, LA Militia	Private	Free Men of Color (FMC)
Carrian, A.		1st Louisiana Native Guards, LA Militia	Private	Free Men of Color (FMC)
Casanave, G.		1st Louisiana Native Guards, LA Militia	Private	Free Men of Color (FMC)
Casimir, Lucien		1st Louisiana Native Guards, LA Militia	Private	Free Men of Color (FMC)
Cassino, Antoine		1st Louisiana Native Guards, LA Militia	Private	Free Men of Color (FMC)
Castaing, Murville		1st Louisiana Native Guards, LA Militia	2nd Lt	Free Men of Color (FMC)
Castille, Raymond		1st Louisiana Native Guards, LA Militia	Private	Free Men of Color (FMC)
Castin, Arthur		1st Louisiana Native Guards, LA Militia	Private	Free Men of Color (FMC)
Catey, Francis		1st Louisiana Native Guards, LA Militia	Private	Free Men of Color (FMC)
Charbonnet, D. L.		1st Louisiana Native Guards, LA Militia	Private	Free Men of Color (FMC)
Charland, Antoine		1st Louisiana Native Guards, LA Militia	Private	Free Men of Color (FMC)
Charles, Joseph		1st Louisiana Native Guards, LA Militia	Private	Free Men of Color (FMC)
Charles, Pierre		1st Louisiana Native Guards, LA Militia	Private	Free Men of Color
Chaumette, Ernest		1st Louisiana Native Guards, LA Militia	Private	Free Men of Color (FMC)
Chauvin, F.		1st Louisiana Native Guards, LA Militia	Private	Free Men of Color (FMC)
Chauvin, J.		1st Louisiana Native Guards, LA Militia	Private	Free Men of Color (FMC)
Chavanne, Francois		1st Louisiana Native Guards, LA Militia	Private	Free Men of Color (FMC)
Chenette, G. J.		1st Louisiana Native Guards, LA Militia	1st Sgt	Free Men of Color (FMC)
Chenot, Louis		1st Louisiana Native Guards, LA Militia	Private	Free Men of Color (FMC)
Cheron, John		1st Louisiana Native Guards, LA Militia	Private	Free Men of Color (FMC)
Chesse, A. L.		1st Louisiana Native Guards, LA Militia	Private	Free Men of Color (FMC)
Chesse, G.		1st Louisiana Native Guards, LA Militia	Private	Free Men of Color (FMC)
Cheval, Ludger		1st Louisiana Native Guards, LA Militia	Private	Free Men of Color (FMC)
Cheval, Angelin		1st Louisiana Native Guards, LA Militia	Corpora	Free Men of Color (FMC)
Chevalier, Alexander		1st Louisiana Native Guards, LA	Private	Free Men of Color (FMC)
Chevalier, Armand		1st Louisiana Native Guards, LA Militia	Private	Free Men of Color (FMC)
Chevalier, Biennimee		1st Louisiana Native Guards, LA Militia	Private	Free Men of Color (FMC)
Chevalier, Jules		1st Louisiana Native Guards, LA Militia	Private	Free Men of Color (FMC)
Chevau, A.		1st Louisiana Native Guards, LA Militia	Private	Free Men of Color C)
Chezan, Sidney		1st Louisiana Native Guards, LA Militia	Private	Free Men of Color (FMC)
Christophe, Firmin C.		1st Louisiana Native Guards, LA Militia	Private	Free Men of Color (FMC)
Clavie, O.		1st Louisiana Native Guards, LA Militia	Private	Free Men of Color (FMC)
Clement, Louis		1st Louisiana Native Guards, LA Militia	Private	Free Men of Color (FMC)
Clement, Pierre		1st Louisiana Native Guards, LA Militia	Private	Free Men of Color (FMC)
Coffy, H.		1st Louisiana Native Guards, LA Militia	Sergean	Free Men of Color (FMC)
Coiron, Stanislas		1st Louisiana Native Guards, LA Militia	Private	Free Men of Color (FMC)
Colas, Raphail		1st Louisiana Native Guards, LA Militia	Private	Free Men of Color (FMC)
Compagnon, J. B.		1st Louisiana Native Guards, LA Militia	Private	Free Men of Color (FMC)
Constant, G. G.		1st Louisiana Native Guards, LA Militia	Private	Free Men of Color (FMC)
Copel, Eugene		1st Louisiana Native Guards, LA Militia	Private	Free Men of Color (FMC)
Cordier, Pierre		1st Louisiana Native Guards, LA	Private	Free Men of Color (FMC)
Coulon, Jean		1st Louisiana Native Guards, LA Militia	Private	Free Men of Color (FMC)
Coulon, Jules		1st Louisiana Native Guards, LA Militia	Private	Free Men of Color (FMC)

Coulon, Prosper	1st Louisiana Native Guards, LAMilitia	Private	Free Men of Color (FMC)
Courcelle, Charles	1st Louisiana Native Guards, LAMilitia	Private	Free Men of Color (FMC)
Craig, J.	1st Louisiana Native Guards, LAMilitia	Private	Free Men of Color (FMC)
Crocker, D.	1st Louisiana Native Guards, LAMilitia	Private	Free Men of Color (FMC)
Dallier, J.	1st Louisiana Native Guards, LAMilitia	Corporal	Free Men of Color (FMC)
Daniel, Armand	1st Louisiana Native Guards, LAMilitia	1st Sgt	Free Men of Color (FMC)
Daquin, Ernest	1st Louisiana Native Guards, LAMilitia	Private	Free Men of Color (FMC)
Daunois, C. J.	1st Louisiana Native Guards, LAMilitia	Private	Free Men of Color (FMC)
Dauphin, Armand	1st Louisiana Native Guards, LAMilitia	Private	Free Men of Color (FMC)
Dauphin, Arthur	1st Louisiana Native Guards, LAMilitia	Private	Free Men of Color (FMC)
Dauphin, P. 0.	1st Louisiana Native Guards, LAMilitia	Private	Free Men of Color (FMC)
David, Belisaire	1st Louisiana Native Guards, LAMilitia	Private	Free Men of Color (FMC)
Davis, E.	1st Louisiana Native Guards, LAMilitia	Captain	Free Men of Color (FMC)
Davison,	1st Louisiana Native Guards, LAMilitia	Private	Free Men of Color (FMC)
Decout, Adolphe	1st Louisiana Native Guards, LAMilitia	Sergeant	Free Men of Color (FMC)
Decout, Armand	1st Louisiana Native Guards, LAMilitia	Private	Free Men of Color (FMC)
Decout, Louis T.	1st Louisiana Native Guards, LAMilitia	Private	Free Men of Color (FMC)
Decout, Numa	1st Louisiana Native Guards, LAMilitia	Private	Free Men of Color (FMC)
Decout, Senneville	1st Louisiana Native Guards, LAMilitia	Private	Free Men of Color (FMC)
Decoux, Charles	1st Louisiana Native Guards, LAMilitia	Private	Free Men of Color (FMC)
Dede, Francois	1st Louisiana Native Guards, LAMilitia	Sergeant	Free Men of Color (FMC)
Dede, Simphorin B.	1st Louisiana Native Guards, LAMilitia	Private	Free Men of Color (FMC)
Delpit, Louis	1st Louisiana Native Guards, LAMilitia	Private	Free Men of Color (FMC)
Depos, Moise	1st Louisiana Native Guards, LAMilitia	Corporal	Free Men of Color (FMC)
Derbigny, Theophile	1st Louisiana Native Guards, LAMilitia	2nd Lt	Free Men of Color (FMC)
Desborde, Joseph	1st Louisiana Native Guards, LAMilitia	Private	Free Men of Color (FMC)
Deslondes, Alcee	1st Louisiana Native Guards, LAMilitia	Sergeant	Free Men of Color (FMC)
Deslondes, Joseph	1st Louisiana Native Guards, LAMilitia	Sergeant	Free Men of Color (FMC)
Dessale, Joseph	1st Louisiana Native Guards, LAMilitia	Sergeant	Free Men of Color (FMC)
Dessalles, Jules	1st Louisiana Native Guards, LAMilitia	Corporal	Free Men of Color (FMC)
Devigne, Armond	1st Louisiana Native Guards, LAMilitia	Private	Free Men of Color (FMC)
Diaz, J.	1st Louisiana Native Guards, LAMilitia	Sergeant	Free Men of Color (FMC)
Dinet, Gustave	1st Louisiana Native Guards, LAMilitia	Sergeant	Free Men of Color (FMC)
Dinet, Joseph	1st Louisiana Native Guards, LAMilitia	Sergeant	Free Men of Color (FMC)
Dinette, Gustav	1st Louisiana Native Guards, LAMilitia	Sergeant	Free Men of Color (FMC)
Dionet, J. M.	1st Louisiana Native Guards, LA Militia	Corporal	Free Men of Color (FMC)
Dome, Leon	1st Louisiana Native Guards, LAMilitia	Private	Free Men of Color (FMC)
Domingue, L.	1st Louisiana Native Guards, LAMilitia	Sergeant	Free Men of Color (FMC)
Dorgan, Armand	1st Louisiana Native Guards, LAMilitia	Sergeant	Free Men of Color (FMC)
Dorson, Andre	1st Louisiana Native Guards, LAMilitia	Sergeant	Free Men of Color (FMC)
D'Orville, A.	1st Louisiana Native Guards, LAMilitia	Sergeant	Free Men of Color (FMC)
Dorville, Edmond	1st Louisiana Native Guards, LAMilitia	Sergeant	Free Men of Color (FMC)
Doyle, H.	1st Louisiana Native Guards, LAMilitia	Sergeant	Free Men of Color (FMC)
Dreux, Edmond	1st Louisiana Native Guards, LAMilitia	Sergeant	Free Men of Color (FMC)
Dubois, Etienne	1st Louisiana Native Guards, LAMilitia	Sgt Maj	Free Men of Color (FMC)
Dubois, L.	1st Louisiana Native Guards, LAMilitia	Sergeant	Free Men of Color (FMC)
Dubuclet, Paular	1st Louisiana Native Guards, LAMilitia	Sergeant	Free Men of Color (FMC)
Dufrene, Jean	1st Louisiana Native Guards, LAMilitia	Private	Free Men of Color (FMC)

Directory of African American Confederates in the U.S. Civil War

Dugue, Charles		1st Louisiana Native Guards, LA	Militia	Sergeant	Free Men of Color (FMC)
Duhart, Armand		1st Louisiana Native Guards, LA	Militia	1st Lt	Free Men of Color (FMC)
Duhart, P. A.		1st Louisiana Native Guards, LA	Militia	Private	Free Men of Color (FMC)
Dunford, T.		1st Louisiana Native Guards, LA	Militia	Sergeant	Free Men of Color (FMC)
Dupard, V.		1st Louisiana Native Guards, LA	Militia	Sergeant	Free Men of Color (FMC)
Dupart, Etienne		1st Louisiana Native Guards, LA	Militia	Corporal	Free Men of Color (FMC)
Dupart, John		1st Louisiana Native Guards, LA	Militia	Private	Free Men of Color (FMC)
Dupart, M. V.		1st Louisiana Native Guards, LA	Militia	Sergeant	Free Men of Color (FMC)
Dupart, Michael		1st Louisiana Native Guards, LA	Militia	Captain	Free Men of Color (FMC)
Duplissis, E.		1st Louisiana Native Guards, LA	Militia	Sergeant	Free Men of Color (FMC)
Duplissis, Michael		1st Louisiana Native Guards, LA	Militia	Sergeant	Free Men of Color (FMC)
Duplissis, Nicolas		1st Louisiana Native Guards, LA	Militia	Sergeant	Free Men of Color (FMC)
Dupre, Cafiste		1st Louisiana Native Guards, LA	Militia	Sergeant	Free Men of Color (FMC)
Dupre, Felix		1st Louisiana Native Guards, LA	Militia	Corporal	Free Men of Color (FMC)
Dupre, Lucien		1st Louisiana Native Guards, LA	Militia	Sergeant	Free Men of Color (FMC)
Dupuis, F. O.		1st Louisiana Native Guards, LA	Militia	2nd Lt	Free Men of Color (FMC)
Duques, Eugene		1st Louisiana Native Guards, LA	Militia	Private	Free Men of Color (FMC)
Duralde, J.		1st Louisiana Native Guards, LA	Militia	Sergeant	Free Men of Color (FMC)
Durand, Charles		1st Louisiana Native Guards, LA	Militia	Private	Free Men of Color (FMC)
Durand, Jean		1st Louisiana Native Guards, LA	Militia	Sergeant	Free Men of Color (FMC)
Durant, Bernard		1st Louisiana Native Guards, LA	Militia	Sergeant	Free Men of Color (FMC)
Durant, Fernando		1st Louisiana Native Guards, LA	Militia	Sergeant	Free Men of Color (FMC)
Durel, Numa		1st Louisiana Native Guards, LA	Militia	Sergeant	Free Men of Color (FMC)
Durie, Georges		1st Louisiana Native Guards, LA	Militia	Sergeant	Free Men of Color (FMC)
Durousseau, Felix		1st Louisiana Native Guards, LA	Militia	Sergeant	Free Men of Color (FMC)
Duthil, Eugene		1st Louisiana Native Guards, LA	Militia	Sergeant	Free Men of Color (FMC)
Dutreuil, P.		1st Louisiana Native Guards, LA	Militia	Sergeant	Free Men of Color (FMC)
Duval, C. D.		1st Louisiana Native Guards, LA	Militia	Sergeant	Free Men of Color (FMC)
Edouard, J. H.		1st Louisiana Native Guards, LA	Militia	Sergeant	Free Men of Color (FMC)
Edouard, Joseph A.		1st Louisiana Native Guards, LA	Militia	Sergeant	Free Men of Color (FMC)
Elf, Homer		1st Louisiana Native Guards, LA	Militia	Sergeant	Free Men of Color (FMC)
Erie, Joseph		1st Louisiana Native Guards, LA	Militia	Sergeant	Free Men of Color (FMC)
Esclavon, Pierre		1st Louisiana Native Guards, LA	Militia	Private	Free Men of Color (FMC)
Esnard, G.		1st Louisiana Native Guards, LA	Militia	Sergeant	Free Men of Color (FMC)
Esnard, T.		1st Louisiana Native Guards, LA	Militia	Sergeant	Free Men of Color (FMC)
Esteve, Charles		1st Louisiana Native Guards, LA	Militia	Private	Free Men of Color (FMC)
Etienne, Leon		1st Louisiana Native Guards, LA	Militia	Private	Free Men of Color (FMC)
Etienne, Vincent		1st Louisiana Native Guards, LA	Militia	Sergeant	Free Men of Color (FMC)
Eugene, Elie 3.		1st Louisiana Native Guards, LA	Militia	Sergeant	Free Men of Color (FMC)
Exavier, Francois		1st Louisiana Native Guards, LA	Militia	Sergeant	Free Men of Color (FMC)
Fagot, Victor		1st Louisiana Native Guards, LA	Militia	Sergeant	Free Men of Color (FMC)
Farr, E.		1st Louisiana Native Guards, LA	Militia	OSgt	Free Men of Color (FMC)
Farrar, Emile		1st Louisiana Native Guards, LA	Militia	Sergeant	Free Men of Color (FMC)
Felix, Joseph		1st Louisiana Native Guards, LA	Militia	Sergeant	Free Men of Color (FMC)
Ferbos, Ulysse		1st Louisiana Native Guards, LA	Militia	Sergeant	Free Men of Color (FMC)
Ferbos, Victor		1st Louisiana Native Guards, LA	Militia	Sergeant	Free Men of Color (FMC)
Ferny, S.		1st Louisiana Native Guards, LA	Militia	Sergeant	Free Men of Color (FMC)
Fernandez, L.		1st Louisiana Native Guards, LA	Militia	Sergeant	Free Men of Color (FMC)

Fernandez, O.	1st Louisiana Native Guards, LA Militia	Sergeant	Free Men of Color (FMC)
Fernandez, P.	1st Louisiana Native Guards, LA Militia	Sergeant	Free Men of Color (FMC)
Fernandez, P. O.	1st Louisiana Native Guards, LA Militia	Corporal	Free Men of Color (FMC)
Ferranti, Bertheleny	1st Louisiana Native Guards, LA Militia	Private	Free Men of Color (FMC)
Ferrand, Buptishe J.	1st Louisiana Native Guards, LA Militia	Corporal	Free Men of Color (FMC)
Ferrand, Buptishe S.	1st Louisiana Native Guards, LA Militia	Sergeant	Free Men of Color (FMC)
Ferrand, Jacques	1st Louisiana Native Guards, LA Militia	Sergeant	Free Men of Color (FMC)
Ferrand, Joseph	1st Louisiana Native Guards, LA Militia	Sergeant	Free Men of Color (FMC)
Ferrand, Joseph J.	1st Louisiana Native Guards, LA Militia	Sergeant	Free Men of Color (FMC)
Ferrand, Louis	1st Louisiana Native Guards, LA Militia	Sgt Maj	Free Men of Color (FMC)
Filie, Joseph	1st Louisiana Native Guards, LA Militia	Private	Free Men of Color (FMC)
Fleming, Jean	1st Louisiana Native Guards, LA Militia	Private	Free Men of Color (FMC)
Fletcher, Jean	1st Louisiana Native Guards, LA Militia	Corporal	Free Men of Color (FMC)
Fleury, E.	1st Louisiana Native Guards, LA Militia	Private	Free Men of Color (FMC)
Fleury, F.	1st Louisiana Native Guards, LA Militia	Private	Free Men of Color (FMC)
Fondal, Joseph	1st Louisiana Native Guards, LA Militia	Corporal	Free Men of Color (FMC)
Fondal, Pierre	1st Louisiana Native Guards, LA Militia	Private	Free Men of Color (FMC)
Forneret, Leonard	1st Louisiana Native Guards, LA Militia	Private	Free Men of Color (FMC)
Fornerette,	1st Louisiana Native Guards, LA Militia	Private	Free Men of Color (FMC)
Forstall, Emile	1st Louisiana Native Guards, LA Militia	Private	Free Men of Color (FMC)
Forstall, L.	1st Louisiana Native Guards, LA Militia	Private	Free Men of Color (FMC)
Forstall, R. F.	1st Louisiana Native Guards, LA Militia	Private	Free Men of Color (FMC)
Forten, Hezekiah	1st Louisiana Native Guards, LA Militia	Private	Free Men of Color (FMC)
Fortune, L.	1st Louisiana Native Guards, LA Militia	Private	Free Men of Color (FMC)
Fouche, George	1st Louisiana Native Guards, LA Militia	Private	Free Men of Color (FMC)
Fouche, Louis N.	1st Louisiana Native Guards, LA Militia	1st Lt	Free Men of Color (FMC)
Foucher, B.	1st Louisiana Native Guards, LA Militia	Sgt Maj	Free Men of Color (FMC)
Fournier, Mitchell	1st Louisiana Native Guards, LA Militia	Private	Free Men of Color (FMC)
Foy, Octave	1st Louisiana Native Guards, LA Militia	1st Lt	Free Men of Color (FMC)
Fraisse, Joseph	1st Louisiana Native Guards, LA Militia	Private	Free Men of Color (FMC)
Francis, Donald	1st Louisiana Native Guards, LA Militia	Private	Free Men of Color (FMC)
Francis, F.	1st Louisiana Native Guards, LA Militia	Private	Free Men of Color (FMC)
Francois, J.	1st Louisiana Native Guards, LA Militia	Private	Free Men of Color (FMC)
Francois, Jean L.	1st Louisiana Native Guards, LA Militia	Private	Free Men of Color (FMC)
Francois, Joseph	1st Louisiana Native Guards, LA Militia	Corporal	Free Men of Color (FMC)
Francois, Ursin	1st Louisiana Native Guards, LA Militia	Private	Free Men of Color (FMC)
Frederick, Leon	1st Louisiana Native Guards, LA Militia	Private	Free Men of Color (FMC)
Frilot, J.	1st Louisiana Native Guards, LA Militia	Private	Free Men of Color (FMC)
Frilot, L.	1st Louisiana Native Guards, LA Militia	Private	Free Men of Color (FMC)
Fuentes, Homer	1st Louisiana Native Guards, LA Militia	Sergeant	Free Men of Color (FMC)
Gabriel, Paul	1st Louisiana Native Guards, LA Militia	Private	Free Men of Color (FMC)
Gabriel, Pierre	1st Louisiana Native Guards, LA Militia	Private	Free Men of Color (FMC)
Gaeton, Charles	1st Louisiana Native Guards, LA Militia	Private	Free Men of Color (FMC)
Gaignard, Charles	1st Louisiana Native Guards, LA Militia	Private	Free Men of Color (FMC)
Gaillard, Armand	1st Louisiana Native Guards, LA Militia	Private	Free Men of Color (FMC)
Gaillard, Dominique	1st Louisiana Native Guards, LA Militia	Private	Free Men of Color (FMC)
Galade, Jean	1st Louisiana Native Guards, LA Militia	Private	Free Men of Color (FMC)
Galatte, Manuel	1st Louisiana Native Guards, LA Militia	Private	Free Men of Color (FMC)

Gallaud, Anatole		1st Louisiana Native Guards, LA	Militia	Private	Free Men of Color (FMC)
Galle, Alfred		1st Louisiana Native Guards, LA	Militia	Private	Free Men of Color (FMC)
Galle, D.		1st Louisiana Native Guards, LA	Militia	Corporal	Free Men of Color (FMC)
Galle, Dermond		1st Louisiana Native Guards, LA	Militia	Private	Free Men of Color (FMC)
Galle, Felix		1st Louisiana Native Guards, LA	Militia	Private	Free Men of Color (FMC)
Galie, L.		1st Louisiana Native Guards, LA	Militia	Private	Free Men of Color (FMC)
Galleau, T.		1st Louisiana Native Guards, LA	Militia	Private	Free Men of Color (FMC)
Galles, Joseph		1st Louisiana Native Guards, LA	Militia	Private	Free Men of Color (FMC)
Garcia, J. B.		1st Louisiana Native Guards, LA	Militia	Private	Free Men of Color (FMC)
Garcia, Piesse		1st Louisiana Native Guards, LA	Militia	Private	Free Men of Color (FMC)
Gardere, Amedie		1st Louisiana Native Guards, LA	Militia	2nd Lt	Free Men of Color (FMC)
Gardette, A.		1st Louisiana Native Guards, LA	Militia	Private	Free Men of Color (FMC)
Gardette, Leonce		1st Louisiana Native Guards, LA	Militia	Private	Free Men of Color (FMC)
Gaspard, Joseph		1st Louisiana Native Guards, LA	Militia	Private	Free Men of Color (FMC)
Gaspard, Lucien		1st Louisiana Native Guards, LA	Militia	Private	Free Men of Color (FMC)
Gaspard, Pierre		1st Louisiana Native Guards, LA	Militia	Private	Free Men of Color (FMC)
Gastram, Leopol		1st Louisiana Native Guards, LA	Militia	Private	Free Men of Color (FMC)
Gaudet, Louis		1st Louisiana Native Guards, LA	Militia	Private	Free Men of Color (FMC)
Gautre, Adolphe		1st Louisiana Native Guards, LA	Militia	Private	Free Men of Color (FMC)
George, Louis		1st Louisiana Native Guards, LA	Militia	Private	Free Men of Color (FMC)
Germain, Anatole		1st Louisiana Native Guards, LA	Militia	Private	Free Men of Color (FMC)
Germain, Jean		1st Louisiana Native Guards, LA	Militia	Private	Free Men of Color
Gignac, Elvard		1st Louisiana Native Guards, LA	Militia	Corporal Farrier	Free Men of Color FMC)
Gilbert, V.		1st Louisiana Native Guards, LA	Militia	Private	Free Men of Color (FMC)
Glapion, C. J.		1st Louisiana Native Guards, LA		Private	Free Men of Color (FMC)
Glapion, Joseph		1st Louisiana Native Guards, LA		Sergeant	Free Men of Color FMC)
Glapion, Pierre		1st Louisiana Native Guards, LA	Militia	Private	Free Men of Color FMC)
Glapion, Telesphose		1st Louisiana Native Guards, LA	Militia	Private	Free Men of Color FMC)
Glaude, P.		1st Louisiana Native Guards, LA	Militia	Private	Free Men of Color (FMC)
Glaudin, M.		1st Louisiana Native Guards, LA	Militia	Orderly Sergeant	Free Men of Color (FMC)
Glaudin, P.		1st Louisiana Native Guards, LA	Militia	Private	Free Men of Color (FMC)
Godefroy, M.		1st Louisiana Native Guards, LA	Militia	Private	Free Men of Color (FMC)
Godfroid, 0.		1st Louisiana Native Guards, LA	Militia	Private	Free Men of Color (FMC)
Golard, Joseph		1st Louisiana Native Guards, LA	Militia	Private	Free Men of Color (FMC)
Golard, Jules		1st Louisiana Native Guards, LA	Militia	Private	Free Men of Color FMC)
Golis, Louis		1st Louisiana Native Guards, LA	Militia	Captain	Free Men of Color (FMC)
Golis, Numa		1st Louisiana Native Guards, LA	Militia	Private	Free Men of Color
Gomez, Jules		1st Louisiana Native Guards, LA	Militia	Private	Free Men of Color
Gondran, D.		1st Louisiana Native Guards, LA	Militia	Private	Free Men of Color
Gonzales, Armand		1st Louisiana Native Guards, LA	Militia	Private	Free Men of Color
Gonzales, Florville		1st Louisiana Native Guards, LA	Militia	1st Sgt	Free Men of Color (FMC)
Gonzales, Gustave		1st Louisiana Native Guards, LA	Militia	Private	Free Men of Color (FMC)
Gonzales, Paul		1st Louisiana Native Guards, LA	Militia	Private	Free Men of Color FMC)
Grace, Alexis		1st Louisiana Native Guards, LA	Militia	Private	Free Men of Color (FMC)
Grandpre, C.		1st Louisiana Native Guards, LA	Militia	Private	Free Men of Color (FMC)
Grandpre, T.		1st Louisiana Native Guards, LA	Militia	Private	Free Men of Color FMC)

Grard, Alfred	A	1st Louisiana Native Guards, LA Militia	Private	Free Men of Color (FMC)
Gravier, Bernard		1st Louisiana Native Guards, LA Militia	Private	Free Men of Color (FMC)
Gravier, T.		1st Louisiana Native Guards, LA Militia	Private	Free Men of Color (FMC)
Greffin, B.		1st Louisiana Native Guards, LA Militia	Private	Free Men of Color (FMC)
Gregoire, A.		1st Louisiana Native Guards, LA Militia	Private	Free Men of Color (FMC)
Gregoire, C.		1st Louisiana Native Guards, LA Militia	Private	Free Men of Color (FMC)
Gregoire, Pierre		1st Louisiana Native Guards, LA Militia	Private	Free Men of Color (FMC)
Guadiz, D.		1st Louisiana Native Guards, LA Militia	2nd Lt	Free Men of Color (FMC)
Guibert, Auguste		1st Louisiana Native Guards, LA Militia	Sergeant	Free Men of Color (FMC)
Guillaume, George		1st Louisiana Native Guards, LA Militia	Private	Free Men of Color (FMC)
Guillaume, J. V.		1st Louisiana Native Guards, LA Militia	Sergeant	Free Men of Color (FMC)
Guillaume, Joseph		1st Louisiana Native Guards, LA Militia	Private	Free Men of Color (FMC)
Guillory, Martin		1st Louisiana Native Guards, LA Militia	Sergeant	Free Men of Color (FMC)
Gustave, Jules		1st Louisiana Native Guards, LA Militia	Private	Free Men of Color (FMC)
Gut, Phillippe		1st Louisiana Native Guards, LA Militia	Private	Free Men of Color (FMC)
Hains, Charles		1st Louisiana Native Guards, LA Militia	Private	Free Men of Color (FMC)
Hains, Manuel		1st Louisiana Native Guards, LA Militia	Private	Free Men of Color (FMC)
Nardi, Evariste		1st Louisiana Native Guards, LA Militia	Private	Free Men of Color (FMC)
Nardi, Robert		1st Louisiana Native Guards, LA Militia	Private	Free Men of Color (FMC)
Hardy, Estes A.		1st Louisiana Native Guards, LA Militia	Private	Free Men of Color (FMC)
Hardy, Paul		1st Louisiana Native Guards, LA Militia	Private	Free Men of Color (FMC)
Harris, Albert		1st Louisiana Native Guards, LA Militia	Private	Free Men of Color (FMC)
Hazeur, Joseph		1st Louisiana Native Guards, LA Militia	Private	Free Men of Color (FMC)
Hecaud, Benjamin		1st Louisiana Native Guards, LA Militia	Private	Free Men of Color (FMC)
Helliot, Louis		1st Louisiana Native Guards, LA Militia	Private	Free Men of Color (FMC)
Heno, Joseph		1st Louisiana Native Guards, LA Militia	Private	Free Men of Color (FMC)
Henry, Joseph		1st Louisiana Native Guards, LA Militia	Private	Free Men of Color (FMC)
Hermann, Ernest		1st Louisiana Native Guards, LA Militia	Corporal	Free Men of Color (FMC)
Hermogene,		1st Louisiana Native Guards, LA Militia	Private	Free Men of Color (FMC)
Herreman, G.		1st Louisiana Native Guards, LA Militia	Private	Free Men of Color (FMC)
Herrere, Jean		1st Louisiana Native Guards, LA Militia	Private	Free Men of Color (FMC)
Hewlett, Ernest		1st Louisiana Native Guards, LA Militia	Corporal	Free Men of Color (FMC)
Hinnigan, H.		1st Louisiana Native Guards, LA Militia	Private	Free Men of Color (FMC)
Hippolyte, Louis		1st Louisiana Native Guards, LA Militia	Private	Free Men of Color (FMC)
Hippolyte, P.		1st Louisiana Native Guards, LA Militia	Private	Free Men of Color (FMC)
Hubbart, William		1st Louisiana Native Guards, LA Militia	Private	Free Men of Color (FMC)
Hubert, Victor		1st Louisiana Native Guards, LA Militia	Private	Free Men of Color (FMC)
Hurbin, Joseph		1st Louisiana Native Guards, LA	Private	Free Men of Color (FMC)
Jacob, William		1st Louisiana Native Guards, LA	Private	Free Men of Color (FMC)
Jacques, Adolph		1st Louisiana Native Guards, LA Militia	Private	Free Men of Color (FMC)
Jacques, Arthur		1st Louisiana Native Guards, LA Militia	Private	Free Men of Color (FMC)
Jacques, Emile		1st Louisiana Native Guards, LA Militia	Sergeant	Free Men of Color (FMC)
Jameson, Eugene		1st Louisiana Native Guards, LA Militia	Private	Free Men of Color (FMC)
Jameson, Felix		1st Louisiana Native Guards, LA Militia	Private	Free Men of Color (FMC)
Janes, Jules		1st Louisiana Native Guards, LA Militia	Private	Free Men of Color (FMC)
Jardell, Jean		1st Louisiana Native Guards, LA Militia	Private	Free Men of Color (FMC)
Jean, Alrein		1st Louisiana Native Guards, LA Militia	Private	Free Men of Color (FMC)
Jean, Henrick		1st Louisiana Native Guards, LA Militia	Private	Free Men of Color (FMC)

Name		Unit	Rank	Status
Johnson, Henry		1st Louisiana Native Guards, LA Militia	Private	Free Men of Color (FMC)
Jolibois, Joseph		1st Louisiana Native Guards, LA Militia	Corporal	Free Men of Color (FMC)
Joly, Joseph		1st Louisiana Native Guards, LA Militia	Captain	Free Men of Color (FMC)
Joly, T.		1st Louisiana Native Guards, LA Militia	Private	Free Men of Color (FMC)
Joseph, A.		1st Louisiana Native Guards, LA Militia	Private	Free Men of Color (FMC)
Joseph, Bazile		1st Louisiana Native Guards, LA Militia	Private	Free Men of Color (FMC)
Joseph, Charles		1st Louisiana Native Guards, LA Militia	Private	Free Men of Color (FMC)
Joseph, Elenne		1st Louisiana Native Guards, LA Militia	Private	Free Men of Color (FMC)
Joseph, Ernest		1st Louisiana Native Guards, LA Militia	Private	Free Men of Color (FMC)
Joseph, 3.		1st Louisiana Native Guards, LA Militia	Private	Free Men of Color (FMC)
Joseph, Louis	L	1st Louisiana Native Guards, LA Militia	Private	Free Men of Color (FMC)
Joseph, Prospero		1st Louisiana Native Guards, LA Militia	Private	Free Men of Color (FMC)
Juin, Andrew		1st Louisiana Native Guards, LA Militia	Private	Free Men of Color (FMC)
Juin, Francis		1st Louisiana Native Guards, LA Militia	Private	Free Men of Color (FMC)
Kata, Alexander		1st Louisiana Native Guards, LA Militia	Private	Free Men of Color (FMC)
Kennedy, E.		1st Louisiana Native Guards, LA Militia	Corporal	Free Men of Color (FMC)
Labatt, C.		1st Louisiana Native Guards, LA Militia	Private	Free Men of Color (FMC)
Labbe, E.		1st Louisiana Native Guards, LA Militia	Private	Free Men of Color (FMC)
Labostrie, F.		1st Louisiana Native Guards, LA Militia	Private	Free Men of Color (FMC)
Lacoste, F. U.		1st Louisiana Native Guards, LA Militia	2nd Lt	Free Men of Color (FMC)
Lacroix, A.		1st Louisiana Native Guards, LA Militia	Private	Free Men of Color (FMC)
Lacroix, E.		1st Louisiana Native Guards, LA Militia	1st Sgt	Free Men of Color (FMC)
Lacroix, V.		1st Louisiana Native Guards, LA Militia	Private	Free Men of Color (FMC)
Lafargue, Hippolite		1st Louisiana Native Guards, LA Militia	Private	Free Men of Color (FMC)
Lafargue, V.		1st Louisiana Native Guards, LA Militia	Private	Free Men of Color (FMC)
Lafferanderie, M.		1st Louisiana Native Guards, LA Militia	Sergeant	Free Men of Color (FMC)
Lafont, Joseph		1st Louisiana Native Guards, LA Militia	Private	Free Men of Color (FMC)
Lafont, Louis		1st Louisiana Native Guards, LA Militia	Sergeant	Free Men of Color (FMC)
Lafrance, Valsin		1st Louisiana Native Guards, LA Militia	Private	Free Men of Color (FMC)
Lajoy, Esteve		1st Louisiana Native Guards, LA Militia	Private	Free Men of Color (FMC)
Lamothe, Martin		1st Louisiana Native Guards, LA Militia	Private	Free Men of Color (FMC)
Lamothe, Merville		1st Louisiana Native Guards, LA Militia	Private	Free Men of Color (FMC)
Lanabere, Jules		1st Louisiana Native Guards, LA Militia	Private	Free Men of Color (FMC)
Lanaux, Paul		1st Louisiana Native Guards, LA Militia	Private	Free Men of Color (FMC)
Lanni, D. A.		1st Louisiana Native Guards, LA Militia	Private	Free Men of Color (FMC)
Lanoy, B.		1st Louisiana Native Guards, LA Militia	Private	Free Men of Color (FMC)
Lanusse, Armand		1st Louisiana Native Guards, LA Militia	Captain	Free Men of Color (FMC)
Lapierre, Francis		1st Louisiana Native Guards, LA Militia	Private	Free Men of Color (FMC)
Larche, Joseph	I	1st Louisiana Native Guards, LA Militia	Private	Free Men of Color (FMC)
Larche, Mathew		1st Louisiana Native Guards, LA Militia	Private	Free Men of Color (FMC)
Laroche, H.	I	1st Louisiana Native Guards, LA Militia	Private	Free Men of Color (FMC)
Larose, Desir		1st Louisiana Native Guards, LA Militia	Private	Free Men of Color (FMC)
Laurent, B.		1st Louisiana Native Guards, LA Militia	Private	Free Men of Color (FMC)
Laurent, Joseph		1st Louisiana Native Guards, LA Militia	Private	Free Men of Color (FMC)
Laurent, P.		1st Louisiana Native Guards, LA Militia	Private	Free Men of Color (FMC)
Laurince, Jean		1st Louisiana Native Guards, LA Militia	Private	Free Men of Color (FMC)
Laveaux, Joseph		1st Louisiana Native Guards, LA Militia	Private	Free Men of Color (FMC)
Lavigne, E.		1st Louisiana Native Guards, LA Militia	Private	Free Men of Color (FMC)

Lavigne, Henry	1st Louisiana Native Guards, LA Militia	Corporal	Free Men of Color (FMC)
Lavigne, Louis	1st Louisiana Native Guards, LA Militia	Private	Free Men of Color (FMC)
Lavigne, V. J.	1st Louisiana Native Guards, LA Militia	Sgt Maj	Free Men of Color (FMC)
Lazare, Louis	1st Louisiana Native Guards, LA Militia	Private	Free Men of Color (FMC)
Lebreton, Clovis	1st Louisiana Native Guards, LA Militia	Private	Free Men of Color (FMC)
Lee, E.	1st Louisiana Native Guards, LA Militia	Private	Free Men of Color (FMC)
Leger, Auguste	1st Louisiana Native Guards, LA Militia	Private	Free Men of Color (FMC)
Leger, Ovide	1st Louisiana Native Guards, LA Militia	Private	Free Men of Color (FMC)
Legras, E.	1st Louisiana Native Guards, LA Militia	2nd Cpl	Free Men of Color (FMC)
Legros, Ernest	1st Louisiana Native Guards, LA Militia	Private	Free Men of Color (FMC)
Legros, Jacques	1st Louisiana Native Guards, LA Militia	Private	Free Men of Color (FMC)
Legros, Louis	1st Louisiana Native Guards, LA Militia	Private	Free Men of Color (FMC)
Leon, Edgurd	1st Louisiana Native Guards, LA Militia	Private	Free Men of Color (FMC)
Leon, Thelesfort	1st Louisiana Native Guards, LA Militia	Private	Free Men of Color (FMC)
Lepine, Frederick	1st Louisiana Native Guards, LA Militia	Sergeant	Free Men of Color (FMC)
Lepine, Joseph	1st Louisiana Native Guards, LA Militia	Private	Free Men of Color (FMC)
Lesassier, Valdes	1st Louisiana Native Guards, LA Militia	Private	Free Men of Color (FMC)
Lesprit, Jules	1st Louisiana Native Guards, LA Militia	Corporal	Free Men of Color (FMC)
Levacher, P. L.	1st Louisiana Native Guards, LA Militia	Private	Free Men of Color (FMC)
Leveille, Gerome	1st Louisiana Native Guards, LA Militia	Private	Free Men of Color (FMC)
Leveille, Louis J.	1st Louisiana Native Guards, LA Militia	Corporal	Free Men of Color (FMC)
Lewis, Alcide	1st Louisiana Native Guards, LA Militia	Captain	Free Men of Color (FMC)
Lewis, Lafayette	1st Louisiana Native Guards, LA Militia	Private	Free Men of Color (FMC)
Lewis, Simon	1st Louisiana Native Guards, LA Militia	Private	Free Men of Color (FMC)
Lherisse, Vincent	1st Louisiana Native Guards, LA Militia	Private	Free Men of Color (FMC)
Lino, Manuel	1st Louisiana Native Guards, LA Militia	Private	Free Men of Color (FMC)
Lopes, Alphonse	1st Louisiana Native Guards, LA Militia	Private	Free Men of Color (FMC)
Lorenz, L.	1st Louisiana Native Guards, LA Militia	Private	Free Men of Color (FMC)
Lorenzo, J.	1st Louisiana Native Guards, LA Militia	Private	Free Men of Color (FMC)
Louck, J.	1st Louisiana Native Guards, LA Militia	C. F.	Free Men of Color (FMC)
Louis, Charles	1st Louisiana Native Guards, LA Militia	Private	Free Men of Color (FMC)
Louis, Joseph	1st Louisiana Native Guards, LA Militia	Private	Free Men of Color (FMC)
Louis, Pierre	1st Louisiana Native Guards, LA Militia	Private	Free Men of Color (FMC)
Lubin, Guillaume	1st Louisiana Native Guards, LA Militia	Private	Free Men of Color (FMC)
MacArty, B.	1st Louisiana Native Guards, LA Militia	Private	Free Men of Color (FMC)
MacArty, Jules	1st Louisiana Native Guards, LA Militia	Private	Free Men of Color (FMC)
MacArty, Prosper	1st Louisiana Native Guards, LA Militia	Private	Free Men of Color (FMC)
Madison, Eugene	1st Louisiana Native Guards, LA Militia	Private	Free Men of Color (FMC)
Magloire, Cosimir	1st Louisiana Native Guards, LA Militia	Private	Free Men of Color (FMC)
Magloire, Joseph	1st Louisiana Native Guards, LA Militia	Private	Free Men of Color (FMC)
Magloire, Louis	1st Louisiana Native Guards, LA Militia	Private	Free Men of Color (FMC)
Mallet, Jules	1st Louisiana Native Guards, LA Militia	Private	Free Men of Color (FMC)
Mansion, Joseph	1st Louisiana Native Guards, LA Militia	Private	Free Men of Color (FMC)
Manuel, Louis	1st Louisiana Native Guards, LA Militia	Private	Free Men of Color (FMC)
Maran, C.	1st Louisiana Native Guards, LA Militia	Private	Free Men of Color (FMC)
Marc, Murville	1st Louisiana Native Guards, LA Militia	Private	Free Men of Color (FMC)
Marcelin, John	1st Louisiana Native Guards, LA Militia	Private	Free Men of Color (FMC)
Marcelin, Joseph	1st Louisiana Native Guards, LA Militia	Private	Free Men of Color (FMC)

Marigny, G.		1st Louisiana Native Guards, LA Militia	Private	Free Men of Color (FMC)
Marine, Joseph		1st Louisiana Native Guards, LA Militia	Private	Free Men of Color (FMC)
Marine, P.		1st Louisiana Native Guards, LA Militia	Private	Free Men of Color (FMC)
Martin, A.		1st Louisiana Native Guards, LA Militia	Sergeant	Free Men of Color (FMC)
Martin, Agenore		1st Louisiana Native Guards, LA Militia	Private	Free Men of Color (FMC)
Martin, Joseph		1st Louisiana Native Guards, LA Militia	Private	Free Men of Color (FMC)
Martin, L.		1st Louisiana Native Guards, LA Militia	Private	Free Men of Color (FMC)
Martin, Louis		1st Louisiana Native Guards, LA Militia	Private	Free Men of Color (FMC)
Martin, Theo		1st Louisiana Native Guards, LA Militia	Private	Free Men of Color (FMC)
Mathe, B.		1st Louisiana Native Guards, LA Militia	Private	Free Men of Color (FMC)
Mathieu, Henrich		1st Louisiana Native Guards, LA Militia	Sergeant	Free Men of Color (FMC)
Mathieu, Henry		1st Louisiana Native Guards, LA Militia	Private	Free Men of Color (FMC)
Mau, Nathaniel G.		1st Louisiana Native Guards, LA Militia	Private	Free Men of Color (FMC)
Maurice, Augustine		1st Louisiana Native Guards, LA Militia	Private	Free Men of Color (FMC)
Maurice, E.		1st Louisiana Native Guards, LA Militia	Private	Free Men of Color (FMC)
Maurice, Michael		1st Louisiana Native Guards, LA Militia	Private	Free Men of Color (FMC)
Maurice, Washington		1st Louisiana Native Guards, LA Militia	Corporal	Free Men of Color (FMC)
McDonnel, Thomas		1st Louisiana Native Guards, LA Militia	Private	Free Men of Color (FMC)
McKenna, William		1st Louisiana Native Guards, LA Militia	Private	Free Men of Color (FMC)
Meide, Arthur		1st Louisiana Native Guards, LA Militia	Private	Free Men of Color (FMC)
Meilleur, F.		1st Louisiana Native Guards, LA Militia	Private	Free Men of Color (FMC)
Meilleur, Gustave		1st Louisiana Native Guards, LA Militia	Sergeant	Free Men of Color (FMC)
Meilleur, Lange		1st Louisiana Native Guards, LA Militia	Private	Free Men of Color (FMC)
Menard, S.		1st Louisiana Native Guards, LA Militia	Private	Free Men of Color (FMC)
Mercada, Francis		1st Louisiana Native Guards, LA Militia	Private	Free Men of Color (FMC)
Merelle, J.		1st Louisiana Native Guards, LA Militia	Private	Free Men of Color FMC)
Merlet,		1st Louisiana Native Guards, LA Militia	Private	Free Men of Color (FMC)
Metoyer, H.		1st Louisiana Native Guards, LA Militia	Private	Free Men of Color (FMC)
Meunier, Henry		1st Louisiana Native Guards, LA Militia	Private	Free Men of Color (FMC)
Michel, Antonio		1st Louisiana Native Guards, LA Militia	Private	Free Men of Color (FMC)
Michel, Marcelain		1st Louisiana Native Guards, LA Militia	2nd Lt	Free Men of Color (FMC)
Milaire, Joseph		1st Louisiana Native Guards, LA Militia	Private	Free Men of Color (FMC)
Mirabin, Alcede		1st Louisiana Native Guards, LA Militia	Private	Free Men of Color (FMC)
Mitchell, Louis		1st Louisiana Native Guards, LA Militia	Private	Free Men of Color (FMC)
Miton, M.		1st Louisiana Native Guards, LA Militia	Private	Free Men of Color (FMC)
Mollay, Pierre		1st Louisiana Native Guards, LA Militia	Corporal	Free Men of Color (FMC)
Mallet, Arthur		1st Louisiana Native Guards, LA Militia	Private	Free Men of Color (FMC)
Monde, Alicde		1st Louisiana Native Guards, LA Militia	Private	Free Men of Color (FMC)
Monde, L.		1st Louisiana Native Guards, LA Militia	Private	Free Men of Color (FMC)
Monde, Lolo		1st Louisiana Native Guards, LA Militia	Private	Free Yen of Color (FMC)
Mondry, Lucien		1st Louisiana Native Guards, LA Militia	Private	Free Men of Color (FMC)
Monette, 3. J.		1st Louisiana Native Guards, LA Militia	Corporal	Free Men of Color (FMC)
Monrose, Eugene		1st Louisiana Native Guards, LA Militia	Private	Free Men of Color (FMC)
Montor, C.		1st Louisiana Native Guards, LA Militia	Private	Free Men of Color (FMC)
Montreuil, J. J.		1st Louisiana Native Guards, LA Militia	Corporal	Free Men of Color (FMC)
Moran, D.		1st Louisiana Native Guards, LA Militia	Private	Free Men of Color (FMC)
Moran, 0. D.		1st Louisiana Native Guards, LA Militia	Private	Free Men of Color (FMC)
Morant, C.		1st Louisiana Native Guards, LA Militia	Private	Free Yen of Color (FMC)

Moret, J. B.		1st Louisiana Native Guards, LA Militia	Private	Free Men of Color (FMC)
Morett, Eugene		1st Louisiana Native Guards, LA Militia	Private	Free Men of Color (FMC)
Morle, Antonio		1st Louisiana Native Guards, LA Militia	Private	Free Men of Color (FMC)
Mornay, Millian		1st Louisiana Native Guards, LA Militia	Private	Free Men of Color (FMC)
Mornet, Augustine		1st Louisiana Native Guards, LA Militia	Private	Free Men of Color (FMC)
Morphy, Jules		1st Louisiana Native Guards, LA Militia	Private	Free Men of Color (FMC)
Muller, Adolph		1st Louisiana Native Guards, LA Militia	Private	Free Men of Color (FMC)
Murley, Francis		1st Louisiana Native Guards, LA Militia	Private	Free Men of Color (FMC)
Narcisse, Honore		1st Louisiana Native Guards, LA Militia	Private	Free Men of Color (FMC)
Nell, L.		1st Louisiana Native Guards, LA Militia	Private	Free Men of Color (FMC)
Nicaud, Alcei		1st Louisiana Native Guards, LA Militia	Private	Free Men of Color (FMC)
Noel, Charles		1st Louisiana Native Guards, LA Militia	Private	Free Men of Color (FMC)
Padoux, Antoine		1st Louisiana Native Guards, LA Militia	Private	Free Men of Color (FMC)
Page, Louis		1st Louisiana Native Guards, LA Militia	Private	Free Men of Color (FMC)
Paton, F.		1st Louisiana Native Guards, LA Militia	Private	Free Men of Color (FMC)
Patron, J. B.	3	1st Louisiana Native Guards, LA Militia	Private	Free Men of Color (FMC)
Patterson, Auguste		1st Louisiana Native Guards, LA Militia	Private	Free Men of Color (FMC)
Patterson, Donatien		1st Louisiana Native Guards, LA Militia	Private	Free Men of Color (FMC)
Patterson, Joseph		1st Louisiana Native Guards, LA Militia	Private	Free Men of Color (FMC)
Peche, Pierre		1st Louisiana Native Guards, LA Militia	Corporal	Free Men of Color (FMC)
Pedesclaux, Bonny		1st Louisiana Native Guards, LA Militia	Private	Free Men of Color (FMC)
Pedesclaux, Charles		1st Louisiana Native Guards, LA Militia	Private	Free Men of Color (FMC)
Pelissier, L.		1st Louisiana Native Guards, LA Militia	Private	Free Men of Color (FMC)
Penas, Charles		1st Louisiana Native Guards, LA Militia	Private	Free Men of Color (FMC)
Penel, Julien		1st Louisiana Native Guards, LA Militia	Private	Free Men of Color (FMC)
Pepe, Hippolyte		1st Louisiana Native Guards, LA Militia	Private	Free Men of Color (FMC)
Perche, Eloie		1st Louisiana Native Guards, LA Militia	2nd Lt	Free Men of Color (FMC)
Perez, A.		1st Louisiana Native Guards, LA Militia	Private	Free Men of Color (FMC)
Perez, Sedro		1st Louisiana Native Guards, LA Militia	Private	Free Men of Color (FMC)
Peroux, Auguste		1st Louisiana Native Guards, LA Militia	Private	Free Men of Color (FMC)
Perrault, Edgard		1st Louisiana Native Guards, LA Militia	Private	Free Men of Color (FMC)
Perrault, S.		1st Louisiana Native Guards, LA Militia	Private	Free Men of Color (FMC)
Perrez, T. M.		1st Louisiana Native Guards, LA Militia	Private	Free Men of Color (FMC)
Petit, Louis		1st Louisiana Native Guards, LA Militia	1st Sgt	Free Men of Color (FMC)
Philippe, Urein		1st Louisiana Native Guards, LA Militia	Private	Free Men of Color (FMC)
Philogene, Jacques		1st Louisiana Native Guards, LA Militia	Private	Free Men of Color (FMC)
Picon, A.		1st Louisiana Native Guards, LA Militia	Private	Free Men of Color (FMC)
Picot, C.		1st Louisiana Native Guards, LA Militia	Private	Free Men of Color (FMC)
Picotte, Ernest		1st Louisiana Native Guards, LA Militia	Private	Free Men of Color (FMC)
Picou, D.		1st Louisiana Native Guards, LA Militia	Private	Free Men of Color (FMC)
Picou, J.		1st Louisiana Native Guards, LA Militia	Private	Free Men of Color (FMC)
Picoux, Octave		1st Louisiana Native Guards, LA Militia	Private	Free Men of Color (FMC)
Piernas, Antoine		1st Louisiana Native Guards, LA Militia	Private	Free Men of Color (FMC)
Pierre, A.		1st Louisiana Native Guards, LA Militia	Private	Free Men of Color (FMC)
Pierre, Alexander		1st Louisiana Native Guards, LA Militia	Private	Free Men of Color (FMC)
Pierre, Eugene		1st Louisiana Native Guards, LA Militia	Corporal	Free Men of Color (FMC)
Pierre, Jacques		1st Louisiana Native Guards, LA Militia	Private	Free Men of Color (FMC)
Pierre, Leon		1st Louisiana Native Guards, LA Militia	Private	Free Men of Color (FMC)

Directory of African American Confederates in the U.S. Civil War

Name		Unit	Rank	Status
Pierre, Theodule		1st Louisiana Native Guards, LA Militia	Corporal	Free Men of Color (FMC)
Pierre, Victor		1st Louisiana Native Guards, LA Militia	Private	Free Men of Color (FMC)
Pinta, Henry		1st Louisiana Native Guards, LA Militia	Private	Free Men of Color (FMC)
Polinard, Pierre		1st Louisiana Native Guards, LA Militia	Private	Free Men of Color (FMC)
Populus, Armand		1st Louisiana Native Guards, LA Militia	Private	Free Men of Color (FMC)
Populus, Joseph		1st Louisiana Native Guards, LA Militia	Private	Free Men of Color (FMC)
Poree, Ernest		1st Louisiana Native Guards, LA Militia	Private	Free Men of Color (FMC)
Poree, F.		1st Louisiana Native Guards, LA Militia	Private	Free Men of Color (FMC)
Poree, Francis		1st Louisiana Native Guards, LA Militia	Private	Free Men of Color (FMC)
Poree, M.		1st Louisiana Native Guards, LA Militia	Private	Free Men of Color (FMC)
Poree, Paul		1st Louisiana Native Guards, LA Militia	Private	Free Men of Color (FMC)
Porree, Nelson		1st Louisiana Native Guards, LA Militia	Private	Free Men of Color (FMC)
Pastille, Leon		1st Louisiana Native Guards, LA Militia	Private	Free Men of Color (FMC)
Patin, Charles		1st Louisiana Native Guards, LA Militia	Private	Free Men of Color (FMC)
Prados, C.		1st Louisiana Native Guards, LA Militia	Private	Free Men of Color (FMC)
Prevost, Francois		1st Louisiana Native Guards, LA Militia	Private	Free Men of Color (FMC)
Quevin, Leonard		1st Louisiana Native Guards, LA Militia	Private	Free Men of Color (FMC)
Quintal, Antoine		1st Louisiana Native Guards, LA Militia	Private	Free Men of Color (FMC)
Ramos, A.		1st Louisiana Native Guards, LA Militia	Private	Free Men of Color (FMC)
Raphael, Aristide		1st Louisiana Native Guards, LA Militia	Private	Free Men of Color (FMC)
Rapp, Eugene		1st Louisiana Native Guards, LA Militia	1st Lt	Free Men of Color FMC
Raymond, Antonio		1st Louisiana Native Guards, LA Militia	Private	Free Men of Color (FMC)
Raynal, A.		1st Louisiana Native Guards, LA Militia	1st Sgt	Free Men of Color (FMC)
Rebouil, Henry		1st Louisiana Native Guards, LA Militia	Corporal	Free Men of Color (FMC)
Reif, Samuel		1st Louisiana Native Guards, LA Militia	Private	Free Men of Color (FMC)
Reif, T. E.		1st Louisiana Native Guards, LA Militia	Corporal	Free Men of Color (FMC)
Remy, A.		1st Louisiana Native Guards, LA Militia	Private	Free Men of Color (FMC)
Remy, F.		1st Louisiana Native Guards, LA Militia	Private	Free Men of Color (FMC)
Remy, J. J.		1st Louisiana Native Guards, LA Militia	1st Sgt	Free Men of Color (FMC)
Remy, 0.		1st Louisiana Native Guards, LA Militia	Private	Free Men of Color (FMC)
Remy, T.		1st Louisiana Native Guards, LA Militia	Private	Free Men of Color (FMC)
Renier, J. B.		1st Louisiana Native Guards, LA Militia	Private	Free Men of Color (FMC)
Revoil, Arthur		1st Louisiana Native Guards, LA Militia	Sgt Maj	Free Men of Color (FMC)
Rey, Armand		1st Louisiana Native Guards, LA Militia	Drummer	Free Men of Color (FMC)
Rey, H. Louis		1st Louisiana Native Guards, LA Militia	Captain	Free Men of Color (FMC)
Rey, Hippolyte		1st Louisiana Native Guards, LA Militia	Corporal	Free Men of Color (FMC)
Rey, Joseph		1st Louisiana Native Guards, LA Militia	Corporal	Free Men of Color (FMC)
Rey, Leon		1st Louisiana Native Guards, LA Militia	Private	Free Men of Color (FMC)
Rey, Octave		1st Louisiana Native Guards, LA Militia	2nd Lt	Free Men of Color (FMC)
Reyes, F.		1st Louisiana Native Guards, LA Militia	2nd Lt	Free Men of Color (FMC)
Riband, Jean		1st Louisiana Native Guards, LA Militia	Private	Free Men of Color (FMC)
Richard, A.		1st Louisiana Native Guards, LA Militia	Private	Free Men of Color (FMC)
Richard, J.		1st Louisiana Native Guards, LA Militia	Private	Free Men of Color (FMC)
Rieffel, Edward		1st Louisiana Native Guards, LA Militia	Private	Free Men of Color (FMC)
Robert, Emile		1st Louisiana Native Guards, LA Militia	Sergeant	Free Men of Color (FMC)
Roche, A.		1st Louisiana Native Guards, LA Militia	Corporal	Free Men of Color (FMC)
Roche, Ialien		1st Louisiana Native Guards, LA Militia	Corporal	Free Men of Color (FMC)
Rochon, Adolph		1st Louisiana Native Guards, LA Militia	Private	Free Men of Color (FMC)

Rock, Sosthene	1st Louisiana Native Guards, LA Militia	1st Lt	Free Men of Color (FMC)
Roland, Charles	1st Louisiana Native Guards, LA Militia	Corporal	Free Men of Color (FMC)
Romain, A.	1st Louisiana Native Guards, LA Militia	Private	Free Men of Color (FMC)
Sabatier, Dursin	1st Louisiana Native Guards, LA Militia	Private	Free Men of Color (FMC)
Sabatier, Paul	1st Louisiana Native Guards, LA Militia	Private	Free Men of Color (FMC)
Sacriste, J. D.	1st Louisiana Native Guards, LA Militia	Private	Free Men of Color (FMC)
Salvador, Gaspard	1st Louisiana Native Guards, LA Militia	Private	Free Men of Color (FMC)
Samuel, Oscar	1st Louisiana Native Guards, LA Militia	Private	Free Men of Color (FMC)
Sannon, Theophiles	1st Louisiana Native Guards, LA Militia	Surgeon	Free Men of Color (FMC)
Santos, Leonard	1st Louisiana Native Guards, LA Militia	Private	Free Men of Color (FMC)
Saragossa, Arthur	1st Louisiana Native Guards, LA Militia	Private	Free Men of Color (FMC)
Sarrazin, A.	1st Louisiana Native Guards, LA Militia	Private	Free Men of Color (FMC)
Saulet, Zenin	1st Louisiana Native Guards, LA Militia	Private	Free Men of Color (FMC)
Saulny, E.	1st Louisiana Native Guards, LA Militia	Private	Free Men of Color (FMC)
Sauvinet, A. G.	1st Louisiana Native Guards, LA Militia	Private	Free Men of Color (FMC)
Sauvinet, G.	1st Louisiana Native Guards, LA Militia	Corporal	Free Men of Color (FMC)
Sauvinet, I.	1st Louisiana Native Guards, LA Militia	Captain	Free Men of Color (FMC)
Savary, Henry	1st Louisiana Native Guards, LA Militia	Private	Free Men of Color (FMC)
Seaux, Eugene	1st Louisiana Native Guards, LA Militia	Private	Free Men of Color (FMC)
Seaux, Gidore	1st Louisiana Native Guards, LA Militia	Private	Free Men of Color (FMC)
Segura, A.	1st Louisiana Native Guards, LA Militia	Private	Free Men of Color (FMC)
Sejour, M.	1st Louisiana Native Guards, LA Militia	Private	Free Men of Color (FMC)
Senac, Antonia	1st Louisiana Native Guards, LA Militia	Private	Free Men of Color (FMC)
Sena, T.	1st Louisiana Native Guards, LA Militia	Private	Free Men of Color FMC)
Sentmanat, Charles	1st Louisiana Native Guards, LA Militia	Captain	Free Men of Color (FMC)
Servan, Paul	1st Louisiana Native Guards, LA Militia	Private	Free Men of Color (FMC)
Severin, Francis	1st Louisiana Native Guards, LA Militia	Private	Free Men of Color (FMC)
Taylor, Charles	1st Louisiana Native Guards, LA Militia	Private	Free Men of Color (FMC)
Terence, Clement	1st Louisiana Native Guards, LA Militia	Private	Free Men of Color (FMC)
Ternoir, Leon	1st Louisiana Native Guards, LA Militia	Private	Free Men of Color (FMC)
Tervalon, A. F.	1st Louisiana Native Guards, LA Militia	Private	Free Men of Color (FMC)
Theodore, C.	1st Louisiana Native Guards, LA Militia	Private	Free Men of Color (FMC)
Thezan, Theodore	1st Louisiana Native Guards, LA Militia	Private	Free Men of Color (FMC)
Thibaut, Dominique	1st Louisiana Native Guards, LA Militia	Private	Free Men of Color (FMC)
Thiot, Armand	1st Louisiana Native Guards, LA Militia	Corporal	Free Men of Color (FMC)
Thomas, Antoine	1st Louisiana Native Guards, LA Militia	Private	Free Men of Color (FMC)
Thomas, Louis	1st Louisiana Native Guards, LA Militia	Private	Free Men of Color (FMC)
Thomas, Pierre	1st Louisiana Native Guards, LA Militia	Private	Free Men of Color (FMC)
Thomassin, Benjamin	1st Louisiana Native Guards, LA Militia	Private	Free Men of Color (FMC)
Thompson, Joseph	1st Louisiana Native Guards, LA Militia	Corporal	Free Men of Color (FMC)
Thompson, Pierre	1st Louisiana Native Guards, LA Militia	Private	Free Men of Color (FMC)
Tomlinson, E.	1st Louisiana Native Guards, LA Militia	Private	Free Men of Color (FMC)
Torresse, Justave	1st Louisiana Native Guards, LA Militia	Private	Free Men of Color (FMC)
Toussaint, Auguste	1st Louisiana Native Guards, LA Militia	Corporal	Free Men of Color (FMC)
Toussaint, Joseph	1st Louisiana Native Guards, LA Militia	Private	Free Men of Color (FMC)
Trepagnier, Francis	1st Louisiana Native Guards, LA Militia	Private	Free Men of Color (FMC)
Turpin, J.	1st Louisiana Native Guards, LA Militia	Private	Free Men of Color (FMC)
Ulysse, Charles	1st Louisiana Native Guards, LAMilitia	Private	Free Men of Color (FMC)

Urquhart, C. V.		1st Louisiana Native Guards, LA Militia	Private	Free Men of Color (FMC)
Valentin, Oscar		1st Louisiana Native Guards, LA Militia	Private	Free Men of Color (FMC)
Valery, Oscar		1st Louisiana Native Guards, LA Militia	Private	Free Men of Color (FMC)
Valet, Desire		1st Louisiana Native Guards, LA Militia	Private	Free Men of Color (FMC)
Ventura,		1st Louisiana Native Guards, LA Militia	Private	Free Men of Color (FMC)
Verdon, L.		1st Louisiana Native Guards, LA Militia	1st Lt	Free Men of Color (FMC)
Victor, Arthur J.		1st Louisiana Native Guards, LA Militia	Private	Free Men of Color (FMC)
Victor, Nicholas		1st Louisiana Native Guards, LA Militia	Private	Free Men of Color (FMC)
Vidal, F.		1st Louisiana Native Guards, LA Militia	Private	Free Men of Color (FMC)
Vidal, J. T.		1st Louisiana Native Guards, LA Militia	Private	Free Men of Color (FMC)
Vierra, Louis		1st Louisiana Native Guards, LA Militia	Private	Free Men of Color (FMC)
Vignaud, Epienne		1st Louisiana Native Guards, LA Militia	Private	Free Men of Color (FMC)
Vignaud, Joseph		1st Louisiana Native Guards, LA Militia	Private	Free Men of Color (FMC)
Vincent, Eugene		1st Louisiana Native Guards, LA Militia	Private	Free Men of Color (FMC)
Vivant, Louis		1st Louisiana Native Guards, LA Militia	Private	Free Men of Color (FMC)
Voisin, Feorand		1st Louisiana Native Guards, LA Militia	Private	Free Men of Color (FMC)
Voltaire, Jacques		1st Louisiana Native Guards, LA Militia	Private	Free Men of Color (FMC)
Wale, William		1st Louisiana Native Guards, LA Militia	Private	Free Men of Color (FMC)
Warburg, Daniel		1st Louisiana Native Guards, LA Militia	Private	Free Men of Color (FMC)
Washington, Baptiste		1st Louisiana Native Guards, LA Militia	Private	Free Men of Color (FMC)

MARYLAND

NAME	CO.	UNIT	RANK	SLAVE / FREE MISC NOTES
Williams, John	A	2nd Battalion Maryland Infantry	Cook	

MISSISSIPPI

A documented case of a Mississippi black confederate man firing a weapon against Northern troops is that of the expert rifleman Holt Collier.

According to records found the state archives, Collier disobeyed his master, Confederate Colonel Howell Hinds of Greenville, and sought to join a Confederate unit.

You probably have no idea what the "Teddy Bear" was all about. The majority of people have never heard of Holt Collier, but those who have may be astonished to read about his past. In 1848 Holt Collier was born into slavery in Mississippi.

He had become an expert on animals in the Mississippi Delta by the age of 15 and was regarded as one of the top bear hunters in the American southeast.

Collier sought to join the Confederacy after being set free prior to the conflict between the North and the South. He was first rejected because of his age, but he was eventually allowed into the 9th Texas Brigade. His service was honorable, and he would serve under Confederate Lt. Gen. Nathan Bedford Forrest as a valued assistant and sniper.

His renown would rise after the war. He claimed to have killed 3,000 bears and to have been the "guide of choice. Men would go long distances to hunt with him, as if they were studying from the master himself. Holt got a request from none other than United States President Teddy Roosevelt in 1902.

"I prepared my belongings and located a lovely camping spot. I was in charge of the hunt. The President arrived with a car-load of security, but he left all except one in the vehicle. In any case, he was safer with me than with all of Washington's cops. "The President was a kind man," Holt later said, "and he'd pause every now and again to solicit other people's opinions."

Roosevelt didn't want to wait more than a week to view a live bear, therefore the hunt was originally set for ten days. The bear was delivered...'popped out of the gap' where it was promised...but the "Colonel" and his company had left the blind for lunch.

Frustrated, Collier determined to take more active measures to bring the bear to the Colonel, despite his exhaustion from his attempts to flesh out the creature. He challenged the bear, but Jocko, Collier's beloved hunting dog, was captured by the bear.

Collier saved him by clubbing the bear with his rifle, then subduing it with a rope around its neck and tying it to a willow tree after a battle. President Roosevelt would be summoned by Collier to show

him the bear he had missed earlier and to put it out of its suffering.

Railroad mogul Stuyvesant Fish and Mississippi Governor Andrew Longino were among those in the party who urged the leader of the free world to shoot the bear.

Mississippi Department of Archives and History, P.O. Box 71 Jackson, MS 39205, Telephone: 601-359-6876, http://www.mdah.state.ms.us/

NAME	CO.	UNIT	RANK	SLAVE / FREE MISC NOTES
Abraham	H	41st Mississippi Infantry	Laundress	
Adam	A	3rd Mississippi Infantry	Cook	
Albert	I	14th Mississippi Infantry	Cook	
Albert	B	23rd Mississippi Infantry	Cook	
Alfred	A,F	23rd Mississippi Infantry	Cook	Slave
Alfred	I	4th Mississippi Infantry	Cook	
Andy	C,G	20th Mississippi Infantry	Cook	
Bill	B	20th Mississippi Infantry	Cook	
Bill (Old Bill)		1st Mississippi Light artillery, Battery A (Wither's Regiment) Served as a Servant to Capt. Samuel Jones Ridley	Cook Servant	Slave From Madison County MS
Blackman	A	7th Mississippi Regiment Served as a Servant to 2nd Cpl John Everly LA Hoiden	Servant	Slave of John E. Holden of Franklin County, MS.
Buck	G	20th Mississippi Infantry	Cook	
Charles	A	13th Mississippi Infantry	Servant Cook	Slave of QM Capt Duncan P. McAllum
Charles	B	23rd Mississippi Infantry	Cook	
Cornelius		Capt. Hoole's Company, Mississippi Light Artillery (The Hudsen Battery)	Teamster	
Edmond	G	3rd Mississippi Infantry	Cook	
Edmond	K	44th Mississippi Infantry	Cook	
Elisha	L	41st Mississippi Infantry	Laundress	
Ellick	F&S F	42nd Mississippi Infantry Regiment 1st Mississippi Infantry Regiment (Johnston's) Served as a servant to 1st Lt (Surgeon) Leander 3. Wilson	Servant	
Flanders	B	23rd Mississippi Infantry	Cook	
Frederick	G	3rd Mississippi Infantry	Cook	
George	B	3rd Mississippi Infantry	Cook	
Henry	I	14th Mississippi Infantry	Chief Cook	
Henry	G	41st Mississippi Infantry	Laundress	
Henry	D	6th Mississippi Infantry Served as a Servant to Capt. William J. Finch	Servant	Saved the life of Capt. Finch by carrying him off the battlefield when he was wounded.
Henry	F	Jeff Davis Legion Mississippi Cavalry	Teamster	
Isaac	D	2nd (Quinn's-State Troops), Mississippi Infantry	Musician	
Jack	E	46th Mississippi Infantry	Cook	
Jess	G	20th Mississippi Infantry	Cook	

War Chicken

A copy is Available at newsonpublishing.com

In July, 1863, the Army of Northern Virginia suffered a defeat at the hands of the Yankees in a place called Gettysburg. As the southern army was preparing to return to Virginia, General Robert E. Lee suddenly realized that his pet was missing from her usual spot.

"Where is the hen?" he asked, in a concerned tone.

By this time, the soldiers knew about the hen, and her absence caused much concern. The retreat came to a halt as the men looked for Nellie. The General himself joined in the hunt.

Here is a strange war time comparison: According to legend, the chickens that saved Western civilization were discovered by the side of a road in a town in Greece in the first decade of the fifth century B.C.

The Athenian navy general and politician, Themistocles, on his way to confront the invading Persian forces, stopped to watch two cocks fighting and summoned his troops, saying:

"Behold, these do not fight for their household gods, for the monuments of their ancestors, for glory, for liberty or the safety of their children, but only because one will not give way to the other."

The tale does not describe what happened to the loser nor explain why the soldiers found this display of instinctive aggression inspirational rather than pointless and depressing.

However, the fate of Western Europe, especially Athenian democracy in Greece, would have taken a turn for the worse had it not been Themistocles and his development of the Greek navy and national politics.

Yes, in like fashion, Lee had a pet and gave the chicken the name "Nellie" and left his tent flap open so she could come and go as she wanted inside. Finally Nellie was found. Little Nellie the Hen travelled with the Army of Northern Virginia for over two years, laying an egg for General Lee almost daily to earn her keep and safe haven.

Jim	A	13th Mississippi Infantry	Servant Cook	Slave of Sgt. Judge Cornwell
John		13th Mississippi Infantry	Servant Cook	Slave of Regimental surgeon Dr. Albert Gallatin Anderson's
John	C	14th Confederate Cavalry Served as a Servant to Zeb Williams	Body Servant	Slave of Bob Williams of Rienzi, Mississippi
John	B	23rd Regiment Mississippi Infantry	Cook	Slave
John	D	2nd (Juinn's-State Troops), Mississippi Infantry	Musician	
Jolly	I	4th Mississippi Infantry	Cook	
Jonah	I	4th Mississippi Infantry	Cook	
Kemp	C	7th Mississippi Infantry		Slave of Pvt. George S. Lea who was killed at the battle of Franklin, Tennessee. Kemp accompanied the body home.
Lewis	A	3rd Mississippi Infantry	Cook	
Major	B	3rd Mississippi Infantry	Cook	
Matt	B	3rd Mississippi Infantry	Cook	
Moses	I	41st Regiment Mississippi Infantry (Capt. Williams' Company)	Laundress	
Owen	B	20th Mississippi Infantry	Cook	
Peter	K	31st Mississippi Infantry	Cook	
Peter	B	41st Mississippi infantry	Laundress	
Peter		Capt. Polk's Independent Company (Polk Rangers), Mississippi Cavalry		
Phill	F	3rd Mississippi Infantry (State Troops)	Cook	
Phillip		13th Mississippi Infantry	Servant Cook	
Sam	F	3rd Mississippi Infantry	Cook	
Sampson	A,B,	23rd Mississippi Infantry	Cook	Slave
Samuel	G	3rd Mississippi Infantry	Cook	
Simon	I	23rd Mississippi Infantry	Cook	
Sinacer	I	4th Mississippi Infantry	Cook	
Solomon	A	3rd Mississippi Infantry	Cook	
Stephen	D	42nd Mississippi Regiment Served as a Servant to Lt. George Adrian Howze	Servant	Lt. Howze was KIA and Stephen retrieved his body from the battlefield taking it to a hospital when he was then buried.
Tom	B	20th Mississippi Infantry	Cook	
Tony	G	20th Mississippi Infantry	Cook	
Aarons, Charlie		Served as a Servant to his master's son John Harris	Bodyguard Servant	Jason Harris Plantation near Meridian, Mississippi.According to his statements in the Alabama Slave Narratives
Abe Sojourner		36th Mississippi Infantry	Cook	Copiah-Clay County, MS Conf Pensioner
Abe Vincent		Seven Stars Mississippi Lt Artillery		Copiah County, MS Conf Pensioner
Abernathy, Simon	B	17th Mississippi Infantry	Cook	
Abram (Abrams)Gus		Quartermaster Dept		Panola County, MS Conf Pensioner

Directory of African American Confederates in the U.S. Civil War

Abschew, Wiley		Wagon Train	Dept Teamster	Yazoo County, MS Conf Pensioner
Adams, Harrison		Unknown Unit	Servant & Cook	Leflore County, MS Conf Pensioner
Adams, Joe		Served as a servant to Capt. R. S. Adams	Servant	Kemper County, MS Conf Pensioner
Adams, Lewis (Louis)		36th Mississippi Infantry	Cook	Hinds County, MS Conf Pensioner
Agee, Eli		6th Mississippi Cavalry		Hinds County, MS Conf Pensioner
Alcorn, Andrew		1st Mississippi Infantry		Quitman County, MS Conf
Aldridge, George		Unknown Unit	Cook	Montgomery County, MS Conf Pensioner
Aldridge, John		3rd Mississippi Cavalry		Grenada County, MS Conf
Aldridge, Johnson		34th Mississippi Infantry	Servant	Wayne County, MS Conf Pensioner
Aldrige, Alfred		Hospital	Attendant	Madison County, MS Conf Pensioner
Allen, Berry		Unknown Unit		Leflore County, MS Conf Pensioner
Allen, Eli		20th Mississippi Infantry		Leflore County, MS Conf Pensioner, wounded in battle.
Allen, James		37th Mississippi Infantry		Yazoo County, MS Conf Pensioner
Allen, Peter	A	1st Mississippi Light Artillery		Madison County, MS Conf Pensioner
Allen, Sam		Unknown Unit		Leake County, MS Conf Pensioner
Allen, Solomon		Breastworks	Laborer	Oktibbeha County, MS Conf Pensioner
Allen, Willis		Jefferson Mississippi Light Artillery	Cook	Yazoo County, MS Conf Pensioner
Alston, Ishman		35th Mississippi Infantry		Attala County, MS Conf Pensioner
Anderson, George		38th Mississippi Infantry		Choctaw County, MS Conf
Anderson, H. W.		20th Mississippi Infantry		Bolivar County, MS Conf
Anderson, Job	I	1st Mississippi Lt Artillery		Yazoo County, MS Conf Pensioner
Anderson, Romeo		Wirt Adams's MS. Cavalry Regt	Cook	Forrest County, MS Conf
Anderson, Santee		27th Mississippi Infantry	Cook	Forrest County, MS Conf
Anderson, Stephen		Stanford's Mississippi Arty Battery	Servant	Grenada County, MS Conf Pensioner
Applewhite, Jerry		7th Mississippi Infantry		Marion County, MS Conf Pensioner
Applewhite, Richard		28th Mississippi Cavalry	Servant	Montgomery County, MS Conf Pensioner
Armstrong, Tucker		2nd Mississippi Infantry	Servant	Monroe County, MS Conf
Arnold, John	A	36th Mississippi Infantry (Mount Zion Guards) Served as a Body Servant to Sgt Albert Brown Douglass	Body Servant	Lincoln County, MS Conf Pensioner
Arnold, Pud	A	1st Mississippi Infantry Battalion	Servant	Marshall County, MS Conf Pensioner
Arrington, Robert		16th Mississippi Infantry		Wilkinson County, MS Conf Pensioner
Askew, Fred		18th Mississippi Cavalry Battalion	Servant	Panda County, MS Conf Pensioner
Atkinson, George		12th Mississippi Battalion Cavalry Partisans		Chickasaw County, MS Conf Pensioner
Atkinson, Jack		8th Mississippi Cavalry		Lee County, MS Conf Pensioner
Atwood, Tom		15th Mississippi Infantry		Attala County, MS Conf Pensioner
Augustus, Dan		Railroad	Worker	Lee County, MS Conf Pensioner
Augustus, January		Railroad	Worker	Lee County, MS Conf Pensioner
Avant, Fed	C	1st Mississippi Light Artillery	Servant	Lafayette County, MS Conf
Avant, Jarret		Commissary Department	Worker	Panola County, MS Conf Pensioner

Name		Unit	Role	County/Notes
Avant, Robert		9th Mississippi Infantry Battalion		Tallahatchie County, MS Conf Pensioner
Avery, Ephraim A.		Wirt Adams's MS. Cavalry Regt		Madison County, MS Conf Pensioner, non-bathe injury.
Ayee, Bob		37th Mississippi Infantry		Smith County, MS Conf Pensioner, non-battle injury
Babbitt, Prince		Commissary Department	Worker	Pontotoc County, MS Conf
Bacon, Tom		26th Mississippi Infantry		Lee County, MS Conf Pensioner
Bailey, Harrison		Unknown Unit		Jones County, MS Conf Pensioner
Baines, Jerry	L	1st Mississippi Light Artillery	Servant	Yazoo County, MS Conf Pensioner
Baker, Gilbert		12th Mississippi Infantry		Hinds County, MS Conf Pensioner
Baker, James		41st Mississippi Infantry		Chickasaw County, MS Conf Pensioner
Baker, Jeremiah		Unknown Unit		Wilkinson County, MS Conf Pensioner
Baker, Tom		6th Mississippi Cavalry		Lowndes County, MS Conf
Baker, Tom		Unknown Unit		Tupelo, MS. Attended the UCV Reunion in Arkansas
Baldwin, Frank		31st Mississippi Infantry		Chickasaw County, MS Conf Pensioner
Ball, Dan		18th Mississippi Infantry		Washington County, MS Conf Pensioner
Ballard, Tobe Cheatham		Hospital	Nurse	Madison County, MS Conf Pensioner
Ballard, Tom		1st Mississippi Cavalry Battalion		Holmes County, MS Conf
Banks, John	A	36th Mississippi Infantry (Capt. John Embry)	Servant	Lincoln County, MS Conf Pensioner, battle injury. Served as a Servant to Dr. D. D. Baker.
Banks, Louis		1st Mississippi Light Artillery		Claiborne County, MS Conf
Banks, Peter		28th Mississippi Cavalry		Adams County, MS Conf
Banks, Sam		1st Mississippi Cavalry	Servant	Bolivar-Quiltman-Yazoo County, MS
Bankston, Lee		3rd Mississippi Infantry		Hinds County, MS Conf Pensioner, battle injury.
Baptist, Bob		Gen Samuel W. Ferguson	Servant	Alcorn County, MS Conf Pensioner, non-battle injury.
Barker, John		11th Mississippi Infantry		Wayne County, MS Conf Pensioner
Barksdale, David		29th Mississippi Infantry		Attala County, MS Conf Pensioner
Barlow, Black		43rd Mississippi Infantry	Servant	Monroe County, MS Conf
Barnes, G. W.		Unknown Unit	Servant	Lee County, MS Conf Pensioner
Barnes, Jack		41st Mississippi Infantry	Horseshoer	Lee County, MS Conf Pensioner, non-battle injury.
Barnes, Thomas		7th Mississippi Infantry	Servant	Marion County, MS Conf Pensioner
Barnett, Allen		46th Mississippi Infantry	Servant	Decatur-Newton County, MS Conf Pensioner, battle injury.
Barnett, Harry		Unknown Unit		Alcorn County, MS Conf Pensioner
Barnett, Henry		Unknown Unit		Sunflower County, MS Conf Pensioner
Barnett, Terral (Bennett)		Turner's Company, Mississippi Light Artillery Served as a Servant to Capt. W.B. Turner and Lt. Charles	Servant	Jasper County, MS Conf Pensioner
Barr, Joe		36th Mississippi Infantry	Messenger	Attala County, MS Conf Pensioner

Baskins, Cap		8th Confederate Cavalry		Chickasaw County, MS Conf Pensioner
Bassett, Allen		Unknown Unit	Cook	Newton County, MS Conf Pensioner
Bassett, Frank		Unknown Unit		Yazoo County, MS Conf Pensioner
Bates, Dock		15th Mississippi Infantry	Servant	Attala County, MS Conf Pensioner
Batey, Washington		39th Mississippi Infantry		Sharkey County, MS Conf Pensioner
Bean, L. W.		24th Mississippi Infantry		Pontotoc County, MS Conf Pensioner
Beanland, Jack		Ballentine's Mississippi Cavalry Regt		Panola County, MS Conf Pensioner, battle injury.
Beaty, Wash		39th Mississippi Infantry		Madison County, MS Conf Pensioner
Beck, Henry	A	42nd Mississippi Infantry		Grenada County, MS Conf Pensioner
Beck, Primus		3rd Mississippi Cavalry		Grenada County, MS Conf Pensioner, non-bathe injury.
Becket, Riley		41st Mississippi Infantry	Servant	Lee County, MS Conf Pensioner
Bedford, Henry		Unknown Unit	Servant	Oktibbeha County, MS Conf Pensioner
Beeson, Ned		31st Mississippi Infantry	Servant	Chickasaw County, MS Conf Pensioner
Bell, Abram	C	2nd Regiment Mississippi Cavalry Served as a servant to Pvt. John W. Bell	Servant	Lauderdale County, MS Conf Pensioner
Bell, Dick	B	1st Mississippi Lt Artillery		Yazoo County, MS Conf Pensioner
Bell, Foster		29th Mississippi Infantry		Yalobusha County, MS Conf Pensioner
Bell, George		14th Mississippi Infantry		Oktibbeha County, MS Conf Pensioner
Bell, Mose		Wirt Adams's MS. Cavalry Regt		Oktibbeha County, MS Conf Pensioner
Belton, Jack		33rd Mississippi Infantry		Franklin-Bolivar County, MS Conf Pensioner
Bender, Wash		Unknown Mississippi Unit Served as a Servant to Griffin Bender	Servant	Jasper County, MS Conf Pensioner
Bennett, Leslie		22nd Mississippi Infantry		Hinds County, MS Conf Pensioner
Bennett, Louis		Seven Stars Mississippi Lt	Cook	Copiah County, MS Conf Pensioner
Bennett, Oston		35th Mississippi Infantry		Clay County, MS Conf Pensioner, non-battle injury.
Benson, Jeff		11th Mississippi Infantry	Servant	Marion County, MS Conf Pensioner
Benson, John		1st Mississippi Cavalry		Panola County, MS Conf Pensioner, battle injury,
Benson, Tom		1st Mississippi Cavalry		Yalobusha County, MS Conf Pensioner
Berry, Charley		8th Confederate Cavalry		Pontotoc County, MS Conf Pensioner
Best (Bess), Nathan		Unknown Unit	Servant	Harrison County, MS Conf Pensioner
Betts, Archie		Quartermaster Dept	Dept Team	Tallahatchie County, MS Conf Pensioner
Bevans, Robert	B	14th Mississippi Artillery Battalion		Panola County, MS Conf Pensioner
Bickerstaff, Duane Harrison		14th Mississippi Infantry		Monroe County, MS Conf Pensioner, battle injury.
Bilbo, Hiram		3rd Mississippi Infantry		Jackson County, MS Conf Pensioner
Billingslea, Taylor	G	1st Mississippi Light Artillery	Servant	Holmes County, MS Conf Pensioner
Binford, Bone		33rd Mississippi Infantry		Holmes County, MS Conf Pensioner

Name	Co.	Unit	Role	Notes
Binford, Chatham	E	15th Mississippi Infantry	Body Servant Laborer	Slave of James and John Binford of Carroll County, MS. Montgomery County, MS Conf Pensioner
Binford, Elisha	E	15th Mississippi Infantry	Body Servant	Slave of James and John Binford of Carroll County, MS.
Bingham, George	K	37th Mississippi Infantry Served as a Servant to Pvt. Lafayette Bingham	Servant	Jasper County, MS Conf Pensioner
Bingham, Pat		31st Mississippi Infantry	Servant	Webster County, MS Conf Pensioner
Binion, Oliver		1st Mississippi Cavalry		Leflore County, MS Conf Pensioner
Bishop, Fed		Unknown Unit	Servant	Panda County, MS Conf Pensioner
Black, Alex		Hospital	Attendant	Yalobusha County, MS Conf Pensioner
Black, Archie		7th Mississippi Infantry		Lincoln County, MS Conf Pensioner, non-bathe injury.
Black, Matthew (Matt)		3rd Mississippi Infantry		Tallahatchie County, MS Conf Pensioner
Blackman, Alex		7th Mississippi Infantry Slave of 2nd Corp. John Everly Holden	Servant	Franklin County, MS Goof Pensioner Slave of John E. Holden of Franklin County, MS.
Blackwell, Charlile		Hospital	Attendant	Tippah County, MS Conf Pensioner
Blackwell, George		Unknown Unit	Servant	Coahoma County, MS Conf Pensioner
Blalock, George		4th Mississippi Infantry		Perry County, MS Conf Pensioner
Bland, Frank		1st Mississippi Infantry Battalion	Servant	Grenada County, MS Conf Pensioner
Bland, Ishmon		28th Mississippi Cavalry	Servant	Claiborne County, MS Goof Pensioner
Blanks, Monroe		Unknown Unit	Servant	Clarke County, MS Conf Pensioner
Blewit, Peter		Unknown Unit	Holster	Slave, His master was KIA, returned to Newton County, MS.
Blue, William Henry		Unknown Unit	Servant And Soldier	Panola County, MS Conf Pensioner
Bluett, Alex Wilson		Gen S. D. Lee	Servant	Lauderdale County, MS Conf Pensioner
Bluntson, George		Unknown Unit	Servant	Hinds County, MS Conf Pensioner
Bob James		29th Mississippi Infantry		Grenada County, MS Conf Pensioner
Boggan, Ben		Unknown Unit		Marshall County, MS Conf Pensioner
Boggan, Jake		6th Mississippi Infantry		Ranking County, MS Conf Pensioner
Bolen, Henry		10th Mississippi Infantry		Lee County, MS Goof Pensioner
Bolls, Charles		4th Mississippi Cavalry	Servant	Hinds County, MS Conf Pensioner
Booker, Ed		1st Mississippi Infantry Battalion	Servant	Grenada-Yalobusha County, MS Conf Pensioner
Booker, Newton		31st Mississippi Infantry	Servant	Lafayette County, MS Conf Pensioner
Booth, John		2nd Mississippi Infantry		Tippah County, MS Conf Pensioner
Boothe, Mills		8th Confederate Cavalry		Tallahatchie County, MS Conf Pensioner
Boulton, Owen	D,F	12th Mississippi 10th Mississippi Cavalry Served as a Servant to A. and C. M. Boulton, and Capt. Dr. G. F. Peek	Servant	Jasper County, MS Conf Pensioner
Bowdry, Andy		23rd Mississippi Infantry		Prentiss County, MS Conf Pensioner
Bowen, Henry		Unknown Unit	Servant	Marshall County, MS Conf Pensioner
Bowen, Stephan		Unknown Unit	Servant	Tate County, MS Conf Pensioner
Bowie, Lewis		Seven Stars Mississippi Lt Artillery		Copiah County, MS Conf Pensioner

Boyd, Abe		14th Confederate Cavalry	Wash And Cook	Attala County, MS Conf Pensioner
Boyd, Granderson		42nd Mississippi Infantry		Yalobusha County, MS Conf Pensioner
Boyd, Henry		28th Mississippi Cavalry		Washington County, MS Conf Pensioner
Boydston, George		15th Mississippi Infantry Battalion	Servant	Yalobusha County, MS Conf Pensioner
Boyles, Edmond		1st Mississippi Cavalry		Tallahatchie County, MS Conf Pensioner
Boyles, Harvey		1st Mississippi Cavalry		Tallahatchie County, MS Conf Pensioner
Bradberry, Sam		4th Mississippi Infantry	Cook	Montgomery County, MS Conf Pensioner
Bradfield, Ammond		Wirt Adams's MS. Cavalry Regt	Servant	Yazoo County, MS Conf Pensioner
Bradford, Elijah		Jefferson Mississippi Light Artillery	Servant	Claiborne County, MS Conf Pensioner
Bradford, Eloda		Unknown Mississippi Unit Served as a cook to his master and nine other soldiers	Cook	Slave, Port Gibson, MS.
Bradford, Peter		Confederate Guards Mississippi Light Artillery	Blacksmith	Pontotoc County, MS Conf Pensioner
Bradley, Burt	E	15th Mississippi Infantry	Servant	Montgomery County, MS Conf Pensioner. Slave of James and John Binford of Carroll County,
Bradley, R. H.	I	29th Mississippi Infantry		Madison County, TN Conf Pension App # C104. Jackson, TN. Attended the UCV Reunion in Arkansas 1928
Bradley, Silas	A	1st Mississippi Light Artillery	Cook	Hinds County, MS Conf Pensioner
Bragg, John		4th Mississippi Cavalry		Claiborne County, MS Conf Pensioner
Bramlette, Miles		11th Mississippi Cavalry		Pontotoc County, MS Conf Pensioner
Brandon, David		18th Mississippi Cavalry Battalion	Servant	Carroll County, MS Conf Pensioner
Brandon, Lee		31st Mississippi Infantry	Servant	Lee County, MS Conf Pensioner
Brannon, John		Unknown Unit		Adams County, MS Conf Pensioner
Brantley, Ceasar		5th Mississippi Infantry		Neshoba County, MS Conf Pensioner
Brantley, Samuel		5th Mississippi Infantry		Montgomery County, MS Conf Pensioner
Brassel, Henry		15th Mississippi Infantry		Panola County, MS Conf Pensioner
Braxton, William		12th Mississippi Infantry	Servant	Yazoo County, MS Conf Pensioner
Brewer, William		7th Mississippi Infantry		Marion County, MS Conf Pensioner
Bridgeman, John A.		Unknown Unit	Servant	Madison County, MS Conf Pensioner
Bridges, Richard		29th Mississippi Infantry		Waithall County, MS Conf Pensioner, battle injury.
Bridges, Sam	F	16th Mississippi Infantry Served as a Servant to 2nd Sgt William Bridges	Servant	Jasper County, MS Conf Pensioner
Briggs, Howard		36th Mississippi Infantry		Hinds County, MS Conf Pensioner
Briscoe, Simon		46th Mississippi Infantry		Bolivar-Washington County, MS Conf Pensioner
Britt, Charlie	B	15th Mississippi Infantry	Servant	Grenada County, MS Conf Pensioner, battle injury.
Britton, Ely	B	1st Mississippi Lt Artillery		Yazoo County, MS Conf Pensioner

Brooks, Jack		Served as a servant to his master	Servant	Slave, Brother of Sam Brooks who also served as a Servant.
Brooks, Ned		4th Mississippi Cavalry	Servant	Claiborne County, MS Conf Pensioner
Brooks, Sam		Served as a servant to his master	Servant	Slave, Brother of Jack Brooks who also served as a Servant.
Brooks, William		28th Mississippi Cavalry		Sharkey County, MS Conf Pensioner
Broome, Bob (1)		Wirt Adams's MS. Cavalry Regt		Hinds County, MS Conf Pensioner
Broome, Bob (2)		16th Mississippi Infantry		Hinds County, MS Conf Pensioner
Brougher, Wesley		29th Mississippi Infantry		Coahoma County, MS Conf Pensioner
Brown, Axton		Gen William H. C. Whiting		Issaquena County, MS Conf Pensioner, injured during the war.
Brown, Ben		10th Mississippi Infantry		Rankin-Sunflower County, MS Conf Pensioner
Brown, Booker	B	1st Mississippi Lt Artillery		Yazoo County, MS Conf Pensioner
Brown, Frank		Unknown Unit	Hostler	Choctaw County, MS Conf Pensioner
Brown, Freeman		38th Mississippi Infantry		Hinds County, MS Conf Pensioner
Brown, George		Breastworks	Laborer	Washington County, MS Conf Pensioner
Brown, Harrison		35th Mississippi Infantry		Hinds County, MS Conf Pensioner
Brown, Henry		3rd Mississippi Cavalry		Tallahatchie County, MS Conf Pensioner
Brown, Hines		4th Mississippi Infantry		Sunflower County, MS Conf Pensioner
Brown, Hiram		Unknown Unit		Claiborne County, MS Conf Pensioner
Brown, Jack		39th Mississippi Infantry		Hinds County, MS Conf Pensioner
Brown, Jacob		4th Mississippi Cavalry		Claiborne County, MS Conf Pensioner, non-battle injury.
Brown, Jeff		11th Mississippi Cavalry		Attala County, MS Conf Pensioner
Brown, John		12th Mississippi Battalion Cavalry Partisans		Monroe County, MS Conf Pensioner
Brown, Lewis		4th Mississippi Cavalry	Servant	Copiah County, MS Conf Pensioner
Brown, Monroe		15th Mississippi Infantry	Servant	Bolivar County, MS Conf Pensioner
Brown, Monroe		Breastworks	Laborer	Washington County, MS Conf Pensioner
Brown, Robert		27th Mississippi Infantry	Cook	Tallahatchie County, MS Conf Pensioner
Brown, Robert		Unknown Unit		Monroe County, NIS Conf Pensioner
Brown, Sam		28th Mississippi Cavalry		Washington County, MS Conf Pensioner
Brown, Sam		Unknown Unit		Hinds County. MS Conf Pensioner
Brown, Scip		Unknown Unit		Montgomery County, MS Conf Pensioner
Brown, Thomas		16th Mississippi Infantry		Ranking County, MS Conf Pensioner
Brown, Thomas		45th Mississippi Infantry		Hinds County, MS Conf Pensioner
Brown, William		Wirt Adams's MS. Cavalry Regt		Hinds County, MS Conf Pensioner, battle injury.
Brunson, George		Unknown Unit	Servant	Leflore County, MS Conf Pensioner
Brunson, Jim		18th Mississippi Cavalry Battalion		Marshall County, MS Conf Pensioner
Bruntson, George		23rd Mississippi Cavalry Battalion		Hinds County, MS Conf Pensioner

Name		Unit	Role	Notes
Bryant, John Coleman	D	33rd Regiment Mississippi Infantry (Franklin Guards) Served as a body servant to William D. Coleman Jr.	Body Servant	Slave, John retrieved William from the battlefield, nursed him back to health and returned him home to his family. William D. Coleman Jr. is the brother of Daniel S. Coleman.
Bryon, Adam		Unknown Unit	Private	Marshall County, MS Conf Pensioner
Buchanan, Ed		Unknown Unit	Servant	Sunflower County, MS Conf Pensioner
Buford, Tom		30th Mississippi Infantry	Servant	Lafayette County, MS Conf Pensioner
Buggy, Levi		34th Mississippi Infantry		Benton County, MS Conf Pensioner
Burdine, Anderson		43rd Mississippi Infantry	Servant	Chickasaw County, MS Conf Pensioner
Burdine, Jim		Mississippi State Troops	Private	Lee County, MS Conf Pensioner
Burgess, Louis	C	14th Mississippi Artillery Battalion	Servant	Panola County, MS Conf Pensioner
Burkhardt, Joseph		16th Mississippi Infantry	Private	Adams County, MS Conf Pensioner
Burks, Anthony		2nd Mississippi Cavalry	Private	Scott County, MS Conf Pensioner
Burks, Dave		Unknown Unit	Private	Scott County, MS Conf Pensioner
Burnett, Henry		Unknown Unit	Private	Monroe County, MS Conf Pensioner
Burney, James		Unknown Unit	Servant	Harrison County, MS Conf Pensioner He is buried at the Beauvoir Confederate Cemetery.
Burns, Hobe		4th Mississippi Cavalry	Private	Wilkinson County, MS Conf Pensioner
Burnside, Tom		Unknown Unit	Servant	Oktibbeha County, MS Conf Pensioner
Burrage, Neal		40th Mississippi Infantry	Servant	Winston County, MS Conf Pensioner
Burrow, Joe		1st Mississippi Infantry Battalion		Hinds County, MS Conf Pensioner
Burt, Edward		Commissary Department	Private	Grenada County, MS Conf Pensioner
Burt, Randle		28th Mississippi Cavalry		Panola County, MS Conf Pensioner, battle injury.
Burton, Edward	C	9th Mississippi Infantry 18th Mississippi Cavalry	Servant	Marshall County, MS Conf Pensioner
Burton, Frank		9th Mississippi Cavalry	Private	Oktibbeha County, MS Conf Pensioner, non-battle injury.
Bush, John		1st Mississippi Infantry Battalion	Servant	Grenada County, MS Conf Pensioner
Butler, Arthur		29th Mississippi Infantry	Servant	Jefferson County, MS Conf Pensioner
Butler, Jim		Breastworks	Laborer	Tallahatchie County, MS Conf Pensioner
Butler, Nathan		Unknown Unit	Servant	Copiah County, MS Conf Pensioner
Butler, Winborn (Winton)		Hospital	Attendant	Jefferson County, MS Conf Pensioner
Byrd, Tony		Unknown Unit	Cook	Copiah County, MS Conf Pensioner
Caffey, Joe		Unknown Unit		Jefferson County, MS Conf Pensioner
Caldwell, John		38th Mississippi Infantry		Hinds County, MS Conf Pensioner
Caldwell, Robert		Commissary Department		Sharkey County, MS Conf Pensioner
Calhoun, Henry		13th Mississippi Infantry		Holmes County, MS Conf Pensioner
Callahan, Alex		18th Mississippi Infantry	Servant	Holmes County, MS Conf Pensioner
Calloway, Walker	G	1st Mississippi Lt Artillery	Cook	Warren County, MS Conf Pensioner
Calomise (Calomese),		1st Mississippi Cavalry		Pontotoc County, MS Conf Pensioner
Campbell, Charles		Bradford's MS. Cavalry Battalion		Hinds County, MS Conf Pensioner

Name		Unit	Role	Location/Notes
Campbell, Henry		12th Mississippi Infantry	Private	Yazoo County, MS Conf Pensioner, battle injury.
Caraway, Simon		2nd Mississippi Infantry Served as a Servant - Jim	Servant	Newton County, MS Conf Pensioner
Carothers, Calvin		11th Mississippi Infantry	Wash And Cook	Lafayette County, MS Conf Pensioner
Carothers, Dennis		28th Mississippi Cavalry	Private	Lafayette County, MS Conf
Carothers, Isom		28th Mississippi Cavalry	Private	Lafayette County, MS Conf
Carothers, Kit		7th Mississippi Cavalry	Private	Lafayette County, MS Conf
Carr, Hampton		21st Mississippi Infantry	Private	Tallahatchie County, MS Conf Pensioner
Carr, John H.		7th Mississippi Infantry	Private	Lauderdale County, MS Conf Pensioner
Carr, Tom		15th Mississippi Infantry		Panola County, MS Conf Pensioner
Carradine, George (1)		Hospital	Attendant	Yazoo County, MS Conf Pensioner
Carradine, George (2)		Wirt Adams's MS. Cavalry Regt	Private	Yazoo County, MS Conf Pensioner
Carruth, Freland C.		34th Mississippi Infantry	Servant	Tippah County, MS Conf Pensioner
Carter, Alex		7th Mississippi Infantry		Perry County, MS Conf Pensioner
Carter, Chance		Hospital Served as a servant to Dr. John Carter	Servant	Kemper County, MS Conf Pensioner
Carter, Emanuel		Commissary Department	Dept Teamste	Yazoo County, MS Conf Pensioner
Carter, Essex		45th Mississippi Infantry	Private	Yazoo County, MS Conf Pensioner
Carter, Joe		6th Mississippi Infantry	Private	Simpson County, MS Conf
Carter, Nelson		1st Mississippi Cavalry Battalion	Private	Bolivar County, MS Conf
Carter, Nick		Served digging breastworks	Laborer	Slave
Cary, Daniel		Wirt Adams's MS. Cavalry Regt	Servant	Yazoo County, MS Conf Pensioner
Cason, Autrey		Unknown Unit	Private	Lee County, MS Conf Pensioner
Chalmers, George		Gen James Chalmers	Private	Bolivar County, MS Conf Pensioner
Chalmers, Thomas		9th Mississippi Infantry	Private	Tunica County, MS Conf Pensioner
Chamberlain, Frank		46th Mississippi Infantry Served as a servant to Bogue Chamberlain	Servant	Kemper County, MS Conf Pensioner
Chambers, Harrison		23rd Mississippi Cavalry Battalion	Servant	Madison County, MS Conf
Chambers, John		18th Mississippi Infantry	Private	Hinds County, MS Conf Pensioner
Chambers, William		1st Mississippi Light Artillery	Private	Madison County, MS Conf
Chambers, William		25th Mississippi Infantry	Servant	Yazoo County, MS Conf Pensioner
Chandler, Silas	F	44th Mississippi Infantry (Blythe's) Served as a servant to Lt. Andrew Martin Chandler 9th Mississippi Cavalry	Servant	Clay County, MS Conf Pensioner, Former Slave, FMC
Chapman, Allen		15th Confederate Cavalry	Private	Wayne County, MS Conf Pensioner
Chapman, Dave		Unknown Unit	Servant	Clarke County, MS Conf Pensioner
Charles, Henry (2)		Madison Mississippi Light	Private	Madison County, MS Conf
Cherry, Arch		18th Mississippi Infantry	Private	Hinds County, MS Conf Pensioner
Cherry, Henry	B	35th Mississippi Regiment Served as a servant to Capt. George W. Oden	Servant	Kemper County, MS Conf Pensioner

Name		Unit	Role	Location / Notes
Childress (Childers), George		40th Mississippi Infantry	Private	Leake County, MS Conf Pensioner
Childress, Frank		Served as a servant to his master Colonel Mark Childress	Courier Servant	Tunica County, MS Conf Pensioner Slave of Mark Childress, he later lived in the Beauvoir, Confederate Soldiers' home in MS. According to his statements in Mississippi Slave Narratives. He is buried at the Beauvoir Confederate Cemetery.
Childress, Isom		3rd Mississippi Cavalry	Servant	Choctaw County, MS Conf Pensioner
Childress, John		Unknown Unit	Dept Teamste	Yalobusha County, MS Conf Pensioner
Childress, Nelson		Breastworks	Laborer	Choctaw County, MS Conf Pensioner
Chiles, George W.		14th Mississippi Infantry	Cook	Oktibbeha County, MS Conf Pensioner
Chilton, Newt		29th Mississippi Infantry	Private	Lafayette County, MS Conf
Claiborne, Wiley	C	43rd Mississippi Infantry 1st Mississippi Cavalry Reserves	Servant	Yazoo County, MS Conf Pensioner
Clark, Hamp		Wirt Adams's MS. Cavalry Regt	Private	Madison County, MS Conf Pensioner
Clark, Jeff		15th Mississippi Infantry	Private	Attala County, MS Conf Pensioner
Clark, John		15th Mississippi Infantry	Private	Leflore County, MS Conf Pensioner
Clark, John		28th Mississippi Cavalry	Servant	Yazoo-Coahoma County, MS Conf Pensioner
Clark, Tony		13th Mississippi Infantry	Servant	Clay County, MS Conf Pensioner Slave of Pvt. George Lafayette
Clay, Henry		36th Mississippi Infantry	Private	Copiah County, MS Conf Pensioner
Clayton, Albert		Commissary Department	Servant	Stone County, MS Conf Pensioner
Clayton, Henry	A	40th Regiment Mississippi Infantry Served as a Servant to Capt. Rufus K. Clayton	Cook Servant	Jasper County, MS Conf Pensioner
Cleveland, Bob		4th Mississippi Cavalry	Servant	Copiah County, MS Conf Pensioner
Cobins (Cobbins), Sam		Wirt Adams's MS. Cavalry Regt	Private	Oktibbeha-Clay County, MS Conf Pensioner
Coffee, John		22nd Mississippi Infantry		Warren County, MS Conf Pensioner
Cohen, Porter		27th Mississippi Infantry	Servant	Tallahatchie County, MS Conf Pensioner
Cole, Anderson		28th Mississippi Cavalry	Private	Perry County, MS Conf Pensioner
Cole, J. M.		Unknown Unit		Pike County, MS Conf Pensioner
Coleman Earls, Charles	D	33rd Regiment Mississippi Infantry (Franklin Guards) Served as a Body Servant to Daniel S. Coleman	Body Servant	Jefferson County, MS Conf Pensioner Slave, Daniel Coleman died August 23, 1864, of disease in a Georgia hospital. Daniel S. Coleman. is the brother of William D. Coleman Jr.
Coleman, Essic		Unknown Unit	Servant	Madison County, MS Conf Pensioner
Coleman, Jack		Unknown Unit	Servant	Oktibbeha County, MS Conf Pensioner
Coleman, Joe		Wirt Adams's MS. Cavalry Regt	Servant	Coahoma County, MS Conf Pensioner
Coleman, Joe		Wirt Adams's MS. Cavalry Regt	Servant	Tallahatchie County, MS Conf Pensioner
Coleman, John		15th Mississippi Infantry	Servant	Yalobusha County, MS Conf Pensioner
Coleman, Jonas		Wirt Adams's MS. Cavalry Regt	Private	Hinds County, MS Conf Pensioner, non-battle injury.

Coleman, Joseph	H	1st Mississippi Cavalry (Adams/Woods) Served as a Body Servant to Dan Wilson	Body Servant	
Coleman, Joseph		20th Mississippi Infantry	Private	Winston County, MS Conf Pensioner
Coleman, Neils (Nelse)		Breastworks	Laborer	Tallahatchie County, MS Conf Pensioner
Coleman, Paul		6th Mississippi Infantry	Servant	Panola County, MS Conf Pensioner
Coleman, Peter		Bradford's MS. Cavalry Battalion	Servant	Tunica County, MS Conf Pensioner
Coleman, Richard		6th Mississippi Cavalry	Private	Oktibbeha County, MS Conf Pensioner
Collier, Marshall		Jefferson Mississippi Light Artillery	Private	Washington County, MS Conf Pensioner
Collier, Merriman		Wirt Adams's MS. Cavalry Regt	Servant	Bolivar-Washington County, MS Conf Pensioner
Collins, James		31st Mississippi Infantry	Private	Lafayette County, MS Conf
Collins, Mose	L	1st Mississippi Lt Artillery	Private	Tallahatchie County, MS Conf Pensioner
Collins, Willis		23rd Mississippi Cavalry Battalion	Private	Copiah County, MS Conf Pensioner
Colston, Thomas		15th Mississippi Infantry	Servant	Madison County, MS Conf Pensioner
Combs, John L.		10th Confederate Cavalry	Private	Franklin County, MS Conf
Commander, Jerry (J. G.)		6th Mississippi Infantry	Private	Coahoma-Madison County, MS Conf Pensioner
Conner, Cicero		14th Mississippi Infantry	Private	Scott County, MS Conf Pensioner
Conway [Coway], Adam		23rd Mississippi Cavalry Battalion	Private	Franklin County, MS Con? Pensioner
Cook, Louis		Unknown Unit	Servant	Franklin County, MS Conf Pensioner
Cooke, Tom	H	1st Mississippi Cavalry (Parson's Regiment) Served as a servant to Pvt. B. T. Worthington but was known to fight by Pvt. Worthington's side in battle.	Servant	Pvt. Ben Taylor Worthington was from Washington County, MS.
Cooley, Berry		Mississippi State Troops	Cook	Clarke County, MS Conf Pensioner
Cooper, Add		37th Mississippi Infantry	Servant	Humphreys County, MS Conf Pensioner
Cooper, Elye		Breastworks	Laborer	Winston County, MS Conf Pensioner
Cooper, Ephriam		44th Mississippi Infantry		Amite County, MS Conf Pensioner
Cooper, Joe		28th Mississippi Cavalry	Servant	Leflore County, MS Conf Pensioner
Cooper, John		40th Mississippi Infantry	Private	Hinds County, MS Conf Pensioner
Cooper, Lige		Wirt Adams's MS. Cavalry Regt	Private	Yazoo County, MS Conf Pensioner
Coppage, Jack		Stanford's Mississippi Artillery	Private	Yalobusha County, MS Conf Pensioner
Cornelius, James	E	16th Mississippi Infantry (Quitman Guards) Under Col. Stockdale. Served as a body servant to his master Pvt. Sam Murray Sandell who was KIA.	Body Servant	Slave of Sam Murray Sandell of Magnolia, MS. According to his statements in Mississippi Slave Narratives. Pike County, MS Conf Pensioner
Cornelius, Jim		4th Mississippi Cavalry	Servant	Pike County, MS Con? Pensioner
Counsell, Isaac		7th Mississippi Cavalry	Private	Tippah County, YS Conf Pensioner
Cowan, Obey		Unknown Unit	Private	Yazoo County, MS Conf Pensioner
Cowan, Willis		29th Mississippi Infantry	Private	Holmes County, MS Con? Pensioner

Directory of African American Confederates in the U.S. Civil War

Cox, Butler C.		3rd Mississippi Cavalry	Private	Harrison County, MS Conf Pensioner
Cox, Fayette		Ferry	Private	Bolivar County, MS Conf Pensioner
Cox, Henry		14th Confederate Regiment	Servant	Grenada County, MS Conf Pensioner
Cox, Henry		Wirt Adams's MS. Cavalry Regt	Servant	Yazoo County, MS Conf Pensioner
Craft, Alexander		8th Mississippi Infantry	Private	Bolivar County, MS Conf Pensioner
Craft, Armstead		Mississippi State Troops	Private	Forrest County, MS Conf Pensioner
Crane, Mack		6th Mississippi Infantry	Private	Ranking County, MS Conf Pensioner
Crawford, Henry		24th Mississippi Infantry	Private	Webster County, MS Conf Pensioner
Crawford, R. B. (Bob)		Wirt Adams's MS. Cavalry Regt	Servant	Leake County, MS Conf Pensioner
Crayton, Phil		26th Mississippi Infantry	Private	Lee County, MS Conf Pensioner
Crigler, Tecumseh		14th Mississippi Infantry	Private	Chickasaw County, MS Conf Pensioner
Critz, Samuel B.		Mississippi State Troops	Private	Oktibbeha County, MS Conf Pensioner
Crosby, Jack	E	8th Regiment Mississippi Infantry Served as a Body Servant to Sgt. Roland Crosby	Servant	Jasper County, MS Conf Pensioner
Cross, Eli		Jeff Davis Mississippi Cavalry Legion	Private	Noxubee County, MS Conf Pensioner, non-battle injury.
Cross, Rueben		1st Mississippi Cavalry	Private	Carroll County, MS Conf Pensioner
Crow, Fred		Quartermaster Dept	Camp Attendan	Chickasaw County, MS Conf Pensioner
Crowder, Manson		40th Mississippi Infantry	Private	Leake County, MS Conf Pensioner, injured during the war.
Crum, Frank		2nd Mississippi Infantry	Private	Benton County, MS Conf Pensioner, wounded in battle
Crump, Levi		Gen S. G. French	Private	Washington County, MS Conf Pensioner
Crump, Willis		12th Mississippi Cavalry	Private	Clay County, MS Conf Pensioner
Cumberlin, Henry		18th Mississippi Infantry	Private	Hinds County, MS Conf Pensioner
Cummings, George	B	17th Mississippi Infantry Served as a Servant to his Master and childhood friend SgtMaj C.C. Cummings.	Body Servant	Slave from the Page farm, KIA, while trying to escape from a Federal Cavalry patrol
Cunningham, Harry		Unknown Unit	Cook	Lee County, MS Conf Pensioner
Cunningham, Major		15th Mississippi Infantry	Private	Leflore County, MS Conf Pensioner
Cunningham, Scipio		12th Mississippi Infantry	Private	Coahoma-Madison County, MS Conf Pensioner
Cunningham, Tom		Ordnance Department	Servant	Humphreys County, MS Conf Pensioner
Curry, Jake		38th Mississippi Infantry	Servant	Newton County, MS Conf Pensioner since 1902
Cyrus, Shedrick		16th Mississippi Infantry	Servant	Lincoln County, MS Conf Pensioner
Dabbs, Steve		7th Mississippi Infantry	Servant	Lee County, MS Conf Pensioner
Dan Leflore		Unknown Unit		Grenada County, MS Conf Pensioner
Dan Melton		22nd Mississippi Infantry	Cook	Grenada County, MS Conf Pensioner, wounded in battle.
Danecy, Wiley		Quartermaster Dept	Private	Tate County, MS Conf Pensioner, non-battle injury
Daniel (Daniels), William (Bill)		15th Mississippi Infantry	Servant	Panola County, MS Conf Pensioner
Daniel, Jordan		8th Mississippi Infantry	Private	Monroe County, MS Conf Pensioner

Name		Unit	Rank	Location
Daniels, Henry		37th Mississippi Infantry	Private	Wayne County, MS Conf Pensioner, wounded in battle.
Daniels, Spencer		Unknown Unit	Private	Scott County, MS Conf Pensioner
Daniels, Tom	C	Jeff Davis Legion, Mississippi Cavalry (Southern Guards) Served as a servant to John Daniels	Servant	Lauderdale County, MS Conf Pensioner
Dansy, Shep		Hospital	Attendant	Oktibbeha County, MS Conf Pensioner
Darty, Isom		Unknown Mississippi Unit Served as a Body Servant to Wilson Darty	Servant	Wayne County, MS
Davenport, Lewis		Unknown Unit	Servant	Hinds County, MS Conf Pensioner
Davis, Byrd		1st Mississippi Cavalry	Private	Tallahatchie County, MS Conf Pensioner
Davis, Edmond (Emanuel)		4th Mississippi Cavalry	Private	Hinds County, MS Conf Pensioner
Davis, Ellis		46th Mississippi Infantry	Servant	Ranking County, MS Conf Pensioner
Davis, Flanders		4th Mississippi Cavalry	Private	Holmes County, MS Conf Pensioner
Davis, George		34th Mississippi Infantry	Private	Tippah County, MS Conf Pensioner, non-battle injury.
Davis, Henry		Unknown Unit	Private	Lee County, MS Conf Pensioner
Davis, Holiday	A	1st Mississippi Lt Artillery	Private	Ranking County, MS Conf Pensioner
Davis, John		1st Mississippi Cavalry	Private	Tallahatchie County, MS Conf Pensioner, battle injury.
Davis, John		Gen S. G. French	Private	Holmes County, MS Conf Pensioner
Davis, John		Unknown Unit	Private	Covington County, MS Conf Pensioner
Davis, Jordan		Jeff Davis Mississippi Cavalry Legion	Servant	Claiborne County, MS Conf Pensioner
Davis, Ned		3rd Mississippi Infantry		Cook-Warren County, MS Conf Pensioner
Davis, Redick		18th Mississippi Infantry	Private	Yazoo County, MS Conf Pensioner
Davis, Robert		Salt Works	Private	Humphreys County, MS Conf Pensioner
Davis, Robert		Served as a Servant to Gen. Dick Taylor	Servant	Adams County, MS Conf Pensioner
Davis, Westiey		Breastworks	Laborer	Copiah County, MS Conf Pensioner
Davis, William		16th Mississippi Infantry	Private	Wilkinson County, MS Conf Pensioner
Davis, William		Jeff Davis Mississippi Cavalry Legion	Servant	Yalobusha County, MS Conf Pensioner
Davis, Willis		36th Mississippi Infantry	Servant	Copiah County, MS Conf Pensioner, non-battle injury.
Davis, Wilson (Wiley)		Unknown Unit	Private	Clay-Sharkey County, MS Conf Pensioner
Dawkins, Tunk		17th Mississippi Infantry	Servant	Jones County, MS Conf Pensioner
Dawson, Barrett		Bradford's MS. Cavalry Battalion	Private	Wilkinson County, MS Conf Pensioner
Dawson, Ferd		Smyth's MS. Cavalry Battalion	Private	Madison County, MS Conf Pensioner
Day, Campbell		18th Mississippi Infantry	Private	Yazoo County, MS Conf Pensioner
Dean, Ben	G	Ballentine's Mississippi Cavalry Regt	Servant	Marshall County, MS Conf Pensioner

Delk, Thomas	A	35th Regiment Mississippi Infantry (Barry Guards) Served as a servant to James Delk	Servant	Lauderdale County, MS Conf Pensioner, he was WIA at Greenwood, MS where he received a flesh wound
Dennis, Adam		29th Mississippi Infantry	Private	Holmes County, MS Conf Pensioner
Dennis, Mose		21st Mississippi Infantry	Private	Wilkinson County, MS Conf Pensioner
Desearn, James		16th Mississippi Infantry	Private	Wilkinson County, MS Conf Pensioner
Dillard, George		6th Mississippi Infantry	Private	Smith County, MS Conf Pensioner
Dillon, Steve		38" Mississippi Infantry	Servant	Walthall County, MS Conf Pensioner
Dinkins, Amos		28th Mississippi Cavalry	Private	Madison County, MS Conf Pensioner
Divine, Bob (Robert)		18th Mississippi Infantry	Cook	Madison County, MS Conf Pensioner
Divinity, Howard H.	D	12th Regiment Mississippi Infantry Served as a Body Servant to Robert "Bob" Marion Scott	Body Servant Cook	Pike-Copiah County, MS Conf Pensioner, battle injury.
Dixon, Alf		23rd Mississippi Cavalry Battalion	Private	Hinds County, MS Conf Pensioner
Dixon, Joe		Unknown Unit	Servant	Harrison County, MS Conf Pensioner
Dixson, Alex		Unknown Unit	Servant	Humphreys County, MS Conf Pensioner
Dobbs, Anthony		Department	Teamster	Panola County, MS Conf Pensioner
Dockery, Tom		Unknown Unit	Servant	Marshall County, MS Conf Pensioner
Dodd, Sam		18th Mississippi Cavalry Battalion	Servant	Attala County, MS Conf Pensioner
Dodson, Henry		16th Mississippi Infantry	Cook	Sharkey County, MS Conf Pensioner, battle injury.
Donahoe, Henry		Unknown Unit	Servant	Coahoma County, MS Conf Pensioner
Donald, Berry		Unknown Unit	Servant	Kemper County, MS Conf Pensioner
Doss, Jerry		14th Mississippi Infantry	Servant	Oktibbeha County, MS Conf Pensioner
Doss, Lige		Unknown Unit	Servant	Clarke County, MS Conf Pensioner
Dotson, Henry		16" Mississippi Infantry	Private	Hinds County, MS Conf Pensioner
Dotson, J. A.		Unknown Unit	Servant	Attala County, MS Conf Pensioner
Dudley, Robert	G	15th Mississippi Infantry (Grenada Rifles)	Servant	Grenada County, MS Conf Pensioner injured during the war.
Dudley, Simon		1st Mississippi Infantry	Private	Ranking County, MS Conf Pensioner, non-battle injury.
Dudley, Thad	B	15th Mississippi Infantry (Grenada Rifles)	Servant	Grenada County, MS Conf Pensioner
Duke, Sam		1st Mississippi Cavalry	Private	Pontotoc County, MS Conf Pensioner
Dulaney, Dave		4th Mississippi Infantry	Private	Holmes County, MS Conf Pensioner
Dumas, Jim		15th Mississippi Infantry	Servant	Webster County, MS Conf Pensioner
Duncan, Ben	E	19th Mississippi Infantry	Servant	Marshall County, MS Conf Pensioner
Dunn, Nelson		15th Mississippi Infantry	Servant	Grenada County, MS Conf Pensioner
Dunnigan, Aaron		12th Mississippi Infantry		Claiborne County, MS Conf Pensioner
Durr, Simon		39th Mississippi Infantry Served as a Body Servant to Capt. Robert Jacob Durr	Servant	Copiah-Simpson County, MS Conf Pensioner, Slave of Michael Durr.
Dyer, John		31st Mississippi Infantry	Private	Wayne County, MS Conf Pensioner
Dyess, William P.		46th Mississippi Infantry	Private	Jefferson Davis County, MS Conf Pensioner
Eans, Fred (John)		Hospital	Servant	LeFlore-Yazoo County, MS Conf Pensioner

Early, John		12th Mississippi Infantry	Private	Leflore County, MS Conf Pensioner
Easley, High		7th Mississippi Cavalry		Prentiss County, MS Conf
Easley, Jeff		3rd Mississippi Infantry	Cook	Hinds County, MS Conf Pensioner
Easton, Alfred		21st Mississippi Infantry	Private	Wilkinson County, MS Conf Pensioner
Eaton, Jim		Department	Dept Teamste	Tallahatchie County, MS Conf Pensioner
Echols, James		Wirt Adams's MS. Cavalry Regt		Hinds County, MS Conf Pensioner
Edison, Burrell		Unknown Unit	Hostler	Bolivar County, MS Conf
Edmondson, John Raymond		Home Service	Nurse Servan	Jasper County, MS Conf Pensioner
Edmonson, John		Unknown Mississippi Unit Served as a Body Servant to James Edmonson	Servant	Clarke County, MS
Edmund Smith		45th Mississippi Infantry	Private	Copiah County, MS Conf Pensioner
Edwards, Ben		5th Mississippi Cavalry	Private	Yalobusha County, MS Conf Pensioner
Edwards, Dan		Wirt Adams's MS. Cavalry Regt	Cook	Clay-Warren County, MS Conf Pensioner
Edwards, George		Hospital	Servant	Leake County, MS Conf Pensioner
Edwards, Peter		15th Mississippi Infantry	Cook	Webster County, MS Conf Pensioner
Edwards, Robert		30th Mississippi Infantry	Private	Yazoo County, MS Conf Pensioner
Edwards, Solomon		15th Mississippi Infantry	Private	Webster County, MS Conf
Edwards, Spencer		15th Mississippi Infantry	Private	Choctaw County, MS Conf
Eiland, Henry		1st Mississippi Cavalry	Private	Winston County, MS Conf Pensioner, non-battle injury.
Ellick,	D	42nd Mississippi Infantry	Cook	
Ellis, Ambrose		40th Mississippi Infantry	Private	Madison County, MS Conf
Enochs, John		28th Mississippi Cavalry	Servant	Calhoun County, MS Conf
Eskridge, Frank		28th Mississippi Cavalry	Cook	Montgomery County, MS Conf Pensioner
Eubanks, Sam		11th Mississippi Cavalry	Private	Attala County, MS Conf Pensioner
Evans, Allen		11th Mississippi Cavalry	Private	Choctaw County, MS Conf Pensioner
Evans, Allen		15th Confederate Cavalry	Private	Webster County, MS Conf
Evans, Andrew		12th Mississippi Infantry	Private	Scott County, MS Conf Pensioner
Evans, Mose		15th Mississippi Infantry	Regt Teamster	Perry-Greene County, MS Conf Pensioner, battle injury.
Evans, Robert		28th Mississippi Cavalry		Holmes County, MS Conf Pensioner
Ewing, Isaac		Gen Braxton Bragg		Lee County, MS Conf Pensioner
Ezelle, Bob		Pettus Mississippi Flying	Servant	Monroe County, MS Conf
Fagan, Benjamin		Unknown Unit	Servant	Yazoo County, MS Conf Pensioner
Falconer, Aaron		7th Mississippi Infantry		Clarke County, MS Conf Pensioner
Farley, James		4th Mississippi Cavalry	Cook	Copiah County, MS Conf Pensioner
Farrow (Farrar), Sam		6th Mississippi Infantry	Private	Ranking County, MS Conf Pensioner
Faust, Ben	C	7th Mississippi Regiment Served as a Servant to Pvt. W. Frank Toler	Private	Amite County, MS Conf Pensioner
Ferguson, Henry		Unknown Unit	Servant	Claiborne County, MS Conf
Field, Edmund		Unknown Unit	Private	Adams County, MS Conf Pensioner

Name		Unit	Role	Location
Fields, Austin		Unknown Unit	Private	Lee County, MS Conf Pensioner
Fields, George		Wirt Adams's MS. Cavalry	Private	Madison County, MS Conf
Fields, Lem		Breastworks	Laborer	Warren County, MS Conf
Fields, Torn		48th Mississippi Infantry	Private	Hinds County, MS Conf
Fields, Torn		Quartermaster Dept	Private	Lee County, MS Conf Pensioner
Figg, Sandy		Unknown Unit	Private	Panola County, MS Conf
Fisher, Charles		2nd Mississippi Cavalry	Wash And Cook	Lauderdale County, MS Conf Pensioner
Fisher, Henry		28th Mississippi Cavalry	Private	Washington County, MS Conf Pensioner
Fisher, Walter	D	1st Mississippi Cavalry- Served as a servant to Capt. C.C. Marshall	Servant	Tallahatchie County, MS Conf Pensioner
Fitzgerald, George		Ballentine's Mississippi Cavalry	Private	Panola County, MS Conf
Flanagan, Bill		Mississippi State Troops	Hostler	Attala County, MS Conf
Flanagan, Green		39th Mississippi Infantry		Scott County, MS Conf Pensioner
Flemins, Robert		Unknown Unit		Tippah County, MS Conf
Fleur, Jal		Unknown Unit	Servant	Jasper County, MS Conf
Flood, Ned		Jeff Davis Mississippi Cavalry Legion	Private	Quitman County, MS Conf Pensioner
Flowers, Harrison		12th Mississippi Infantry	Private	Claiborne County, MS Conf Pensioner Servant, battle injury.
Fondren, Patrick		20th Mississippi Infantry	Servant	Attala County, MS Conf
Fontaine, Peter		1st Mississippi Cavalry	Servant	Pontotoc County, MS Conf
Foote, Richard		7th Mississippi Cavalry	Servant	Union County, MS Conf
Ford, Albert		Unknown Unit	Servant	Tallahatchie County, MS Conf Pensioner
Ford, Emma		Hospital	Attendant	Warren County, MS Conf Pensioner
Fore, Sam		28th Mississippi Cavalry	Private	Ranking County, MS Conf
Fortune, Charley		Smyth's MS. Cavalry Battalion	Private	Leake County, MS Conf
Fortune, Moses		40th Mississippi Infantry	Servant	Leake County, MS Conf
Foster, G. L.		15th Confederate Cavalry	Private	Jackson County, MS Conf Pensioner, battle injury.
Foster, Sam		Wirt Adams's MS. Cavalry Regt	Private	Yazoo County, MS Conf
Fountain, Willis		6th Mississippi Infantry	Private	Lake County, TN Conf Pensioner # C184
Fox, Turner		Commissary Department	Corn Miller	Quitman County, MS Conf
Frank Rans		Unknown Unit	Servant	Panola County, MS Conf Pensioner
Franklin, John		38th Mississippi Infantry	Private	Lincoln County, MS Conf Pensioner, non-battle injury.
Franklin, Ned		Wirt Adams's MS. Cavalry Regt	Cook	Hinds County, MS Conf
Franks, Pet		Served as a servant to his master Jimmy Tatum in Corinth, MS. He	Nurse Servant	Slave of Jimmy Tatum, According to his statement in Mississippi Slave Narratives.
Frazier, Bailey		28th Mississippi Cavalry	Hostler	Washington County, MS Conf Pensioner
Freeman, Nathan		1st Mississippi Cavalry	Private	Lee County, MS Conf Pensioner
Frierson, Sam		Quartermaster Dept	Shoemaker	Lee County, MS Conf Pensioner

Funches, J. R. (Rome)		36th Mississippi Infantry	Private	Lincoln County, MS Conf Pensioner
Fuqua, Henry		12th Mississippi Infantry	Private	Yazoo County, MS Conf Pensioner
Furlong, Hamilton Ward		24th Mississippi Infantry	Private	Monroe County, MS Conf Pensioner
Gadberry, Dennis	I	1st Mississippi Lt Artillery	Private	Yazoo County, MS Conf Pensioner
Gaddy, Bob		37th Mississippi Infantry	Servant	Jasper County, MS Conf Pensioner
Gage, Elias	A	13th Mississippi Infantry	Servant Cook	Slave of Pvt. James W. Gage.
Gamage, Edwards		Unknown Unit	Servant	Smith County, MS Conf Pensioner
Gant, William	H	22nd Mississippi Infantry Regiment (Rodney Guards) Served as a servant to Pvt. Richard C. Gant	Servant	Attended the Veterans Reunion at Vicksburg 1890
Gant, William		9th Mississippi Infantry	Private	Quitman County, MS Conf Pensioner
Gardner, Mitchell		1st Mississippi Light Artillery	Cook	Jefferson-Adams County, MS Conf Pensioner
Garrett, Hardy	B	23rd Mississippi	Servant	Marshall County, MS Conf Pensioner
Garrison, George		Bureau Of Mines		Tunica County, MS Conf Pensioner
Gary, Andrew	I	1st Mississippi Lt Artillery	Servant	Yazoo County, MS Conf Pensioner
Gassaway, Sam		Unknown Unit	Servant	Lee County, MS Conf Pensioner
Gaston, W. M.		44th Mississippi Infantry	Private	Calhoun-Tallahatchie County, MS Conf Pensioner
Gaston, William		22nd Mississippi Infantry	Private	Copiah County, MS Conf Pensioner
Gatewood, Wesley	G	17th Mississippi Infantry Served as servant to Cpl. Lafayette Gatewood and Pvt. Thomas Gatewood	Servant	Shelby County, TN Conf Pensioner # C131
Gattis, Jack		29th Mississippi Infantry	Servant	Yalobusha County, MS Conf Pensioner
Gavin, Tony		13th Mississippi Infantry	Private	Jasper County, MS Conf Pensioner, battle injury.
George Ivey		Unknown Unit		Grenada County, MS Conf Pensioner
George, Richard		Commissary Department	Private	Madison County, MS Conf Pensioner
Gerald, Charles		18th Mississippi Infantry		Yazoo County, MS Conf Pensioner
Geren, Charles	E	15th Mississippi Infantry	Body Servant	Slave
Gholston, Nathan		12th Mississippi Cavalry	Private	Chickasaw County, MS Con? Pensioner
Gibbs, Lit		30th Mississippi Infantry	Private	Yazoo County, MS Con? Pensioner
Gibson, Alfred		Wirt Adams's MS. Cavalry	Hostler	Warren County, MS Conf Pensioner
Gilbert, Wash		Unknown Unit	Servant	Newton County, MS Conf Pensioner since 1902
Gill, Griffin		Unknown Unit	Servant	Lee County, MS Conf Pensioner
Gill, Henry		Breastworks	Laborer	Leake County, MS Conf Pensioner
Gill, Simon		Unknown Unit	Private	Tate County, MS Conf Pensioner
Gillespie, John T.		43rd Mississippi Infantry	Private	Oktibbeha County, MS Conf Pensioner
Gilliam, Richard		1st Mississippi Cavalry	Private	Pontotoc County, MS Conf Pensioner
Gilmer, George		1st Mississippi Infantry	Servant	Lafayette County, MS Conf Pensioner
Gilmer, Rube		11th Mississippi Infantry	Private	Lafayette County, MS Conf Pensioner
Gilmore, Harrison		11th Mississippi Infantry	Private	Monroe County, MS Conf Pensioner

Name		Unit	Role	Location / Notes
Ginyard, Commodore		1st Mississippi Infantry	Servant	Wilkinson County, MS Conf Pensioner
Givens, Mack		7th Mississippi Infantry	Private	Pike County, MS Conf Pensioner
Gladney, Dan		5th Mississippi Infantry	Private	Attala County, MS Conf Pensioner
Golden, China		Unknown Unit	Camp Attendant	Quitman County, MS Conf Pensioner
Gooch, Jordan		Breastworks	Laborer	Tallahatchie County, MS Conf Pensioner
Goode, Chesterfield		3rd Mississippi Infantry	Servant	Harrison County, MS Conf Pensioner
Gooden (Gordon), Matt		Henderson's Mississippi Cavalry Scouts	Private	Adams County, MS Cent Pensioner
Goodridge, Jake		He was captured with his master and was made a waiter by the Union soldiers.	Private	Slave, P.O.W.
Goodwin, William		Gen Wade Hampton	Servant	Washington County, MS Conf Pensioner
Gordan, Julius	C I	2nd Regiment, Mississippi Cavalry 8th Regiment, Mississippi Cavalry Served as a servant to Cornelius Gordon and his master Pvt. A. D. Gordon	Servant	Lauderdale County, MS Conf Pensioner, Slave of A. D. Gordon,
Gordon, Austin		23rd Mississippi Cavalry Battalion	Servant	Adams County, MS Conf Pensioner
Gordon, James		Ashcraft's Mississippi Cavalry Regt	Servant	Lafayette County, MS Conf Pensioner, battle injury.
Gordon, Robert	B	14th Mississippi Artillery Battalion	Private	Monroe County, MS Conf Pensioner
Gordon, Wade		Unknown Unit	Private	Lee County, MS Conf Pensioner
Gordon, William		4th Mississippi Cavalry	Private	Pontotoc County, MS Conf Pensioner
Gosa (Gaza), Frank		13th Mississippi Infantry	Private	Chickasaw County, MS Conf Pensioner
Graham, Jack		22nd Mississippi Infantry	Servant	Lafayette County, MS Conf Pensioner
Gray, Simon		7th Mississippi Infantry	Private	Hinds County, MS Conf Pensioner
Greaves, Wilson		Confederate Guards Mississippi Light Artillery		Hinds County, MS Conf Pensioner
Green, Abram		28th Mississippi Cavalry	Servant	Ranking County, MS Conf Pensioner
Green, Abram		36th Mississippi Infantry	Private	Lincoln County, MS Conf Pensioner
Green, Pleasant		20th Mississippi Infantry	Servant	Claiborne County, MS Conf Pensioner
Greer, Wash		15th Mississippi Infantry	Private	Attala County, MS Conf Pensioner
Griffin, Anthony		28th Mississippi Cavalry	Private	Holmes County, MS Conf Pensioner
Griffin, Ed		16th Mississippi Infantry	Wash & Cook	Leake County, MS Conf Pensioner
Griffin, Eli (Ely)		42nd Mississippi Infantry	Private	Monroe-Tallahatchie County, MS Conf Pensioner
Griffin, Wilson		1st Mississippi Cavalry	Private	Panola County, MS Cant Pensioner
Griffith, Archie		Unknown Unit	Hostler	Warren County, MS Conf Pensioner
Griggs, Mack		Unknown Unit	Private	Chickasaw County, MS Conf Pensioner
Grimes, Joe		Unknown Unit	Drummer Boy	Warren County, MS Conf Pensioner
Grissom, Charley		33-d Mississippi Infantry		Coahoma County, MS Conf Pensioner
Gully, Ike		40th Mississippi Cavalry Served as a servant to Capt. Slake Gully	Servant	Kemper County, MS Conf Pensioner
Gunn, Bob		Unknown Unit	Private	Calhoun County, MS Conf Pensioner

Name		Unit	Rank/Role	County/Notes
Guyton, Giles		Commissary Department	Private	Tippah County, MS Conf Pensioner
Hall II, Turner	E	41st Mississippi Infantry Served as a Servant to his master Judge Trice	Servant	
Hall, Henry		33rd Mississippi Infantry	Private	Leake County, MS Conf Pensioner
Hamblen, Charley		18th Mississippi Infantry	Private	Madison County, MS Conf Pensioner
Hamilton, Albert		44th Mississippi Infantry	Servant	Yalobusha County, MS Conf Pensioner
Hamilton, Jeff		Ashcraft's Mississippi Cavalry Regt	Private	Lee County, MS Conf Pensioner
Hampton, Joseph		23rd Mississippi Cavalry Battalion	Private	Wilkinson County, MS Conf Pensioner
Hampton, William		35th Mississippi Regiment Served as a servant to G. B. (Pat) Hampton	Servant	Kemper County, MS Conf Pensioner
Hankens, Thad		15th Mississippi Infantry	Servant	Grenada County, MS Conf Pensioner, battle injury.
Hanson, Henry	A	14th Mississippi Artillery Battalion		Panola County, MS Conf Pensioner
Hardeman, Lem		Henderson's Mississippi Cavalry Scouts	Private	Grenada County, MS Conf Pensioner
Hardy, Mitchell		16th Mississippi Infantry		Covington County, MS Conf Pensioner, battle injury.
Hardy, Uncas		Confederate Guards Mississippi Light Artillery	Servant	Lawrence County, MS Conf Pensioner
Harman, Dick		15th Mississippi Infantry		Holmes County, MS Conf Pensioner, non-battle injury.
Harmon, Joe		4th Mississippi Cavalry	Servant	Tate County, MS Conf Pensioner
Harper, Alford		6th Mississippi Infantry	Private	Madison County, MS Conf Pensioner
Harper, Anderson		Unknown Unit	Servant	Lee County, MS Conf Pensioner
Harper, Bob		27th Mississippi Infantry	Private	Leake County, MS Conf Pensioner
Harper, Calvin		43rd Mississippi Infantry	Private	Lee County, MS Conf Pensioner
Harper, Jeff		Commissary Department	Private	Madison County, MS Conf Pensioner
Harper, Wallace		Wirt Adams's MS. Cavalry Regt	Private	Claiborne County, MS Conf Pensioner
Harrall (Harrel), Jerry		24th Mississippi Cavalry Battalion	Servant	Grenada County, MS Conf Pensioner
Harrel, Jerry		Unknown Unit	Private	Grenada County, MS Conf Pensioner
Harrell, Sam		Commissary Department	Drover	Bolivar County, MS Conf Pensioner
Harris, Albert		Pettus Mississippi Flying Artillery	Wash & Cook	Leake County, MS Conf Pensioner
Harris, Albert		Unknown Unit	Servant	Monroe County, MS Conf Pensioner
Harris, Ambrose H.		21st Mississippi Infantry	Private	Wilkinson County, MS Conf Pensioner
Harris, Bob		Unknown Unit	Servant	Panola County, MS Conf Pensioner
Harris, Henry		22nd Mississippi Infantry	Private	Washington County, MS Conf Pensioner
Harris, Jack		44th Mississippi Infantry	Private	Yazoo County, MS Conf Pensioner
Harris, Jack "Army Jack"		Served as a bodyguard to Capt W. B. Harris	Body Guard	Slave
Harris, John F.		Unknown Unit	Private	Served in the Mississippi House of Representatives in 1890, made famous speech for Confederate Memorial
Harris, Martin Van Buren		15th Confederate Cavalry	Private	Forrest County, MS Conf Pensioner

Name		Unit	Role	County / Notes
Harris, Ned		Unknown Unit	Private	Leflore County, MS Conf Pensioner, battle injury.
Harris, Ned H.		27th Mississippi Infantry	Private	Lafayette County, MS Conf Pensioner
Harris, Wade		40th Mississippi Infantry	Servant	Madison County, MS Conf Pensioner
Harrison, Ephraham (Eph) Radford		Hospital	Attendant	Sunflower County, MS Conf Pensioner
Harrison, Lewis		18th Mississippi Cavalry Battalion	Private	Coahoma County, MS Conf Pensioner
Harry, Pompey		7th Mississippi Infantry	Private	Marion County, MS Conf Pensioner
Hartfield, Alex		27th Mississippi Infantry	Private	Perry County, MS Conf Pensioner
Harwell, Mose		32nd Mississippi Infantry	Private	Lee County, MS Conf Pensioner
Harwood, Milus		9th Mississippi Cavalry	Private	Monroe County, MS Conf Pensioner
Haskins, William	E	15th Mississippi Infantry	Body Servant	Slave
Hatch, Clay		Unknown Unit	Hostler	Quitman County, MS Conf Pensioner
Hatcher, Ed		41st Mississippi Infantry	Private	Forrest County, MS Conf Pensioner
Hatchey (Hatcher), Thomas		48th Mississippi Infantry	Cook	Hinds County, MS Conf Pensioner
Hathorn, Lewis		Breastworks	Laborer	Winston County, MS Conf Pensioner
Hawkins [Hankins], Thad		15th Mississippi Infantry	Private	Montgomery County, MS Conf Pensioner
Haynes, Sam		Unknown Unit	Servant	Wilkinson County, MS Conf Pensioner
Hays (Hayes), Jackson (Jack)		12th Mississippi Infantry	Servant	Claiborne County, MS Conf Pensioner
Hays (Hayes), Lyttleton		38th Mississippi infantry	Private	Wilkinson County, MS Conf Pensioner
Hays, Daniel		40th Mississippi Infantry	Private	County, MS Conf Pensioner
Hays, Mose		8th Mississippi Cavalry	Cook	Leake County, MS Conf Pensioner
Hays, Sam		18th Mississippi Infantry	Private	Yazoo County, MS Conf Pensioner
Haywood, Henderson		Unknown Unit	Cook	Grenada County, MS Conf Pensioner
Hemphill, Ben		15th Mississippi Infantry	Private	Choctaw County, MS Conf Pensioner
Hemphill, Ransom		Hospital	Private	Claiborne County, MS Conf Pensioner
Henderson, Ed		Unknown Unit	Cook	Calhoun County, MS Conf Pensioner
Henderson, Henry		Mississippi State Troops	Servant	Hinds County, MS Conf Pensioner
Henderson, Napoleon		29th Mississippi Infantry	Private	Yazoo County, MS Conf Pensioner
Hendricks, Andy		5th Mississippi Infantry	Private	Oktibbeha County, MS Conf Pensioner
Henor, Archie		Unknown Unit	Private	Tallahatchie County, MS Conf Pensioner
Henry Sojourner		36th Mississippi Infantry	Private	Copiah County, MS Conf Pensioner, battle injury.
Henry, Carroll		Turner's Company, Mississippi Light Artillery, Served as a servant to his master S2Lt W. W. Henry	Servant	Lauderdale County, MS Conf Pensioner, Slave of Lt. W. W. Henry,
Hentz, John		1st Mississippi Cavalry	Private	Panola County, MS Conf Pensioner
Hentz, Moses		Ballentine's Mississippi Cavalry Regt	Private	Panola County, MS Conf Pensioner
Herd, Prior		Unknown Unit	Private	Covington County, MS Conf Pensioner

Herndon, Oliver		Unknown Unit	Servant	Lauderdale County, MS Conf Pensioner
Herrin, Gilbert		39th Mississippi Infantry	Private	Ranking County, MS Conf
Herrod, Jeff		Breastworks	Laborer	Calhoun County, MS Conf
Hervey, James	C	18th Mississippi Cavalry	Servant	Killed at the Battle of Shiloh
Hickingbottom, Jake		14th Confederate Cavalry	Private	Franklin County, MS Conf
Hicks, Ransom		Unknown Unit	Wash And Cook	Clarke County, MS Conf Pensioner
Hill, David		3rd Mississippi Cavalry	Servant	Marshall County, MS Conf
Hill, Jack		14th Mississippi Infantry	Private	Attala County, MS Conf
Hill, James		Served as a Body Servant to John H. Hill and W. B. Hill	Body Servant	Slave of Mr. J. Hill, Marshall County, MS.
Hill, Monroe		9th Mississippi Infantry	Servant	Marshall County, MS Conf
Hill, Will		Unknown Unit	Hostler	Tate County, MS Conf Pensioner
Hines, Houston		12th Mississippi Infantry	Private	Claiborne County, MS Conf
Hinton, Jim (James)		9th Mississippi Cavalry	Private	Perry County, MS Conf Pensioner
Hinton, Willis		Hospital	Attendant	Lee County, MS Conf Pensioner
Hodges, Jake		9th Mississippi Cavalry	Cook	Monroe County, MS Conf
Hodges, Rayford	D	1st Mississippi Light Artillery	Servant	Lee County, MS Conf Pensioner
Hodo, Anderson		Unknown Unit	Private	Coahoma County, MS Conf
Hoffman, George		7th Mississippi Cavalry	Private	Bolivar County, MS Conf
Hoges, John		32nd Mississippi Infantry	Private	Covington County, MS Conf Pensioner
Hoke, William		1st Mississippi Cavalry	Private	Tallahatchie County, MS Conf Pensioner
Holden, Thomas		22nd Mississippi Infantry	Private	Amite County, MS Conf Pensioner
Holiday (Holladay), Henry		9th Mississippi Infantry	Private	Yazoo County, MS Conf Pensioner
Holliman (Holloman),		22nd Mississippi Cavalry Battalion	Private	Wilkinson County, MS Conf Pensioner
Hollingsworth, Andy		3rd Mississippi Infantry	Cook	Washington-Hinds County, MS Conf Pensioner
Hollins, Squire		11th Mississippi Infantry	Private	Clay County, MS Conf Pensioner, he was wounded in battle
Holloway, Nick		43rd Mississippi Infantry	Servant	Lee County, MS Conf Pensioner
Holly (Holley), Peter		Home Service	Dept Teamste	Ranking County, MS Conf Pensioner
Holmes, Sterling		28th Mississippi Cavalry	Private	Issaquena County, MS Conf Pensioner
Holmes, Sterling		Harvey's Mississippi Cavalry	Private	Warren County, MS Conf
Holston, Martin		Unknown Unit	Hostler	Humphreys County, MS Conf Pensioner
Hood, Sam		Unknown Unit	Servant	Panola County, MS Conf
Hooks, Rafe		27th Mississippi Infantry	Private	Monroe County, MS Conf
Hoover, Aaron		14th Confederate Cavalry	Private	Franklin County, MS Conf
Hopson, Milton		23rd Mississippi Infantry	Private	Coahoma County, MS Conf Pensioner, battle injury.
Horace, Jordan		18th Mississippi Cavalry Battalion	Private	Coahoma County, MS Conf
Horn, Macon		13th Mississippi Infantry	Private	Oktibbeha County, MS Conf Pensioner
Hoskins, Clark		16th Mississippi Infantry	Servant	Yalobusha County, MS Conf Pensioner

Hoskins, Jack		15th Mississippi Infantry	Horseshoer	Montgomery County, MS Con? Pensioner
Hough, Jac		Unknown Unit	Private	Wayne County, MS Conf Pensioner
Houston, Dan		Unknown Unit	Servant	Smith County, MS Conf Pensioner
Houston, Sam		12th Mississippi Battalion Cavalry Partisans	Private	Washington County, MS Conf Pensioner, non-battle
Howard, Bob	D	1St Mississippi Light Artillery	Servant	Holmes County, MS Conf Pensioner
Howard, Henry		2-th u Mississippi	Private	Monroe County, MS Conf Pensioner
Howard, Hull		31St Mississippi Infantry	Private	Webster County, MS Conf Pensioner
Howard, Mack		Salt Works	Salt Maker	Lee County, MS Conf Pensioner
Howard, Roach		Gen A. C. Vaughan	Servant	Benton County, MS Conf Pensioner
Howcott, Willis		Black Cavalry of Harvey's Scouts, Served as a Servant to H.W. Howcott	Servant	KIA, was only 14 yrs old. H.W. Howcott later built a memorial to his servant and childhood friend Willis Howcott. Madison County, MS.
Howell, Tobe		Unknown Unit	Servant	Marshall County, MS Conf Pensioner
Howery, Cage		11th Mississippi Infantry	Private	Tallahatchie County, MS Conf Pensioner
Howze, Floyd		8th Mississippi Infantry	Cook	Clarke County, MS Conf Pensioner
Howze, Stephen	D	42nd Mississippi Infantry	Servant	
Huddleston, Scipio	A	44th Mississippi Infantry	Private	
Hudson, Lem [Lin]		Jefferson Mississippi Light Artillery	Servant	Jefferson County, MS Conf Pensioner
Hudson, Tillman		35th Mississippi Infantry	Servant	Winston County, MS Conf Pensioner
Huggins, Joe		16th Mississippi Infantry	Private	Washington County, MS Conf Pensioner
Hughes, Jessey		35th Mississippi Infantry	Servant	Winston County, MS Conf Pensioner
Hughes, Sam	A	6th Mississippi Infantry	Servant	Grenada County, MS Conf Pensioner
Hughes, Tom		2nd Mississippi Cavalry	Private	Scott County, MS Conf Pensioner
Hughes, Wilson		46th Mississippi Infantry	Private	Hinds County, MS Conf Pensioner
Hughey, Bill		Hospital	Attendant	Hinds County, MS Conf Pensioner
Hulett (Hulet), Hiram		16th Mississippi Infantry	Private	Hinds County, MS Conf Pensioner
Hunter, Dick		31st Mississippi Infantry	Private	Webster County, MS Conf Pensioner
Hunter, George		31st Mississippi Infantry	Cook	Webster County, MS Conf Pensioner
Hunter, Mack		39th Mississippi Infantry	Private	Hinds County, MS Conf Pensioner
Hutchins, Charlie		Gen Douglas H Cooper	Cook	Bolivar County, MS Conf Pensioner
Ike (Isaac) Johnson		8th Mississippi Cavalry	Private	Grenada County, MS Conf Pensioner
Ingram, Joe		29th Mississippi Infantry	Servant	Montgomery County, MS Conf Pensioner
Ingram, Tony		Unknown Unit	Servant	Marshall County, MS Conf Pensioner
Isham, Preston		35th Mississippi Infantry	Private	Oktibbeha County, MS Conf Pensioner, battle
Isom, Joe	F&S	17th Regiment, Mississippi Infantry Hospital Served as a servant to Dr. Thomas D. Isom (Surgeon)	Servant Attendant	Lafayette County, MS Conf Pensioner, battle injury.
Isom, William		24th Mississippi Cavalry Battalion	Servant	Hinds County, MS Conf Pensioner
Ivey, George		Unknown Unit	Servant	Grenada County, MS Conf Pensioner
Ivy, Elijah		Breastworks	Laborer	Noxubee County, MS Conf Pensioner
I Jack, Ceasar		35th Mississippi Infantry	Servant	Newton County, MS Conf Pensioner

Name		Unit	Rank	Location
Jack, James	B	35th Mississippi Regiment Served as a servant to Capt. Abb M. Jack	Servant	Kemper County, MS Conf Pensioner
Jackson, Andrew		35th Mississippi Infantry	Private	Washington County, MS Conf Pensioner
Jackson, Andrew		7th Mississippi Infantry	Private	Amite County, MS Conf Pensioner
Jackson, Andrew		Wirt Adams's MS. Cavalry Regt	Private	Franklin County, MS Conf Pensioner
Jackson, Andrew		Wirt Adams's MS. Cavalry Regt	Private	Yazoo County, MS Conf Pensioner
Jackson, Ben		28th Mississippi Cavalry	Private	Sunflower County, MS Conf Pensioner, battle injury.
Jackson, Burl (Burwell)		38th Mississippi Infantry	Servant	Holmes County, MS Conf Pensioner
Jackson, Calvin		26th Mississippi Infantry	Servant	Yazoo County, MS Conf Pensioner, battle injury.
Jackson, Charles		38th Mississippi	Private	Holmes County, MS Conf Pensioner
Jackson, Clark		1st Mississippi Cavalry	Private	Yazoo County, MS Conf Pensioner
Jackson, General		19th Mississippi Infantry	Servant	
Jackson, Henry		18th Mississippi Infantry	Private	Madison County, MS Conf Pensioner
Jackson, Henry		18th Mississippi Infantry	Servant	Yazoo County, MS Conf Pensioner
Jackson, Isaac		Smyth's MS. Cavalry Battalion	Private	Madison County, MS Conf Pensioner
Jackson, John		22nd Mississippi Infantry	Private	Hinds County, MS Conf Pensioner
Jackson, Reese		1st Mississippi Cavalry	Private	Clay County, MS Conf Pensioner
Jackson, Sam		33rd Mississippi Infantry	Private	Pike County, MS Conf Pensioner
Jackson, Sandy		22nd Mississippi Infantry	Private	Amite County, MS Conf Pensioner
Jackson, Squire		38th Mississippi Infantry	Private	Claiborne County, MS Conf Pensioner, wounded in battle.
Jackson, William		19th Mississippi Infantry	Private	Warren County, MS Conf Pensioner
Jaggers, Ben		46th Mississippi Infantry		Madison County, MS Conf Pensioner
Jake White		Mississippi State Troops	Servant	Copiah County, MS Conf Pensioner
James, Henry		1st Mississippi Cavalry		Jasper County, MS Conf Pensioner
James, Bob	G	29th Mississippi Infantry	Servant	Grenada County, MS Conf Pensioner
James, Henry		13th Mississippi Infantry	Private	Clarke County, MS Conf Pensioner
James, Sterling		15th Mississippi Infantry	Private	Grenada County, MS Conf Pensioner
James, Tony		18th Mississippi Cavalry Battalion	Private	Grenada County, MS Conf Pensioner
Jamison (Jimmerson), Abe		28th Mississippi Cavalry	Private	Hinds County, MS Conf Pensioner
Jamison, Mat		16th Mississippi Infantry	Private	Chickasaw County, MS Conf Pensioner
Jefferson, Edmond	A	1st Mississippi Light Artillery	Private	Madison County, MS Conf Pensioner
Jefferson, Green		18th Mississippi Infantry	Private	Yazoo County, MS Conf Pensioner
Jefferson, Thomas		44th Mississippi Infantry	Private	Clay County, MS Conf Pensioner
Jeltz, Dan		Unknown Unit	Private	Leflore County, MS Conf Pensioner
Jenkins, Boney		14th Mississippi Infantry	Private	Wayne County, MS Conf Pensioner
Jenkins, Frank		1st Mississippi Cavalry	Private	Washington County, MS Conf Pensioner
Jenkins, George		Unknown Unit	Servant	Bolivar County, MS Conf Pensioner
Johnson, Alfred		29th Mississippi infantry	Servant	Tallahatchie County, MS Conf Pensioner
Johnson, Allen		Unknown Unit	Private	Leflore County, MS Conf Pensioner
Johnson, Anderson		45th Mississippi Infantry	Servant	Holmes County, MS Conf Pensioner
Johnson, Armstead		28th Mississippi Cavalry	Private	Holmes County, MS Conf Pensioner

Directory of African American Confederates in the U.S. Civil War

Name		Unit	Role	County
Johnson, Bob		1st Mississippi Cavalry		Pontotoc County, MS Conf Pensioner, battle injury.
Johnson, Bob		Unknown Unit		Prentiss County, MS Conf
Johnson, Clark		9th Mississippi Infantry		Copiah County, MS Conf Pensioner
Johnson, Dick	A	1st Mississippi Light Artillery	Servant	Madison County, MS Conf
Johnson, Fiddler		33rd Mississippi Infantry		Panola County, MS Conf Pensioner
Johnson, Henry	A	1st Mississippi Lt Artillery		Yazoo County, MS Conf Pensioner
Johnson, Henry		4th Mississippi Infantry		Holmes County, MS Conf
Johnson, J.		Unknown Unit	Servant	Grenada County, MS Conf
Johnson, Jack	H	1st Mississippi Light Artillery	Servant	Copiah County, MS Conf Pensioner
Johnson, Jerre		Commissary Department		Lee County, MS Conf Pensioner
Johnson, John		Unknown Unit	Cook	Leflore County, MS Conf Pensioner
Johnson, Jordan		8thMississippi Infantry		Wayne County, MS Conf Pensioner
Johnson, Joseph		Wirt Adams's MS. Cavalry Regt		Yazoo County, MS Conf Pensioner
Johnson, Judge		23rd Mississippi Infantry	Servant	Clarke County, MS Conf Pensioner
Johnson, Landry		12th Mississippi Cavalry		Marion County, MS Conf Pensioner
Johnson, Leggett		Unknown Unit	Servant	Lamar County, MS Conf Pensioner
Johnson, Mark		1st Mississippi Cavalry		Benton County, MS Conf Pensioner
Johnson, Marshall		22nd Mississippi Infantry	Servant	Amite County, MS Conf Pensioner
Johnson, Matt		Jefferson Mississippi Light		Adams County, MS Conf Pensioner
Johnson, Richard		23rd Mississippi Cavalry Battalion	Servant	Wilkinson County, MS Conf Pensioner
Johnson, Robert		18th Mississippi Cavalry Battalion		Panola County, MS Conf Pensioner
Johnson, Rubin		18th Mississippi Infantry		Yazoo County, MS Conf Pensioner
Johnson, Sam		Wirt Adams's MS. Cavalry Regt	Servant	Madison County, MS Conf Pensioner
Johnson, Samuel		Unknown Unit	Servant	P.O.W. at Camp Morton, Indiana Died there and now buried at Greenfield Park, Indianapolis
Johnson, Tillman (1)		6th Mississippi Cavalry		Chickasaw County, MS Conf Pensioner
Johnson, Tillman (2) (Tilman)		8th Mississippi Cavalry	Servant	Chickasaw County, MS Conf Pensioner
Johnson, Tom		11th Mississippi Infantry		Hinds County, MS Conf Pensioner
Johnson, Tom		8th Mississippi Cavalry		Coahoma County, MS Conf
Johnson, Tom		Unknown Unit	Servant	Tate County, MS Conf Pensioner
Johnson, Wallace		Hospital	Attendant	Yazoo County, MS Conf Pensioner
Johnson, Wiley		31st Mississippi Infantry		Chickasaw County, MS Conf Pensioner
Johnson, William			Servant	Monroe County, MS Conf Pensioner
Johnson, William		Wirt Adams's MS. Cavalry Regt		Madison County, MS Conf
Johnson, William L.		9th Mississippi Cavalry	Servant	Lamar County, MS Conf Pensioner
Johnson, Logan		Pettus Mississippi Flying Artillery		Monroe County, MS Conf
Joiner, Fayett		Unknown Unit	Servant	Monroe County, MS Conf Pensioner
Joiner, Ned		1st Mississippi Cavalry		Noxubee County, MS Conf Pensioner, non-battle injury.
Jolla, Soloman		28th Mississippi Cavalry	Servant	Wilkinson County, MS Conf Pensioner, non-battle injury.
Jolley, John		17th Mississippi Infantry	Servant	Yalobusha County, MS Conf Pensioner
Jones, Albert		Wirt Adams's MS. Cavalry Regt		Oktibbeha County, MS Conf Pensioner

Name		Unit	Role	Location/Notes
Jones, Ben		1st Mississippi Light Artillery		Hinds County, MS Conf Pensioner, battle injury
Jones, Bill Sam		36th Mississippi Infantry	Servant	Jones County, MS Conf Pensioner
Jones, Dan		40th Mississippi Infantry	Servant	Jasper County, MS Conf Pensioner
Jones, Frank		33rd Mississippi Infantry		Amite County, MS Conf Pensioner
Jones, Frank		Unknown Unit	Laborer	Runaway Slave, of Chesterfield Mississippi. According to Avalena McConico in Arkansas Slave Narratives.
Jones, George		11th Mississippi Infantry		Oktibbeha County, MS Conf Pensioner
Jones, George (1)		Madison Mississippi Light Artillery		Panola County, MS Conf Pensioner
Jones, George (2) W.		Unknown Unit		Panola County, MS Conf Pensioner
Jones, Gus		23th Mississippi Cavalry Battalion	Regt Teamste	Bolivar-DeSoto County, MS Conf Pensioner
Jones, Harris		Unknown Unit	Servant	Bolivar County, MS Conf Pensioner
Jones, Henry		Unknown Unit		Leflore County, MS Conf Pensioner, battle injury.
Jones, Joe		18th Mississippi Cavalry Battalion	Servant	Panola County, MS Conf Pensioner
Jones, John H.		37th Mississippi Infantry	Servant	Jasper County, MS Conf Pensioner
Jones, Math		20th Mississippi Infantry	Servant	Smith County, MS Conf Pensioner
Jones, Monroe	A	1st Mississippi Light Artillery Served as a Surgeon's Assistant and lost both legs at Snyder's Bluff in the Vicksburg campaign.	Surgeon's Assistant Servant	Warren County, MS Conf Pensioner, battle injury.
Jones, N. J.		31st Mississippi Infantry		Chickasaw County, MS Conf Pensioner
Jones, Peter		14th Mississippi Infantry		Lee County, MS Conf Pensioner
Jones, Peter		Madison Mississippi Light Artillery		Panda County, MS Conf Pensioner,
Jones, Sam		Unknown Unit	Servant	Lee County, MS Conf Pensioner
Jones, Simon		Wirt Adams's MS. Cavalry Regt		Madison County, MS Conf
Jones, Wallace		3rd Mississippi Infantry	Servant	Leflore County, MS Conf Pensioner
Jordan, Ben		Smith's-Turner's Mississippi Arty		Clarke County, MS Conf Pensioner
Jordan, Horace		15th Mississippi Cavalry Battalion		Coahoma County, MS Conf
Jordan, Neut		Ordnance Department	Dept Teamste	Washington County, MS Conf Pensioner
Jordon, Surry R.		Breastworks		Wayne County, MS Conf Pensioner
Joyner, William		17th Mississippi Infantry	Servant	Marshall County, MS Conf
Julian, Alexander		29th Mississippi Infantry		Tallahatchie County, MS Conf Pensioner, battle injury.
Keelin, B. F.	D	27th Mississippi Infantry	Private	P.O.W. at Camp Morton, Indiana Died there and now buried at Greenfield Park,
Keller, Elijah		Unknown Unit	Cook	Sunflower County, MS Conf Pensioner
Keller, Robert		16th Mississippi Infantry		Wilkinson County, MS Conf Pensioner
Kelley, Abe		7th Mississippi Cavalry	Servant	Tippah County, MS Conf Pensioner
Kelly, Anderson		Unknown Unit	Servant	Yalobusha County, MS Conf Pensioner, battle injury.
Kelly, Dave		Ballentinet's Mississippi Cavalry Regt		Attala County, MS Conf Pensioner

Name		Unit	Role	Location/Notes
Kelly, Isaac (Ike)		Wirt Adams's MS. Cavalry Regt	Private	Yazoo County, MS Conf Pensioner
Kennedy, Manuel		15th Mississippi Calvary	Private	Shelby County, TN Conf Pension App # C161, application rejected.
Kennedy, Robert	B	14th Mississippi Infantry Served as a servant to his master Dr. John F. Kennedy (Surgeon)	Servant	Lauderdale County, MS Conf Pension denied for lack of proof
Kilgore, Sam		Served building breastworks and hedges in Alabama, Tennessee and Kentucky.	Laborer Servant	Slave of Lt. John Peacock, who became a Colonel and was killed in battle in Florida. According to his statements in Texas Slave Narratives.
Kimbel, Charlie		7th Mississippi Cavalry	Servant	Humphreys County, MS Conf Pensioner
Kinard (Kinnard), Jack		8th Mississippi Infantry	Private	Wayne County, MS Conf Pensioner
Kinchloe, Dallas		28th Mississippi Cavalry	Private	Tate County, MS Conf Pensioner
King, Anderson		46th Mississippi Infantry	Servant	Smith County, MS Conf Pensioner, battle injury.
King, John		8th Mississippi Cavalry	Private	Lee County, MS Conf Pensioner
King, Mose		20th Mississippi Infantry	Servant	Jasper County, MS Conf Pensioner
King, Randal		16th Mississippi Infantry	Servant	Jasper County, MS Conf Pensioner, battle injury.
Kinion (Kenyon), Simon		5th Mississippi Cavalry	Private	Leflore County, MS Conf Pensioner
Kinney, Edward		16th Mississippi Infantry	Private	Hinds County, MS Conf Pensioner
Kirkland, Harrison		38th Mississippi Infantry	Private	Hinds County, MS Conf Pensioner
Kline, Mason		37th Mississippi Infantry	Cook	Hinds County, MS Conf Pensioner
Knight, Peter		Ballentine's Mississippi Cavalry Regt	Regt Teamster	Smith County, MS Conf Pensioner
Knight, Peter		Unknown Unit	Cook	Forrest County, MS Conf Pensioner
Knight, Trip		Unknown Unit	Cook	Perry-Pike County, MS Conf Pensioner
Kuykendall, Wilson		Ballentine's Mississippi Cavalry	Private	Panola County, MS Conf Pensioner
Lambert, Isaac		7th Mississippi Cavalry	Private	Alcorn County, MS Conf Pensioner
Lambeth, Hal		14th Mississippi Infantry	Private	Monroe County, MS Conf Pensioner
Lampley, Eli	C	1st Mississippi Cavalry Reserves 43rd Mississippi Infantry Served as a servant to Capt. Benjamin L. Lampley and Capt. Henry Gully	Servant	Kemper County, MS Conf Pensioner
Lampley, Phillip		46th Mississippi Infantry	Private	Wayne County, MS Conf Pensioner
Land, Charles		28th Mississippi Cavalry	Private	Holmes County, MS Conf Pensioner
Lane, Frank		28th Mississippi Cavalry	Private	Lafayette County, MS Conf Pensioner
Lane, Sweet		30th Mississippi Infantry	Cook	Montgomery County, MS Conf Pensioner
Latham, Jacob		Unknown Unit	Cook	Oktibbeha County, MS Conf Pensioner
Lawless, Horace		1st Mississippi Light Artillery	Cook	Hinds County, MS Conf Pensioner
Laws, George		1st Mississippi Cavalry		Hinds County, MS Conf Pensioner
Laws, Robert (Hooter)		Unknown Unit	Drover	Yazoo County, MS Conf Pensioner
Lay, Richard		Unknown Unit	Servant	Marshall County, MS Conf Pensioner
Leach, Ed		Wirt Adams's MS. Cavalry Regt	Cook	Copiah County, MS Conf Pensioner

Name	Co.	Unit	Role	Notes
Leake Leek), George	I	1st Mississippi Lt Artillery	Private	Yazoo County, MS Conf Pensioner, non-battle injury.
Leatherwood, Henry		10th Mississippi Infantry	Servant	Tippah County, MS Conf pensioner
Ledbetter, Edmon		Gen Ambrose R. Wood	Horseshoer	Alcorn County, MS Conf Pensioner
Lee, Albert		36th Mississippi Infantry	Servant	Copiah County, MS Conf Pensioner
Lee, George		10th Mississippi Infantry	Servant	Adams County, MS Conf Pensioner
Lee, Green		15th Mississippi Infantry	Private	Attela County, MS Conf Pensioner
Lee, Ottoway L.		Unknown Unit	Servant	Grenada County, MS Conf Pensioner
Lee, Sonnie	I	17th Mississippi Infantry	Private	Arkansas, Monroe County Conf Pensioner, application #25163. His widow Susan later received his pension.
Lee, T. H.		4th Mississippi Cavalry	Private	Jefferson Davis County, MS Conf Pensioner
LeFlare, Dan		Unknown Unit	Servant	Grenada County, MS Conf Pensioner
Leflore, Crockett		Breastworks	Laborer	Leake County, MS Conf Pensioner
Leggett, Hardy		Unknown Unit	Private	Lamar County, MS Conf Pensioner
Leggett, Martin		Mississippi State Troops	Attendant	Marshall County, MS Conf
Leland, Richard		Madison Mississippi Light Artillery	Private	Panola County, MS Conf Pensioner, battle injury.
Lemon, Scott		36th Mississippi Infantry	Servant	Lafayette County, MS Conf
Lester, Abe Patterson		1st Mississippi Cavalry	Servant	Yalobusha County, MS Conf Pensioner
Lester, Coleman	A	1st Mississippi Lt Artillery	Cook	Marshall County, MS Conf
Lester, Coleman	K	22nd Regiment, Mississippi Infantry (Pegues Defenders) Served as a servant to Capt. George Lester	Servant	Lafayette County, MS Conf Pensioner, was WIA by a piece of shell, battle injury.
Lester, Pattison		1st Mississippi Cavalry	Servant	Yalobusha County, MS Conf Pensioner
Lester, William Harrison		Unknown Unit	Servant	Panola County, MS Conf Pensioner
Lewellen, Lewis (Louis)		31st Mississippi Infantry		Lee County, MS Conf Pensioner
Lewis, Ed		15th Mississippi Infantry	Servant	Grenada County, MS Conf
Lewis, Jule		20th Mississippi Infantry	Private	Harrison County, MS Conf
Lewis, Nat		28th Mississippi Cavalry	Private	Leflore County, MS Conf Pensioner
Lewis, Robert		Ballentine's Mississippi Cavalry Regt	Private	Panola County, MS Conf Pensioner
Lewis, Thomas		35th Mississippi Infantry	Private	Hinds County, MS Conf Pensioner
Liggans (Liggins), Cyrus		4th Mississippi Cavalry	Servant	Claiborne County, MS Conf Pensioner
Lighter (Litter), Jack		Wirt Adams's MS. Cavalry Regt	Private	Hinds County, MS Conf Pensioner
Lindsey, Nathan		Railroad	Worker	Yazoo County, MS Conf Pensioner
Lindsy, Coleman		14th Confederate Cavalry	Regt Teamst	Yazoo County, MS Conf Pensioner
Linebarger, Lawson		6th Mississippi Cavalry	Private	Leflore County, MS Conf Pensioner
Lipsey, Alfred		4th Mississippi Infantry	Private	Montgomery County, MS Conf Pensioner
Littleton, Solomon		3rd Mississippi Infantry	Servant	P.O.W. at Camp Morton, Indiana Died there and now buried at Greenfield Park, Indianapolis
Lochman, Alex		28th Mississippi Cavalry	Private	Rankin County, MS Conf Pensioner

Lockhart, Peter		Lindsay's Mississippi Cavalry Regt	Camp Attendant	Montgomery County, MS Conf Pensioner, battle injury.
Logan, Branch		2nd Mississippi Cavalry	Private	Tate County, MS Conf Pensioner
Logan, Henry		Unknown Unit	Servant	Panola County, MS Conf Pensioner
Loggins, Lee		15th Mississippi Infantry	Private	Webster County, MS Conf Pensioner
Loggins, Miles		30th Mississippi Infantry	Private	Webster County, MS Conf Pensioner
Long, Edmund		7th Mississippi Cavalry	Private	Lee County, MS Conf Pensioner
Longstreet, Hudson		13th Regiment Mississippi Volunteers (Barksdale's Regiment, and under Gen. Walthall) 11th Mississippi Infantry Also served as a servant to Gilbert Longstreet	Servant	Lafayette County, MS Conf Pensioner, was WIA in the neck by a bullet, enlisted in Yalobusha County, MS.
Love, George		5th Mississippi Cavalry	Private	Attala County, MS Conf Pensioner
Loving, Henry	G	1st Mississippi Lt Artillery	Private	Warren County, MS Conf Pensioner
Lucas, Lawrence		Unknown Unit	Servant	Hinds County, MS Conf Pensioner
Lumford, Anthony		Ordnance Department	Dept Teamste	Simpson County, MS Conf Pensioner
Lundie, Reuben	E	19th Regiment, Mississippi Infantry (McClung Rifles) Served as a servant to Cpl. William H. Lundie	Servant	Lafayette County, MS Conf Pensioner
Luster, Joe		Wirt Adams's MS. Cavalry Regt	Servant	Hinds County, MS Conf Pensioner
Mackey, Isaac		1st Mississippi Infantry	Private	Panola County, MS Conf Pensioner
Magee, Emp		4th Mississippi Cavalry	Private	Covington County, MS Conf Pensioner, battle injury.
Mallory, Jim		26th Mississippi Infantry.	Private	Attala County, MS Conf Pensioner
Mann, Tony	A	1st Mississippi Light Artillery	Cook	Leake County, MS Conf Pensioner
Manning, George		Unknown Unit	Private	Monroe County, MS Conf Pensioner
Manuel, Stephen		Unknown Unit	Servant	Quitman County, MS Conf Pensioner
Manuel, Steve		Gen. Price (Pap)	Cook Forager	Mark, MS. Attended the UCV Reunion in Arkansas 1928
Marion, Andy		Served as a bodyguard to his master	Bodyguard	Slave
Markham, Alexander	F I	1st Mississippi Light Artillery 12th Mississippi Infantry Served as a Servant to Pvt. Henry C. Covington	Body Servant	
Marrs, Jack		Unknown Unit	Servant	Lee County, MS Conf Pensioner
Marshall, Aaron (Aron)		5th Mississippi Cavalry	Private	Webster County, MS Conf Pensioner
Marshall, Albert		Conscript Service	Camp Attendan	Yazoo County, MS Conf Pensioner
Marshall, Isham		Wirt Adams's MS. Cavalry Regt	Private	Warren County, MS Conf Pensioner
Marshall, Jim		Seven Stars Mississippi Lt Artillery	Private	Chickasaw County, MS Conf Pensioner
Martin, Butler		24th Mississippi Cavalry Battalion	Servant	Hinds County, MS Conf Pensioner
Martin, Cisley		37th Mississippi Infantry	Private	Smith County, MS Conf Pensioner
Martin, Green		6th Mississippi Infantry	Private	Madison County, MS Conf Pensioner
Martin, Hanable		37th Mississippi Infantry	Private	Smith County, MS Conf Pensioner

Name		Unit	Rank/Role	Location/Notes
Martin, J. B.		45th Mississippi Infantry	Private	Pike County, MS Conf Pensioner, battle injury.
Martin, John		Unknown Unit	Private	Washington County, MS Conf Pensioner
Martin, Will		Wirt Adams's MS. Cavalry Regt	Private	Madison County, MS Conf
Marvel, Martin		Served under his master Sheriff Carson of Washington County, Mississippi	Slave	He was entrusted with the county records which he saved from being burnt by Federal
Mason, Julia (Female)		Hospital	Attendant	Warren County, MS Conf Pensioner, battle injury.
Mason, Neal	I	Ballentine's Mississippi Cavalry Regt	Servant	Grenada County, MS Conf Pensioner
Massengale, William		18th Louisiana Infantry	Wash And	Noxubee County, MS Conf Pensioner
Massey, Alex	I	1st Mississippi Lt Artillery	Private	Yazoo County, MS Conf Pensioner
Massey, Daniel		Unknown Unit	Private	Webster County, MS Conf Pensioner
Mathews (Mathis), Andrew		8th Confederate Cavalry	Private	Prentiss County, MS Conf Pensioner
Matthews, C. L.		Unknown Unit	Servant	P.O.W. at Camp Morton, Indiana Died there and now buried at Greenfield Park,
Matthews, Fed		23rd Mississippi Cavalry Battalion	Servant	Lee County, MS Conf Pensioner
Matthews, Manuel		4th Mississippi Cavalry	Cook	Marshall County, MS Conf Pensioner
Matthews, Manuel		Unknown Unit	Servant	Marshall County, MS Conf Pensioner
Maxey, Columbus		12th Mississippi Cavalry	Servant	Rankin County, MS Conf Pensioner
Mayes, Romulus		28th Mississippi Cavalry	Servant	Lafayette County, MS Conf Pensioner
Mayfield, Jacob		27th Mississippi Infantry	Servant	Chickasaw County, MS Conf Pensioner
Mayo, Romulus		28th Mississippi Infantry Served as a servant to William Mayo	Servant	Lafayette County, MS Conf Pensioner
McAllum, Unknown		Served as a servant to his master Mr. McAllum who was WIA at Manasas Gap, and died after he was accompanied home	Servant	Slave of McAllum of Kemper, MS. According to his step-son Sam McAllum, in Mississippi Slave Narratives.
McBeath, Dan		33rd Mississippi Infantry	Cook	Leake County, MS Conf Pensioner
McCaleb, Hayse	A B	11th Mississippi Infantry Regiment 35th Mississippi Infantry Regiment Served as a servant to Capt. Calvin B. McCaleb	Servant	Kemper County, MS Conf Pensioner
McCall, Richard (Dick)		10th Mississippi Infantry 14th Mississippi Infantry Served as a servant to Capt. Bill Jarvis	Servant	Kemper County, MS Conf Pensioner
McCamery, John		Unknown Unit	Private	Lee County, MS Conf Pensioner
McCarty, Handy		37th Mississippi Infantry	Private	Clarke County, MS Conf Pensioner
McCaskill, Willis		11th Mississippi Infantry	Servant	Carroll County, MS Conf Pensioner
McClendon, Frank		12th Mississippi Cavalry		Monroe County, MS Conf
McCollum, Isom		1st Mississippi Cavalry	Servant	Yalobusha County, MS Conf Pensioner
McCoy, Evander (Evando)		28th Mississippi Cavalry	Private	Hinds County, MS Conf Pensioner

Name		Unit	Role	Location
McCoy, Gus	I	24th Mississippi Infantry (Kemper Rebels) Served as a servant to Pvt. John L. McCoy	Servant	Lauderdale County, MS Conf Pensioner
McCray, Henry		18th Mississippi Infantry	Cook	Madison County, MS Conf Pensioner
McCree, Cornelius		37th Mississippi Infantry	Private	Clarke County, MS Conf Pensioner, non-battle injury.
McCree, Samuel		1st Mississippi Cavalry	Private	Yazoo County, MS Conf Pensioner
McCullough, James		Madison Mississippi Light Artillery	Servant	Madison County, MS Conf Pensioner, battle injury.
McDonald, Major		Unknown Unit	Wash And Cook	Winston County, MS Conf Pensioner
McEwen, Winnie	K	4th Mississippi Cavalry 1st Battalion, Mississippi Cavalry (Miller's), Bowles Company Served as a servant to (Dr.) Capt. John B. McEwen	Servant	Lafayette County, MS Conf Pensioner
McFarland, Frank		15th Mississippi Infantry	Servant	Yalobusha County, MS Conf Pensioner
McFields, Lewis		4th Mississippi Cavalry	Private	Wilkinson County, MS Conf Pensioner
McGaughy, George		Unknown Unit	Servant	Lee County, MS Conf Pensioner
McGee, E. D.		32nd Mississippi Infantry	Private	Prentiss County, MS Conf Pensioner
McGee, Julius		36th Mississippi Infantry	Cook	Yazoo County, MS Conf Pensioner
McGee, Mize		Unknown Unit	Servant	Clarke County, MS Conf Pensioner
McGee, Reuben		Seven Stars Mississippi Lt	Servant	Lee County, MS Conf Pensioner
McGehee, Moses		7th Mississippi Infantry	Private	Panola County, MS Conf Pensioner
McGill, Anthony		7th Mississippi Cavalry	Private	Lafayette County, MS Conf Pensioner
McGowan (McGowen),		45th Mississippi Infantry	Servant	Hinds County, MS Conf Pensioner
McGowen, Dempsey		36th Mississippi Infantry	Private	Copiah-Hinds County, MS Conf Pensioner, battle injury.
McJunkin, Tom		11th Mississippi Infantry	Private	Chickasaw County, MS Conf Pensioner
McKinney, Felix G.		27th Mississippi Infantry	Cook	Calhoun County, MS Conf Pensioner
McKinney, John		Unknown Unit	Servant	Winston County, MS Conf Pensioner
McKinney, Robert		18th Mississippi Cavalry Battalion		Panola County, MS Conf Pensioner
McKissack, Norwood		9th Mississippi Infantry	Servant	Marshall County, MS Conf Pensioner
McLaughlin, Jack	H	14th Regiment Mississippi Infantry Served as a servant to his master J2Lt William J. McLaughlin	Servant	Lauderdale County, MS Conf Pensioner
McLaurin, Silas		28' Mississippi Cavalry	Servant	Hinds County, MS Conf Pensioner
McLaurin, Ves		38th Mississippi Infantry	Private	Hinds County, MS Conf Pensioner
McLendon, Caesar		8th Mississippi Cavalry	Private	Chickasaw County, MS Conf Pensioner
McMath, Singleton	E	15th Mississippi Infantry	Cook Servant	Grenada County, MS Conf Pensioner
McMichael, Ben		5th Mississippi Infantry	Private	Attala County, MS Conf Pensioner
McMillan, Clem		2nd Mississippi Cavalry	Servant	Leake County, MS Conf Pensioner
McMorris, Seab		Unknown Unit	Private	Pike County, MS Conf Pensioner, battle injury.
McMullan, Wilson		Col. Wilburn's Cavalry Regiment	Servant	Lafayette County, MS Conf Pensioner

McMurtry, Sanford		Breastworks	Laborer	Leake County, MS Conf Pensioner
McNair, Amos		4th Mississippi Cavalry	Servant	Simpson County, MS Conf Pensioner
McNairy, Anderson		Ordnance Department	Dept Team	Monroe County, MS Conf Pensioner, non-battle injury.
McNeal, James		38th Mississippi Infantry	Private	Hinds County, MS Conf Pensioner
McNeil, Lake		38th Mississippi Infantry	Cook	Copiah County, MS Conf Pensioner
McNeil, Port (John Culver)	A	1st Mississippi Light Artillery (Ridley's Company) Served as a Body Servant to George A. McNeill	Body Servant	
McQuiston, Andrew (Anderson)	E	15th Mississippi Infantry	Body	Montgomery County, MS Conf Pensioner, Slave.
McWilliams, Ira	L	1st Mississippi Light Artillery	Servant	Forrest County, MS Conf Pensioner
Medley, Jordan		Unknown Unit	Private	Lee County, MS Conf Pensioner
Meek, Jacob		22nd Mississippi Infantry	Private	Yazoo-Holmes County, MS Conf Pensioner
Meek, Zack		4th Mississippi Cavalry	Servant	Panola County, MS Conf Pensioner
Melton, Dan	B	22nd Mississippi Infantry	Servant	Grenada County, MS Conf Pensioner
Merrell, Jake (Jack)		37th Mississippi Infantry	Servant	Jasper County, MS Conf Pensioner
Merriweather, Ned		Unknown Unit	Private	Lamar County, MS Conf Pensioner
Middlebrooks, Frank		8th Mississippi Infantry	Private	Chickasaw County, MS Conf Pensioner
Middleton, Fed		18th Mississippi Cavalry Battalion	Servant	Panola County, MS Conf Pensioner
Middleton, Gran		4th Mississippi Cavalry		Franklin County, MS Conf Pensioner
Middleton, John		Commissary Department	Servant	Madison County, MS Conf Pensioner
Miles, Jack		Pettus Mississippi Flying Artillery	Private	Panola County, MS Conf Pensioner
Miles, Nelson		Unknown Unit	Servant	Lafayette County, MS Conf Pensioner
Miliam, Spence		Wirt Adams's MS. Cavalry Regt	Private	Tate County, MS Conf Pensioner
Miller, Andrew	K	1st Mississippi Lt Artillery	Cook	Oktibbeha County, MS Conf Pensioner
Miller, Hazzard		Unknown Unit	Servant	Hinds County, MS Conf Pensioner
Miller, Henry		3rd Mississippi Cavalry	Cook	Forrest County, MS Conf Pensioner
Miller, Jerrymire (Jerry)		11th Mississippi Cavalry	Servant	Winston County, MS Conf Pensioner
Miller, Patrick		1st Mississippi Cavalry	Private	Pontotoc County, MS Conf Pensioner
Miller, Warn		30th Mississippi Infantry	Servant	Lee County, MS Conf Pensioner
Mills, Charles (Charley)		Wirt Adams's MS. Cavalry Regt	Private	Yazoo County, MS Conf Pensioner
Mills, John		Wirt Adams's MS. Cavalry Regt	Private	Yazoo County, MS Conf Pensioner
Minor, Elijah		27th Mississippi Infantry	Private	Monroe County, MS Conf Pensioner
Minor, Tom		Commissary Department	Private	Warren County, MS Conf Pensioner
Minter, Fannie (Female)		Served nursing wounded soldiers	Nurse	Slave
Minter, Manuel		1st Mississippi Cavalry	Private	Tallahatchie County, MS Conf Pensioner
Minter, Tom		1st Mississippi Cavalry	Private	Tallahatchie County, MS Conf Pensioner
Mitchell, Alonzo		31st Mississippi Infantry	Private	Washington County, MS Conf Pensioner
Mitchell, Charley		Unknown Unit	Private	Holmes County, MS Conf Pensioner, battle injury.

Name		Unit	Role	Location
Mitchell, Dan		Breastworks	Laborer	Yalobusha County, MS Conf Pensioner
Mitchell, Handy		Ordnance Department	Cartridge Maker	Bolivar County, MS Conf Pensioner
Mitchell, Ike		36th Mississippi Infantry	Servant	Copiah County, MS Conf Pensioner
Mitchell, Irvin		Bradford's MS. Cavalry Battalion		Rankin County, MS Conf Pensioner
Mitchell, Robert		Wirt Adams's MS. Cavalry Regt	Cook	Yazoo County, MS Conf Pensioner
Mitchell, Steve		Unknown Unit	Cook	Bolivar County, MS Conf Pensioner, wounded in battle
Mobley, Nance		Unknown Unit	Private	Yazoo County, MS Conf Pensioner
Moffett, D.		Unknown Unit	Cook	Clarke County, MS Conf Pensioner
Moman, John		20th Mississippi Infantry	Servant	Madison County, MS Conf
Montgomery,	C	1st Mississippi Light Artillery	Servant	Lee County, MS Conf Pensioner
Montgomery, Sarah (Female)		Unknown Unit	Wash & Cook	Sunflower County, MS Conf Pensioner
Montgomery, Thad		Gen John C. Pemberton	Servant	Chickasaw County, MS Conf Pensioner
Moore, Andy		Unknown Unit	Servant	Tippah County, MS Conf Pensioner
Moore, Ben		11th Mississippi Infantry	Private	Chickasaw County, MS Conf Pensioner
Moore, George		8th Mississippi Infantry	Private	Tallahatchie County, MS Conf Pensioner
Moore, Harry		15th Mississippi Infantry	Private	Yalobusha County, MS Conf Pensioner
Moore, Harvey		Unknown Unit	Private	Lee County, MS Conf Pensioner
Moore, Ike		Wirt Adams's MS. Cavalry Regt	Servant	Bolivar County, MS Conf Pensioner
Moore, Jesse		2nd Mississippi Cavalry	Cook	Scott County, MS Conf Pensioner
Moore, Jesse		9th Mississippi Infantry		Madison County, MS Conf Pensioner
Moore, Jim		Mississippi Stare Troops	Private	Hinds County, MS Conf Pensioner
Moore, Marion		21st Mississippi Infantry	Private	Wilkinson County, MS Conf Pensioner
Moore, Peter		Unknown Unit	Servant	Yalobusha County, MS Conf Pensioner
Moore, Pomp		Unknown Unit	Cook	Montgomery County, MS Conf Pensioner
Moore, Shep	A	1st Mississippi Light Artillery	Wash And Cook	Hinds County, MS Conf Pensioner
Moore, Smith		11th Mississippi Infantry	Private	Clay County, MS Conf Pensioner
Moore, Tom		1st Mississippi Cavalry	Servant	Carroll County, MS Conf Pensioner
Mordecai, Lank		1st Mississippi Cavalry	Private	Washington County, MS Conf Pensioner
Morgan, Dempsey		Unknown Unit	Camp Attenda	Jasper County, MS Conf Pensioner
Morgan, Zack		9th Mississippi Cavalry		Monroe County, MS Conf Pensioner
Morman, Burt (Bert)		Unknown Unit	Servant	Prentiss County, MS Conf Pensioner battle injury.
Morris, Charles		Wirt Adams's MS. Cavalry Regt	Wash & Cook	Oktibbeha County, MS Conf Pensioner
Morris, Duke		Unknown Unit	Servant	Hinds County, MS Conf Pensioner
Morris, Paden		Unknown Unit	Servant	Lee County, MS Conf Pensioner
Morris, Tom		Unknown Unit	Wash & Cook	Jefferson Davis County, MS Conf Pensioner

Morrison, Alex		8th Mississippi Cavalry		Lafayette-Pontotoc County, MS Conf Pensioner
Morton, Rederich	F	3rd Mississippi Cavalry Served as a servant to Thomas H. Morton	Servant	Lauderdale County, MS Conf Pensioner
Moseley, Abe		34th Mississippi Infantry	Cook	Union County, MS Conf Pensioner
Moseley, James	D A	Perrin's Battalion, Mississippi State Cavalry 1st Regiment, Mississippi Infantry (Johnston's)	Servant	Lafayette County, MS Conf Pensioner Served as a servant to Capt. George M. Moseley and Maj. Flemmings, also served as a servant in the Commissary
Mosely, Gilbert		17th Mississippi Infantry		Quitman County, MS Conf Pensioner
Mosley, Harrison	A	35th Regiment Mississippi Infantry (Barry Guards) Served as a servant to his master Pvt. William C. Mosley	Servant	Lauderdale County, MS Conf Pensioner
Mosley, Louis		Unknown Unit	Servant	Hinds County, MS Conf Pensioner
Motley, Charley		Seven Stars Mississippi Lt Artillery		Copiah County, MS Conf Pensioner
Mullen, Larkin		Unknown Unit	Servant	Pontotoc County, MS Conf Pensioner
Mullins, Mart		19th Mississippi Infantry		Lafayette County, MS Conf Pensioner
Murdough, Horace		32nd Mississippi Infantry	Servant	Alcorn County, MS Conf Pensioner
Murff, Austin		20th Mississippi infantry		Attila County, MS Conf Pensioner
Murphy, Jason		Unknown Unit		Yazoo County, MS Conf Pensioner
Murphy, Solomon		4th Mississippi Infantry	Servant	Holmes County, MS Conf Pensioner
Murray, Henry		39th Mississippi Infantry	Cook	Simpson County, MS Conf Pensioner
Musgraves, Billie	A	18th Mississippi Cavalry	Servant	
Myers, Code		Wirt Adams's MS. Cavalry Regt		Rankin County, MS Conf Pensioner
Myers, Handy		13th Mississippi Infantry		Rankin County, MS Conf Pensioner, battle injury.
Myers, Handy		7th Mississippi Infantry		Forrest [Perry] County, MS Conf Pensioner, battle injury.
Myers, Harry		7th Mississippi Infantry		Perry County, MS Conf Pensioner
Myers, Wesley		39th Mississippi Infantry		Madison County, MS Conf Pensioner
Nabors, Berry		Served as a servant to J. W. Nabors who was WIA at Tupelo MS by a bursting shell	Servant	Lafayette County, MS Conf Pensioner, battle injury.
Name not known	D	19th Mississippi Infantry Served as a body servant to Capt. Chesley S. Coffee	Body Servant	Both were captured at the battle of Williamsburg.
Name not known	D	19th Mississippi Infantry Served as a body servant to Pvt. Samuel B. Stampley	Body Servant	He was disabled at Chancellorsville
Name not known	D	28th Mississippi Cavalry Regiment Served as a servant to 2nd Lt. William Nugent	Servant	Slave of Abram F. Smith of Greenville, Washington County, MS.
Name not known	E	2nd Battalion Mississippi Infantry Served as a servant to his master's son, Capt. Will	Servant	Slave of Capt. Will Crutcher's father
Name not known	K	7th Mississippi Regiment Served as a Servant to Pvt. George P. Claughton	Servant	Slave of George P. Claughton who was WIA, his servant was taking him home when he died at Summit, MS.
Nash, Abraham (Abe)		Unknown Unit	Cook	Leake County, MS Conf Pensioner
Nash, Frank		40th Mississippi Infantry		Madison County, MS Conf Pensioner

Name		Unit	Role	Location
Nash, Marsh	D	1st Mississippi Cavalry	Servant	Grenada County, MS Conf Pensioner
Nash, Orange	D	40th Mississippi Infantry 24th Mississippi Infantry Served as a Body Servant to Pvt. George Nash	Body Servant Cook	Leake County, Mississippi. MS Conf Pension Applicant. Slave
Neal, Ben		Wirt Adams's MS. Cavalry Regt	Private	Hinds County, MS Conf Pensioner
Neal, James	F	1st Mississippi Light Artillery	Private	Lawrence County, MS Conf Pensioner
Neal, Nelson		Ballentine's Mississippi Cavalry Regt 29th Mississippi Infantry	Cook Servant	Grenada County, MS Conf Pensioner
Neely, H. M.		48th Mississippi Infantry	Servant	Oktibbeha County, MS Conf Pensioner
Neely, H. M. (Rev)		Unknown Unit	Private	Columbus, MS. Attended the UCV Reunion in Arkansas 1928
Nelson, Abram		48th Mississippi Infantry	Servant	Tallahatchie County, MS Conf Pensioner, battle injury.
Nelson, Ben		Unknown Unit	Private	Copiah County, MS Conf Pensioner
Nelson, John		35th Mississippi Infantry	Servant	Copiah County, MS Conf Pensioner
Nelson, Reeves		Unknown Unit	Cook	Marion County, MS Conf Pensioner
Nesbit, George		Unknown Unit	Servant	Union County, MS Conf Pensioner
Netter, Elijah		23rd Mississippi Cavalry Battalion	Private	Jefferson County, MS Conf Pensioner
Netterville, Joe		Unknown Unit	Private	Wilkinson County, MS Conf Pensioner, non-battle
Nettles, Frank		Wirt Adams's MS. Cavalry Regt	Private	Clay County, MS Conf Pensioner, non battle injury.
Nettles, Hampton		14th Mississippi Infantry	Private	Oktibbeha County, MS Conf Pensioner, non-battle
Newell, Tom		Unknown Unit	Cook	Attala County, MS Conf Pensioner
Newsom (Newsome), Wiley		Quartermaster Dept	Cook	Yazoo County, MS Conf Pensioner
Newsom, Stephen		Unknown Unit		Marion County, MS Conf Pensioner
Newsome, Adam		39th Mississippi Infantry		Hinds County, MS Conf Pensioner
Newton, George		7th Mississippi Infantry	Servant	Jefferson Davis County, MS Conf Pensioner
Nichols, Albert		39th Mississippi Infantry	Private	Hinds County, MS Conf Pensioner
Nicholson, Isaac		Unknown Unit	Servant	Clarke County, MS Conf Pensioner
Nicholson, William		Hospital	Attendant	Kemper County, MS Conf Pensioner
Nixon, Book		Unknown Unit	Hostler	Jasper County, MS Conf Pensioner
Noel, Frank		1st Mississippi Cavalry	Private	Tallahatchie County, MS Conf Pensioner
Nolan, Cornelius	I	1st Mississippi Lt Artillery	Private	Yazoo County, MS Conf Pensioner
Norman, Elbert		39th Mississippi Infantry	Cook	Rankin County, MS Conf Pensioner
Norman, Henry		39th Mississippi Infantry	Servant	Newton County, MS Conf Pensioner
Nunn, Alex		5th Mississippi Infantry	Private	Rankin County, MS Conf Pensioner
Nunn, Peter		Unknown Unit	Horseshoer	Noxubee County, MS Conf Pensioner
O'Neal, Zeke		16th Mississippi Cavalry	Private	Prentiss County, MS Conf Pensioner
Oatis, Pharaoh		22nd Mississippi Infantry	Private	Lawrence County, MS Conf
Odum, Mose		Unknown Unit	Servant	Tippah County, MS Conf Pensioner
Oglesby, Jack	F	17th Mississippi Infantry	Servant	
Orr, Alfred		31st Mississippi Infantry	Private	Lee County, MS Conf Pensioner
Orr, Matt		Breastworks	Laborer	Chickasaw County, MS Conf Pensioner

Orr, Perry		31st Mississippi Infantry	Cook	Pontotoc County, MS Conf Pensioner
Osborn, Ben		Gen John S. Marmaduke	Private	Bolivar County, MS Conf Pensioner
Otterway Leigh		Wagon Train	Dept Teamster	Grenada County, MS Conf Pensioner
Outlaw, Alex		35th Mississippi Infantry	Private	Oktibbeha County, MS Conf Pensioner
Outlaw, William		Wirt Adams's MS. Cavalry Regt	Cook	Oktibbeha County, MS Conf Pensioner
Owen, Willis		8th Mississippi Infantry	Private	Clarke County, MS Conf Pensioner
Owens, Lewis		18th Mississippi Infantry	Private	Hinds County, MS Conf Pensioner
Pack, Jim		Unknown Unit	Cook	Lauderdale County, MS Conf Pensioner
Page, Charles		8th Mississippi Infantry	Servant	Smith County, MS Conf Pensioner
Page, Charley		Unknown Unit	Servant	Jasper County, MS Conf Pensioner
Page, George		24th Mississippi Infantry	Private	Bolivar County, MS Conf Pensioner
Page, Steve		8th Mississippi Infantry	Servant	Covington County, MS Conf Pensioner
Parchman, Lum		43rd Mississippi Infantry	Servant	Lee County, MS Conf Pensioner
Parish (Parrish), Chesley		12th Mississippi Infantry		Copiah County, MS Conf Pensioner
Park, Richard		12th Mississippi Battalion Cavalry Partisans	Private	Monroe County, MS Conf Pensioner
Parker, Esaw		5th Mississippi Infantry	Cook	Scott County, MS Conf Pensioner
Parker, Jim		Breastworks	Laborer	Leake County, MS Conf Pensioner, non-battle injury.
Parker, William	K	15th Mississippi Infantry	Body Servant	Slave
Parker, William		5th Mississippi Cavalry		Grenada County, MS Conf Pensioner
Parmore, Dave		Unknown Unit		Webster County, MS Conf Pensioner
Parnell, Henry		Unknown Mississippi Unit Served as a laborer cutting down timber, worked under a young man named Tom.	Laborer Servant	Slave of Henry Parnell of Carroll County MS. According to his son Austin Per Parnell in Arkansas Slave Narratives.
Parrott (Parret),		40th Mississippi Infantry	Drummer	Scott County, MS Conf Pensioner
Pasley (Posley), Peter		Wirt Adams's MS. Cavalry Regt	Private	Panola County, MS Conf Pensioner
Patterson, Aaron	I	1st Mississippi Light Artillery	Servant	Jasper County, MS Conf Pensioner
Patterson, Roadman		Salt Works	Salt Maker	Lee County, MS Conf Pensioner
Patterson, Robert		Mississippi State Troops	Servant	Madison County, MS Conf Pensioner
Patterson, Sonny		25th Mississippi Infantry		Oktibbeha County, MS Conf Pensioner
Patton, Jim	F&S A	13th Mississippi Infantry Served as a servant to LtCol. (Judge) M. H. Whittaker 37th Regiment Mississippi Infantry Served as a servant to Col. William S. Patton	Servant	Lauderdale County, MS Conf Pensioner, battle injury.
Payton, Henry		Unknown Unit	Private	Tate County, MS Conf Pensioner
Peal, Alfred		Unknown Unit	Servant	Marshall County, MS Conf Pensioner
Peebles Peobles), Jonas (Jonah)		14th Mississippi Infantry	Wash And Cook	Oktibbeha County, MS Conf Pensioner

Name		Unit	Role	Location/Notes
Peeples, Andrew		Unknown Unit	Private	Leflore County, MS Conf Pensioner, battle injury.
Pendelton, Ausbon		Unknown Unit		Copiah County, MS Conf Pensioner
Perkins, Henderson		46th Mississippi Infantry	Hostler	Yazoo County, MS Conf Pensioner, non-battle injury.
Perkins, Henry		48th Mississippi Infantry	Private	Clay County, MS Conf Pensioner, non battle injury.
Perkins, James		18th Mississippi Infantry	Cook	Sunflower County, MS Conf Pensioner
Perkins, Renza	B	1st Mississippi Light Artillery	Cook	Humphreys County, MS Conf Pensioner
Perry, Fred		15th Mississippi Infantry	Servant	Grenada County, MS Conf Pensioner, battle injury.
Perry, Tom	K	22nd Regiment, Mississippi Infantry (Pegues Defenders) Served as a servant to Frank	Servant	Lafayette County, MS Conf Pensioner
Perryman, Eli		23rd Mississippi Cavalry Battalion	Servant	Copiah County, MS Conf Pensioner, battle injury.
Peters, Jim		27th Mississippi Infantry	Private	Monroe County, MS Conf Pensioner
Peterson, Simon		Unknown Unit	Private	Yazoo County, MS Conf Pensioner
Petree, Frank		Unknown Unit	Servant	
Pettus, Pleasant		Served as a servant to Gen. Ed Pettus	Servant	Kemper County, MS Conf Pensioner
Phillips, Benjamin		4th Mississippi Cavalry	Private	Hinds County, MS Conf Pensioner
Phillips, Fletcher		Unknown Unit	Servant	Marshall County, MS Conf
Phillips, Hogan		Unknown Unit	Servant	Covington County, MS Conf Pensioner
Pittman, Charles		Unknown Unit	Cattle Drover	Wayne County, MS Conf Pensioner
Pittman, John A.		Mississippi State Troops	Private	Jefferson Davis County, MS Conf Pensioner
Pittman, Milton		Unknown Unit	Servant	Lauderdale County, MS Conf Pensioner
Pittman, Russell		15th Mississippi Infantry	Servant	Grenada County, MS Conf
Pittman, Wesley		4tl Mississippi Infantry	Servant	Montgomery County, MS Conf Pensioner
Pitts, Dempsey		Served hauling food for Confederate soldiers	Teamster	Slave
Pitts, John		Unknown	Private	Madison County, MS Conf
Poe, Sol	K	15th Mississippi Infantry	Body Servant	Slave
Poe, Tom		33rd Mississippi Infantry	Cook	Webster County, MS Conf
Polk, John		1st Mississippi Cavalry	Servant	Yazoo County, MS Conf Pensioner
Pon (Pan), Jacob		24th Mississippi Infantry	Servant	Wayne County, MS Conf Pensioner
Pon, Henry		13th Mississippi Infantry	Private	Wayne County, MS Conf Pensioner
Pool, Unknown (Smith)		Unknown Mississippi Unit Served with his master Mr. Pool.	Servant	He changed his last name back to Smith after he was freed. Smith was his father's surname.
Poole, Gilbert		Breastworks	Laborer	Lawrence County, MS Conf Pensioner
Pope, Noah		39th Mississippi Infantry	Private	Washington County, MS Conf Pensioner
Porter, Rasberry		9th Mississippi Infantry	Private	Hinds County, MS Conf Pensioner

Directory of African American Confederates in the U.S. Civil War

Porterfield, Jacob		16th Mississippi Regiment Served under Lt. William Jefferson	Cook	Slave of Evans Jefferson Augusta County, Virginia Conf Pensioner
Pound Pounds), William		1st Mississippi Infantry	Private	Lee County, MS Conf Pensioner
Pounds, John		Unknown Unit	Private	Tallahatchie County, MS Conf Pensioner, battle injury.
Powe, Mallie		24th Mississippi Cavalry Battalion	Private	Wayne County, MS Conf Pensioner
Pratt, Henry P.		Unknown Unit	Cook	Calhoun County, MS Conf Pensioner
Prescott, Jake		Unknown Unit	Servant	Calhoun County, MS Conf Pensioner
Preston, Isom		Gen Richard S. Ewell	Private	Washington County, MS Conf Pensioner
Price, George		Mississippi State Troops	Servant	Copiah County, MS Conf Pensioner
Price, Peter		Unknown Unit	Servant	Monroe County, MS Conf Pensioner
Prince, Aaron		11th Mississippi Infantry	Private	Noxubee County, MS Conf Pensioner
Prince, Jerry		11th Mississippi Infantry	Cook	Attala County, MS Conf Pensioner
Prince, John		12th Mississippi Infantry	Servant	Noxubee County, MS Conf Pensioner
Pringle, Isaac (Ike)	A	24th Mississippi Infantry Served as a servant to his master's son Frank M. Pringle	Body Servant Wash And Cook	Lauderdale County, MS Conf Pensioner, Slave of W.S. Pringle. Meridian, MS. Attended the UCV Reunion in Arkansas 1928. Also gave statement in the Mississippi Slave narratives, Lauderdale County. He was a member of the Walthall United Confederate Veterans Camp.
Pryor, Adam	I	19th Mississippi Infantry	Cook Servant	Marshall County, MS Conf Pensioner
Pulley, Jim		44th Mississippi Infantry	Servant	Yalobusha County, MS Conf Pensioner
Pulliam, Jim		31st Mississippi Infantry	Servant	Chickasaw County, MS Conf Pensioner
Purify, John		Unknown Unit	Private	Neshoba County, MS Conf Pensioner
Quarles, Barney	A,E	7th Regiment Mississippi Infantry (Franklin Rifles)Served as a Body Servant to Lt. James A. Lee	Body Servant	Franklin County, MS Conf Pensioner
Quinn, Doc		Ogburn's Regiment, Mississippi Served as a Bodyguard to his Master Col. Joe Ogburn who he grew up with as a child.	Body Guard	Slave of Col. Joe Ogburn of Monroe County, MS. According to his statements in Arkansas Slave Narratives.
Ragsdale, George		23' Mississippi Infantry	Private	Coahoma County, MS Conf Pensioner
Rail (Rails) (Rawl), Alex		Iron Works	Iron Worker	Bolivar County, MS Conf Pensioner
Rails, Prince		le Confederate Cavalry	Private	Franklin County, MS Conf Pensioner
Ramsburg (Ramburg), Pat		Unknown Unit	Servant	Warren County, MS Conf Pensioner
Rance, Calvin		Unknown Unit	Servant	Yazoo County, MS Conf Pensioner
Randle, Willis		Unknown Unit	Servant	Monroe County, MS Conf Pensioner
Rankin, Ed		281-n Mississippi Cavalry	Private	Washington County, MS Conf Pensioner
Rappan, John (Riffan)	C	4th Mississippi Infantry (Consolidated)	Slave	Slave, P.O.W.
Ratliff, Roy		28th Mississippi Cavalry	Servant	Rankin County, MS Conf Pensioner

Rawls, George W.	B	7th Mississippi Infantry	Private	Slave of Benjamin Rawles III Both men enlisted in the Confederate Army into Company B, 7th Mississippi Infantry; Benjamin as an officer and George as a private.
Rayburn, Allen		Breastworks	Laborer	Tallahatchie County, MS Conf Pensioner
Redditt, Jesse		20th Mississippi Infantry	Private	Leflore County, MS Conf Pensioner
Redmond, Wesley		Unknown Unit	Private	Holmes County, MS Conf Pensioner
Reed, Dock		Unknown Unit	Cook	Clarke County, MS Conf Pensioner
Reed, James		Served as a servant to Milton Reed and Jeff Cala	Servant	Tunica County, MS Conf Pensioner
Reed, Sam		Unknown Unit	Servant	Kemper County, MS Conf Pensioner
Reed, Sampson		Mississippi State Troops	Drover	Copiah County, MS Conf Pensioner
Reese, March		15th Mississippi Infantry	Private	Calhoun County, MS Conf Pensioner
Reese, Clem		Breastworks	Laborer	Covington County, MS Conf Pensioner, battle injury.
Rennels, Albert		26th Mississippi Infantry	Private	Forrest County, MS Conf Pensioner
Reynolds, Green		30th Mississippi Infantry	Private	Leflore County, MS Conf Pensioner
Reynolds, James		7th Mississippi Infantry	Private	Pike County, MS Conf Pensioner
Rhodes, Jerry		Unknown Unit	Servant	Harrison County, MS Conf Pensioner
Rhodes, William		39th Mississippi Infantry	Private	Hinds County, MS Conf Pensioner
Rice, Thomas H.		Unknown Unit	Servant	Claiborne County, MS Conf Pensioner
Richardson, Allen		Wirt Adams's MS. Cavalry Regt		Clay County, MS Conf Pensioner
Richardson, Susan (female)		Unknown Unit	Servant	Yazoo County, MS Conf Pensioner
Richardson, Unknown	A	9th Mississippi Infantry Served as a servant to his master's son Samuel L. Scott.	Servant	Slave of Jake/Jim Scott of the Scott Plantation in Franklin County, MS. According to Mrs. Canduce Richardson his wife's statements in Indiana Slave Narratives.
Riddick, Alex		15th Mississippi Infantry	Private	Quitman County, MS Conf Pensioner
Riddick, Jack		29th Mississippi Infantry	Private	Yalobusha County, MS Conf Pensioner
Ridley, Jim		Unknown Unit	Private	Oktibbeha County, MS Conf Pensioner
Rigmar, Andrew		Unknown Unit	Cook	Copiah County, MS Conf Pensioner
Riley, Charles		16th Mississippi Infantry	Private	Copiah County, MS Conf Pensioner
Riley, James R.		Unknown Unit	Private	Attala County, MS Conf Pensioner
Rives, Spencer		Unknown Unit	Servant	Oktibbeha County, MS Conf Pensioner
Robert, Israil		Unknown Unit	Servant	Humphreys County, MS Conf Pensioner
Roberts, Erwin		3rd Mississippi Cavalry	Private	Jackson County, MS Conf Pensioner
Roberts, Richard		Breastworks	Laborer	Sunflower County, MS Conf Pensioner
Robertson (Roberson), Ephram		12th Mississippi Infantry	Servant	Hinds County, MS Conf Pensioner
Robertson, Henry		Unknown Unit	Servant	Marion County, MS Conf Pensioner
Robertson, Isaac		29th Mississippi Infantry	Private	Panola County, MS Conf Pensioner
Robinson, Bob		44th Mississippi Infantry	Private	Clay County, MS Conf Pensioner, wounded in battle
Robinson, Ike		4th Mississippi Cavalry	Servant	Hinds County, MS Conf Pensioner

Robinson, James		Unknown Unit	Servant	Hinds County, MS Conf Pensioner
Robinson, Jim	B	1st Mississippi Lt Artillery	Private	Yazoo County, MS Conf Pensioner
Robinson, Jim		36th Mississippi Infantry	Private	Copiah County, MS Conf Pensioner
Robinson, Lewis		Unknown Unit	Private	Hinds County, MS Conf Pensioner
Robinson, Lit		Unknown Unit	Private	Choctaw County, MS Conf Pensioner
Robinson, Samson (Sampson)		Wirt Adams's MS. Cavalry Regt	Servant	Hinds County, MS Conf Pensioner
Robinson, Spencer		Breastworks	Laborer	Madison County, MS Conf Pensioner
Rodgers, Isom		1st Mississippi Cavalry	Private	Panola County, MS Conf Pensioner
Rodgers, Monroe		4th Mississippi Infantry	Private	Holmes County, MS Conf Pensioner
Rogers, Ben		Wagon Train	Dept Teamste	Wayne County, MS Conf Pensioner, non-battle injury.
Rogers, George		Stayed with his master until the master died, George then went over to the Union side.	Private	Slave
Rogers, Jack		Unknown Unit	Servant	Lee County, MS Conf Pensioner
Ross, Henry		Commissary Department	Helper	Hinds County, MS Conf Pensioner
Ross, Jerry "Old Jerry"	C	3rd Mississippi Infantry Served as a Servant to Pvt. Henry Clay Sharkey	Cook	Slave of Henry C. Sharkey of Hinds County, MS.
Rossom, C. L.		37th Mississippi Infantry	Wash And Cook	Smith County, MS Conf Pensioner
Royals, A. G.		Unknown Unit	Servant	Jasper County, MS Conf Pensioner
Ruffin, Albert		36th Mississippi Infantry	Private	Claiborne County, MS Conf Pensioner, wounded in battle.
Rundles, Washingto		4th Mississippi Cavalry	Cook	Claiborne County, MS Conf Pensioner
Runnel's, Marshall		Unknown Unit	Servant	Yazoo County, MS Conf Pensioner
Russell, Iron		Unknown Unit	Servant	Oktibbeha County, MS Conf Pensioner
Russell, Warren		15th Mississippi Infantry	Private	Sunflower County, MS Conf Pensioner
Russum, Daniel		6th Mississippi Infantry	Private	Scott County, MS Conf Pensioner
Russum, Joe		39th Mississippi Infantry	Private	Scott County, MS Conf Pensioner
Ryan, Warren		14th Mississippi Infantry	Servant	Jasper County, MS Conf Pensioner
Saddler, George		22nd Mississippi Infantry	Servant	Yazoo County, MS Conf Pensioner
Sales, William		Unknown Unit	Private	Madison County. MS Conf Pensioner, battle injury.
Sallis, Jerry		15th Mississippi Infantry	Private	Attala County, MS Conf Pensioner
Salter, Cason		Unknown Unit	Servant	Hickory, Newton County, MS Conf Pensioner
Sam Hughes		6th Mississippi Cavalry	Cook	Grenada County, MS Conf Pensioner, non-battle injury.
Sampson, Anthony		2nd Mississippi Infantry	Servant	Lee County, MS Conf Pensioner
Sanders, Douglas		Wirt Adams's MS. Cavalry Regt4th Mississippi Cavalry	Servant	Adams County, MS Conf Pensioner
Sanders, James		7th Mississippi Infantry	Helper	Tippah County, MS CD -if Pensioner
Sanders, Jim		9th Mississippi Infantry	Private	Madison County, MS Conf Pensioner
Sanders, Ned		10th Mississippi Infantry	Private	Adams County, MS Conf Pensioner
Sandifer, Emanuel		4th Mississippi Cavalry	Private	Lincoln County, MS Conf Pensioner
Sanford, John		Unknown Unit	Private	Grenada County, MS Conf Pensioner
Sargent, Edman		2nd Mississippi Cavalry	Private	Lee County, MS Conf Pensioner

Name		Unit	Role	Location / Notes
Sargent, Mat		Unknown Unit	Servant	Prentiss County, MS Conf Pensioner
Saunders (Sanders), Sam		6th Mississippi Infantry	Private	Oktibbeha County, MS Conf Pensioner
Scales, Cicero		11th Mississippi Infantry	Private	Lowndes County, MS Conf
Scales, David (Dave)		1st Mississippi Infantry	Servant	Lee County, MS Conf Pensioner
Scales, Marshall		Unknown Unit	Servant	Alcorn County, MS Conf Pensioner
Scott, Albert		18th Mississippi Infantry	Servant	Scott County, MS Conf Pensioner
Scott, Alex		1st Mississippi Infantry	Cook	Pontotoc County, MS Conf Pensioner, battle injury.
Scott, Alex		Unknown Unit	Servant	Leflore County, MS Conf Pensioner
Scott, Charles		Quartermaster Dept	Dept Teamster	Madison County, MS Conf Pensioner
Scott, Hal		18th Mississippi Infantry	Servant	Madison County, MS Conf Pensioner
Scott, John		Unknown Unit	Private	Claiborne County, MS Conf Pensioner
Scott, Taylor		Unknown Unit	Cook	Copiah County, MS Conf Pensioner
Seals, Nelson		9th Mississippi Cavalry	Private	Forrest County, MS Conf Pensioner, non-battle injury.
Searcy, Daily (Dailey)		Unknown Unit	Servant	Sharkey County, MS Conf Pensioner, non-battle injury
Sears, Alex		Hospital	Attendant	Humphreys County, MS Conf Pensioner
Segers (Seagers), Harrison		15th Mississippi Infantry	Private	Attala County, MS Conf Pensioner
Sellers, Frank		3rd Mississippi Cavalry	Private	Grenada County, MS Conf Pensioner
Selvy, Louis H.		11th Mississippi Infantry	Private	Rankin County, MS Conf Pensioner
Semmes, Andrew		Wirt Adams's MS. Cavalry Regt	Regt Teamste	Madison County, MS Conf Pensioner
Sewell, George W.		14th Mississippi Infantry	Private	Hamilton County, TN Conf Pension App #C129, application
Seymour, William		Unknown Unit	Private	Yazoo County, MS Conf Pensioner
Shackelford, Frank	H	11th Mississippi Infantry 42nd Mississippi Infantry	Servant	Grenada County, MS Conf Pensioner
Shannon, Bill		11th Mississippi Infantry	Wash And Cook	Clarke County, MS Conf Pensioner
Shannon, Granville D.		Unknown Unit	Hostler And Horseshoer	Lee County, MS Conf Pensioner
Shannon, Newell		Unknown Unit	Cook	Sunflower County, MS Conf Pensioner
Shaw, Isaac		Unknown Unit	Private	Calhoun County, MS Conf Pensioner
Shaw, John		18th Mississippi Infantry	Servant	Panola County, MS Conf Pensioner
Shaw, Minter Ervin		14th Mississippi Infantry	Servant	Oktibbeha County, MS Conf Pensioner
Shelby, Willis		Hospital	Servant	Hinds County, MS Conf Pensioner
Shelton, Charlie		6th Mississippi Infantry	Private	
Sheppard, Gibbs	K	7th Mississippi Regiment 23rd Mississippi Cavalry Battalion Served as a Servant to Maj. Joseph Ferdinand Sessions	Servant	Slave of Joseph F. Sessions of Franklin County, MS. Franklin County, MS Conf Pensioner
Shippens, George		Unknown Unit	Servant	Hinds County, MS Conf Pensioner
Shoemaker, William		Bradford's MS. Cavalry Battalion	Servant	Copiah-Clay County, MS Conf Pensioner

Name		Unit	Role	Location / Notes
Sim, Lane		Unknown Unit	Servant	DeSoto County, MS Conf Pensioner in the 1938 List.
Simmons, Ed		29th Mississippi Infantry	Servant	Panola County, MS Conf Pensioner
Simmons, Levi		16th Mississippi Infantry	Servant	Jasper County, MS Conf Pensioner
Simpson, Archie		Wirt Adams's MS. Cavalry Regt	Private	Madison County, MS Conf Pensioner
Simpson, Cyrus		7th Mississippi Infantry	Private	Wayne County, MS Conf Pensioner
Sims, Andrew		Wirt Adams's MS. Cavalry Regt	Private	Madison County, MS Conf Pensioner
Sims, Dick		29th Mississippi Infantry	Private	Attala County, MS Conf Pensioner
Singleton, William		Wirt Adams's MS. Cavalry Regt	Servant	Adams County, MS Conf Pensioner, he suffered a non battle injury.
Skillman, Bill		11th Mississippi Cavalry	Servant	Prentiss County, MS Conf Pensioner
Skinner, Grant		Unknown Unit	Servant	Rankin County, MS Conf Pensioner
Slaughter, George		1st Mississippi Cavalry	Private	Neshoba-Attala County, MS Conf Pensioner
Sledge, Prince		12th Mississippi Infantry	Private	Tate County, MS Conf Pensioner
Small, Joe		4th Mississippi Infantry	Cook	Montgomery County, MS Conf Pensioner
Small, Pompey		28th Mississippi Cavalry	Private	Coahoma County, MS Conf Pensioner
Smith, Albert		18th Mississippi Infantry	Private	Madison County, MS Conf Pensioner
Smith, Allen		Unknown Unit	Camp Attendant	Madison County, MS Conf Pensioner
Smith, Ananias		Wirt Adams's MS. Cavalry Regt	Servant	Panola County, MS Conf Pensioner
Smith, Andrew		Hospital	Attendant	Washington County, MS Conf Pensioner
Smith, Arch		11th Mississippi Cavalry	Private	Covington County, MS Conf Pensioner
Smith, Bill		Gen B. G. Humphreys	Servant	Leflore County, MS Conf Pensioner
Smith, Braxton		Unknown Unit	Cook	Leflore County, MS Conf Pensioner
Smith, Coleman		Gen Braxton Bragg	Servant	Tate County, MS Conf Pensioner
Smith, Dave		Unknown Unit	Servant	Monroe County, MS Conf Pensioner
Smith, Henderson		Unknown Unit	Dept Teamste	Quitman County, MS Conf Pensioner
Smith, Isham		6th Mississippi Infantry	Private	Lincoln County, MS Conf Pensioner
Smith, J. S.		Unknown Unit	Servant	Grenada County, MS Conf Pensioner
Smith, Jack		Unknown Unit	Servant	Warren County, MS Conf Pensioner, battle injury.
Smith, Jake	K	1st Mississippi Light Artillery	Servant	Hinds County, MS Conf Pensioner
Smith, James	K	11th Mississippi Infantry	Servant	Grenada County, MS Conf Pensioner
Smith, James		42nd Mississippi Infantry		Grenada County, MS Conf Pensioner
Smith, James		Unknown Unit	Servant	Marshall County, MS Conf Pensioner
Smith, Jim		Unknown Unit	Cook	Bolivar County, MS Conf Pensioner
Smith, John		Madison Mississippi Light		Madison County, MS Conf Pensioner
Smith, Josh		25th Mississippi Infantry	Servant	Panola County, MS Conf Pensioner
Smith, Lewis		Unknown Mississippi Unit	Body Servant	Slave of Jim and Louisa Smith Served as a Body Servant, According to his sister Rachel Harris in Arkansas Slave Narratives.
Smith, Marcus		29th Mississippi Infantry	Cook	Yalobusha County, MS Conf Pensioner
Smith, Monroe		40th Mississippi Infantry	Servant	Leake County, MS Conf Pensioner

Smith, Nelson		29th Mississippi Infantry	Private	Tate County, MS Conf Pensioner, battle injury.
Smith, Reddick		Unknown Unit	Private	Hinds County, MS Conf Pensioner
Smith, Rederic		44th Mississippi Infantry	Private	Coahoma County, MS Conf Pensioner
Smith, Robert Harris		Unknown Unit	Servant	Jefferson County, MS Conf Pensioner, battle injury.
Smith, Sam		Commissary Department	Private	Panola County, MS Conf Pensioner
Smith, Shelby		4th Mississippi Cavalry	Cook	Copiah-Clay County, MS Conf Pensioner
Smothers, Armstead Hoskins		Unknown Unit	Servant	Holmes County, MS Conf Pensioner
Sorey, W. L.		Ashcraft's Mississippi Cavalry Regt	Servant	Smith County, MS Conf Pensioner
Spearman, Abraham		2nd Mississippi Cavalry	Private	Lee County, MS Conf Pensioner
Spearman, Steve		4th Mississippi Cavalry	Private	Monroe County, MS Conf Pensioner
Spears, George		Unknown Unit	Private	Marshall County, MS Conf Pensioner
Spears, Jesse		Quartermaster Dept	Servant	Yazoo County, MS Conf Pensioner
Spellman, Abe		19th Mississippi Infantry	Servant	Adams County, MS Conf Pensioner
Spencer, Seborn (Sebon)		Choctaw Agency	Servant	Oktibbeha County, MS Conf Pensioner
Spencer, Will		Commissary Department	Drover (Cattle)	Jasper County, MS Conf Pensioner
Spight, Tuck	B	34th Mississippi Infantry Served as a Body Servant to Capt. Thomas Spight	Body Servant	Slave, Tippah County, MS Conf Pensioner
Spight, Tucker		34th Mississippi Infantry	Servant	Tishomingo County, MS Conf Pensioner
Stamps, Milton		28th Mississippi Cavalry	Servant	Hinds County, MS Conf Pensioner
Stamps, Robert		22nd Mississippi Infantry		Hinds County, MS Conf Pensioner
Staples, Bill		24th Mississippi Infantry	Servant	Montgomery County, MS Conf Pensioner
Starks, Thad		23rd Mississippi Cavalry Battalion 14th Mississippi Infantry	Private	Franklin-LeFlore County, MS Conf Pensioner
Staten, Riley		9th Mississippi Infantry	Servant	Tallahatchie County, MS Conf Pensioner
Steele, Henry		24th Mississippi Infantry		Neshoba County, MS Conf
Stephenson, Frank		Unknown Unit	Servant	Attala County, MS Conf Pensioner
Stevens, Alex		11th Mississippi Cavalry	Servant	Winston County, MS Conf
Stevens, Charlie		3rd Mississippi Infantry		Hinds County, MS Conf Pensioner
Stewart, Jack		Commissary Department		Lee County, MS Conf Pensioner
Stier, Isaac		1st Mississippi Infantry (Patton's) (Army of 10,000) Served with Pvt. J. H. Stier	Servant	Slave of James Stowers, From Adams County, MS. Also made statements in Mississippi Slave Narratives.
Stingley, Al		46th Mississippi Infantry	Private	Scott County, MS Conf Pensioner
Stokes, John		18th Mississippi Cavalry Battalion	Private	Quitman County, MS Conf
Stovall, Andrew		Unknown Unit	Private	Union County, MS Conf Pensioner
Stovall, Louis		24th Mississippi Infantry	Private	Lafayette County, MS Conf
Stowers, Elias		41st Mississippi Infantry	Private	Noxubee County, MS Conf Pensioner
Strong, Harrison		9th Mississippi Cavalry	Wash & Cook	Clay County, MS Conf Pensioner
Strong, Joe		11th Mississippi Infantry	Servant	Monroe County, MS Conf Pensioner, non-battle injury.

Name		Unit	Role	Location
Stuart, Frank	C	45th Mississippi Regiment 3rd Battalion Mississippi Infantry Served as a servant to Capt. Elias F. Nunn	Servant	Kemper County, MS Conf Pensioner
Sturdivant, Bill	C	14th Mississippi Artillery Battalion	Private	Tallahatchie County, MS Conf Pensioner
Sudduth, Monroe		11th Mississippi Cavalry	Private	Choctaw County, MS Conf
Summers, Green		Unknown Unit	Private	Madison County, MS Conf
Sykes, Joe		43rd Mississippi Infantry	Private	Monroe County, MS Conf Pensioner
Sykes, Wesley		43rd Mississippi Infantry	Private	Monroe County, MS Conf Pensioner
Table, Alex		Unknown Unit	Dept Teamster	Grenada County, MS Conf Pensioner
Talbert (Talbot), Randolph		29th Mississippi Infantry	Private	Tallahatchie County, MS Conf Pensioner
Talbert, Burrell (Burl)		11th Mississippi Infantry	Servant	Grenada County, MS Conf Pensioner
Talbert, Israel		Unknown Unit	Private	Humphreys County, MS Conf Pensioner
Talbert, Randall		Unknown Unit	Servant	Grenada County, MS Conf
Tally, Adam		18th Mississippi Infantry	Servant	Benton County, MS Conf Pensioner
Tarkington, Sam		Unknown Unit	Private	Clay County, MS Conf Pensioner
Tate, John		Unknown Unit	Servant	DeSoto County, MS Conf Pensioner in the 1938 List.
Tate, Reuben	A	42nd Mississippi Infantry 30th Mississippi Infantry	Servant	Grenada County, MS Conf Pensioner
Tate, Steve		11th Mississippi Infantry	Cook	Lee County, MS Conf Pensioner
Tatum, Bob		Unknown Unit	Servant	Jasper County, MS Conf Pensioner
Taylor, Arter		6th Mississippi Infantry	Cook	Rankin County, MS Conf Pensioner
Taylor, B. J.		Unknown Unit	Private	Tallahatchie County, MS Conf Pensioner
Taylor, Berry		1st Mississippi Cavalry	Private	Pontotoc County, MS Conf Pensioner, battle injury.
Taylor, Bob		11th Mississippi Cavalry	Private	Lee County, MS Conf Pensioner
Taylor, Dempsey		5th Mississippi Cavalry	Private	Attala County, MS Conf Pensioner
Taylor, Osbron		Commissary Department	Dept Teamste	Yazoo County, MS Conf Pensioner
Taylor, Reddock		6th Mississippi Infantry	Servant	Rankin County, MS Conf Pensioner
Taylor, Robert		3rd Mississippi Cavalry	Private	Hinds County, MS Conf Pensioner
Taylor, Shed		Bradford's MS. Cavalry Battalion	Private	Wilkinson County, MS Conf Pensioner
Taylor, Tom		12th Mississippi Infantry	Private	Copiah County, MS Conf Pensioner
Tee, Tom		Unknown Unit	Servant	Tate County, MS Conf Pensioner
Terrell, Wallace		Unknown Unit	Private	Grenada County, MS Conf Pensioner
Terry, William		23rd Mississippi Cavalry	Private	Lincoln County, MS Conf Pensioner
Thames, Ben		13th Mississippi Infantry	Servant	Newton County, MS Conf Pensioner
Thauss, Jacob		12th Mississippi Infantry	Private	Lincoln County, MS Conf Pensioner
Thomas, Allen	A	14th Mississippi Artillery	Private	Panola County, MS Conf Pensioner
Thomas, Bally		Unknown Unit	Private	Yazoo County, MS Conf Pensioner
Thomas, Ed		Gen Robert Toombs	Servant	Harrison County, MS Conf
Thomas, George		Ballentine's Mississippi	Private	Grenada County, MS Conf
Thomas, Henry		Unknown Unit	Servant	Hinds County, MS Conf Pensioner

Thomas, Jack		16th Confederate Cavalry	Servant	Clay County, MS Conf Pensioner
Thomas, Jordan		5th Mississippi Infantry	Private	Oktibbeha County, MS Conf Pensioner
Thomas, Nathan		28th Mississippi Cavalry	Private	Leflore County, MS Conf Pensioner
Thomas, Neil		Unknown Unit	Private	Smith County, MS Conf Pensioner
Thomas, Riddick		18th Mississippi Infantry	Private	Madison County, MS Conf Pensioner
Thomas, William		Ballentine's Mississippi Cavalry	Servant	Grenada County, MS Conf Pensioner
Thomas, William		Gen John C. Pemberton	Private	Leflore County, MS Conf Pensioner
Thomas, William Blewett		Mississippi State Troops	Servant	Noxubee County, MS Conf Pensioner
Thomas, Wilson		Unknown Unit	Private	Yazoo County, MS Conf Pensioner
Thomason, Joe		41st Mississippi Infantry	Private	Lee County, MS Conf Pensioner
Thompson, Dave		5th Mississippi Infantry	Servant	Winston County, MS Conf Pensioner
Thompson, Hammond		Unknown Unit	Cook	Sunflower County, MS Conf Pensioner
Thompson, Henry		16th Mississippi Infantry	Servant	Wilkinson County, MS Conf Pensioner
Thompson, Lindsey		19th Mississippi Infantry	Camp Attendant	Tallahatchie County, MS Conf Pensioner
Thompson, Morris		4th Regiment, Mississippi Cavalry Served as a Body Servant to his master Elijah C. Miller	Body Servant	Lincoln County, MS Conf Pensioner App #
Thompson, Robert		291h Mississippi Infantry	Private	Yalobusha County, MS Conf Pensioner
Thompson, Rufus		Ballentine's Mississippi Cavalry	Private	Lafayette County, MS Conf Pensioner
Thompson, Smith		Quartermaster Dept	Private	Madison County, MS Conf Pensioner
Thompson, Wes		36th Mississippi Infantry	Servant	Copiah-Clay County, MS Conf Pensioner
Thornton, Horace		5th Mississippi Cavalry	Servant	Panola County, MS Conf Pensioner
Thornton, Jeff		Unknown Unit	Private	Panola County, MS Conf Pensioner
Tillman, Sam	F	1st Mississippi Light Artillery	Cook	Hinds County, MS Conf Pensioner
Tinnin, Dick		6th Mississippi Infantry	Private	Hinds County, MS Conf Pensioner, battle injury.
Tinsley, Ned		13th Mississippi Infantry	Private	Kemper County, MS Conf Pensioner
Torrey, Peter		1st Mississippi Infantry Battalion	Private	Holmes County, MS Conf Pensioner, battle injury.
Townsend, Frank	B	35th Mississippi Regiment Served as a servant to Capt. George W. Oden and Pvt. Andrew Jack Townsend	Servant	Kemper County, MS Conf Pensioner
Townsend, John		9th Mississippi Cavalry	Private	Clay County, MS Conf Pensioner
Townsend, Johnson		11th Mississippi Infantry	Cook	Montgomery County, MS Conf Pensioner
Trantham, Calvin		Pettus Mississippi Flying	Private	Panola County, MS Conf Pensioner
Triplett, Ike		Breastworks	Laborer	Winston County, MS Conf Pensioner
Triplett, Pierce		14th Mississippi Infantry	Private	Winston County, MS Conf Pensioner
Trotter, Charley		28th Mississippi Cavalry	Private	Lafayette County, MS Conf Pensioner
Trotter, Issac	B	15th Mississippi Infantry	Body Servant	Slave
Trotter, Judge		Unknown Unit	Servant	Leflore County, MS Conf Pensioner
Truitt, Henry		26th Mississippi Infantry	Private	Claiborne County, MS Conf Pensioner

Truly, George		Breastworks	Laborer	Humphreys County, MS Conf Pensioner
Tucker, Adam		30th Mississippi Infantry		Panola County, MS Conf Pensioner, battle injury.
Tucker, Henderson		Jefferson Mississippi Light Artillery		Yazoo County, MS Conf Pensioner, battle injury.
Tucker, Remulus		11th Mississippi Infantry		Chickasaw County, MS Conf Pensioner, wounded
Turner, Anderson		Unknown Unit	Servant	Winston County, MS Conf
Turner, Dred		Commissary Department		Bolivar County, MS Conf
Turner, Henry		Served with General Patrick Cleburne		Slave
Turner, Hinds		23rd Mississippi Cavalry Battalion		Franklin County, MS Conf
Turner, John		16th Mississippi Infantry	Servant	Jasper County, MS Conf Pensioner
Turner, Tom		Hospital	Attendant	Winston County, MS Conf
Turnipseed, Sam		33rd Mississippi Infantry		Pike County, MS Conf Pensioner
Tyler, Jim	E	15th Mississippi Infantry	Servant	Grenada County, MS Conf
Unknown Name		13th Mississippi Infantry	Servant Cook	Slave of Major Isham D. Harrison Jr.,
Unknown Name	K	7th Mississippi Infantry	Servant	Slave of Pvt. George P. Claughton was ill and not required to go into battle at Shiloh but went in and was wounded in the breast. His servant was bringing him home when he died at Summit, Ms
Unknown Name (Female)		Served as a Cook in Littlerock where the Confederate Army was building forts.	Cook	Slave of Tom Warren from Greenville, MS.According to her daughter Mrs. Cora C. Gillam, in Arkansas Slave Narratives.
Vallentine,	A	14th Mississippi Artillery Battalion		Panola County, MS Conf Pensioner
Vance, Archer	G	1st Mississippi Lt Artillery		Yazoo County, MS Conf Pensioner
Vance, Robert		Unknown Unit	Servant	P.O.W. at Camp Morton, Indiana Died there and now buried at Greenfield Park,
Vaughan, Bob		Unknown Unit		Yazoo County, MS Conf Pensioner, non-battle injury.
Vaughan, Charles		Ordnance Department	Blacksmith	Lee County, MS Conf Pensioner
Vick, Sam	D	1st Mississippi Light Artillery		Attala County, MS Conf Pensioner
Vickman, Sex		Unknown Unit	Servant	Adams County, MS Conf
Wade, Chapman		Hospital	Attendant	Sunflower County, MS Conf Pensioner
Wade, Frank		Unknown Unit	Servant	Quitman County, MS Conf
Wade, George		14th Mississippi Infantry		Prentiss County, MS Conf Pensioner battle injury.
Wade, Newt	L	1st Mississippi Lt Artillery	Servant	Union County, MS Conf Pensioner
Wade, Walter		38th Mississippi Infantry		Claiborne County, MS Conf Pensioner, wounded in battle.
Waits (Waites), Houston		39th Mississippi Infantry		Scott County, MS Conf Pensioner
Walker, Amos		28th Mississippi Cavalry		Leflore County, MS Conf Pensioner
Walker, Anthony		12th Mississippi Infantry		Leflore-Holmes County, MS Conf Pensioner, battle injury.
Walker, Arther		Breastworks	Laborer	Monroe County, MS Conf Pensioner

Directory of African American Confederates in the U.S. Civil War

Name		Unit	Role	County / Pension
Walker, Charlie	A	14th Mississippi Artillery Battalion	Private	Hinds County, MS Conf Pensioner
Walker, Felix		Breastworks	Laborer	Monroe County, MS Conf Pensioner
Walker, Henry		1st Mississippi Cavalry	Private	Benton County, MS Conf Pensioner, wounded in battle
Walker, John		20th Mississippi Infantry	Private	Pontotoc County, MS Conf Pensioner
Walker, Ned		8th Confederate Cavalry	Servant	Monroe County, MS Conf Pensioner, battle injury.
Walker, Robert		9th Mississippi Infantry	Private	Marshall County, MS Conf Pensioner
Wall, Pete		34th Mississippi Infantry	Private	Benton County, MS Conf Pensioner
Wallace, Phillip	A	14th Mississippi Arty Battalion	Regt Teamster	Lauderdale County, MS Conf Pensioner
Wallace, Rolla		Unknown Unit	Servant	Newton County, MS Conf Pensioner
Wallace, Tom		33rd Mississippi Infantry	Private	Panola County, MS Conf Pensioner
Walson, Alfred		22nd Mississippi Infantry	Private	Holmes County, MS Conf Pensioner
Walton, Allen Brady		Pettus Mississippi Flying Artillery	Private	Panola County, MS Conf Pensioner
Walton, Arthur	A	14th Mississippi Artillery	Private	Hinds County, MS Conf Pensioner
Walton, Stephen		Unknown Unit	Servant	Monroe County, MS Conf Pensioner
Ward, Green		Unknown Unit	Servant	Carroll County, MS Conf Pensioner
Ward, Moses		Wirt Adams's MS. Cavalry Regt	Servant	Oktibbeha County, MS Conf Pensioner
Ware, Frank		Unknown Unit	Servant	Holmes County, MS Conf Pensioner
Waffleld, Henry		He was from Vicksburg, Mississippi, Served as a Body Servant to his Master	Body Servant	From Warren County, MS
Warren, Frank		46th Mississippi Infantry	Private	Wayne County, MS Conf Pensioner
Warren, Frank		Commissary Department	Private	Panola County, MS Conf Pensioner
Wash, Gilbert		13th Mississippi Infantry	Private	Newton County, MS Conf Pensioner, battle injury.
Washington, George		28th Mississippi Cavalry	Private	Hinds County, MS Conf Pensioner
Washington, Isaac	A	14th Mississippi Artillery Battalion	Private	Hinds County, MS Conf Pensioner, non-battle injury.
Washington, J. W.		Jackson, Mississippi Served nursing Confederate soldiers	Nurse	Slave of Perkins Family
Washington, Levi		48th Mississippi Infantry	Servant	Bolivar County, MS Conf Pensioner
Washington, Rolly		Gen P. T. Beauregard	Private	Adams County, MS Conf Pensioner, wounded in battle.
Washington, William		Bradford's MS. Cavalry Battalion	Private	Hinds County, MS Conf Pensioner, battle injury.
Wasser, Alfred		22nd Mississippi Infantry	Servant	Holmes County, MS Conf Pensioner
Waters, Louis		Unknown Unit	Servant	Jasper County, MS Conf Pensioner
Watkins, Ben		Unknown Unit	Private	Hinds County, MS Conf Pensioner
Watkins, Charley		13th Mississippi Infantry	Servant	Newton County, MS Conf Pensioner
Watkins, Nep		1st Mississippi Cavalry	Private	Sunflower County, MS Conf Pensioner, battle injury.
Watkins, Peter		Ballentine's Mississippi Cavalry Regt	Private	Tallahatchie County, MS Conf Pensioner, battle
Watkins, Sim		Bradford's MS. Cavalry Battalion	Private	Rankin County, MS Conf Pensioner
Watson, Charley		14th Mississippi Infantry	Servant	Bolivar County, MS Conf Pensioner
Watson, Coleman		35th Mississippi Infantry	Private	Attala County, MS Conf Pensioner, wounded in battle.

Name		Unit	Rank/Role	Location/Notes
Watson, Constance	A	14th Mississippi Arty Battalion	Male Servant	Bolivar County, MS Conf Pensioner
Watson, Eli		Unknown Unit	Private	Yazoo County, MS Conf Pensioner
Watson, Frank		Unknown Unit	Private	Montgomery County, MS Conf Pensioner
Watson, Henry		Unknown Unit	Private	Tunica County, MS Conf Pensioner, battle injury.
Watson, Peter		12th Mississippi Battalion Cavalry Partisans	Private	Monroe County, MS Conf Pensioner, non-battle injury.
Watson, Wade		7th Mississippi Infantry	Private	Claiborne County, MS Conf Pensioner
Watts, Felix		Jefferson Mississippi Light	Private	Jefferson County, MS Conf Pensioner
Watts, Henry Booth		36th Mississippi Infantry	Servant	Bolivar County, MS Conf Pensioner
Watts, Sam		Gen William E Baldwin	Private	Rankin County, MS Conf Pensioner
Watts, Simon		4th Mississippi Cavalry	Servant	Covington County, MS Conf Pensioner
Watts, Wesley (Westly)		1st Mississippi Cavalry	Servant	Pontotoc County, MS Conf Pensioner
Weatherall, Harvey		31st Mississippi Infantry	Cook	Pontotoc County, MS Conf Pensioner
Weathersby, Dave		Unknown Unit	Private	Rankin County, MS Conf Pensioner
Weathersby, George		4th Mississippi Cavalry	Private	Jefferson Davis County, MS Conf Pensioner
Webster, Dan		39th Mississippi Infantry	Private	Franklin County, MS Conf Pensioner
Weeks, Baker		18th Mississippi Infantry	Private	Franklin County, MS Conf Pensioner
Weems, Andrew Jackson		Hospital	Attendant	Madison County, MS Conf Pensioner
Wesley, Ned		14th Mississippi Infantry	Private	Clay County, MS Conf Pensioner
West, Ed		13th Mississippi Infantry	Cook	Clarke County, MS Conf Pensioner
Westbrooks, Ben		14th Mississippi Infantry	Private	Monroe County, MS Conf Pensioner
Westley, Ned		48th Mississippi Infantry	Private	Oktibbeha County, MS Conf Pensioner
Wheeler, Silas		Unknown Unit	Private	Forrest-Jefferson Davis County, MS Conf Pensioner
Wheeler, William		Unknown Unit	Private	Yazoo County, MS Conf Pensioner
White, Bill		35' Mississippi Infantry	Servant	Winston County, MS Conf Pensioner
White, Gloster		Unknown Unit	Cook	Claiborne County, MS Conf Pensioner
White, Henderson		22'd Mississippi Infantry	Servant	Hinds County, MS Conf Pensioner
White, Peter		Unknown Unit	Private	Adams County, MS Conf Pensioner
White, Ruben		Commissary Department	Dept Teamste	Madison County, MS Conf Pensioner
White, Wyatt N.		Unknown Unit	Private	Marshall County, MS Conf Pensioner
Whitehead, Joe	H	4th Mississippi Infantry	Private	P.O.W.
Whitesides, Alex			Blacksmith	Lee County, MS Conf Pensioner
Whiting, Beverly		4th Mississippi Cavalry	Private	Jefferson County, MS Conf Pensioner
Wiggins, Peter		4th Mississippi Cavalry	Private	Adams County, MS Conf Pensioner
Wilburn, Henderson		35th Mississippi Infantry	Private	Webster County, MS Conf Pensioner
Wiley, Anderson		1st Mississippi Cavalry	Private	Lafayette County, MS Conf Pensioner
Wiley, Mount		30th Mississippi Infantry	Private	Lafayette County, MS Conf Pensioner, non-battle injury.
Wiley, Sidney		Unknown Unit	Servant	Lafayette County, MS Conf Pensioner

Directory of African American Confederates in the U.S. Civil War

Name		Unit	Role	Notes
William, James		Unknown Unit	Servant	P.O.W. at Camp Morton, Indiana Died there and now buried at Greenfield Park, Indianapolis
Williams, Anderson		36th Mississippi Infantry	Private	Copiah-Clay County, MS Conf Pensioner
Williams, Anderson		36th Mississippi Infantry	Servant	Copiah County, MS Conf Pensioner
Williams, Andrew		16th Mississippi Infantry	Cook	Warren County, MS Conf Pensioner
Williams, Anthony		22nd Mississippi Infantry	Servant	Hinds County, MS Conf Pensioner
Williams, Bill		Unknown Unit	Servant	Sunflower County, MS Conf Pensioner
Williams, Billie		Unknown Unit	Private	Coahoma County, MS Conf Pensioner, battle injury.
Williams, Charles		15th Mississippi Infantry	Private	Holmes County, MS Conf Pensioner
Williams, Charles		4th Mississippi Cavalry		Hinds County, MS Conf Pensioner
Williams, Charles		4th Mississippi Cavalry	Private	Pike County, MS Conf Pensioner
Williams, Colbert		28th Mississippi Cavalry	Private	Sharkey County, MS Conf Pensioner
Williams, Frank		28th Mississippi Cavalry	Private	Hinds County, MS Conf Pensioner
Williams, Green		Wirt Adams's MS. Cavalry Regt	Private	Yazoo County, MS Conf Pensioner
Williams, Harrison		16th Mississippi Infantry	Cook	Copiah-Clay County, MS Conf Pensioner
Williams, Henry	B	1st Mississippi Lt Artillery	Private	Madison County, MS Conf Pensioner
Williams, Henry		28th Mississippi Cavalry	Private	Madison County, MS Conf Pensioner
Williams, Hosea		Wirt Adams's MS. Cavalry Regt	Private	Hinds County, MS Conf Pensioner
Williams, Houston (Huston)		33rd Mississippi Infantry	Private	Franklin County, MS Conf Pensioner
Williams, Huston		33rd Mississippi Infantry	Servant	Jefferson County, MS Conf Pensioner
Williams, J. A.		7th Mississippi Infantry	Private	Clarke County, MS Conf Pensioner
Williams, Jack		1st Mississippi Cavalry	Servant	Lafayette County, MS Conf Pensioner
Williams, Jack		Served as a servant to Jeff Payne	Servant	Kemper County, MS Conf Pensioner
Williams, Joe		Unknown Unit	Servant	Jasper County, MS Conf Pensioner
Williams, John		18th Mississippi Infantry	Private	Yazoo County, MS Conf Pensioner
Williams, John		1st Mississippi Cavalry	Servant	Yalobusha-Tate County, MS Conf Pensioner
Williams, Jordan		Unknown Unit	Servant	Claiborne County, MS Conf Pensioner
Williams, Lee	A	15th Mississippi Infantry	Servant	Grenada County, MS Conf Pensioner
Williams, Merritt	K	1st Mississippi Light Artillery	Private	Hinds County, MS Conf Pensioner
Williams, Nelson		18th Mississippi Infantry	Private	Tate County, MS Conf Pensioner, non-battle injury
Williams, Owen		Wirt Adams's MS. Cavalry Regt	Servant	Yazoo County, MS Conf Pensioner
Williams, Perry		36th Mississippi	Servant	Hinds County, MS Conf Pensioner
Williams, Sam	B	1st Mississippi Light Artillery	Private	Holmes County, MS Conf Pensioner, non-battle injury.
Williams, Sam		5th Mississippi Cavalry	Cook	Carroll County, MS Conf Pensioner
Williams, Samuel		Madison Mississippi Light	Private	Madison County, MS Conf Pensioner
Williams, Sandy		Unknown Unit	Private	Madison County, MS Conf Pensioner
Williams, Thomas		Unknown Unit	Servant	Lee County, MS Conf Pensioner
Williams, Tom		Labor Detail, Captain West Dobbs	Servant Laborer	Grenada-Tallahatchie County, MS Conf Pensioner
Williams, Will	K	1st Mississippi Light Artillery		Claiborne County, MS Conf Pensioner

Williams, William		18th Mississippi Infantry	Servant	Hinds County, MS Conf Pensioner
Williamson, Bob		Unknown Unit		Grenada County, MS Conf Pensioner
Williamson, Jesse		14th Mississippi Artillery Battalion	Servant	Tallahatchie County, MS Conf Pensioner
Williamson, Tyler		Served as a Body Servant to Gen. H. E. Williamson	Body Servant	Slave of Gen. H. E. Williamson
Willis, Austin	A	30th Mississippi Infantry 42nd Mississippi Infantry	Servant	Grenada County, MS Conf Pensioner, non-battle injury.
Willis, Dick		Unknown Unit	Servant	Hinds County, MS Conf Pensioner
Willis, Edmond		42" Mississippi Infantry	Servant	Grenada County, MS Conf Pensioner
Willis, Phil		Unknown Unit	Servant	Lee County, MS Conf Pensioner
Willis, Spencer		20th Mississippi Infantry	Private	Lowndes County, MS Conf Pensioner
Willis, Tom		14th Mississippi Infantry	Private	Monroe County, MS Conf Pensioner
Wilson (Harris), Ellison		Unknown Unit	Private	Quitman County, MS Conf Pensioner
Wilson, Alex		1st Mississippi Cavalry	Private	Panola-Tallahatchie County, MS Conf Pensioner
Wilson, Amos		37th Mississippi Infantry	Servant	Jasper County, MS Conf Pensioner
Wilson, Edward		45th Mississippi Infantry		Hinds County, MS Conf Pensioner
Wilson, Elick		1st Mississippi Cavalry	Private	Panola County, MS Conf Pensioner
Wilson, George		Unknown Unit		Neshoba County, MS Conf Pensioner
Wilson, Henry		Hospital	Attendant	Yazoo County, MS Conf Pensioner
Wilson, J. M.		Unknown Unit	Private	Smith County, MS Conf Pensioner
Wilson, Jackson		4th Mississippi Infantry	Private	Attala County, MS Conf Pensioner, wounded in battle.
Wilson, Joe		4th Mississippi Cavalry	Cook	Lafayette-Marshall County, MS Conf Pensioner
Wilson, Meredith		46t" Mississippi Infantry	Private	Yazoo County, MS Conf Pensioner
Wilson, Nat		Unknown Unit	Private	Claiborne County, MS Conf Pensioner
Wilson, Orange (Oran)		Hospital	Attendant	Holmes County, MS Conf Pensioner
Wilson, R. T.		24th Mississippi Infantry	Private	Chickasaw County, MS Conf Pensioner
Wilson, S. H.		11th Mississippi Infantry		Chickasaw County, MS Conf Pensioner, wounded in battle.
Wilson, Sam		12th Mississippi Infantry		Claiborne County, MS Conf
Wilson, Walter		Unknown Unit		Panola County, MS Conf Pensioner
Winfield, Archie		7th Mississippi Infantry	Servant	Jefferson County, MS Conf Pensioner
Wingo, Seborn		5th Mississippi Cavalry		Leake County, MS Conf Pensioner
Winn, Richard		15th Mississippi Infantry	Private	Attala County, MS Conf Pensioner
Winters, A. 3.		1st Mississippi Infantry Battalion	Private	Attala County, MS Conf Pensioner
Winters, Essex		5th Mississippi Cavalry		Attala County, MS Conf Pensioner
Witty, Henry		30th Mississippi Infantry	Cook	Montgomery County, MS Conf Pensioner
Wood, Daniel		Quartermaster Dept	Helper	Smith County, MS Conf Pensioner
Wood, Isaac		14th Va Infantry	Private	Oktibbeha County, MS Conf Pensioner
Woodley, Balum		Mississippi State Troops	Private	Yazoo County, MS Conf Pensioner
Woods, Harry		33rd Mississippi Infantry	Regt Teamste	Pike County, MS Conf Pensioner

Name		Unit	Rank	Location
Woods, Jasper		11th Mississippi Infantry	Private	Chickasaw County, MS Conf Pensioner
Woods, Louis		Unknown Unit	Private	Bolivar County, MS Conf Pensioner
Woodside, Archy		4th Mississippi Cavalry	Private	Wilkinson County, MS Conf Pensioner
Woodward, Aaron		44th Mississippi Infantry	Private	Webster-Calhoun County, MS Conf Pensioner
Woodward, Ike Lee		Unknown Unit	Servant	Calhoun County, MS Conf Pensioner
Worley, Henry		21st Mississippi Infantry	Private	Tallahatchie County, MS Conf Pensioner
Worthy, Dave		1st Mississippi Cavalry	Private	Winston County, MS Conf Pensioner
Wren, George		Unknown Unit	Private	Sunflower County, MS Conf Pensioner
Wright, Henry Clay		Breastworks	Laborer	Tallahatchie County, MS Conf Pensioner
Wright, Jack		15th Mississippi Infantry	Private	Panola County, MS Conf Pensioner
Wright, Robert		Unknown Unit	Private	Humphreys County, MS Conf Pensioner
Wright, Tom		Breastworks	Laborer	Holmes County, MS Conf Pensioner
Wright, William		Served as a Servant to Brigadier General Marcus J.	Servant	Grenada County, MS Conf Pensioner
Wyatt, Henry	E	21st Mississippi Infantry Served as a servant to his master who was KIA.	Servant	Wilkinson County, MS Conf Pensioner. Attended the Veterans Reunion at Vicksburg in 1890
Wynn, Richard		15th Mississippi Infantry	Private	Bolivar County, MS Conf Pensioner
Yarbrough, Abram	A	13th Mississippi Infantry	Servant Cook	Slave of SgtMaj Robert E. Yarbrough
Yarbrough, William		16th Mississippi Infantry	Private	Washington County, MS Conf Pensioner
Yates, Frank		8th Mississippi Infantry	Servant	Prentiss County, MS Conf Pensioner, battle injury.
Yates, George	C	32nd Mississippi Infantry Served as a servant to Lt. J. H. Yates	Servant	Prentiss County, MS Conf Pensioner, battle injury.
Yates, Jake		36th Mississippi Infantry	Private	Jones County, MS Conf Pensioner
Yates, Lawrence		36th Mississippi Infantry	Private	Hinds County, MS Conf Pensioner
Yeates, Boon		Wirt Adams's MS. Cavalry Regt	Private	Oktibbeha County, MS Conf Pensioner
Yeates, John		Unknown Unit	Private	Oktibbeha County, MS Conf Pensioner
Young, Ben		Unknown Unit	Servant	Oktibbeha County, MS Conf Pensioner
Young, Jacob		45th Mississippi Infantry	Private	Madison County, MS Conf Pensioner
Young, Lee		48th Mississippi Infantry	Wash And Cook	Calhoun County, MS Conf Pensioner
Young, Mat		Unknown Unit	Servant	Simpson County, MS Conf Pensioner
Young, Taylor		39th Mississippi Infantry	Servant	Warren County, MS Conf Pensioner
Younger, Burwell	B	1st Mississippi Lt Artillery		Yazoo County, MS Conf Pensioner

MISSOURI

Missouri began awarding annuities to destitute Confederate veterans only in 1911; widows received none. African-Americans, it appears, were also denied pensions. A home for disabled Confederate veterans existed in Missouri.

Black Confederates and free African Americans who filled a number of different positions in support of the Confederate States of America during the American Civil War (1861–1865). Most often this assistance was coerced rather than offered voluntarily.

Male slaves were either hired out by their owners or impressed to work in various departments of the Confederate army. Free black men were also routinely impressed or otherwise forced to perform manual labor for the army.

The government's use of black labor, whether free or slave, followed patterns established during the antebellum period,

when county governments routinely engaged the service of black men to help maintain local roads and other public property. While large numbers of black men thus accompanied every Confederate army on the march or in camp, those men would not have been considered soldiers. Only a few black men were ever accepted into Confederate service as soldiers, and none did any significant fighting.

Missouri began awarding annuities to destitute Confederate veterans only in 1911; widows received none. African-Americans, it appears, were also denied pensions. A home for disabled Confederate veterans existed in Missouri. The pension and veterans' home applications are filed together at;

Missouri State Archives, 600 W. Main, P.O. Box 1747, Jefferson City, MO 65102, Telephone: 573-751-3280 Web Site https://www.sos.mo.gov/archives/

NAME	CO.	UNIT	RANK	SLAVE / FREE MISC NOTES
John	F	5th Missouri Infantry Served as a servant to LtCol. Robert S. Bevier	Cook	Mulatto
Sam		McNeill's Partisan Rangers Served as a servant to his master Capt. John Hanson	Servant	Slave of Capt. John Hanson McNeil of Daviess County, Missouri
Sid		Parson's Brigade, Missouri Served as a Servant to Gen. M. M. Parsons	Cook Servant	Slave of Gen. Mosby Monroe Parsons
Zack		Quantrill's Raiders	Servant	He became an orderly for Quantrill and Todd after his capture at Baxter Spring, 6 Oct. 1863. Also known as Rube
Brent, Burr C.		2nd Missouri State Guards	Cook	
Charles, Henry (1)		1st Missouri Infantry		Madison County, MS Conf Pensioner
Garrett, Willis		Unknown Missouri Unit	Servant	P.O.W. at Camp Morton, Indiana Died there and now buried at Greenfield Park,
Lobb, John		Quantrill's Raiders, He served as a Spy, spying in Lawrence, Kansas before Quantrill and his men did a raid	Scout Spy	
McDonald, George	B	16th Missouri Infantry Regiment	Private	S. Claire County, WIA at Wilson's Creek, Attended the 1903 Conf reunion at Columbia , MO
Noland, John		Quantrill's Raiders, Negro Spy sent to spy in Lawrence, Kansas.	Hostler Scout Spy	FMC, From Kansas City, KS. Attended the Eighth Annual Reunion of Quantrill's Guerrillas, Independence, MO., August 25 and 26, 1905.
Parker, A. J.		2nd Missouri Cavalry	Servant	Leflore County, MS Conf Pensioner, battle injury.

A copy is Available at newsonpublishing.com

Possess

Uncle Gregory's "Possess"

This publisher don't want to call it a conspiracy to ignore the role of Blacks below the Mason-Dixon line, but it was definitely a tendency, which began around 1910."

Historian, Erwin L. Jordan, Jr., calls it a "cover-up" which started back in 1865. He writes, "During my research, I came across instances where Black men stated they were soldiers, but you can plainly see where 'soldier' is crossed out and 'body servant' inserted, or 'teamster' on pension applications." Another black historian, Roland Young, says he is not surprised that blacks fought.

He explains that "…some, if not most, Black southerners would support their country" and that by doing so they were "demonstrating it's possible to hate the system of slavery and love one's country." This is the very same reaction that most African Americans showed during the American Revolution, where they fought for the colonies, even though the British offered them freedom if they fought for them. The "Richmond Howitzers" were partially manned by black militiamen. They

saw action at 1st Manassas (or 1st Battle of Bull Run) where they operated battery no. 2. In addition two black "regiments", one free and one slave, participated in the battle on behalf of the South. "Many colored people were killed in the action", recorded John Parker, a former slave.

At least one Black Confederate was a non-commissioned officer. James Washington, Co. D 34th Texas Cavalry, "Terrell's Texas Cavalry" became it's 3rd Sergeant. In comparison, The highest-ranking Black Union soldier during the war was a Sergeant Major.

Frederick Douglas reported, "There are at the present moment many Colored men in the Confederate Army doing duty not only as cooks, servants and laborers, but real soldiers, having musket on their shoulders, and bullets in their pockets, ready to shoot down any loyal troops and do all that soldiers may do to destroy the Federal government and build up that of the rebels." For go to: www.scv.org

Simms, Bill		Served as a laborer after he was sent by his master to work for the Confederate Army. He served for three years off and on, hauling canons, driving mules, hauling ammunition, and provisions.	Laborer	Slave of Mr. Simms of Osceola, Missouri, according to statements in Kansas Slave Narratives. He then ran away and served the Union army, after the war he returned to his old master who hired him as a laborer, and gave his mother 40 acres of land with a cabin on it. His master was then killed fearing he would give away all his land to his former slaves.
Sparks, George Washington		Bulbridge's Missouri Cavalry		Arkansas, Miller County Conf Pensioner, application #29029. Application
Wilson Jr., Frank	C	Quantrill's Raiders Col Shank's 2nd Missouri Cavalry	Scout Spy	
Wood, Jim	A	2nd Missouri Cavalry Regiment	Cook Servan	Grenada County, MS Conf Pensioner
Wyatt, William (Billie)		3rd Missouri Calvary		Lake County, TN Conf Pension #C165, application rejected.

NORTH CAROLINA

In 1867, North Carolina began granting Confederate soldiers pensions. Only those who had been blinded or had lost a limb during their duty were eligible. All other disabled destitute Confederate soldiers or widows were granted eligibility in 1885 by the state. The North Carolina Division of Archives and History in Raleigh has both the pension applications and an index, but they are not currently available anywhere else. North Carolina was one of just a few states to offer a pension to African American servants.

"Confederate Negro" used in North Carolina refer to blacks who made significant contributions to the Confederacy during the Civil War. Some slaves served in noncombatant roles, such as nurses in government hospitals, supply wagon and ambulance drivers, and cooks. At times slaves carried news from home and delivered supplies and food to their masters on the battlefield, or they brought home the wounded and dead.

As Confederate military fortunes continued to fall, more and more southern whites began to contemplate changes in the slave system, including sending black men—the last source of troops—to fight

North Carolina State Archives
109 East Jones Street
Raleigh, NC 27601-2807
Telephone: 919-733-7305
Web Site: https://archives.ncdcr.gov/media

NAME	CO.	UNIT	RANK	SLAVE / FREE MISC NOTES
Henry		Ray's Company, 33rd North Carolina Militia	Drummer	
Jim	H	51st Infantry Regiment North Carolina 18th Infantry Regiment North Carolina	Cook	Liberty Mills, Virginia
Mat	I	13th North Carolina Infantry Served as a body servant to Capt. Chalmers Glenn	Body Servant	Captain Glenn's was killed at the battlefield of Boonsboro, or South Mountain.
Monroe	B	12th North Carolina Infantry	Cook	
Sam	D	1st Regiment North Carolina Infantry (6 months, 1861) (Bethel Regiment Wythe Rifles) Served as a Servant to his Master Capt. Richard J. Ashe	Servant	Sam help shoot and kill a Union officer during the war, abolitionist Major Theodore Winthrop

I wish i had coffee

Aside from the severe limits of the economic, technological and medical advances of an era, the Civil War imbued the century with its own brand of hardship.

Coffee was a hot commodity that the Union troops was guzzling down more quickly than the Confederates and civilians could keep up with, and food was rationed. In an article regarding coffee's role in the Civil War, the New York Times stated, "Nobody can 'soldier' without coffee." and "Union troops drank coffee from canteens and puddles, brackish bays, and Mississippi dirt—liquid their horses wouldn't drink."

When the beans ran out, though, consumers had to think out-side the box. For example, consider the following paragraph from a recipe article from the Weekly Arkansas Gazette in Little Rock on June 15, 1861, the first day of the Civil War: "Mix one spoonful of coffee with one spoonful of toasted corn meal, boil well, then clear in the usual method, and you've got yourself a very fine coffee for only $1.12 cents."

"Confederate Coffee," as this concoction described above was called in most cases, didn't contain any caffeine and was more like a tea. Before steeping or dissolving these components in hot water to form "coffee," they were either dried, browned, roasted or ground.

Directory of African American Confederates in the U.S. Civil War

Wash		43rd North Carolina Infantry Served as a body servant to Lt. George W. Wills	Body Servant	Slave
, William	D	6' North Carolina Cavalry Regiment	Private	Henderson County, N.C.
Abbott, George	B	Clark's Special Battalion, North Carolina Militia	Musician	
Allen, Henry		Hauled Supplies	Laborer	Slave, Vance County, NC Conf Pensioner. Attended the Zeb Vance Camp, UCV Conference May 1930
Alston, Isaac	D	39th North Carolina Infantry Served as a Body Servant to Capt. William (Bill) Allen	Body Servant	Slave, Wake County, NC Conf Pensioner. Attended the Zeb Vance Camp, UCV Conference May 1930
Anderson, Sam		6th North Carolina Infantry Served as a Body Servant to his master Quinten Anderson	Body Servant	Slave, Johnston County, NC Conf Pensioner
Anthony, Henry		Served helping her master Orderly Sgt. Jason Robertson driving wagons hauling ammunition and provisions.	Teamster	Slave, Jackson North Carolina
Armstrong, Moses	K	3rd North Carolina Infantry Served as a Body Servant to Capt. Thomas J. Armstrong	Body Servant	
Ashcraft, Wilson C.	I	53rd North Carolina Infantry Served as a Body Servant to Capt. Thomas Ellison Ashcraft	Body Servant	Slave, Union County, NC Conf Pensioner Attended Zeb Vance Camp, UCV Conference May 1930
Atwater, Alexander	H	43rd North Carolina Infantry Hauled supplies for soldiers around Wilmington, N.C.	Teamster	Slave of William Stroud, Durham County, NC Conf Pensioner. Attended Zeb Vance Camp, UCV Conference May 1930
Baird, Gilbert	C	18th North Carolina Infantry Served his master Pvt. James A. Baird	Body Servant	Slave, Buncombe County, NC Conf Pensioner Attended Zeb Vance Camp, UCV Conference May 1930
Ballentine, George	F	15t' North Carolina Infantry. Served with his Master Sgt. Allison (Aisle) Holland	Body Guard Teamster	Slave, Wake County, NC Conf Pensioner Attended Zeb Vance Camp, UCV Conference May 1930
Barringer, Alfred	F	1st North Carolina Cavalry. (9 State Troops.) Served as a servant to his master	Gen. Rufus R. Barringer Servant	Slave, Mecklenburg County, NC Conf Pensioner
Beard, Yancey	F	37th North Carolina Infantry Served as a servant to his master Lt. William Beard	Servant	Slave, Halifax County, VA Conf Pensioner
Beebe, Sam	D	2'd North Carolina Cavalry Served as a servant to John, Edmond and George Waddell	Body Servant	Slave, Bladen County, NC Conf Pensioner Attended Zeb Vance Camp, UCV Conference May 1930
Bennett, John	B	12th North Carolina Infantry Served as a body guard to his master Pvt. Solomon H. Philpott	Body Guard	Slave, Granville, County, NC Conf Pensioner Attended Zeb Vance Camp, UCV Conference May 1930

Best, Nathan (Bess, Nathan)		Served as a servant to his master's son Captain Rufus Best	Servant	Slave of Henry Best, of Greene County, NC. He attended a Confederate Reunion in Montgomery, MS. He later lived in the Beauvoir, Confederate Soldiers' home in MS. According to his statements in Mississippi Slave Narratives. He was WIA, losing an arm. He is buried at the Beauvoir Confederate Cemetery.
Bizzell, Agrippa	A	30th North Carolina Infantry Regiment Served with his master	Servant	Slave, His wife Mrs. Edith Bizzell applied for his Conf Pension in Sampson County, NC Attended Zeb Vance Camp, UCV Conference May 1930
Blackburn, Alfred T. (Teen)	FB	41st North Carolina Troops 38th North Carolina Regiment Served as a Body Guard to his master 2" Lt. Augustus W. Blackburn	Body Guard Cook	Slave, of 2.'d Lt. Augustus W. Blackburn. He grabbed his master's sword when he was shot, fought off a charging federal soldier, and saved his life Yadkin County, NC Conf Pensioner. Attended Zeb Vance Camp, UCV Conference May 1930
Blackburn, Wiley	B	38th North Carolina Regiment Served as a Body Guard to his master 2" Lt. Augustus W. Blackburn	Body Guard	Slave, Iredell County, NC Conf Pensioner Attended Zeb Vance Camp, UCV Conference May 1930
Boney, Joe	E	30tk North Carolina Infantry Regiment Served with his master Pvt. James Daniel Boney	Servant	Slave, Duplin County, NC Conf Pensioner
Boney, Oliver		Served as a Body Servant to his master Col. L. A. Powell and Col. A. A. McKay	Servant	Slave, Sampson County, NC Conf Pensioner
Boykin, Isaac	A	61st North Carolina Infantry Regiment Served as a servant to his master Pvt. Abraham Boykin	Servant	Slave, Sampson County, NC Conf Pensioner
Breedlove, Tom Lewis	G	23rd North Carolina Infantry Regiment Served as a servant to his master Capt. James Breedlove	Servant	Slave, Granville County, NC Conf Pensioner
Bridges, Nathan		Cooked and helped construct breastworks	Cook Laborer	Cleveland County, NC Conf Pensioner
Brown, Enoch	M	22' North Carolina Infantry Regiment Served as a cook and servant to his master Capt. John M. Odell	Cook Launderer	Slave, Randolph County, NC Conf Pensioner
Brown, Malcolm	B	2" North Carolina Artillery (36th State Troops) Helped build breastworks at Fort Fisher under Col. Peter Campbell	Laborer	Slave, Hoke County, NC Conf Pensioner
Bruce, Edmond		45rd Regiment North Carolina Infantry	Servant	
Bryan, Lee	F	3" North Carolina Cavalry Served with his master Pvt. E. 3. Bryan	Servant	Rutherford County, NC Conf Pensioner
Bryson, Steve		Served With His Master In South Carolina	Servant	Slave, Swain County, North Carolina Conf Pensioner. His widow Jane Bryson Submitted for a pension too.

Burrell, Billie		Served with his master John Burrell. Served as a laborer at Fort Fisher, Fort Caswell and Baldhead Island.	Laborer	Slave of John Burrell of Granville County. Vance County, NC Conf Pensioner
Bynum, Brinkley	A	1st North Carolina Infantry 15th North	Private	Orange County, NC Conf Pensioner
Byrd, Ned		Served as a servant to his master King Byrd	Body Servant	Slave, Union County, NC Conf Pensioner
Cabaniss, Sam		Served under "Kinsey" at Baldhead Island and Fort Fisher	Laborer	Cleveland County, NC Conf Pensioner
Caeser, Phillip		Served by building breastworks	Laborer	Surry County, NC Conf Pensioner
Calvert, Butler	F&S	56th Regiment North Carolina Infantry Served with his master Capt. Samuel J. Calvert	Servant	Northampton County, NC Conf Pensioner
Campbell, Henry		Served as a body servant to his master William S. Campbell	Body Servant	Slave, Hoke County, NC Conf Pensioner
Canedy, Simeon (Kennedy, Simon)	G	10th Battalion Heavy Artillery Regiment North Carolina	Servant	
Carlton, W. C.	A G	3rd North Carolina Artillery (40 State Troops) 44th North Carolina Infantry Served with his Master Pvt. Washington Johnson	Private	Slave, Sampson County, NC Conf Pensioner
Carr, Blount		Served with Confederate troops in Virginia and Maryland		Slave, Pitt County, NC Conf Pensioner
Carter, Hawkins W.	C	46th Regiment North Carolina Infantry Served as a cook, constructed breastworks and as a combat soldier alongside white soldiers	Private	Warren County, NC Conf Pensioner
Carver, Nicholas	F	24th Regiment North Carolina Infantry Served as a servant with his master Capt. Jonathan Evans	Servant	Slave, Cumberland County, NC Conf Pensioner
Cass, Hunter		Served with his master Arthur Barlow Treadwell doing labor in and around Mobile, Alabama	Laborer	Slave, Orange County, NC Conf Pensioner
Cathey, J. C.	A	20th Regiment North Carolina Infantry Served as a servant with his master Capt. John D. Irvin	Servant	Slave, Gaston County, NC Conf Pensioner
Chandler, Silas		21st North Carolina Infantry	Private	Former Slave, FMC
Clark, Tom		Unknown Unit	Servant	Slave. Lincoln County, NC Conf Pensioner
Clay, C. Thomas	E G	56th Regiment North Carolina Infantry 58th Regiment North Carolina Infantry Served as a servant with his master Pvt. John W. Lawrence	Servant	Slave, Granville County, NC Conf Pensioner
Clyburn, Wary D.	E	12th North Carolina Regiment Served as a body servant to Capt. Frank Clyburn	Body Servant	Slave, Union County, NC Conf Pensioner
Collins, Harvey		Served as an aide to his master Robert Laws.	Servant	Slave, Person County, NC Conf Pensioner

Cooper, Ed	E	33rd Regiment North Carolina Infantry Served under his master Lt. J. C. Cooper	Servant	Slave, Granville County, NC Conf Pensioner Attended Zeb Vance Camp, UCV Conference May 1930
Cossens, Franklin	A	37th North Carolina State Troops (Ashe Beauregard Riflemen)	Pvt	FMC
Cowan, Harry		Served as a body servant to Gen. Joseph Johnston	Body Servant	Slave of Thomas L. Cowan of Salisbury, N.C.
Crawford, John		Served hauling provisions under the supervision of his master Thomas Crawford	Servant	Slave, Surry County, NC Conf Pensioner
Crudup, Clark	D	12th Regiment North Carolina Infantry Served as a laborer under his master Pvt. Josiah Crudup.	Laborer	Slave, Vance County, NC Conf Pensioner. His wife Marina applied for a pension.
Crudup, Hilyard		Served as a laborer at Fort. Fisher	Laborer	Slave, Vance County, NC Conf Pensioner
Cuthbertson, Hamp	I G	53rd North Carolina Infantry 1st North Carolina Detailed Men Served as a laborer at Ft. Fisher under Lt.'s Moses and John D. Cuthbertson	Servant	Slave, Union County, NC Conf Pensioner
Daniel, Pope Whitehead		Served as a laborer building breastworks under Mr. Kirkland	Laborer	Halifax County, NC Conf Pensioner
Darden, Needham	D	8th Battalion Partisan Rangers, North Carolina Capt. Bass' Company, North Carolina Served at Ft. Fisher	Servant	Slave of J. K. Darden, Sampson County, NC Conf Pensioner
Demory, John	F	1st North Carolina Infantry Served as a servant to Col. John A. McDowell and later to Dr. Jim Robinson	Servant	Bladen County, NC Conf Pensioner
Dempsey, Charles	F	36th North Carolina Regiment (2nd North Carolina Artillery)	Cook Servant	FMC, Captured at Ft. Fisher on January 15, 1865, POW at Point Lookout, MD. Refused to take the oath of allegiance. Paroled and exchanged at Coxes Landing, James River, VA, February 14-15, 1865.
Dempsey, Eli	G	1st North Carolina Artillery	Servant	FMC, Captured at Ft. Fisher on January 15, 1865, POW at Point Lookout, MD. Refused to take the oath of allegiance. Paroled and exchanged at Coxes Landing, James River, VA, February 14-15, 1865.
Dempsey, Henry	F	36th North Carolina Regiment (2nd North Carolina Artillery)	Cook Servant	Captured at Ft. Fisher on January 15, 1865, POW at Point Lookout, MD. Refused to take the oath of allegiance. Paroled and exchanged at Coxes Landing, James River, VA, February 14-15, 1865.
Dew, Jim Ellis		Served in Jonathan Dew's place during the war.	Private	Slave of Hickman Ellis, Wilson County, NC Conf Pensioner
Dixon, Nelson		27th North Carolina Infantry	Private	Leflore County, MS Conf Pensioner

Directory of African American Confederates in the U.S. Civil War

Douglas, Lewis		1st Confederate Infantry Served as body servant to Dr. William R. Capehart, Chief Surgeon of the Seventh Army Corps.	Body Servant	Slave, Bertie County, NC Conf Pensioner
Dove, William H.	E	5th North Carolina Cavalry (Barringers	Cook	
Dove, Willis	E	63' North Carolina Infantry 5th North Carolina Cavalry (Barringers Brigade)	Cook	
Downs, Harvey	C F	1st North Carolina Infantry 5th North Carolina Cavalry Served with his master Sgt. J. T. Downs	Servant	Slave, Mecklenburg County, NC Conf Pensioner
Doyle, I.	C	3rd North Carolina Artillery	Cook Servant	
Doyle, James	E	40th North Carolina Regiment 3rd North Carolina Artillery	Cook Servant	Captured at Ft. Fisher on January 15, 1865, POW at Point Lookout, MD. Refused to take the oath of allegiance. Paroled and exchanged at Boulware's Wharf, James River, VA, March 16, 1865.
Dublin, Austin		5th North Carolina Infantry	Private	Coahoma County, MS Conf Pensioner, battle injury.
Dunn, Abon		Served building breastworks	Laborer	Slave
Dunston, Tom	F	8th North Carolina Infantry	Cook	
Eaton, Allen P.	E D E	6th North Carolina Cavalry 7th Battalion North Carolina Cavalry Served with his master Pvt. John S. Young	Servant	Slave, Vance County, NC Conf Pensioner
Evans, Jackson	H F	2nd Battalion North Carolina Infantry 3rd Battalion North Carolina Infantry Served with Daniel 3. Evans	Private	
Farrington, Joe	E	5th North Carolina Cavalry (Barringers Brigade) Served as a servant to his master John Ferrington	Servant	Slave, Lake County, TN Conf Pension #C9
Feimster, William	C	4th North Carolina Infantry Served with his master Sgt Rufus P. Feimster	Laborer	Slave, Iredell County, NC Conf Pensioner
Fletcher, Sandy	D	23rd North Carolina Infantry Served as a Servant to Sgt. William C. Covington, Ben Covington and J. M. Covington	Servant	Slave of Calvin Covington, Richmond County, NC Conf Pensioner Attended Zeb Vance Camp, UCV Conference May 1930
Fogg, Isaac	E G	28th Regiment North Carolina Infantry 43rd Regiment North Carolina Infantry Served as a servant to Capt. Thomas Green	Servant	Slave, Wake County, NC Conf Pensioner
Forester, Jeff	B	55th North Carolina Infantry Served with his Master Samuel J. Forester	Servant	Slave, Wilkes County, NC Conf Pensioner
Foust, James	C G	2nd Battalion North Carolina Local Defense Troops 44th Regiment North Carolina Infantry	Private	Slave of George and Thomas Foust, Rockingham County, NC Conf Pensioner

Directory of African American Confederates in the U.S. Civil War

Name	Co.	Unit / Service	Role	Status
Foust, John		Was drafted as a Teamster	Teamster	Slave, Alamance County, NC Conf Pensioner
Fraser, Mose	I	22nd Regiment North Carolina Infantry Served as a Body Servant to his master Elias Fraser	Body Servant	Slave, Union County, NC Conf Pensioner
French, John	K	3rd Battalion, North Carolina Junior Reserves	Cook	
Fugit, Henry	D	33rd Regiment North Carolina Infantry Served with his master Lt. Joines and served under Capt. Oliver Parks	Private	Slave, Wilkes County, NC Conf Pensioner
Galloway, Charlie	H H	Snead's Company, North Carolina Local Defense 3rd Regiment North Carolina Infantry Served as a cook to Capt Swift Galloway	Cook	Slave, New Hanover County, NC Conf Pensioner
Gibson, Stephen	D	46th Infantry Regiment North Carolina	Private	FMC, Buncombe County and Swain County, NC Conf Pensioner
Gillespie, Mack	C	49th Regiment North Carolina Infantry Served as a Body Servant to his master Maj. Pinkney B. Chambers	Body Servant	Slave, Montgomery County, NC Conf Pensioner
Gilmer, John	B	27th Regiment North Carolina Infantry Served as a Body Servant to his master Col. John A. Gilmer Jr.	Body Servant	Slave, Forsyth County, NC Conf Pensioner
Glass, Samuel		Served as a Body Servant to Capt. Joshua Glass	Body Servant	Slave, Rockingham County, NC Conf Pensioner
Glenn, Dudley		Served as a Body Servant to his master Joseph Williams	Body Servant	Slave, Yadkin County, NC Conf Pensioner
Goins, Hilliard		Enlisted in the North Carolina State Troops	Private	Halifax County, NC Conf Pensioner
Gooding, John	A F	8th Battalion Part, Cavalry Regiment North Carolina 66th Infantry Regiment North Carolina Served as a Body Servant to Capt. Rhinhart and Maj. McNeil	Body Servant	Slave, Lenoir County, NC Conf Pensioner
Gorham, Mark	I, S	4th Cavalry Regiment North Carolina Served as a Servant to Capt. William Jordan	Servant	Slave, Pitt County, NC Conf Pensioner
Graham, John M.	F	18th Infantry Regiment North Carolina Served as a Servant to Capt. William H. McLaurin	Servant	Hoke County, NC Conf Pensioner
Green, John		Unknown North Carolina Unit	Private	Hamblen County, TN Conf Pension Rcd # C261, application rejected.
Greenwood, Hampton	H	54th Regiment North Carolina Infantry Served as a Body Servant to his master Pvt. William B. Greenwood	Body Servant	Slave, Granville County, NC Conf Pensioner
Griffin, Sam		24th North Carolina Infantry Served as a body servant to his master Pressly Griffin	Body Servant	Slave, Wake County, NC Conf Pensioner

Haith, William	A	21st Regiment North Carolina Infantry Served as a Body Servant to Nick Mebane	Body Servant Private	Slave, Alamance County, NC Conf Pensioner
Haley, Torn		Served as a Laborer on infantry fortifications building breastworks, at Weldon, N.C.	Laborer	Slave of Holladay Haley (Halley)., Nansemond County, VA Conf Pensioner
Harris, Alfred J.	E	9th Regiment North Carolina Troops (1st Cavalry) Served as a Body Servant to James H. Harris	Body Servant Cook	Slave, Warren County, NC Conf Pensioner
Harris, Peter Lomax	F	37th Regiment North Carolina Infantry Served as a Body Servant to Captain James Nickerson (Surgeon)	Body Servant	Slave, Yadkin County, NC Conf Pensioner
Harris, William R.		Served as a Body Servant to his master Thomas Paine Harris	Body Servant	Slave, Bertie County, NC Conf Pensioner
Hawkins, Sam	E	2nd Battalion, North Carolina Infantry Served as an attendant to a wounded officer Lt. James M. Bonner	Attendant	Franklin County, NC Conf Pensioner
Hayes, Sidney		Unknown North Carolina Unit	Private	Slave of Zack Rich, Durham County, NC Conf Pensioner
Hays, Everett	F	1st North Carolina Artillery	Cook	
Henlsey, Lee		Unknown North Carolina Unit		Slave, Caswell County, NC Conf Pensioner
Herring, Daniel	F	36th North Carolina Regiment (2nd North Carolina Artillery)	Cook	Captured at Ft. Fisher on January 15, 1865, POW at Point Lookout, MD. Released after taking Oath of Allegiance June 19, 1865. The official surrender was in April, 1865.
Hicks, Jerry	S	23rd Infantry Regiment North Carolina Medical Staff Regiment Confederate States Served as an attendant to Dr. Robert (Bob) Hicks	Attendant	Slave, Vance County, NC Conf Pensioner
Hicks, Judson		Unknown Unit	Laborer	Slave of Dr. Thomas Hicks, Wake County, NC Conf Pensioner
Hicks, Wesley	F	14th Regiment, North Carolina Infantry Served as a servant to his master 2nd Lt Thomas Dillard	Body Servant	Slave of Thomas D. Johnston of Haywood County, NC
High, Isaac		Served as a laborer building breastworks	Laborer	Slave of Green High, Wake County, NC Conf Pensioner
Hinton, Donaldson		Served as a laborer building breastworks	Laborer	Slave of Maj. David Hinton, Wake County, NC Conf Pensioner
Holland, Clairborne		Served building breastworks in North Carolina	Laborer	Slave
Holland, Cornelius		General and Staff Officers, Corps, Division and Brigade Staffs, Non-com. Staffs and Bands, Enlisted Men, Staff Department Served under Maj. Corn. Jubal Early	Cook	Slave
Holland, Creed		Unknown North Carolina Unit	Teamster	Slave

Horton, Charles	A	32nd North Carolina Infantry Served as a Body Servant to Maj. Henry G. Lewis	Body Servant	Slave, Washington County, NC Conf Pensioner
Howard, Elisha		15th North Carolina Infantry Served as an assistant to W. S. Corbet	Servant	Slave, Randolph County, NC Conf Pensioner Attended Zeb Vance Camp, UCV Conference May 1930
Hunt, Primus		Served as a Servant to Gen. Stephens and Lt. Corner	Servant	Slave, Franklin County, NC Conf Pensioner
Hunter, Frank	K	23rd Regiment North Carolina State Troops Served as Servant to his master Stanhope Hunter	Laborer Servant	Slave, Lincoln County, NC Conf Pensioner
Hunter, Porter		Served as a Laborer building breastworks	Laborer	Slave
Ingram, Jack	C	14th Regiment North Carolina Infantry Was taken to Ft. Fisher by Thomas B. Crump and helped build breastworks	Laborer	Slave, Surry County, NC Conf Pensioner
Jackson, James H.	C	2nd North Carolina Artillery, (36th State Troops)	Bugler	
Jacobs, Enos	I	2nd Battalion North Carolina Local Defence Troops Served as a cook for Pvt's Walter Draughon and Buckner Peterson, also helped build breastworks at Ft. Caswell	Cook Laborer	Sampson County, NC Conf Pensioner
James, Hampton		Served as a cook and building breastworks at Ft. Fisher	Cook Labore	New Hanover County, NC Conf Pensioner
Jarvis, Cornelius	B	8thRegiment North Carolina Troops	Private	Currituck County, NC Conf Pensioner
Jeffers, Marchael		Unknown North Carolina Unit		Alamance County, NC Conf Pensioner
Jeffries, Bedford		Served as a cook for B. G. Mebane	Cook	Alamance County, NC Conf Pensioner
Jeffries, James		Was sent by his master to serve building breastworks	Laborer	Slave of S. S. Lea, Caswell County, NC Conf Pensioner
Johnson, Andrew		Served as a cook and building breastworks	Cook Labore	Cleveland County, NC Conf Pensioner
Jones, Jacob		Served as a Body Servant to his master Col. E. P. Jones	Body Servan	Slave, Guilford County, NC Conf Pensioner
Jones, Joseph		Served under Quartermaster Thomas Sloan in Greensboro,	Servant	Guilford County, NC Conf Pensioner
Jones, Rilla Patterson (Female)		Served her Master Frank Patterson by taking him a note advising of Federal Soldiers nearby so that Frank Patterson's unit could attack them.	Courier	Slave of Frank Patterson
Jones, Willis (Willie)	E	26th North Carolina Infantry	Private	Crockett County, TN Conf Pension Rcd # C278, application rejected.
Judd, Stokes		Served as a Body Servant to Capt. Davis	Body Servant	Lee County, NC Conf Pensioner
Kendall, George W.		Served as a laborer and teamster at Ft. Fisher	Laborer Teamster	Slave of Reuben Kendall, Stanly County, NC Conf Pensioner

Kendall, Weldon	C	14th Infantry Regiment North Carolina Served as a Body Servant to his master Henry Kendall	Body Servant	Slave of Henry Kendall, Anson County, NC Conf Pensioner
Kennedy, Lorenzo Dow	B	Clark's Special Battalion, North Carolina Militia	Servant	
Leach, Needham	C	53rd North Carolina Infantry Served as a servant to 1st Lt. George T. Leach	Servant	
Ledbetter, Press		Served under H. B. Billingsley at Ft. Fisher	Laborer	Slave of Col. Henry W. Ledbetter, Anson County, NC Conf Pensioner
Lewis, Grand	E	2nd North Carolina Cavalry Served as a Body Servant to David Cooper	Body Servant	Slave of James Cooper, Vance County, NC Conf Pensioner
Liggins, Will		13th North Carolina Infantry Served as a servant to Col. James E. Boyd, Clay Hazell, and Jim Vincent	Body Servant	Slave, Alamance County, NC Conf Pensioner Attended Zeb Vance Camp, UCV Conference May 1930
Lilly, Lewis	C	14th Regiment North Carolina Infantry Served as a Body Servant to his master Capt. Robert Lilly	Body Servant	Slave, Robeson County, NC Conf Pensioner
Love, Peter M.	L F& S	16th Regiment North Carolina Infantry 62nd Regiment North Carolina Infantry Served as a Servant to Col. R. G. Love	Servant	Gaston County, NC Conf Pensioner
Lowder, Sr., Caleb (Lauder, Caleb)	K F&S	1st Regiment North Carolina Infantry (6 months, 1861) 21st Regiment North Carolina Infantry 33rd Regiment North Carolina Infantry Served as a cook under BGen.Robert Fredrick Hoke	Cook	Fannie Lowder his widow submitted for a pension, Lincoln County, NC Conf Pensioner
Lynch, William	E	5th North Carolina Cavalry. (63 State Troops.) (Barringers Brigade)	Cook	
Majors, William		Served as a Body Servant to his Master Sam Majors.	Body Servant	Slave of Sam Majors, Person County, NC Conf Pensioner
Massenburg, Oscar		Served as a Teamster	Teamster	Wake County, NC Conf Pensioner
Maynor, George W.		Served building breastworks at Ft. Caswell and Ft. Fisher	Laborer	FMC, Harnett County, NC Conf Pensioner
McDaniel, J. M.		Served when he was sent to Wilmington, N.C. to load and unload freight cars.	Laborer	Rarcolph County, NC Conf Pensioner
McDowell, Fred		Served helping build Ft. Fisher under Capt. Middleton	Laborer	Bladen County, NC Conf Pensioner
McGhee, Frank	G	30th Regiment North Carolina Infantry Served as a Body Servant to Capt. Richard P. Taylor	Body Servant	Granville County, NC Conf Pensioner
McGill, Lewis		Served As A Body Servant To His Master Ellis Frazier who he served with in South Carolina	Body Servant	Slave of Ellis Frazier, Union County, North Carolina Conf Pensioner

Name		Unit	Role	Notes
McLelland, Isaac	A	48th Regiment North Carolina Infantry Served with his masters Pvt. John and Fess McLelland	Servant	Iredell County, NC Conf Pensioner
McMillan, Bill (Bill Stallings)	C	2nd Battalion, North Carolina Local Defense Troops Served as a cook and servant to his master Pvt. John C. McMillan	Cook Servant	Slave of John C. McMillan, Duplin County, NC Conf Pensioner
Mendenhall, M. H.	A	4th Regiment North Carolina Cavalry (59th North Carolina State Troops) Served as a Body Servant to his master W. A. Mendenhall	Body Servant	Slave, Anson County, NC Conf Pensioner
Miller, William(Bill)		Served as Willmington, N.C. building breastworks	Laborer	Slave of Veteran Daniel E. Guerrant, Rockingham County, NC Conf Pensioner
Mills, George		16th, 25th, and 35th North Carolina Infantry Served as a Body Servant to his master Capt. Walter M. Bryson	Body Servant	Slave of Capt. Walter M. Bryson, Henderson County, NC Conf Pensioner. Capt. Bryson was killed in the Battle of Antietam, Md. George recovered the body, then made the trip home to Hendersonville, N.C., so that his master would not be buried in a ditch with the 24,000 Union and Confederate soldiers who died in battle that day
Moore, Adam		Was sent by his master to serve as a wagoner.	Teamster	Slave of Moses Roberts, Lincoln County, NC Conf Pensioner
Moore, Adam (Miller)	M	16th North Carolina Regiment Served as Servant to Pvt. Adam Miller Roberts	Body Servant	Slave, Lincoln County, NC Conf Pensioner
Moore, Harvey		3rd North Carolina Light Artillery Served as a body servant to Maj. John W. Moore	Body Servant	Slave of Maj. John W. Moore of Murfreesburo, NC.
Morrisette, Redic		Unknown North Carolina Unit	COOK	Camden County, NC Conf Pensioner
Name not known	H	2nd Regiment North Carolina Cavalry Served as a Servant to Capt. John Randolph	Servant	FMC,
Name not known		Plaque placed at Walker Top Church on Burkemont Mountain in the South Mountains State Park, N.C.	Servant	
Nelson, Alex	D	52nd Regiment North Carolina Infantry Served as a Body Guard to his master 1st Lt. Isaac Nelson	Body Guard Servant	Father of Anderson G. Nelson.
Nelson, Anderson G.	D	52nd Regiment North Carolina Infantry Served as a Body Guard to his master 1st Lt. Isaac Nelson	Body Guard Servant	Guilford County, NC Conf Pensioner. Son of Alex Nelson
Osburne, Cye	C,H	4th Regiment North Carolina Infantry Served as a body servant to Col. Edwin A. Osburne and Thomas Osburne	Body Servant	Wake County, NC Conf Pensioner
Owen, Joseph	I	22nd Regiment North Carolina Infantry	Private	FMC, McDowell County, NC Conf Pensioner

Parker, Buck		Served as a servant to his master H. Clay King	Servant	Slave of H. Clay King, Alamance County, NC Conf Pensioner
Payne, Unknown		Unknown North Carolina Unit Served for four years.	Servant	Slave, Son of John Payne and Sarah Hadyn. According to his brother Larkin Payne, in Arkansas Slave Narratives.
Payne, Unknown		Unknown North Carolina Unit Served for two years.	Servant	Slave, Son of John Payne and Sarah Hadyn. According to his brother Larkin Payne, in Arkansas Slave Narratives.
Paythress, Wiley	K L	32nd Regiment North Carolina Infantry (Lenoir Braves) 15th Regiment North Carolina Infantry Served as a servant to his master Pvt. Washington L. Branch	Servant	Slave of Washington L. Branch, Franklin County, NC Conf Pensioner
Perry, Aaron	B	37th Regiment North Carolina Infantry Served as a body servant to his master Lt. Col. John B. Ashcroft	Body Servant	Union County, NC Conf Pensioner
Pettiford, Silas	I	55th Regiment North Carolina Infantry Served as a body servant to his master Sgt. Shimuel C. Blackley	Body Servant	Franklin County, NC Conf Pensioner
Phelps, Abner		Unknown North Carolina Unit	Private	Slave, Caswell County, NC Conf Pensioner
Plummer, Frank		Served building breastworks	Laborer	Slave of Dr. Alfred Plummer, Granville County, NC Conf Pensioner
Poisson, James	D	10th Battalion North Carolina Heavy Artillery	Musician	
Polk, John	E I	Infantry Regiment Thomas' Legion, North Carolina Also served 63rd Tennessee Infantry. (Fain's Regiment 74th Tennessee Infantry) Served as a body servant to Samuel Love	Body Servant	Lincoln County, NC Conf Pensioner
Potts, Milas		Served building breastworks at Wilmington, N.C.	Laborer	Cabarrus County, NC Conf Pensioner
Powell, Amos	D	23rd Infantry Regiment North Carolina Served as a body servant to Cpl. Charles P. Powell	Private	Anson County, NC Conf Pensioner
Prince, Malcolm M.	H G	3rd North Carolina Junior Reserves 61st North Carolina Infantry Served with his master's son Pvt. William R. Prince, helping building breastworks.	Servant	Slave, Wake County, NC Conf Pensioner
Pulley, John	B	47th North Carolina Infantry Served under Capt. A. D. Crudup	Private	Submitted for a Confederate Pension. State Auditor Baxter Durham denied the claim, saying that the Confederacy had no Negro troops.
Ransom, M. C.	E	15th North Carolina Infantry Served as a servant to Capt. William Ballard, Lt. Henry Kearney and Lt. John Morris	Body Servant	Granville County, NC Conf Pensioner

Ratliff, William	I	43rd North Carolina Infantry Served as a cook to his master Pvt. Nelson P. Hildreth	Cook	Slave of Nelson P. Hildreth, Anson County, NC Conf Pensioner
Reed, Arthur	D	3rd North Carolina Artillery	Private	
Reed, Henry		Served as a body servant to Dr. Condy Boyd and building breastworks	Laborer	Halifax County, NC Conf Pensioner
Reed, Miles	D	3rd North Carolina Artillery	Private	
Revels, Henry	F	51st North Carolina Infantry	Private	
Revels, Henson	A	1st Battalion North Carolina Heavy Artillery	Private	
Revels, Jonathan	F	51st North Carolina Infantry Capt. McDugald's Co., North Carolina.	Private	
Revels, William Galen	H	21st North Carolina Infantry	Fifer	NC Conf Pensioner Attended Zeb Vance Camp, UCV Conference May 1930
Richardson, Jack		Unknown North Carolina Unit		From Johnston County, NC
Richardson, Wylie		Served building breastworks	Laborer	Slave
Robinson,		1st North Carolina Cavalry Served as a bodyguard of Capt. John Nichols	Bodyguard	Slave, KIA
Robinson, Jane (female)		Washed And Ironed For Soldiers In The Pettegrew Hospital	Laundress	Her Husband Was A Bodyguard Of Captain John Nichols Of The First North Carolina Cavalry
Rogers, George		Served as a servant to his master William Rogers, after his masters death he helped build breastworks at Natural Gap	Laborer Servant	Slave of William Rogers, Wake County, NC Conf Pensioner
Rudd, William	E	5th North Carolina Cavalry (63rd Slave Troops.) (Barringers Brigade)	Cook	
Russell, Frank	B	7th Infantry Regiment North Carolina Served as a servant to Capt. James Harris	Servant	Cabarrus County, NC Conf Pensioner
Sampson, David Sellars		Company Batty D, 2nd Light Artillery Regiment North Carolina Served as a servant to this master Col. William Sellars, Herman Register and Henry Lee.	Servant	Slave, Sampson County, NC Conf Pensioner
Scales, Porter		Served building breastworks at Fort Fisher	Laborer	Rockingham County, NC Conf Pensioner
Sellars, Jerry		Served as a servant to James Moore and Capt.	Servant	Alamance County, NC Conf Pensioner
Singleton, William Henry	K / H	2-" North Carolina Infantry Served as a servant to his master **ALSO SERVED THE UNION 10th Regiment Connecticut Infantry Served as a servant to Capt. Robert Leggett**	Servant	Slave of John Hancock Nelson. Attended the Blue-Gray Gettysburg Reunion 1938.
Smallwood, Mat		Served hauling provisions for soldiers	Teamster	Slave of Thomas Smallwood, Cabarrus County, NC Conf
Smith, George		Served as a body servant to Lt. Joseph Smith	Body Servant	Washington County, NC Conf Pensioner

Spears, Elic		Served as a Laborer working on fortifications (Breastworks) in North Carolina and served under Capt. John Pharr	Laborer Servant	Lafayette County, MS Conf Pensioner
Spelman, John	A	56th Infantry Regiment North Carolina	Cook	Camden County, NC Conf Pensioner
Stewart, Peter	B	2nd Infantry Regiment North Carolina Enlisted and served as a servant to Capt. David Cooper	Servant	Surry County, NC Conf Pensioner
Streeter, Shadrack	I D	43rd Infantry Regiment North Carolina 37th Infantry Regiment North Carolina Served as a servant to 3rd Lt. Welsey Battle, Lt. Battle died of his wounds as a POW at Gettysburg, PA. Shadrack then helped build breastworks at Frazier's Point.	Laborer Servant	Anson County, NC Conf Pensioner
Strowd, Aaron		Served as a servant to his master Capt. C. Pinkney Strowd, he went with his master to build breastworks at Wilmington, N.C.	Laborer Servant	Slave of Capt. C. Pinkney Strowd, Wake County, NC Conf Pensioner
Swinson, Sam		Served with his master John Swinson at Baldhead Island	Laborer	Slave of John Swinson, Wayne County, NC Conf Pensioner
Sykes, Caleb	G D	4th_ Regiment North Carolina Cavalry (59th North Carolina State Troops) 10th Regiment North Carolina Heavy Artillery	Musician	
Taylor Amos Jones	G	48th Infantry Regiment North Carolina Served as a servant to Capt. William H. Jones	Servant	Chatham County, NC Conf Pensioner
Thomas, Cudge	D	21st Regiment North Carolina Infantry Served as a servant to his master William H. Thomas	Servant	Slave, Jackson County, NC Conf Pensioner
Thomas, John	L	15th Infantry Regiment North Carolina Served as a servant to his master Capt. Charles Thomas	Servant	Franklin County, NC Conf Pensioner
Thompson, Armstead		Served building breastworks at Wilmington, N.C.	Laborer	Slave of Gen Nicholas Thompson, Orange County, NC Conf Pensioner
Tomlinson, Louis		Served building breastworks at Wilmington, N.C.	Laborer	Slave of Capt. Sam Tomlinson, Anson County, NC Conf Pensioner
Turner, Ben		Served as a body servant to his master Simon S. Turner	Servant	Slave of Simon Turner, Wake County, NC Conf Pensioner
Turner, John		Served as a Teamster hauling provisions	Teamster	Slave of Simon Turner, Wake County, NC Conf Pensioner
Turner, Thomas		Served manufacturing salt petre during the war.	Laborer	Orange County, NC Conf Pensioner
Tyler, George		25th North Carolina Infantry		Yalobusha County, MS Conf Pensioner
Underwood, Sandey	K	51st North Carolina Infantry Served as a body servant to Capt. Joseph B. Underwood.	Body Servant	Sampson County, NC Conf Pensioner

Venable, John W.	H	21st Regiment North Carolina Troops	Private	Forsyth County, NC Conf Pensioner application. His wife Sarah Venable also submitted for a widow's pension after he died. Both pension applications were disallowed with a reply "No law for this".
Walker, Andrew	F	3rd North Carolina Cavalry Served as a body servant to Maj. Benjamin Walker (Surgeon)	Body Servant	Washington County, NC Conf Pensioner
Walker, Brown	H	6th North Carolina Infantry Served as a servant to David A. Walker	Servant	Alamance County, NC Conf Pensioner
Watson, Giles	C	50th North Carolina Infantry Served with his master Lt. G. W. Watson	Servant	Slave of Lt. G. W. Watson, Johnston County, NC Conf Pensioner
Wells, Major Bartlett	G	52nd North Carolina Infantry Served with his master Capt. James Wells	Servant	Slave of Capt. James Wells, Jackson County, NC Conf Pensioner
White, George	B	1st North Carolina Junior Reserves Served with his master's son Ben F. Lawrence	Servant	Slave of John G. Lawrence, Wake County, NC Conf Pensioner
Whitfield, Luke		Unknown North Carolina Unit Served as a Blacksmith	Blacksmith	Slave of Bill Carraway of New Bern, NC. According to his son J. W. Whitfield, Arkansas, in Arkansas Slave Narratives.
Williams, Ed		Served As A Servant To Reverand John J. Landrum In South Carolina	Servant	Gaston County, North Carolina Conf Pensioner
Williams, Francis		Served building breastworks	Laborer	Slave of Argustus High
Williams, Henry Andrew (Tip)		49th Regiment North Carolina Infantry Served as a Teamster under Gen. Matt W. Ransom	Teamster	Slave of Jason and Betsy Williams of Jackson, NC. According to his statements, in Arkansas Slave Narratives.
Wilson, James	K	6th Regiment North Carolina Infantry Served as a cook and attendant to Capt. James W. Lea	Cook Servant	Alamance County, NC Conf Pensioner
Wilson, Jerry		Served as a servant to Col. R. N. Wilson	Servant	Gaston County, NC Conf Pensioner
Wilson, John		Served building breastworks at Fort Fisher	Laborer	Cleveland County, NC Conf Pensioner
Wilson, John	K	Thomas Legion Infantry Regiment North Carolina Served as a servant to Col. Tom Butler	Servant	Cabarrus County, NC Conf Pensioner
Wilson, William	F	6th Regiment North Carolina Infantry Served with Lt. George Bason	Servant	Alamance County, NC Conf Pensioner
Wolfe, Houston		Served carrying messages for the Home Guard	Mail Carrier	Gaston County, NC Conf Pensioner
Yarborough, Henry H.	G	47th Regiment North Carolina Infantry Served as a servant to his master 2nd Lt. Richard F. Yarborough	Servant	Slave of Richard F. Yarborough, Franklin County, NC Conf Pensioner
Young, Mark	C	16th Regiment North Carolina Infantry Served as a servant to Capt. Creed F. Young and Wesley Young	Servant	Yancey County, NC Conf Pensioner

Young, Peter		Served as a servant to his master Samuel Young	Servant	Slave of Samuel Young, Mitchell County, NC Conf Pensioner

OKLAHOMA TERRITORY

When the Choctaw Nation was forcibly resettled in Indian Territory in present-day Oklahoma in the 1830s, it was joined by enslaved Black people—the tribe had owned enslaved Blacks since the 1720s. By the eve of the Civil War, 14 percent of the Choctaw Nation consisted of enslaved Blacks. Avid supporters of the Confederate States of America, the Nation passed a measure requiring all whites living in its territory to swear allegiance to the Confederacy and deemed any criticism of it or its army treasonous and punishable by death. Choctaws also raised an infantry force and a cavalry to fight alongside Confederate forces.

Although some may have served with Confederate Indian Forces such as the Choctaw or Cherokee Nations, I was unable to locate any African-Americans who served from the Oklahoma Territory.

In 1915, Oklahoma began paying annuities to Confederate veterans and widows. There is a searchable index available online. Department of Libraries of Oklahoma n Oklahoma, the first provision for Confederate veterans was made in 1915. Approximately two-thirds of the applications were denied in the first year. The inability to verify eligibility and the state's lack of cash were among the reasons for these rejections.

On 21 rolls of microfilm, the Historical Genealogy Department has a copy of these applications, with the last two reels being supplemental applications. The index to this information is like wise owned by the Department. The Oklahoma Genealogical Society published Submitted by Confederate Soldiers, Sailors, and their widows.

Oklahoma Department of Libraries
Archives and Records Management Divisions
200 Northeast 18th Street
Oklahoma City, OK 73105
Telephone: 1-800-522-8116 (nationwide) ext. 209

Oklahoma Department of Libraries
Archives and Records Management Divisions
Index to Oklahoma Confederate Pension Records

SOUTH CAROLINA

C. M. Douglas of Columbia, South Carolina, published "A Notable Colored Man" in 1894:

Old William Rose, a courier for the Governor's office in every Democratic administration since 1876, is one of Columbia's most well-known freedmen. William Rose was born in Charleston in 1813, and was a slave of the Barrett family of that city. He was 85 years old at the time of thE article and still at his station of duty every day, and nothing pleases him more than to take part in any Confederate protest.

When he was twelve years old, he was transported to Columbia and taught the carpenter and tinner skills. In his earlier days, he served as a drummer in Capt. Elmore's company, the Richland Volunteers, in the Florida War, an organization that is still active and has a proud record in three wars. Following that, he served as a servant for Capt. (later Col.) Butler of the legendary Palmetto Regiment during the Mexican War.

However, he is most proud of his service during the Confederacy.

He was the body servant of that illustrious Carolinian, Gen. Maxey Gregg, and as soon as he learned that his loving master had fallen on the field at Fredericksburg, he went to his side as quickly as a horse could carry him, and stayed with him to the end. His account of Gen. Gregg's death, his reunion with Stonewall Jackson, and his courageous final letter to the Governor of South Carolina are all tragic in the extreme, and the elderly man never tells the story without passion.

William saw the inauguration of [Grover] Cleveland, as well as the unveiling of the soldiers' monument in Richmond and the recent big Confederate reunion in Birmingham.

He returned laden with badges from the latter, which he treasures as mementos of the experience. He's been associated with the Richland Volunteers for sixty years, yet they never parade.

He never forgets Memorial Day, and since the war's end, the 10th of May has never gone by without a tribute from him being put on the Gregg memorial in Elmwood. The United States awarded him a pension for his service in the Florida War.

Old "Uncle" William belongs to a generation that has died out. They will not have a hero as such , but until the last of them crosses the "black river," the world may see benefactors in grateful Southern whites.

Directory of African American Confederates in the U.S. Civil War

South Carolina began granting pensions to needy Confederate veterans and their widows in 1887, but initially limited the pensions to veterans who were disabled by loss of limb or other injury during the war and widows of soldiers or sailors who had died in service. Both had to meet means tests, which were made even more restrictive in 1900. Responding to a provision of the 1895 State Constitution, the General Assembly in 1896 expanded eligibility to poor uninjured veterans over 60 and poor widows over 60 and ushered in a major growth period for both pension funding and the number of applicants. Revisions enacted in 1900 refined the classification and procedures for pensions, defining a system that would remain in force until 1919. Unfortunately, few applications for Confederate pensions under any of the pre-1919 acts survive either at the state or local level.

The state board appointed a three-member board for each county to approve applications from local residents. Eligible pensioners included all veterans and widows over the age of sixty who had married veterans before 1890. The General Assembly provided $500,000 to pay for pensions. Changes the following year , eliminated the state board, named the comptroller general as pension commissioner, and authorized the local veterans camp to hear appeals of each county board's decision.

Act No. 63, 1923 S.C. Acts 107 allowed African Americans who had served at least six months as cooks, servants, or attendants to apply for a pension. Then in 1924, apparently because there were too many applications, the act was amended to eliminate all laborers, teamsters, and non-South Carolinians by extending eligibility only to South Carolina residents who had served the state for at least six months as "body servants or male camp cooks."

NAME	CO.	UNIT	RANK	SLAVE / FREE MISC NOTES
Abram	I	11th South Carolina Infantry (9th South Carolina Volunteers)	Musician	
Ace	F	Holcombe Legion, South Carolina Infantry Regiment	Private	
Alec	T	16th Regiment South Carolina Militia	Cook	
Alick	B	1st Battalion South Carolina Sharp Shooters	Cook	
Alick	F	27th South Carolina Infantry (Gaillard's Regiment)	Cook	
Ance		5th Regiment South Carolina Infantry Served As A Servant To Pvt. James Michael Barf	Servant	Slave
Andrew		16th Regiment South Carolina Militia	Musician	
Andrew	F&S	18th Regiment South Carolina Militia	Musician	
Andrew (Andy)	H	Hampton Legion South Carolina Infantry Regiment	Cook Servant	
Ansel	I	27th South Carolina Infantry (Gaillard's Regiment)	Drummer	
Ben	B	1st Regiment Artillery South Carolina Militia	Drummer	
Ben		Capt. Meichers' Company (German Artillery) South Carolina Artillery	Drummer	
Ben	A	1st (Charleston) Battalion South Carolina Infantry (Gaillard's Battalion)	Cook	
Ben	I	27th South Carolina Infantry (Gaillard's Regiment)	Cook	
Ben	C, D	Holcombe Legion, South Carolina Cavalry Battalion	Cook	
Ben	F&S	Holcombe Legion, South Carolina Infantry Regiment	Drummer	

The History of the Life of **Rev. William. Mack Lee** states he lived between (1835-1932), was a body servant and cook for General Robert E. Lee during the Civil War and until the general's death in 1870. According to W. M. Lee's story, he was raised at the General's Arlington Heights estate, where he served "Marse Robert, even after being legally emancipated in 1865.

W.M. Lee's History portrays him as having been ordained "a Missionary Baptist preacher" in Washington, D.C., in 1881 and having gone on to found four separate congregations in southern Maryland and northern Virginia. The History also states that in 1887, W.M. Lee organized the State Benevolent Association of Virginia, an organization dedicated to relieving the physical needs of the poor. In 1912, W.M. Lee, according to the History, successfully raised the funds to build a stone and brick church for his fourth and final congregation in Churchland, Virginia.

W.M Lee published his History to help him raise money from white southerners to complete the financing for his Churchland, Virginia, pastorate.He was wounded by a Yankee bullet and having served Robert E. Lee himself during the Civil War got the attention of southern whites whom W.M. Lee solicited for funds.

On May 4, the eve of the fighting, General Lee invited some people over for dinner. According to the memoirs of his slave and cook William Mack Lee: On dat day–we was all so hongry and I didn't have nuffin in ter cook, dat I was jes' plumb bumfuzzled. I didn't know what to do.

Marse Robert, he had gone and invited a crowd of ginerals to eat wid him, an' I had ter git de vittles. and Marse A. P. Hill, and Marse D. H. Hill, and Marse Wade Hampton, Gineral Longstreet, and Gineral Pickett and sum others.

When asked by the general where had such a plump little chicken come from? Surely not from foraging! And the General Lee kept up the pressure. Upon questioning, William admitted to the deed. After hearing the sad truth, Lee asked, " "No, you didn't, William; and the general's reply I'm going to write Miss Mary about you. I'm going to tell her you have killed Nellie. William, now that you have killed Nellie, what are we going to do for eggs?"

"I jes' had ter do it, Marse Robert," William replied.

Often times, throughout human history, the fates of entire nations or regions of the world have been shaped by the least expected figures or transformative events whether they were

slaves or low-wage workers or household pets.

Similarly but on an incomparably much grander scale, notable African-American slaves played a crucial role in Lee's successes.

According to The Greenville News in South Carolina, "Uncle William Mack Lee" left behind "the chapel he had built, a small brochure issued in praise of Marse Robert E. Lee, and the friendships not just of members of his race but a wide circle of acquaintances among the 'white folks'" when he died in 1932.

In 1921, The Roanoke News identified "Uncle William Mack Lee" as "one of the best known colored men in the South" and "a Negro of the old kind, distinguished looking, polite in demeanor ... " in the Old North state.

He was "the body servant and cook for Robert E. Lee" and a "old darkie" who was "the center of a throng of veterans and members of the Daughters of the Confederacy all day and until late in the evening" at the soldiers' reunion in New Orleans in 1923, according to the Associated Press (via an article in the San Francisco Chronicle dated April 13 of that year).

Benjamin	A	1st (McCreary's) South Carolina Infantry	Cook	
Bill	D	Holcombe Legion, South Carolina Cavalry Battalion	Cook	
Bristol		Walter's Company, South Carolina Light Artillery (Washington	Teamster	
Bristow (Bristol)?		Capt. J. T. Kanapauxs Company (Lafayette Artillery), South Carolina Light Artillery	Hired Teamster	
Cage "Uncle"		3rd Regiment South Carolina	Cook	
Charles		Capt. Gilchrist's Company, South Carolina Heavy Artillery (Gist Guard)	Musician	
Charles		Served as a servant to Adjutant B. H. Burk	Servant	He captured a Federal soldier at Manassas Junction, VA and turned him over to Brig. General Milledge L. Bonham
Daton	C	Holcombe Legion, South Carolina Cavalry Battalion	Cook	
Dick	A	Holcombe Legion, South Carolina Infantry Regiment	Cook	
Edmond	C, E	Holcombe Legion, South Carolina Cavalry Battalion	Cook Servant	
Edward	B	1st (Charleston) Battalion South Carolina Infantry (Gaillard's Battalion)	Drummer	
Edward	B	27th South Carolina Infantry	Drummer	
Edward		Capt. J. T. Kanapauxs Company (Lafayette Artillery), South Carolina Light Artillery	Musician	
Ellick		Capt. Mayham Ward's Company, (Waccawaw Light Artillery) South Carolina Light Artillery	Teamster	
, Ellick	E,F	Hampton Legion South Carolina Infantry Regiment	Private	Servant
, Fevers	A	1st (Charleston) Battalion South Carolina Infantry (Gaillard's Battalion)	Cook	
, Fevers	I	27th South Carolina Infantry (Gaillard's Regiment)	Cook	
, Fortune	C	25th Regiment South Carolina Infantry (Eutaw	Cook	
, Frank	D	21st South Carolina Volunteers Served as a Laborer at Fort Sumter and Fort Johnson, S.C.	Slave	Slave of Rev. James Wilson Burn
, Frank	C	Holcombe Legion, South Carolina Cavalry Battalion	Cook	
, Gallant	B	Holcombe Legion, South Carolina Cavalry Battalion	Cook	
, George		16th Regiment South Carolina Militia (Friest's Company)	Under Cook	
, George	A	1st (Charleston) Battalion South Carolina Infantry	Cook	

Directory of African American Confederates in the U.S. Civil War

John		16th Regiment South Carolina Militia	Musician	
John	B	1st Battalion South Carolina Sharp Shooters	Musician	
John	M	1st South Carolina Infantry (6 Months, 1861)	Musician	
John		Capt. Gilchrist's Company (Gist Guard), South Carolina Heavy Artillery	Musician	
John	F F&	Holcombe Legion, South Carolina Cavalry Battalion	Cook Drumme	
Jordon		Waccarnaw Light Artillery, South Carolina Light Artillery, (Capt. Mayhem Ward's Company)	Musician	
Josey		3rd Regiment South Carolina	Cook	
Joshua		16th Regiment South Carolina Militia (Prendergats'	Cook	
Larcomb	F&S	1st Regiment South Carolina Infantry	Musician	
Leroy	E	Holcombe Legion, South Carolina Infantry Regiment	Cook	
Lotte		Walter's Company, South Carolina Light Artillery (Washington Artillery)	Cook	
Madison	E	Holcombe Legion, South Carolina Infantry Regiment	Cook Privat	
Manley	B	1st (Charleston) Battalion South Carolina Infantry (Gaillard's Battalion)	Cook	
Manley	K	27th South Carolina Infantry (Gaillard's Regiment)	Cook	
March	A	1st (Charleston) Battalion South Carolina Infantry (Gaillard's Battalion)	Musician	
May	A	Holcombe Legion, South Carolina Cavalry Battalion	Cook	
Middleton	A	1st (Charleston) Battalion South Carolina Infantry (Gaillard's Battalion)	Drummer	
Milton	E	Holcombe Legion, South Carolina Infantry Regiment	Cook	
Moses	A	27th South Carolina Infantry (Gaillard's	Cook	
Ned	D	Holcombe Legion, South Carolina Cavalry Battalion	Cook	
Oliver	F&S	1st Regiment South Carolina Infantry	Musician	
Pete		Capt. Walter's Company (Washington Artillery), South Carolina Light	Cook	
Peter	C	1st (Charleston) Battalion South Carolina Infantry	Cook	
Peter	A	27th South Carolina Infantry	Drummer	
Peter	A	Holcombe Legion Cavalry Battalion Infantry Regiment South Carolina	Cook Teamster	

Directory of African American Confederates in the U.S. Civil War

John		16th Regiment South Carolina Militia	Musician	
John	B	1st Battalion South Carolina Sharp Shooters	Musician	
John	M	1st South Carolina Infantry (6 Months, 1861)	Musician	
John		Capt. Gilchrist's Company (Gist Guard), South Carolina Heavy Artillery	Musician	
John	F F&	Holcombe Legion, South Carolina Cavalry Battalion	Cook Drumme	
Jordon		Waccarnaw Light Artillery, South Carolina Light Artillery, (Capt. Mayhem Ward's Company)	Musician	
Josey		3rd Regiment South Carolina	Cook	
Joshua		16th Regiment South Carolina Militia (Prendergats'	Cook	
Larcomb	F&S	1st Regiment South Carolina Infantry	Musician	
Leroy	E	Holcombe Legion, South Carolina Infantry Regiment	Cook	
Lotte		Walter's Company, South Carolina Light Artillery (Washington Artillery)	Cook	
Madison	E	Holcombe Legion, South Carolina Infantry Regiment	Cook Privat	
Manley	B	1st (Charleston) Battalion South Carolina Infantry (Gaillard's Battalion)	Cook	
Manley	K	27th South Carolina Infantry (Gaillard's Regiment)	Cook	
March	A	1st (Charleston) Battalion South Carolina Infantry (Gaillard's Battalion)	Musician	
May	A	Holcombe Legion, South Carolina Cavalry Battalion	Cook	
Middleton	A	1st (Charleston) Battalion South Carolina Infantry (Gaillard's Battalion)	Drummer	
Milton	E	Holcombe Legion, South Carolina Infantry Regiment	Cook	
Moses	A	27th South Carolina Infantry (Gaillard's	Cook	
Ned	D	Holcombe Legion, South Carolina Cavalry Battalion	Cook	
Oliver	F&S	1st Regiment South Carolina Infantry	Musician	
Pete		Capt. Walter's Company (Washington Artillery), South Carolina Light	Cook	
Peter	C	1st (Charleston) Battalion South Carolina Infantry	Cook	
Peter	A	27th South Carolina Infantry	Drummer	
Peter	A	Holcombe Legion Cavalry Battalion Infantry Regiment South Carolina	Cook Teamster	

Philip	B	Holcombe Legion, South Carolina Cavalry Battalion	Cook	
Primus	A	27th South Carolina Infantry (Gaillard's	Cook	
Ralph D.	B	1st (Charleston) Battalion South Carolina Infantry	Cook	
Richard	T	16th Regiment South Carolina Militia	Cook	
Sam		17th Regiment South Carolina Militia (Field Artillery) Served as a Servant to Lt. Webb	Servant	
Sam	A	Holcombe Legion, South Carolina Cavalry Battalion	Cook	
Samuel	K	18th Regiment South Carolina		POW At Fort McHenry Prison Camp, captured on 6 Apr, 1865 at Harpers Farm, VA.
Scott	E	3rd Regiment South Carolina Cavalry	Teamster	
Sempie	C	27th South Carolina Infantry (Gaillard's Regiment)	Cook	
Simon	H	Hampton Legion South Carolina Infantry Regiment	Cook Servant	
Stephen	F&S	12th Regiment South Carolina Infantry	Fifer	
Stephen	B	Holcombe Legion, South Carolina Cavalry Battalion	Cook	
Stokes	F	Holcombe Legion, South Carolina Infantry Regiment		
Stuart	F&S	1st Regiment South Carolina Infantry	Musician	
Swinton	F&S	1st Regiment South Carolina Infantry (Hagood's)	Musician	
Thomas	1	4th Regiment South Carolina Cavalry		POW At Fort McHenry Prison Camp, captured on 28May, 1864.
Thomas	G	1st (Charleston) Battalion South Carolina Infantry (Gaillard's Battalion)	Cook	
Thomas	B	Holcombe Legion, South Carolina Cavalry Battalion	Cook	
Titus		Unknown South Carolina Unit		Captured at Gettysburg and refused to fight against the south.
Tom		Capt. Gilchrist's Company, (Gist Guard) South Carolina Heavy Artillery	Musician	
Tom		Capt. Wafter's Company, Washington Artillery, South Carolina Light	Cook	
William	E	10th Battalion South Carolina Cavalry		
William	Eas	16th Regiment South Carolina	Cook	
William	K,B		Cook	
Willie		Served as a servant to his master George Crawford.	Servant	Slave of George Crawford of Chester County, S.C. According to Charlie Davis another slave of the same plantation, in South Carolina Slave Narratives.

Directory of African American Confederates in the U.S. Civil War

Abel, Anderson	G	6th Regiment South Carolina Cavalry Served Under Ed Mobley	Cook	Richland County, South Carolina Conf Pensioner App # 9850
Abercrombie, Edom		Listed on the 1926 S. C. Comptroller General's List to the General Assembly		Greenville County, South Carolina Conf Pensioner
Abercrombie, Silas		Listed on the 1926 S. C. Comptroller General's List to the General Assembly		Greenville County, South Carolina Conf Pensioner
Abercrombie, Tom (Thomas)		Served as a Laborer working on Fortifications along the Seacoast	Laborer	Laurens County, South Carolina Conf Pensioner App # 6943
Abraham, Needham	I	1st Regiment South Carolina Cavalry Served As A Laborer Under Capt. Daniel Hutson	Laborer	Lee County, South Carolina Conf Pensioner App # 7405
Adair, Alford	I	3rd Regiment South Carolina Infantry (Capt. B. S. Jones Company) Served As A Cook For Edmond Adair	Cook	Laurens County, South Carolina Conf Pensioner App # 6944
Adams, W. P.	E	1st South Carolina Lt Artillery	Wash	Tate County, MS Conf Pensioner
Agurs, Samuel W.	A	17th Regiment South Carolina Infantry Served Under Capt. John R. Culp	Cook	York County, South Carolina Conf Pensioner
Alton, Thomas L.	G	7th Regiment South Carolina Infantry	Corporal	
Albert, Henry		Served Under Capt. Devereaux, Castle Pinckney Breastworks, (Bishopville)	Laborer	Lee County, South Carolina Conf Pensioner App # 7406
Alfred, Thomas M.	K	7th Regiment South Carolina Served Under Capt. Jack Burris	Servant	McCormick County, South Carolina Conf Pensioner App 8120
Allston, Jim	F&S	25th Regiment North Carolina Infantry Served as an Attendant to Col. H. M. Rutledge	Camp Attendant	Charleston County, South Carolina Confederate Pensioner #1736
Anderson, Burckett (Anderson, Burkett)	G	2nd Regiment South Carolina Artillery (Capt. George W. Stallings Company) Served Under G. W. Anderson	Cook	Barnwell County, South Carolina Conf Pensioner App # 1315
Anderson, Cato		Listed on the 1926 S. C. Comptroller General's List to the General Assembly		Darlington County, South Carolina Conf Pensioner
Anderson, David		Worked On Fortifications On The Sea Coast And Islands. Served Under Capt. Lipscomb	Laborer	Laurens County, South Carolina Conf Pensioner App # 6952
Anderson, Friday		Listed on the 1926 S. C. Comptroller General's List to the General Assembly		Florence County, South Carolina Conf Pensioner
Anderson, George		Served working as a Laborer on fortifications on the Sea Coast	Laborer	Laurens County, South Carolina Conf Pensioner App # 6953
Anderson, U. A.		Served working as a Laborer on fortifications on the Sea Coast Served under Charles Simmons the overseer	Laborer	Laurens County, South Carolina Conf Pensioner App # 6956

Andrews, Allen		Served as a servant to his master He was at Columbia with the Conf troops when Sherman burnt the place. They were captured and taken to Richmond Va. They escaped and walked back home.	Servant	Slave, POW, Captured and taken to Richmond Va. They escaped and walked back home. According to his wife Frances Andrews of Newberry, S.C. In South Carolina Slave Narratives.
Arch, Tom	B	1st Regiment South Carolina Cavalry (Nesbitt's Company) Served Under Capt. Nesbitt	Private	Spartanburg County, South Carolina Conf Pensioner App # 10519
Archer, Reuben		Listed on the 1926 S. C. Comptroller General's List to the General Assembly	Private	Chester County, South Carolina Conf Pensioner
Archer, Thad		South Carolina Reserves		York County, South Carolina Conf Pensioner
Armstrong, Charlie		1st South Carolina Infantry	Servant	Tate County, MS Conf Pensioner
Ashford, James	G	7th Battalion South Carolina Infantry Served Under Capt. Augustus P. Irby	Cook	Richland County, South Carolina Conf Pensioner App # 9852
Avery, Andrew	A	15th Battalion, South Carolina Heavy Artillery (Lucas') Served as a Laborer under Dr. Edward Avery	Laborer Private	York County, South Carolina Conf Pensioner
Avery, John		Listed on the 1926 S. C. Comptroller General's List to the General Assembly	Private	Georgetown County, South Carolina Conf Pensioner
Bacot, Mitchell		Listed on the 1926 S. C. Comptroller General's List to the General Assembly	Private	Darlington County, South Carolina Conf Pensioner
Baldric, Abraham	F	2nd Regiment South Carolina Artillery (Capt. Rufus LeGree's Company) Served under Pvt. Rufus Whitmore	Cook	Orangeburg County, South Carolina Conf Pensioner App # 9183
Banks, Noah	C H	14th Regiment South Carolina Infantry 17th Regiment South Carolina Infantry Served under Pvt. William L. Avery	Private	York County, South Carolina Conf Pensioner
Barabaha, James		Gen. Martin W. Gary's Cavalry Brigade, Quartermaster Department	Guard	Surrendered at Appomattox
Barfield, Jacob B.		Cavalry Battalion, Holcombe Legion, South Carolina (Capt. Bartley's Company) Served As A Servant Under Sgt. Joseph Harvey	Servant	Berkeley County, South Carolina Conf Pensioner App # 1574
Barksdale, Wash	G	3rd Regiment South Carolina Infantry (Capt. R. P. Todd's Company) Served as a cook and attendant to Cpl. Thomas B. Barksdale	Cook Attendant	Laurens County, South Carolina Conf Pensioner App # 6981
Barnes, Robert		Listed on the 1926 S. C. Comptroller General's List to the Gere-al Assembly	Private	Lancaster County, South Carolina Conf Pensioner
Barnett, Anthony	B	15th Regiment South Carolina Infantry Served Under Col. Allison And Captain Steel	Servant	York County, South Carolina Conf Pensioner

Directory of African American Confederates in the U.S. Civil War

Barrett, Emmett	C	8th Battalion, South Carolina Reserves (Stalling's) (Capt. William W. Hutto's Company) Served Under John E. Gardner	Cook	Aiken County, South Carolina Conf Pensioner App # 252
Barron, Harney		Served As A Servant For The Commander of Fort Sumter	Servant	York County, South Carolina Conf Pensioner
Bates, Anderson		He served as a laborer at Hopewell, Virginia, and worked in the DuPonts factory in the acid area. The atmosphere burned off all the skin from his face and arms, but he stuck it out until the end of the war. After the war the factory was dismantled.	Laborer	Slave of Dr. S. Furman from Jenkinsville, S. C., According to his statements in South Carolina Slave Narratives.
Bates, Jilson	B	Holcombe Legion, South Carolina Infantry Regiment	Cook	
Baxter, Charles		21st Regiment South Carolina Served as a cook for Dr. Andrew F. Crum in South Carolina and in Virginia	Cook	Slave of Rev. L. J. Crum. Orangeburg County, South Carolina Conf Pensioner App # 9187
Beamer, T.	K	3rd Regiment South Carolina Cavalry	Teamster	
Beatty, J. Han	B	18th Regiment South Carolina Volunteers	Private	York County, South Carolina Conf Pensioner
Bellinger, Daniel		Served as a servant to his master Lt. Bellinger.	Servant	Slave of Lt. Bellinger killed while bringing the Lt. his sword in the fort at Secessionville.
Beon, Joe B.		Listed on the 1926 S. C. Comptroller General's List to the General Assembly	Private	Florence County, South Carolina Conf Pensioner
Best, Ben		Listed on the 1926 S. C. Comptroller General's List to the General Assembly	Private	Barnwell County, South Carolina Conf Pensioner
Bing, Tom	K	3rd Regiment South Carolina (Colcock's Regiment) (Capt. William Peeples' Company)	Private	Hampton County, South Carolina Conf Pensioner App # 6082
Bird, George	A	12th South Carolina Volunteers (Palmer Guards) Served Under James Chancely Chambers	Cook	FMC, York County, South Carolina Conf Pensioner
Bittle, Isaac	A	4th Regiment South Carolina Cavalry (Rutledge's) Served With His Master Pvt. John Wesley Bittle	Body Servant	Anson County, North Carolina Conf Pensioner Attended Zeb Vance Camp, UCV Conference May 1930
Bivings, Patrick		Served as a cook under Ed Bivings	Cook	Spartanburg County, South Carolina Conf Pensioner App # 10557
Black, Jefferson (Jeff)		1st Regiment South Carolina Infantry (Butler's) (1st Regulars) (Capt. J. W. Perrin's Company) Served under Capt. Lewis Perrin	Cook Laborer	Abbeville County, South Carolina Conf Pensioner App # 16
Blakeney, Alfred		Listed on the 1926 S. C. Comptroller General's List to the General Assembly	Private	Lancaster County, South Carolina Conf Pensioner

Blume, Wash	D	20th Regiment South Carolina Infantry (Capt. Richard V. (Dick) Danelly's Company) Served under Sgt. John H. Livingston	Body Servant	Orangeburg County, South Carolina Conf Pensioner App # 9192
Bogan, Edwin		Unknown South Carolina Unit	Servant	Slave of Doctor Bogan of Union County, SC.
Bold, Sam		Stuart's Company, South Carolina Artillery (Beaufort Volunteer Artillery)(Capt. H. M. Stuart's Company) Served as a Servant of Pvt. Michael Jenkins	Servant	Beaufort County, South Carolina Conf Pensioner App # 1520
Boulware, Ed	B	17th Regiment South Carolina Infantry Served Under Pink Boulware	Cook Laundryman	Fairfield County, South Carolina Conf Pensioner App # 3672
Bowen, Burress		Gen. Martin W. Gary's Cavalry Brigade, Quartermaster Department	Teamster	Surrendered at Appomattox
Bowen, John		Gen. Martin W. Gary's Cavalry Brigade, Quartermaster Department	Teamster	Surrendered at Appomattox
Bowen, Thomas		Gen. Martin W. Gary's Cavalry Brigade, Quartermaster	Teamster	Surrendered at Appomattox
Bower, Nathan		Listed on the 1926 S. C. Comptroller General's List to the General Assembly	Private	Chester County, South Carolina Conf Pensioner
Bowie, Jefferson	B	7th Regiment South Carolina Infantry Served Under J. W. Bush	Servant	Greenwood County, South Carolina Conf Pensioner App # 5824
Boyd, Richard Sidney		Served as a Laborer under Col. Davis	Laborer	Richland County, South Carolina Conf Pensioner App
Boykin, Henry		Listed on the 1926 S. C. Comptroller General's List to the General Assembly		Kershaw County, South Carolina Conf Pensioner
Brannon, John	A	3rd Battalion South Carolina Reserves Served as a Laborer under Jim Cromer	Laborer	Richland County, South Carolina Conf Pensioner App # 9890
Briggs, George		16th Regiment South Carolina Infantry Also served under Capt. Franklin Bailey.	Private	Slave of Jesse Briggs (Black Jesse) of Union County, S.C. According to his statements in South Carolina Slave Narratives. Union County, South Carolina Conf Pensioner Listed on the 1926 S. C. Comptroller General's List to the General Assembly
Bright, James	F	1st Regiment South Carolina Volunteer Infantry	Musician	
Brister, Commeclore	K	3rd Regiment South Carolina Cavalry (Capt. William B. Peeples' Company) Served Under Pvt. L. Alonzo Ashley	Cook	Barnwell County, South Carolina Conf Pensioner App # 1335

Bristow, McDonald	E	19th Regiment South Carolina Infantry Served Under Pvt. William C. Luckey	Servant	Lee County, South Carolina Conf Pensioner
Brobham, Ervin (Brabham, Ervin)	C,I	1st Regiment, South Carolina Infantry (Hagood's) Served as a servant to Capt. John F. Brabham	Servant	Bamberg County, South Carolina Conf Pensioner App # 1176
Brogdon, William		Listed on the 1926 S. C. Comptroller General's List to the General Assembly	Private	Williamsburg County, South Carolina Conf Pensioner
Brown, Anderson		Listed on the 1926 S. C. Comptroller General's List to the General Assembly	Private	Barnwell County, South Carolina Conf Pensioner
Brown, Andrew	B	2nd Regiment South Carolina Artillery (Capt. I. W. Lancaster's Company) Served Under J. E. Templeton	Cook	Barnwell County, South Carolina Conf Pensioner App # 1336
Brown, Green		18th Regiment South Carolina Infantry Served Under Capt. Willis	Cook	Spartanburg County, South Carolina Conf Pensioner App # 10575
Brown, Henry	E / I	1st Regiment South Carolina (Darlington Guards) 8th Regiment South Carolina 21st Regiment South Carolina (Capt. S.H. Wilds' Co.)	Drummer	FMC
Brown, Henry	F&S	21st Regiment South Carolina Infantry (Hagwood's Brigade)	Hq Staff	
Brown, Leonard		Listed on the 1926 S. C. Comptroller General's List to the General Assembly		Florence County, South Carolina Conf Pensioner
Brown, Middleton		Unknown South Carolina Unit		
Brown, Nelson	C	7th Regiment South Carolina Infantry (Capt. Patrick H. Bradley's Company) Served as a cook under John F. Calhoun, Ed Calhoun	Cook	McCormick County, South Carolina Conf Pensioner App # 8131
Brown, Quakoo		Listed on the 1926 S. C. Comptroller General's List to the General Assembly	Private	Georgetown County, South Carolina Conf Pensioner
Brown, S. Sebastian		Unknown South Carolina Unit	Private	
Brown, Tom		Unknown South Carolina Unit	Private	
Brown, Zack	B	4th Regiment South Carolina Cavalry (Capt. Robert F. Coleman's Company) Served as a body servant to Pvt. Robert F. Cameron	Body Servant	Fairfield County, South Carolina Conf Pensioner App # 3680
Buckner, John Wilson	I	1st Regiment South Carolina Artillery Served under Capt. P.O. Gaillard and Capt. Boykin	Private	FMC, WIA. Was wounded at Ft. Wagner repulsing the U.S. (Colored) 54th Massachusetts Regiment.
Bugg, Jim	A	1st Regiment South Carolina Cavalry Served Under Pvt. George Patterson	Cook	Abbeville County, South Carolina Conf Pensioner App # 31

Bunch, Joseph	A	8th Battalion South Carolina Reserves Confederate States Army Served Under Pvt. A. A. Way	Cook	Orangeburg County, South Carolina Conf Pensioner App # 9211
Bunch, Simon		Listed on the 1926 S. C. Comptroller General's List to the General Assembly	Private	Dorchester County, South Carolina Conf Pensioner
Burgess, William Thomas	A,C	3rd Regiment, South Carolina Infantry (Capt. Thomas J. Maffett's Company) Served as a Servant to Pvt. Frank Moon	Servant	Orangeburg County, South Carolina Conf Pensioner App # 9214
Burns, Wallace	D	21st South Carolina Volunteers Served as a Laborer at Fort Sumter and Fort Johnson, S.C. under Frank Burn.	Slave	Slave of Rev. James Wilson Burn
Burnside, Sam		Serving as a Laborer on fortifications on the Sea Coast.	Laborer	Laurens County, South Carolina Conf Pensioner App
Burris, Hiram B.	I	18th South Carolina Infantry Served With His Master Pvt. William Burris	Servant	Slave, Gaston County, North Carolina Conf Pensioner
Burton, James (Burton, Larkin)	A	Hampton Legion South Carolina Infantry Regiment Served as a cook and servant to his master Henry Seigler	Servant Cook	Slave of Pvt. Henry Seigler. Aiken County, South Carolina Conf Pensioner App # 1523
Bush, Aderson		Battery And Building Bomb Troop Served under Capt. Hatcher In Charleston	Laborer	Barnwell County, South Carolina Conf Pensioner App # 1339
Butler, Ed		2nd Regiment South Carolina Cavalry Served as a servant to Frank R. Lipscomb and as an Orderly to Gen. M. C. Butler	Orderly Servant	Greenwood County, South Carolina Conf Pensioner App # 5844
Bynes, Titus		Served as a servant to his master Gabriel Flowden.	Servant	Slave of Gabriel and Diana Flowden of Clarendon County, S.C., According to his statements in Florida Slave Narratives
Byrd, Cain	K	15th Regiment South Carolina Infantry Served under Capt. Hobson Byrd	Servant	Edgefield County, South Carolina Conf Pensioner App # 3482
Caldwell, Gilbert		Listed on the 1926 S. C. Comptroller General's List to the General Assembly		Chester County, South Carolina Conf Pensioner
Caldwell, Jack		Gen. Martin W. Gary's Cavalry Brigade, Quartermaster Department	Teamster	Surrendered at Appomattox
Campbell, Paul	G	7th Regiment South Carolina Cavalry (Capt. W. H. Jefford's Company) Served as a body servant to Lt. W. G. Hinson	Body Servant	Charleston County, South Carolina Conf Pensioner App # 1773
Campbell, Tom		2nd Regiment South Carolina Cavalry (Capt. Heywards Company) Served Under William Norton	Cook	Hampton County, South Carolina Conf Pensioner

Cannon, Josh	C,F	20th Regiment South Carolina Volunteers (Capt. John M. Kinnard's Company) Served as a cook under Pvt. Henry Stone	Cook	Newberry County, South Carolina Conf Pensioner App # 8441
Cannon, L. G. W.		Served building fortifications on Sea Coast And Islands of South Carolina	Laborer	Laurens County, South Carolina Conf Pensioner App # 7019
Cannon, Press		20th Regiment South Carolina Volunteers (Capt. Ellison S. Keitt's Company) Served Under Bill Stone	Cook	Newberry County, South Carolina Conf Pensioner App # 8442
Canon, Marcus		Listed on the 1926 S. C. Comptroller General's List to the General Assembly	Private	Darlington County, South Carolina Conf Pensioner
Capers, Scipio	F	21st South Carolina Regiment Infantry (Hagwood's)	Cook	
Carmichael, Elijah	L	21st South Carolina Regiment (Capt. Hannibal Legette's Company) Served Under A.B. Carmichael	Cook	Dillon County, South Carolina Conf Pensioner App # 3187
Casey, Scipio		Served Under Charles Snowden Of Blue Hole Plantation	Body Servant	Charleston County, South Carolina Conf Pensioner App # 1776
Cave, W. T.		Unknown South Carolina Unit	Private	In 1958 his widow Minne Cave, received a pension from the U.S. Federal Government for the service of W.T. Cave during the Chill War however Mr. Cave was a Confederate Soldier. Buried at Olar, S.C.
Chambers, Anderson		Served As A Servant For The Commander of Fort Sumter	Servant	York County, South Carolina Conf Pensioner
Chance, Lloyd		Listed on the 1926 S. C. Comptroller General's List to the General Assembly	Private	Barnwell County, South Carolina Conf Pensioner
Chandler, Caesar		Listed on the 1926 S. C. Comptroller General's List to the General Assembly	Private	Williamsburg County, South Carolina Conf Pensioner
Chandler, Steve		He was sent to Virginia, and served building forts and breastworks around Petersburg, VA. He was described as a tall black man over six feet high, with broad shoulders.	Laborer	Slave of Nick Collins of Chester County, S.C. According to his son John Collins, in South Carolina Slave Narratives.
Chapman, General		3rd South Carolina Infantry Regiment Served Under Capt. George Haltiwanger	Cook	Richland County, South Carolina Conf Pensioner App # 9913
Chappell, Ben	B F	5th Regiment South Carolina Reserves 1st South Carolina State Troops Served Under Sgt. Milton Coleman	Servant	Greenwood County, South Carolina Conf Pensioner App # 5849
Charles, Jesse	I	23rd Regiment South Carolina Volunteers (Capt. H. H. Lesesne's Company) Served Under William R. Coskrey	Body Servant	Clarendon County, South Carolina Conf Pensioner App # 2765
Chase, W.	B,D	1st (Charleston) Battalion South Carolina Infantry (Gaillard's Battalion)	Musician	

Name		Service	Role	Location
Chavis, Ransom	C	2nd Regiment South Carolina Cavalry Served Under Capt. Meyer Meighan	Cook	Richland County, South Carolina Conf Pensioner App # 9915
Cherry, J. E.	D	1st Regiment, South Carolina Rifles (Orr's) (Capt. F. E. Harrison's Company)	Servant Cook	Oconee County, South Carolina Conf Pensioner App # 8910
Chiles, Wade (Childs, Wade)	B	1st Regiment, South Carolina Rifles (Orr's) (Capt. James S. Cothran's Co.) Served as a servant to J. C. Chiles, Dr. T. C. Chiles and J. S. Chiles. Gov. B. L. Bonham submitted an affidavit so support Wade Chiles pension application.	Servant	Anderson County, South Carolina Conf Pensioner App # 734
Christie, Sam		Listed on the 1926 S. C. Comptroller General's List to the General Assembly	Private	Greenwood County, South Carolina Conf Pensioner
Clardy, Yancy		Listed on the 1926 S. C. Comptroller General's List to the General Assembly	Private	Greenville County, South Carolina Conf Pensioner
Clark, Henry		Listed on the 1926 S. C. Comptroller General's List to the General Assembly	Private	Orangeburg County, South Carolina Conf Pensioner
Clark, Tom		Infantry Regiment, Holcombe Legion, South Carolina	Private	First wounded at Second Manasas. He was wounded again in Kingston, N.C. According to his son Charlie Jeff Harvey in South Carolina Slave Narratives.
Clary, Santanna	G	7th Regiment South Carolina (Capt. J. Hampden Brook's Company) Served Under Cpl. M. Wells Clary	Cook	Saluda County, South Carolina Conf Pensioner App # 10328
Clyburn, Joe		Listed on the 1926 S. C. Comptroller General's List to the General Assembly	Private	Lancaster County, South Carolina Conf Pensioner
Clyburn, Sam Sr.	G	2nd Regiment South Carolina Infantry (2" Palmetto Regiment) (Capt. C. C. Haile's Company) Servant Under 1st Lt. Thomas J. Clyburn	Body Servant	Clarendon County, South Carolina Conf Pensioner App # 2766
Cohen, Abram		Served Under Capt. Hughet	Servant	Greenwood County, South Carolina Conf Pensioner App # 5856
Coleman, Fred		Listed on the 1926 S. C. Comptroller General's List to the General Assembly	Private	Darlington County, South Carolina Conf Pensioner
Coleman, William P.		7th Regiment South Carolina Infantry Served as a cook and laundryman under W. P. Coleman	Cook Laundryman	Fairfield County, South Carolina Conf Pensioner App # 3690
Collins, Jim	E	5th Regiment South Carolina Cavalry Served Under Capt. Cornelius Sams	Cook	Charleston County, South Carolina Conf Pensioner App # 1780
Conway, Laurence (Conway, Lonnie)	F	3rd Regiment South Carolina Infantry Served Under Captain John Nance	Cook Attendant	Slave of H. J. Bailey Sr. Laurens County, South Carolina Conf Pensioner

Cooper, Amos	B	Capt. Melchers' Company (German Artillery) South Carolina Artillery Served Under Pvt. H. J. Bailey, Jr.	Cook	Georgetown County, South Carolina Conf Pensioner App # 4050
Cooper, Daniel		Brown's Battalion Reserves Guarding Prisoners At Florence, South Carolina Served Under Lt. W. A. Cooper	Servant	Sumter County, South Carolina Conf Pensioner App #11276B. Application was submitted by Probate Judge Thomas E. Richardson
Copeland, Spencer	A	3rd Regiment South Carolina Infantry (C. Garland) Worked On Fortifications On Coasts And Islands of South Carolina Served Under John Sullivan	Servant Laborer	Laurens County, South Carolina Conf Pensioner App # 7040 and # 7314
Corry, Jake		Listed on the 1926 S. C. Comptroller General's List to the General Assembly	Private	Cherokee County, South Carolina Conf Pensioner
Craig, Sam		Listed on the 1926 S. C. Comptroller General's List to the General Assembly		Fairfield County, South Carolina Conf Pensioner
Crawford, Hansel		South Carolina State Troops Served as a servant to his master Ed Crawford	Servant	Slave, Gaston County, North Carolina Conf Pensioner
Crawford, Peter	A	17th Regiment South Carolina Infantry (Capt. John R. Culp's Company) Served as a cook for Pvt. William G. Crawford	Cook	York County, South Carolina Conf Pensioner
Crawford, Sanders	A	15th Regiment, South Carolina Infantry Served as a servant to Pvt. Lawrence Beckwith	Servant	
Crawford, Scott		Listed on the 1926 S. C. Comptroller General's List to the General Assembly	Private	Chester County, South Carolina Conf Pensioner
Crayton, Jake	K	1st Regiment, South Carolina Rifles (Orr's) (Capt. Robert S. Cheshire's Company) Served Under Lt. Gus Lewis	Servant	Oconee County, South Carolina Conf Pensioner App ± 8925
Crosby, Isaac		Listed on the 1926 S. C. Comptroller General's List to the General Assembly		Colleton County, South Carolina Conf Pensioner
Cross, Council	D	3rd South Carolina Cavalry, Coicocks Regiment, (Capt. P. M. Willis' Company) Served Under R. W. McCreary	Cook	Barnwell County, South Carolina Conf Pensioner App # 1358
Cuffie, A.		Capt. Walter's Company (Washington Artillery), South Carolina Light Artillery	Cook	
Cunningham, Wyatt		South Carolina State Troops Served As A Laborer	Laborer	Slave, Union County, North Carolina Conf Pensioner
Cureton, George	E H	7th South Carolina Cavalry Infantry Regiment Holcombe Legion South Carolina Served With His Master Capt. James L. Doby	Servant	Slave, Union County, North Carolina Conf Pensioner

Daniels, Jake		(No Details provided)		Lee County, South Carolina Conf Pensioner
Daniels, Marcus	H	17th Regiment South Carolina Infantry Served Under Capt. H. M. Ray	Cook	Barnwell County, South Carolina Conf Pensioner App # 1359
Darby, Jim		1st Regiment, South Carolina Cavalry Served as a servant to Capt. James Davis Trezevant	Servant	Calhoun County, South Carolina Conf Pensioner App # 8459
Darby, Newton	A	4th Battalion South Carolina Reserves (Capt. H. C. Mosely's Company) Served Under Henry Simms	Cook	Newberry County, South Carolina Conf Pensioner App # 8459
Daton, Servant	C	Holcombe Legion, South Carolina Cavalry Battalion	Cook	
Datt, Lazarus (Datta, Lazarus)		3rd Regiment South Carolina Cavalry (Capt. Alfred Martin's Company) Servant under Elliott Solomons	Servant	Hampton County, South Carolina Conf Pensioner App # 6106
Davis, Beverly (Female)		Listed on the 1926 S. C. Comptroller General's List to the General Assembly	Private	Florence County, South Carolina Conf Pensioner
Davis, Harry		Served working as a Laborer on fortifications on the Sea Coast Served under Charles Simmons	Laborer	Laurens County, South Carolina Conf Pensioner App # 7050
Davis, Henry	K	1st Regiment South Carolina Cavalry (Capt. A. P. Brown's Company) Served under J. W. Lyles	Cook Servant	Fairfield County, South Carolina Conf Pensioner App # 3692
Davis, Isham (Davis, Isom)	I	Holcombe Legion, South Carolina Cavalry Battalion Served under Lt. John Bankston Davis	Servant	Spartanburg County, South Carolina Conf Pensioner App # 10662
Davis, June	F&S C	2nd Regiment South Carolina Cavalry (Capt. Thomas E. Scriven's Company) Cavalry Battalion, Hampton Legion, South Carolina Served under Pvt. Wiley W. McTeer	Cook	Slave of W. W. McTeer, Hampton County, South Carolina Conf Pensioner App # 6108
Davis, Nelson		7th Regiment South Carolina Cavalry Servant To Pvt. John C. Davis And Robert C. Davis	Servant Cook	Greenville County, South Carolina Conf Pensioner App # 11548D
Davis, Sam		Served as a servant and body guard to his master Thomas Sloan. He was also a forager for food.	Body Guard Servant	Slave of Thomas Sloan of Fairfield, S.C. According to his wife Louisa Davis, in South Carolina Slave
Davis, Stephens		Listed on the 1926 S. C. Comptroller General's List to the General Assembly	Private	Dillon County, South Carolina Conf Pensioner
Dawkins, John (James)		Listed on the 1926 S. C. Comptroller General's List to the General Assembly	Shoemaker	Union County, South Carolina Conf Pensioner
Dawkins, Mallory	E	15th Regiment South Carolina Infantry (Kershaw's Brigade) Served as a Servant to Col. Bunyan Davis	Body Servant Cook	Greenville County, South Carolina Conf Pensioner App # 5783

Deal, James (Jim)		South Carolina State Troops Served As A Body Servant And Body Guard To Col. Clinton Eugee	Bodyguard	Slave, Macon County, North Carolina Conf Pensioner. Resident of West's Mill, Macon County, North Carolina 1937.
Dean, Aaron	K	15th Regiment South Carolina Infantry Served as a cook under Pvt. A. Bryant Dean	Cook	Edgefield County, South Carolina Conf Pensioner App # 3509
Dean, Bob	E	2nd Regiment South Carolina Cavalry Served Under Capt. A. H. Dean	Cook	
Dean, Elias		Hoods Company, Hawthorns Regiment (Capt. Tom Denby's Company) Served under Jessie Wilbling	Waitman	Greenwood County, South Carolina Conf Pensioner App # 5877
Dean, Henry	E	2nd Regiment South Carolina Cavalry Served Under Capt. George B. Dean	Cook	Spartanburg County, South Carolina Conf Pensioner App # 10666
DeLoach, Richard	D	3rd Regiment South Carolina Cavalry (Capt. G. W. Kirkland's Company) Served as a Cook Under Sgt. Bower	Cook	Allendale County, South Carolina Conf Pensioner App # 574
Dennis, Henry		Listed on the 1926 S. C. Comptroller General's List to the General Assembly		Darlington County, South Carolina Conf Pensioner
Dennis, Jackson	A	15th Battalion, South Carolina Heavy Artillery (Lucas'), (Capt. Robertson's Company) Served under Pvt. Edward J. Brady	Cook	Abbeville County, South Carolina Conf Pensioner App # 98
Dennis, Wesley		Listed on the 1926 S. C. Comptroller General's List to the General Assembly	Private	Lexington County, South Carolina Conf Pensioner
Desaussure, Albert	K	3rd South Carolina Infantry Regiment Served under Edgar Clarkson And Eugene Clarkson	Servant	Richland County, South Carolina Conf Pensioner App # 9950
Dickerson, Robert	G	17th Regiment South Carolina Infantry Served under Capt. Josiah Dickinson	Cook	Barnwell County, South Carolina Conf Pensioner App # 1363
Donnelly, Ben	C	2nd Regiment South Carolina Volunteers (Capt. W. F. Davis' Company)	Cook	Marion County, South Carolina Conf Pensioner App # 7991
Douglas, Simon		Served as a laborer building trenches and shod horses. **ALSO SERVED The Union with the cavalry shoding horses.**	Laborer Holster	
Dozier, Mims		7th South Carolina Cavalry	Private	Hinds County, MS Conf Pensioner
Drakeford, Washington	E	2nd Regiment South Carolina Infantry (2nd Palmetto Regiment) Served as a cook under Capt. Joseph J. Drakeford	Cook	Kershaw County, South Carolina Conf Pensioner App # 6597
Drayton, Cato L.		Capt. Ed L. Parkers Battery, (Marion Artillery), South Carolina Light Artillery Served Under J. R. P. Ravenel	Cook	Charleston County, South Carolina Conf Pensioner App # 1803

Drayton, Isaac	A	Manigault's Battalion, South Carolina Volunteers (Infantry, Artillery and Cavalry) (Capt. Elias Venning's Company) Served Under Pvt. Philip Pepper	Servant	Charleston County, South Carolina Conf Pensioner App # 1804
Drummond, Milton	E	Capt. Hamilton's Company Provost Guard, South Carolina 2nd Regiment South Carolina (Capt. George B. Dean's Company) Served Under Pvt. H. E. Drummond	Laborer	Spartanburg County, South Carolina Conf Pensioner App # 10681
Duff, Rose (Female)		1st (Orr's) South Carolina Rifles	Cook Laundres	
Dunbar, Boston	G	2nd Regiment South Carolina Artillery Served working on Battery under Capt. Alexander Willingham and 2-a Lt George Black	Laborer	Barnwell County, South Carolina Conf Pensioner App # 1364
Edward, Cold	B	27th South Carolina infantry (Gaillard's Regiment) Lafayette Artillery, South Carolina Artillery (Capt. J. T. Kanapaux's Company)	Drummer	
Edwards, Bright		Listed on the 1926 S. C. Comptroller General's List to the General Assembly	Private	Florence County, South Carolina Conf Pensioner
Edwards, Ned		Listed on the 1926 S. C. Comptroller General's List to the General Assembly	Private	Chester County, South Carolina Conf Pensioner
Egleston, Sam	C	6th Regiment South Carolina Cavalry (Aiken's Partisan Rangers) (1st Partisan Rangers) (Capt. Goodwin, Col. Aiken's Regiment, Butler's Brigade) Served as a servant under Pvt. J. W. Coleman	Waitman	Fairfield County, South Carolina Conf Pensioner App # 3702
Ellerbe, Isaac	G H	21st Regiment South Carolina Infantry 6th Regiment South Carolina Cavalry Served Under Zachariah (Zack) Ellerbe	Cook	Chesterfield County, South Carolina Conf Pensioner App # 2615E
Hick, E.	F	Holcombe Legion, South Carolina Infantry Regiment	Servant-	
Elliott, Gas	C	5th Regiment South Carolina Reserves (90 Days, 1862-3.), (Capt. T. W. Whatley's Company) Served Under David (Dave) Shaw	Servant	Aiken County, South Carolina Conf Pensioner App # 306
Ellis, Calep		No other Information provided	Servant	Orangeburg County, South Carolina Conf Pensioner App # 9269
Feaster, Jerry		Listed on the 1926 S. C. Comptroller General's List to the General Assembly	Private	Chester County, South Carolina Conf Pensioner
Feaster, Robert		Listed on the 1926 S. C. Comptroller General's List to the General Assembly	Private	Chester County, South Carolina Conf Pensioner
February, Cold	B	27th South Carolina Infantry (Gaillard's Regiment)	Cook	

Felder, Henry		Listed on the 1926 S. C. Comptroller General's List to the General Assembly	Private	Bramberg County, South Carolina Conf Pensioner
Fewell, Samuel		Listed on the 1926 S. C. Comptroller General's List to the General Assembly	Private	Cherokee County, South Carolina Conf Pensioner
Field, Joe		Listed on the 1926 S. C. Comptroller General's List to the General Assembly	Private	Darlington County, South Carolina Conf Pensioner
Finley, Amos	E	11th South Carolina Infantry (9th South Carolina Volunteers) (Capt. Mikler) Served under Augustus Finley (Capt. John H. Mickler's Company)	Cook Servant	Hampton County, South Carolina Conf Pensioner App # 6118
Floyd, Henry	C	1st Battalion, South Carolina Sharpshooters Served As A Servant Under Capt. Henry Buist	Cook Servant	Barnwell County, South Carolina Conf Pensioner App # 1372
Floyd, William	G	27th South Carolina Infantry (Gaillard's Regiment)	Cook	
Footman, Josh	❏	1st Regiment South Carolina Infantry Served Under Capt. John Sellers (Col. Olin Dantzler's Company)	Cook	Dorchester County, South Carolina Conf Pensioner App # 3353
Ford, Edwin P.	A	21st Regiment South Carolina Infantry (Col. Graham, Gen. Harley) Served Under J. Harieston Read	Cook Drummer	Georgetown County, South Carolina Conf Pensioner App # 4061
Ford, Frederick		Served Under Shackelford In Confederate Army (Capt. Brown, Gen. Napier) Pvt. Benjamin P. Fraser submitted affidavit	Cook Wagon Driver	Georgetown County, South Carolina Conf Pensioner App # 4062
Ford, Henry James	A	7th Regiment South Carolina Cavalry Served under Capt. John Tucker In Marions Men Of Winyah.	Cook	Georgetown County, South Carolina Conf Pensioner App # 4063
Foxworth, William H.	D	12th Battalion South Carolina Cavalry Served As A Laborer On Breastworks In Charleston Under 1stLt E. A. Coleman	Laborer	Marion County, South Carolina Conf Pensioner App # 7999
Franklin, Jerry D.		Listed on the 1926 S. C. Comptroller General's List to the General Assembly	Private	Colleton County, South Carolina Conf Pensioner
Franklin, Trus	F	10th Regiment South Carolina Volunteers (Capt. Miller) Served Under Capt. B. Frank Davis	Cook	Marion County, South Carolina Conf Pensioner App # 8000
Franks, Ben	D	3rd Battalion, South Carolina Infantry Served Under John M. Franks	Cook Attendant	Laurens County, South Carolina Conf Pensioner App # 7085
Franks, Benjamin	A	1st Regiment South Carolina Infantry (McCreary's) (1st	Cook	
Frasier, Henry		Listed on the 1926 S. C. Comptroller General's List to the General Assembly	Private	Darlington County, South Carolina Conf Pensioner

Directory of African American Confederates in the U.S. Civil War

Frazier, Marcus (Markus)		Served As An Attendant To Capt. James Frazier	Attendant	Abbeville County, South Carolina Conf Pensioner App
Fuller, Dan	D	4th Battalion South Carolina Reserves Served Under 1st Lt James	Cook Attendant	Laurens County, South Carolina Conf Pensioner App # 7090
Funchess, July		Confederate States Army Served Under Col. D. R.	Servant	Orangeburg County, South Carolina Conf Pensioner
Gaillard, Philip		104th Regiment South Carolina (Capt. Manigault) I believe this is a U.S. Unit. (U.S.C.T.)? However he submitted for and received a Confederate Pension.	Wagoner	Georgetown County, South Carolina Conf Pensioner App # 4064
Galluchat, July		Served as a Laborer on the fortifications at Charleston, was wounded at Fort Sumter.	Laborer	Clarendon County, South Carolina Conf Pensioner
Gantt, Ed		1st Battalion South Carolina Sharpshooters (Capt. Black) Serving As A Cook Under John Aaron	Cook	Barnwell County, South Carolina Conf Pensioner App # 1373
Gantt, F. W.	A	4th Regiment South Carolina Served Under Capt. Robinson	Helper	Aiken County, South Carolina Conf Pensioner
Gantt, Will		Listed on the 1926 S. C. Comptroller General's List to the General Assembly	Private	Aiken County, South Carolina Conf Pensioner
Gardner, Seymour	H	1st Regiment South Carolina Infantry (Gregg's)	Musician	
Garland, Prince		Listed on the 1926 S. C. Comptroller General's List to the Genera. Assembly	Private	Florence County, South Carolina Conf Pensioner
Garner, James		Served at Fort Sumter as a Laborer	Laborer	Richland County, South Carolina Conf Pensioner App
Garrett, George W.		1st Colored Company, South Carolina	Private	Shelby County, TN Conf Pensioner App # C244,
Garrett, Robert		Listed on the 1926 S. C. Comptroller General's List to the General Assembly	Private	Greenville County, South Carolina Conf Pensioner
Garris, George	C,D	Manigault's Battalion, South Carolina Artillery	Chief Teamste	
Gasque, John	A	Garys Regiment, South Carolina (Capt. Albert Thomas) Served Under James Williams	Cook	Georgetown County, South Carolina Conf Pensioner App # 4065
Gass, Elliott		Listed on the 1926 S. C. Comptroller General's List to the General Assembly	Private	Aiken County, South Carolina Conf Pensioner
Gaston, James		Listed on the 1926 S. C. Comptroller General's List to the General Assembly	Private	Chester County, South Carolina Conf Pensioner
Gentry, Samuel		Listed on the 1926 S. C. Comptroller General's List to the General Assembly	Private	Greenville County, South Carolina Conf Pensioner
Geter, Peter		Listed on the 1926 S. C. Comptroller General's List to the General Assembly	Private	Barnwell County, South Carolina Conf Pensioner
Gethers, Sandy		2nd Regiment South Carolina Artillery Served Under Capt. Bacon	Cook	Barnwell County, South Carolina Conf Pensioner App # 1375

Giles, Charlie R.	D	5th South Carolina Infantry Served as a bodyguard to his master Capt. John	Bodyguard	Slave of Capt. John Giles
Giles, James	1	3rd Regiment, South Carolina Cavalry (Capt. J. Seabrook's Company) Served Under Townsend Mikell	Cook	Charleston County, South Carolina Conf Pensioner App # 1816
Ginn, Ransom		3rd South Carolina Cavalry (Kirks Squadron) (Capt. J. Manning) Served Under Samuel J. Lewis	Cook Servant	Hampton County, South Carolina Conf Pensioner App # 6120
Givins, George		Listed on the 1926 S. C. Comptroller General's List to the General Assembly	Private	Barnwell County, South Carolina Conf Pensioner
Glover, Frank	F	2nd Regiment South Carolina Artillery (Fredericks' Regiment) (Capt. Thomas Legare) Served Under 2nd Lt. J. B. Connor	Body Servant	Orangeburg County, South Carolina Conf Pensioner App # 9309
Gold, Smith		Listed on the 1926 S. C. Comptroller General's List to the General Assembly	Private	Bramberg County, South Carolina Conf Pensioner
Gooding, Joe	D,G	11th Regiment, South Carolina Infantry (9th Volunteers) Served Under Maj. John J. Gooding	Servant	Allendale County, South Carolina Conf Pensioner App # 577
Goodwin, Kit		2nd Regiment South Carolina Cavalry Served Under Col. Frank Hampton	Servant	Richland County, South Carolina Conf Pensioner App # 9994
Gothers, Sandy		Listed on the 1926 S. C. Comptroller General's List to the General Assembly	Private	Barnwell County, South Carolina Conf Pensioner
Grant, Alfred		Served as a Laborer in the Confederate Government Hospital, at James Island	Laborer	Laurens County, South Carolina Conf Pensioner App # 7110
Grant, Fred		Served as an attendant to Capt. Glick	Attendant	Abbeville County, South Carolina Conf Pensioner App
Grant, Wesley		Served as a Laborer on Fortifications In Charleston and adjacent islands	Laborer	Laurens County, South Carolina Conf Pensioner App # 7111
Grantham, John		Listed on the 1926 S. C. Comptroller General's List to the General Assembly	Private	Colleton County, South Carolina Conf Pensioner
Graves, John	F	1st Regiment South Carolina Volunteer Infantry (Gregg's)	Musician	
Gray, George	K	2nd Regiment South Carolina Cavalry	Cook	Greenville County, South Carolina
Green, Elijah	D	2nd Regiment, South Carolina Artillery Served as a servant to his master's son 1stLt. William H. Jones	Servant	Slave of Lt. William H. Jones who deserted and hid in his attic until the end of the war. According to his statement in the South Carolina Slave Narratives.
Green, Jacob	A	5th Regiment South Carolina Cavalry (Capt. Craig And Capt. Henry McIver) Served with his master William Benton and as a cook in the company mess.	Cook	Slave of William Benton. Chesterfield County, South Carolina Conf Pensioner App # 2612

Green, P.	F&S	1st Regiment South Carolina Infantry (Hagood's)	Musician	
Green, Richard	K	5th Regiment South Carolina Served as a servant to his master Gen. Jim Green	Servant	Slave of Gen. Jim Green. Spartanburg County, South Carolina Conf Pensioner App # 10720
Greene, Charles		Listed on the 1926 S. C. Comptroller General's List to the General Assembly	Private	Barnwell County, South Carolina Conf Pensioner
Gregory, Coleman	A	18th Regiment South Carolina Infantry (Capt. Robert McBeth's Company) Served as a cook and servant to Pvt. Harvey Gregory	Cook Servant	Spartanburg County, South Carolina Conf Pensioner App # 10723
Gregory, John		Listed on the 1926 S. C. Comptroller General's List to the General Assembly	Private	Union County, South Carolina Conf Pensioner
Grice, Joe	D	8th Regiment South Carolina Served Under J. W. Singletory	Bodyguard Forager	Dillon County, South Carolina Conf Pensioner App # 3216
Gridison, William		Served Under Capt. Haskell And Capt. Huffman	Laborer	Richland County, South Carolina Conf Pensioner App
Griffin, Ben P.	H	4th Regiment South Carolina (Capt. James A. Griffin) Served as a laborer at Fort	Laborer	Pickens County, South Carolina Conf Pensioner App # 9667
Gunter, Harry		Served as a Laborer around Charleston, South Carolina	Laborer	Slave of Dr. William Weston. Richland County, South Carolina Conf Pensioner App
Guy, Adam		Served Under Capt. Roberson	Servant	York County, South Carolina Conf Pensioner
Haltiwanger, Abe	E	3rd Regiment South Carolina wilkes Served Under J. 0. Turnipseed and Capt. James D. Nance	Cook	Newberry County, South Carolina Conf Pensioner App # 8507
Hampton, James (Jim)		4th Regiment South Carolina Served Under Capt. Samuel Wilkes who was Killed in Action, Jim Hampton accompanied the body home.	Servant	Anderson County, South Carolina Conf Pensioner App # 850. He is buried at the Welfare Church in the Neal's Creek area of Belton, in Anderson County.
Hardy, Derry (Hardee, Derry)	D I	3rd Regiment Infantry North Carolina 44th Regiment Infantry North Carolina Served Under Capt. Calvin Mills	Servant	Georgetown County, South Carolina Conf Pensioner App # 4070
Harmon, Elisha	B	26th Regiment, South Carolina Infantry	Private	Died as a P.O.W. at Douglas Hospital,
Harmon, John		Served as a servant under Mid Singley	Servant	Richland County, South Carolina Conf Pensioner App
Harrell, Scip	D	12th Battalion South Carolina Cavalry Served As A Laborer On Breastworks In Charleston Under 1stLt E. A. Coleman	Laborer	Marion County, South Carolina Conf Pensioner App # 8015
Harris, Henry	A	1st Regiment, South Carolina Rifles (Orr's) Served as a Laborer under Pvt. Samuel Hester	Laborer	Oconee County, South Carolina Conf Pensioner App # 8980
Harris, James	E	5th Regiment South Carolina Infantry Served Under William Crosby	Cook	Slave, York County, South Carolina Conf Pensioner

Harris, Joe	C	19th Regiment South Carolina Infantry (Capt. John Quattlebaum's Company) Served as a Servant to 1st Lt. John B. Harris	Servant	Saluda County, South Carolina Conf Pensioner App # 10371
Harrison, Alex	B	2r Regiment South Carolina Infantry Capt. P. A. McMichael's Company) Served Under Col. Olin Dantzen	Servant	Aiken County, South Carolina Conf Pensioner App # 354
Harrison, Gus		Served as a servant to Guss White	Servant	Aiken County, South Carolina Conf Pensioner App # 355
Harrison, Joe		Listed on the 1926 S. C. Comptroller General's List to the General Assembly	Private	Colleton County, South Carolina Conf Pensioner
Harrison, March Sr.	B	14th Regiment South Carolina Infantry (Capt, Tillman Watson's Company) Servant Under James Foster And Haus Boatwright	Servant	Aiken County, South Carolina Conf Pensioner App # 356
Harrison, Warren	B	Hampton Legion South Carolina Infantry Regiment Served under General Martin W. Gary, Capt. Summerfield Gary	Servant	Greenwood County, South Carolina Conf Pensioner App # 5920
Hart, Tillman	K	7th Regiment South Carolina (Capt. Bradley) Served Under John W. Bartley	Cook	Edgefield County, South Carolina Conf Pensioner App # 3545
Hartley, Robert		Listed on the 1926 S. C. Comptroller General's List to the General Assembly	Private	Lexington County, South Carolina Conf Pensioner
Harvey, Unknown		Holcombe Legion, South Carolina Cavalry Battalion	Private	WIA. He was the father of Jeff Charlie Harvey
Hay, Cato		Served As A Laborer Under Easterling And Weathersbee. Easterling was the overseer.	Laborer	Barnwell County, South Carolina Conf Pensioner App # 1403
Haynes, Jenkins	A	3rd Regiment South Carolina Cavalry (Capt. Lowery) Served Under Claudius Haynes	Cook	Hampton County, South Carolina Conf Pensioner App # 6136
Hearne, Sam		1st South Carolina Infantry (Rifles)	Servant	Grenada County, MS Conf Pensioner
Hearst, Wesley	A	Confederate Army Served Under Capt. Tim Lipscomb	Cook	Greenwood County, South Carolina Conf Pensioner App # 5924
Hemphill, Burrei		Slave Who Stayed at Home to Protect The Home and family.	Servant	Slave. Of Robert Hemphill, Chester County, Was Killed By Gen. Sherman's Soldiers For Refusing to turn over his Master's Silverware.
Henry, Addison	A	3rd Battalion South Carolina Infantry (Capt. Townsend) Served Under Sudy Teague, John Finley, And William Finley	Cook Attendant	Laurens County, South Carolina Conf Pensioner App # 7135
Hiers, Lawton (Hiero, Lawton)	C	1st Regiment, South Carolina Infantry (Hagood's) (Capt. Isaac S. Bamberg's Company)	Laborer	Bamberg County, South Carolina Conf Pensioner App # 1214

Hill, Adam	C	6th Regiment South Carolina Cavalry (Capt. Peter W. Goodwin's Company) Served Under John Kellar	Cook	Saluda County, South Carolina Conf Pensioner App # 10375
Hinds, Smart		Listed on the 1926 S. C. Comptroller General's List to the General Assembly	Private	Florence County, South Carolina Conf Pensioner
Hinton, Joseph	M	7th Regiment South Carolina (Capt. Brooks) Served Under William F. Seay	Servant	Richland County, South Carolina Conf Pensioner App # 10029
Hobson, Sylvester	B	4th Regiment South Carolina State Troops Served Under Capt. William S. Hobson	Servant	Spartanburg County, South Carolina Conf Pensioner App # 10771
Hodges, George	G	1st Regiment, South Carolina Rifles (Orr's) Served Under Capt. William W. Higgins	Cook Laundryman	Greenwood County, South Carolina Conf Pensioner App # 5929
Holmes, Gilbert	G	20th Regiment, South Carolina Infantry Served Under Pvt. Edward (Eddie) Andrews	Servant	Orangeburg County, South Carolina Conf Pensioner App # 9336
Hood, Thomas		Served as a Laborer On Fortifications Of Charleston and surrounding Islands.	Laborer	Laurens County, South Carolina Conf Pensioner App # 7143
Hook, William (Dannelly, Daniel)	D	20th Regiment, South Carolina Infantry Served Under Capt. (Dr.) Richard (Dick)V. Dannelly building breastworks on James and Sullivan Island's under Capt. Gregg	Servant	Orangeburg County, South Carolina Conf Pensioner App # 9338
Howard, Stephen (Steven)		Served Under Capt. Williams	Laborer Cook	Greenwood County, South Carolina Conf Pensioner App # 5932
Howell, Samuel		Served as a servant under Townsend	Servant	Calhoun County, South Carolina Conf Pensioner App
Hudley, Henry		Listed on the 1926 S. C. Comptroller General's List to the General Assembly	Private	Chesterfield County, South Carolina Conf Pensioner
Hunter, Tom	G	3rd Regiment South Carolina Infantry (Capt. R. P. Todd's Company) Served under (Dr.) Pvt. J. P. Hunter	Cook Servant	Laurens County, South Carolina Conf Pensioner App # 7149
Hutcherson, Charles (Hutchinson, Charlie)	F	2nd Regiment South Carolina Infantry (Capt. W. C. Vance's Company) Served Under Sole Hutcherson	Cook	Greenwood County, South Carolina Conf Pensioner App # 5934
Ingram, Sandy		South Carolina State Troops Served With His Master Maj. Thomas J. Ingram, Helped Build Breastworks At Frazier's Point, South Carolina	Laborer	Slave Of Maj. Thomas J. Ingram. Anson County, North Carolina Conf Pensioner
Isom, Hall		6th South Carolina Infantry	Private	Attala County, MS Conf Pensioner
Ison, Isaac		Listed on the 1926 S. C. Comptroller General's List to the General Assembly	Private	Florence County, South Carolina Conf Pensioner
Jackson, Berryman		Holcombe Legion, South Carolina Infantry Regiment	Teamster	

Jackson, Dennis		Listed on the 1926 S. C. Comptroller General's List to the General Assembly		Abbeville County, South Carolina Conf Pensioner
Jackson, Griffin (Jackson, Griffith)	A	2nd Regiment South Carolina Rifles Served as a cook under Sgt. John W. Calvert	Cook	Greenwood County, South Carolina Conf Pensioner App # 5936
Jacobs, Richard		Served As A Laborer Under Government Control.	Laborer	Barnwell County, South Carolina Conf Pensioner App # 1409
Jaggers, Charles	H	7th Battalion South Carolina Infantry (Rions Battalion) Served Under Capt. Boyd	Teamster	Richland County, South Carolina Conf Pensioner App # 10054
James, Charles	A A	9th Regiment, South Carolina Reserves 3rd Regiment, South Carolina Infantry Gunells Battalion South Carolina Served Under William T. Chappell	Cook	Spartanburg County, South Carolina Conf Pensioner App # 10793
Jamison, Aaron (Jemerson, Aaron)	K	3rd Regiment South Carolina Cavalry (Capt. William B. Peeples Company) Served Under Capt. Estes	Cook	Allendale County, South Carolina Conf Pensioner App # 589
Jenkins, Esaw	D	2nd Regiment South Carolina Infantry (Capt. H. H. Hydrick's Company) Served Under Pvt. John H. Nettles	Cook	Dorchester County, South Carolina Conf Pensioner App # 3372
Jenkins, Jeff	H	20th Regiment, South Carolina Infantry Served as a servant to Dr. Thomas Zimmerman.	Servant	Spartanburg County, South Carolina Conf Pensioner App # 10797
Jenkins, Jethro	C	20th Regiment, South Carolina Infantry Served as a servant to Capt. Cornelius Sams and Capt. Elias Venning	Servant	Charleston County, South Carolina Conf Pensioner App # 1843
Jenkins, Nelson		Listed on the 1926 S. C. Comptroller General's List to the General Assembly		Orangeburg County, South Carolina Conf Pensioner
John, Jack		Listed on the 1926 S. C. Comptroller General's List to the General Assembly		Florence County, South Carolina Conf Pensioner
Johnson, Albert		Listed on the 1926 S. C. Comptroller General's List to the General Assembly		Lexington County, South Carolina Conf Pensioner
Johnson, Edward	H	2nd Regiment South Carolina Cavalry Served Under Pvt. Toland R. Bass	Cook	Calhoun County, South Carolina Conf Pensioner App # 1699
Johnson, Hector, R.	B,D, G	11th Regiment, South Carolina Infantry (9th Volunteers) (90 days 1862-63) Served under Capt. W. D. McMillan		Dorchester County, South Carolina Conf Pensioner App # 3371
Johnson, Henry	H	11th Regiment, South Carolina Infantry (9th Volunteers), (Capt. Christopher Gaillard's Company) Served Under Pvt. Oliver Russell	Laborer	Berkeley County, South Carolina Conf Pensioner App # 1612

Johnson, Merriman	B	44th South Carolina Militia Regiment (Capt. D. J. Bradham's Company) Served As A Servant o Ellison H. Smyth	Servant	Clarendon County, ,South Carolina Conf Pensioner App # 2767
Johnson, Noh (Noah)	C	2nd Regiment South Carolina Cavalry Served Under Capt. James P. McFie	Servant	Richland County, South Carolina Conf Pensioner App # 10057
Johnson, Preston		Served Building Fortifications In Charleston, South Carolina	Laborer	Marion County, South Carolina Conf Pensioner
Johnson, Robert	E	3rd Regiment South Carolina Infantry (Capt. James D. Nance's Company) Served Under Dr. David E. Ewart (Surgeon)	Cook	Newberry County, South Carolina Conf Pensioner App # 8541
Johnson, William		Listed on the 1926 S. C. Comptroller General's List to the General Assembly	Private	Clarendon County, South Carolina Conf Pensioner
Jones, Henry		Served under Capt. White	Cook	Abbeville County, South Carolina Conf Pensioner App
Jones, Isiah		Listed on the 1926 S. C. Comptroller General's List to the General Assembly	Private	Lexington County, South Carolina Conf Pensioner
Jones, Jackson		Listed on the 1926 S. C. Comptroller General's List to the General Assembly	Private	Lexington County, South Carolina Conf Pensioner
Jones, William	A	1st Regiment, South Carolina Infantry (Hagood's) (Capt. Alfred J. Frederick's Company) Served as a cook under Cpl. Benjamin Izlar	Cook	Orangeburg County, South Carolina Conf Pensioner App # 9375
Jordan, Cold		Ward's Battery South Carolina Light Artillery Captain Mayham Ward's Company	Musician	
Jordan, Luke		Listed on the 1926 S. C. Comptroller General's List to the General Assembly	Private	Chester County, South Carolina Conf Pensioner
July, Galluchut		Served as a Laborer in The Charleston Area Fortifications, Wounded At Ft. Sumter, Sept. 1863	Laborer	Clarendon County, South Carolina Conf Pensioner
Kearse, Preston		Served as a servant to Tom Ealy and worked on building fortifications.	Servant	Bamberg County, South Carolina Conf Pensioner App # 1230
Keel, Daniel	F	2nd Regiment South Carolina Artillery (Capt. Lagree's Company) Served as a cook under Mike Odowd	Cook	Barnwell County, South Carolina Conf Pensioner App # 1420
Keith, Elias	A	1st Regiment South Carolina Infantry	Cook	Greenville County, South Carolina Conf Pensioner
Keith, Ferdinand		Listed on the 1926 S. C. Comptroller General's List to the General Assembly	Private	Darlington County, South Carolina Conf Pensioner
Kelly, Ansel	G	2nd Regiment South Carolina Artillery Served as a cook under Capt. George W. Stallings	Cook	Aiken County, South Carolina Conf Pensioner App # 396

Directory of African American Confederates in the U.S. Civil War

Kelly, Carolina (Female)		Listed on the 1926 S. C. Comptroller General's List to the General Assembly	Private	Florence County, South Carolina Conf Pensioner
Kennedy, D. R.	F	3rd South Carolina Infantry South Carolina State Troops Served As A Servant To William McClure	Servant	Slave, Gaston County, North Carolina Conf Pensioner
Kershaw, Eli	B	Holcombe Legion, South Carolina Cavalry Battalion	Teamster	
King, Adam	H	17th South Carolina Infantry Served As A Body Servant To His Master Frank Love Of York County, South Carolina	Body Servant	Slave, Cleveland County, North Carolina Conf Pensioner
Knight, L. K.	A	Hampton Legion, South Carolina Artillery Battalion, Served as a servant to his master Dr. James Perry Knight,	Cook	Slave of Dr. J. P. Knight. Oconee County, South Carolina Conf Pensioner App # 9009. He was wounded at Petersburg, Virginia
Ladson, S. W.		Washington's Artillery (Capt. George H. Waiter's Company)	Cook	Charleston County, South Carolina Conf Pensioner App # 1849
Laney, Isaac		Listed on the 1926 5. C. Comptroller General's List to the General Assembly		Florence County, South Carolina Conf Pensioner
Lark, Summerfield (Lark, Sumer L.)	B	3rd Regiment South Carolina Cavalry (Capt. Gary) Served Under Cpl. Dennis Lark	Cook	Newberry County, South Carolina Conf Pensioner App # 8559
Laurel', Bill	C	3rd Regiment South Carolina (Capt. Gregory) Served Under J. E. Robinson	Cook	Jasper County, South Carolina Conf Pensioner App # 6504
Lawrence, Esau	A	7th Regiment South Carolina Cavalry (Capt. John Tucker's Company) Served under Cpl. G. G. Ford.	Hostler	Georgetown County, South Carolina Conf Pensioner App # 4077
Lawton, Charles (Lawton, Charlie)		Beaufort Light Artillery Battery, South Carolina (Capt. Stephen Elliott's Company) Served Under William Hutson Townsend	Cook	Orangeburg County, South Carolina Conf Pensioner App # 9389
Lee, Isaac		Listed on the 1926 S. C. Comptroller General's List to the General Assembly		Florence County, South Carolina Conf Pensioner
Lee, Jacob	D	2nd Regiment South Carolina Infantry (Capt. H. H. Hydrick's Company) Served as a servant to John Henry Browning, J. Browning, and Stephen Browning.	Servant	Dorchester County, South Carolina Conf Pensioner App # 3380
Lee, Samuel Jones	F	14th Regiment South Carolina Infantry	Servant	FMC
Lee, William M.		7th South Carolina Cavalry	Servant	Pearl River County, MS Conf Pensioner
Leech, Sam		Served As A Servant For The Commander of Fort Sumter	Servant	York County, South Carolina Conf Pensioner
Lemon, Willis		(Capt. Isaac Johnston's Company) Served as a servant to Dr. Aquilla Johnston	Servant	Dorchester County, South Carolina Conf Pensioner App # 3382

Name		Service	Role	Notes
Lewis, Peter		Served with has master Evans Lewis at Fort Sumter for four years.	Servant	Slave of Evans Lewis, of the Evans Lewis Plantation. According to his daughter, Heddie Davis, in South Carolina Slave Narratives.
Lightener, Frank		Listed on the 1926 S. C. Comptroller General's List to the General Assembly	Private	Chester County, South Carolina Conf Pensioner
Lightner, Alex (Leitner, Alex)		3rd Battalion South Carolina Reserves (Capt. John McLurkin, Maj. Giles) Served Under Butler Estes	Cook	Fairfield County, South Carolina Conf Pensioner App # 3736
Linsay, E. J.		Listed on the 1926 S. C. Comptroller General's List to the General Assembly	Private	Union County, South Carolina Conf Pensioner
Littlejohn, Elijah		Listed on the 1926 S. C. Comptroller General's List to the General Assembly	Private	Cherokee County, South Carolina Conf Pensioner
Lloyd, Chance	C	8th Battalion, South Carolina Reserves (Stalling's) (Capt. C. C. Cooper's Company) Served as a cook under Maj. W. W. Hutto	Cook	Barnwell County, South Carolina Conf Pensioner App # 1426
Loadholt, Miles	F	3rd Regiment South Carolina Cavalry (Smart's Company) Served under D.O. Loadholt And A. R. Loadholt	Cook	Allendale County, South Carolina Conf Pensioner App # 601
Logan, Dick	F&S	3rd Regiment South Carolina Reserves (90	Musician	
Logan, James Scott	F	17th Regiment South Carolina Infantry "Evans Tramp Brigade" Served as a Body Servant to Lt. D. J. Logan	Body Servant	
Logan, West	F	2nd Regiment South Carolina Volunteers (Capt. Bill Perriman's Company) Served Under Jim, Bill And Pinkney Morrow And Ed Smith	Cook Laundryman	Greenwood County, South Carolina Conf Pensioner App # 8925
Logan, William B.		25th Regiment South Carolina Volunteers (Capt. Sellers) Served as a servant to R. D. Zimmerman, Also served at a hospital after his master was killed at Petersburg, Virginia.	Servant	Sumter County, South Carolina Conf Pensioner App #11276B. Application was submitted by Probate Judge Thomas E. Richardson
Long, Daniel Albright	C	2nd Regiment North Carolina Service Under Col. Wash	Private	Florence County, South Carolina Conf Pensioner App
Lyman, T. M.	D	2nd Regiment South Carolina Infantry (2 Palmetto Regiment)	Cook	
Mack, Daniel		Listed on the 1926 S. C. Comptroller General's List to the General Assembly		Charleston County, South Carolina Conf Pensioner
Mack, Sam	K	4th Regiment South Carolina Infantry Served as a servant to his master Capt. Julius Lewis Shanklin	Cook	Charleston County, South Carolina Conf Pensioner App # 1862

Mackey, Jeff		3rd Battalion South Carolina Infantry 2nd Regiment South Carolina Infantry	Cook	Slave Of Dr. J. F. Mackey, York County, South Carolina Conf Pensioner
Makin, Matthew		Col. Butlers Regiment South Carolina Served as a servant to A. W. Moore	Servant	Greenwood County, South Carolina Conf Pensioner App # 5957
March, Cold	A	1st (Charleston) Battalion South Carolina Infantry (Gaillard's Battalion)	Musician	
Marshall, Heyward (Marshall, Haywood)	S	5th Regiment South Carolina Infantry Served Under Dr. J. Rufus Bratton	Servant	York County, South Carolina Conf Pensioner
Martin, W. M.		Listed on the 1926 S. C. Comptroller General's List to the General Assembly		Colleton County, South Carolina Conf Pensioner
Martin, William		Listed on the 1926 S. C. Comptroller General's List to the General Assembly		Edgefield County, South Carolina Conf Pensioner
Masterman, Jacob	B	1st (Charleston) Battalion South Carolina Infantry (Gaillard's Battalion)	Cook	
Mattison, Marshall		Provost Guard, Columbia South Carolina (Capt. R. D. Senn's Company) Served Under Wyatt Mattison ,	Cook	Anderson County, South Carolina Conf Pensioner App #939. He was the son of Docie and Nelson Mattison and was born April 2, 1850. He is buried at Mt. Zion Church in Belton, SC.
Maysant, William	F,G	3rd Regiment South Carolina Reserves (90 Days	Musician Nurse	
Mazyck, Peter	H	1st Regiment South Carolina Infantry (Gregg's) 1st Regiment South Carolina Infantry (Hagood's)	Musician	
McAllister, Andrew	G	1st Regiment South Carolina Cavalry (Capt. J. L. Johnson's Company)	Cook	Abbeville County, South Carolina Conf Pensioner App # 128
McBride, Porter		Listed on the 1926 S. C. Comptroller General's List to the General Assembly		Williamsburg County, South Carolina Conf Pensioner
McCant, Alex	A	5th Regiment South Carolina Cavalry (Capt. John C. Edward's Company) Served as a servant to Charles S. Edwards	Servant	Berkeley County, South Carolina Conf Pensioner App # 1619
McClintock, Perry		Served working on James Island Fortifications	Laborer	Slave of Robert McClintock. Laurens County, South Carolina Conf Pensioner
McClinton, Jack	G	1st Regiment South Carolina Rifles (Orr's) (Capt. T. S. Ellis' Company)	Cook	Abbeville County, South Carolina Conf Pensioner App # 130
McCrea, Peter		Listed on the 1926 S. C. Comptroller General's List to the General Assembly		Williamsburg County, South Carolina Conf Pensioner
McCullough, Anthony		Listed on the 1926 S. C. Comptroller General's List to the General Assembly		Williamsburg County, South Carolina Conf Pensioner

McCutcheson, George		Listed on the 1926 S. C. Comptroller General's List to the General Assembly	Private	Williamsburg County, South Carolina Conf Pensioner
McDonald, Bob		Served as a servant no other information	Servant	Richland County, South Carolina Conf Pensioner App
McDonald, Bristow	E	19th Regiment South Carolina Infantry (Capt. Addison Clinkscales) Served as a servant to Pvt. William C. Luckey.	Servant	Lee County, South Carolina Conf Pensioner App # 7488
McDonald, Mitchell		Served as a laborer under Capt. Dave Anderson	Laborer	Lee County, South Carolina Conf Pensioner App # 7487
McElrath, Tom	E	2nd Regiment South Carolina Cavalry Served under Capt. George B. Dean	Servant	Spartanburg County, South Carolina Conf Pensioner App # 10887
McFadden, Rufus		Lancaster Graves Regiment South Carolina (Capt. Landing) Served Under Capt/Q.M. Thomas B. Fraser	Cook	Dorchester County, South Carolina Conf Pensioner App # 3386
McKey, Jeff		Listed on the 1926 S. C. Comptroller General's List to the General Assembly	Private	York County, South Carolina Conf Pensioner
McKinley, John		14th Regiment South Carolina (Charleston Riflemen) (Capt. Joe Johnson's Company)	Private	Charleston County, South Carolina Conf Pensioner App # 1872
McKinney, Unknown		Served as a Laborer building forts	Laborer	From Edgefield County, South Carolina, According to his son Warren McKinney in Arkansas Slave Narratives.
McLendon, Curtis		Listed on the 1926 S. C. Comptroller General's List to the General Assembly	Private	Darlington County, South Carolina Conf Pensioner
McLeod, John	K	2nd Regiment South Carolina Cavalry (Capt. William Company) Served Under Dr. B. H. Knotts	Servant	Orangeburg County, South Carolina Conf Pensioner App # 9400
McNeill, Hector	I	20th Regiment South Carolina (Capt. A. D. Sparks' Company) Served Under James Manning	Waltman	Dillon County, South Carolina Conf Pensioner App # 3258
McTeer, Caesar	A	3rd Regiment South Carolina Cavalry (Capt. Lowery) Served Under Edwin McTeer	Cook	Hampton County, South Carolina Conf Pensioner App # 6150
Melton, George		General and Staff Officers, Non-Regimental Enlisted Men, CSA Served Under Major Samuel Melton	Cook	Slave, York County, South Carolina Conf Pensioner
Metz, E.		1st Regiment South Carolina Artillery Militia	Musician	
Middleton, Louis	A	South Carolina Seige Train (Capt. B. C. Webb) Served Under R. B. Simons	Cook	Charleston County, South Carolina Conf Pensioner App # 1981
Middleton, Stuart	A I	1st (Charleston) Battalion South Carolina Infantry 27th Regiment, South Carolina Infantry (Gaillard's)	Drummer	

Name		Service	Role	Location / Pension
Mikell, Wallace		Served Under Sidney Legare In Signal Corps, Capt. Micah Jenkins	Camp Attendant	Charleston County, South Carolina Conf Pensioner App # 1879
Milans, Nelson		Serving building Sea Island fortifications	Laborer	Laurens County, South Carolina Conf Pensioner App # 7203
Miley, James		Colcock's Regt, South Carolina Volunteers (Capt. Henry Smart's Company) Served as a servant to his master John Wiley	Servant	Slave of John Wiley. Aiken County, South Carolina Conf Pensioner App # 421
Miller, Berry	B	10th Regiment South Carolina Volunteers Served Under Capt. Miller	Servant	Dillon County, and Marion County, South Carolina Conf Pensioner App # 8044
Miller, Kelly	F	12th Regiment South Carolina Infantry (Capt. Harpie McMekin's Company) Served Under Capt. John Bell	Servant	Fairfield County, South Carolina Conf Pensioner App # 3757
Mims, Dallas	K	7th Regiment South Carolina (Capt. Jack Burriss' Company) Served Under Luke Shibley	Servant	McCormick County, South Carolina Conf Pensioner App # 8190
Mitchell, June (Rev.)		Fort Matte Rangers (Capt. Trezevant) General and Staff Officers, Non-Regimental Enlisted Men, CSA Served under Dr. Albert Tabor (Assistant Surgeon)	Servant	Slave of Dr. Albert Tabor. Orangeburg County, South Carolina Conf Pensioner App # 9408
Mitchell, Theordon (Mitchell, Theodore)	B	1st Regiment, South Carolina Rifles (Orr's) (Capt. James M. Perrin's Company) Served Under Riley	COOK	Newberry County, South Carolina Conf Pensioner App # 8600
Mobley, Harrison		Service In Confederate Army		Fairfield County, South Carolina Conf Pensioner App # 3758
Mobley, Richmond	E	1st Regiment, South Carolina Infantry (Butler's) (1st Regulars) (Capt. John P. Mickler's Company) Served Under Billie Mobley	Cook	Saluda County, South Carolina Conf Pensioner App # 10414
Moore, Hiram		Served as a cook under Capt. Mike Moore	Cook	Fairfield County, South Carolina Conf Pensioner App # 3759
Morgan, Alford		Unknown South Carolina Unit Served Under Three Beams Boys	Cook	Newberry County, South Carolina Conf Pensioner App
Mortimer, Jack	A	25th Regiment South Carolina Infantry (Eutaw Regiment)	Cook	
Moseley, Ed		Listed on the 1926 S. C. Comptroller General's List to the General Assembly		Lexington County, South Carolina Conf Pensioner
Moultrie, Sheddrick		Trapier's Company Served Under Capt. James Trapier	Orderly	Georgetown County, South Carolina Conf Pensioner App #
Murphy, Jim		Listed on the 1926 S. C. Comptroller General's List to the General Assembly		Union County, South Carolina Conf Pensioner
Murphy, Robert	D	15th Regiment South Carolina Infantry (Capt. Thomas Warren's Company) Served Under 1st Sgt Joe J. Huckabee	Cook	Kershaw County, South Carolina Conf Pensioner App # 6660

Myers, Robert	I	49th Regiment South Carolina (Capt. Mills) Served As A Body Servant To Capt. Spratts	Servant	Lee County, South Carolina Conf Pensioner App # 7495
Name not known		Served as a Servant to his master Cooke McKie.	Body Servant	Slave Cooke McKie in Edgefield County, South Carolina. According a statement of his daughter Margaret Green in Georgia Slave narratives.
Neal, Charlie		Listed on the 1926 S. C. Comptroller General's List to the General Assembly		Aiken County, South Carolina Conf Pensioner
Nimmons, Will		2nd Battery, South Carolina Artillery James Island	Laborer	Barnwell County, South Carolina Conf Pensioner App # 1451
Noble, Isaac		Listed on the 1926 S. C. Comptroller General's List to the General Assembly		Abbeville County, South Carolina Conf Pensioner
Norton, John	E	21st Regiment South Carolina Infantry Served With His Master Pvt. Burrell Merriman	Servant	Slave Of Burrell Merriman, Anson County, North Carolina Conf Pensioner
Oliver, Solomon		Listed on the 1926 S. C. Comptroller General's List to the General Assembly		Lee County, South Carolina Conf Pensioner App #
Owens, Starling		4th Regiment South Carolina Cavalry (Capt. Rivers) Served Under B. L. Thompson	Cook	Anderson County, South Carolina Conf Pensioner App # 1002. He was the son of Annie and George Owens, and is buried at Mt. Pisgah Church.
Parker, Edmund		Served at Charleston, South Carolina building breastworks	Laborer	Slave of Col. Rice of Waterloo, S.C. According to his J. M. Parker in Arkansas Slave Narratives.
Pearson, Warren	E	3rd Regiment South Carolina State Troops (Capt. Bradley) Served As A Servant To James B. Fort	Servant Cook	Sumter County, South Carolina Conf Pensioner App #11276B. Application was submitted by Probate Judge Thomas E. Richardson
Perrineau, J.	A	25th Regiment South Carolina Infantry (Eutaw Regiment)	Under COOK	
Pettiford, T. Wade	F&S	21st Regiment, South Carolina Infantry (Hagwood's Brigade)	Musician	
Phoenix, C.	B	1st (Charleston) Battalion South Carolina Infantry (Gaillard's Battalion)	Cook	
Pitts, Hessie	B	3rd Regiment South Carolina Infantry (Capt. John G. Williams Company) Served under Pvt. Washington Pitts	Cook	Newberry County, South Carolina Conf Pensioner App # 8624
Poinsette, Peter		4th Regiment South Carolina Cavalry Served Under Capt. B. H. Rutledge	Servant	Charleston County, South Carolina Conf Pensioner App # 1902
Polite, Paul		3rd South Carolina Cavalry (Kirks Squadron) Served Under Capt. J. Manning	Servant	Jasper County, South Carolina Conf Pensioner App # 6517
Pollock, John	F	12th Regiment South Carolina Infantry (Capt. Harpie McMekin's Company) Served as a servant to 2nd Lt. David L. Glenn	Servant	Richland County, South Carolina Canf Pensioner App # 10160

Pooler, J. B.		Listed on the 1926 S. C. Comptroller General's List to the General Assembly		Darlington County, South Carolina Conf Pensioner
Porter, James	C	18th Regiment, South Carolina Infantry Served under Pvt. J.F. Bailey and others	Cook	Union County, South Carolina Conf Pensioner, Listed on the 1926 S. C. Comptroller General's List to the General Assembly
Pou, Louis	D	22nd South Carolina Infantry (Dantzler Regiment) 20th South Carolina Infantry (Keitts Regiment) Served as a servant to Pvt. William Pou	Servant	Slave of Mrs. Mary Pou, Orangeburg County, South Carolina Conf Pensioner App # 9435
Power, Ben	D, G	7th Regiment South Carolina Infantry Served as a cook under Pvt. J. W. Power and Capt. Johnson	Cook	Abbeville County, South Carolina Conf Pensioner App # 156
Pratt, Hugh		Listed on the 1926 S. C. Comptroller General's List to the General Assembly		Chester County, South Carolina Conf Pensioner
Pressley, John		Listed on the 1926 S. C. Comptroller General's List to the General Assembly		Williamsburg County, South Carolina Conf Pensioner
Prince, Hiram	D B	5th Battalion North Carolina Cavalry 6th North Carolina Cavalry Served Under Pvt. John F. Hartzog	Servant	Orangeburg County, South Carolina Conf Pensioner App # 1440
Pringle, Sr., Aaron	A	10th Regiment South Carolina Infantry Served Under Capt. J. F. Carraway	Servant	Georgetown County, South Carolina Conf Pensioner App # 4096
Pringle, Stewart		Unknown South Carolina Unit		Slave, also served as a servant to Col. Butler of the Palmetto Regiment during the Mexican-American War.
Prophet, Frank	A	Hampton Legion, South Carolina Artillery Battalion, Served Under Pvt. Henry F. Sally	Servant	Aiken County, South Carolina Conf Pensioner App # 439
Quarles, Richard (Christopher Columbus)	K D	7th Regiment South Carolina Infantry 14th Regiment S. C. Served Under Capt. Penion	Cook	McCormick County, South Carolina Conf Pensioner App # 8204
Quarrels, Hort	D	5th Regiment, South Carolina Reserves (90 days 1862-63) Served as a servant under Capt. G. W. Turner and Capt. Hard	Servant	Aiken County, South Carolina Conf Pensioner App # 441
Reaves, Simuel		Served Building Fortifications In Charleston, South Carolina	Laborer	Marion County, South Carolina Conf Pensioner App # 8104
Rector, Will		Listed on the 1926 S. C. Comptroller General's List to the General Assembly		Greenville County, South Carolina Conf Pensioner
Reed, Yancy (Reid, Yancey)		Unknown South Carolina Unit	Cook	Abbeville County, South Carolina Conf Pensioner App #164
Reese, Arthur		South Carolina Cavalry	Hostler	Was captured and made a servant for a Col. Putney of a Wisconsin Cavalry Unit
Renwick, George Washington	D	13th Regiment South Carolina Infantry (Capt. Isaac F. Hunt's Company) Served Under George Lawson	Cook	Newberry County, South Carolina Conf Pensioner App # 8642

Rhodes, Primus	E	3rd Battalion, South Carolina Infantry (Lauren's) (James') Served under Pvt. Wiley	Cook Attendant	Laurens County, South Carolina Conf Pensioner App # 7275
Rice, James		Enlisted At Charleston, South Carolina Helping Build Breastworks at Sullivan Island And Mount Pleasant, South Carolina	Laborer	Cleveland County, North Carolina Conf Pensioner
Rice, Jim		Served as a laborer at Charleston working on breastworks	Laborer	
Rice, Sarah (Female)		Listed on the 1926 S. C. Comptroller General's List to the General Assembly	Private	Colleton County, South Carolina Conf Pensioner
Richardson, James		Served as a servant with Virginia Troops	Servant	Forsyth County, North Carolina Conf Pensioner
Rilley, William	A	1st Regiment South Carolina Infantry (Hagood's) Served as a Servant to Milton Dantzler	Cook Servant	Orangeburg County, South Carolina Conf Pensioner App # 9448
Ring, Frank	C	3rd Regiment South Carolina Served Under Capt. Maffett	Servant	Greenville County, South Carolina Conf Pensioner App
Ring, Peter		Listed on the 1926 S. C. Comptroller General's List to the General Assembly	Private	Greenville County, South Carolina Conf Pensioner
Rivers, Joseph		Listed on the 1926 S. C. Comptroller General's List to the General Assembly	Private	Chesterfield County, South Carolina Conf Pensioner
Rivers, Josiah	C	1st Regiment South Carolina Infantry (Hagood's) Served As A Laborer Under Capt. Isaac S. Bamberg	Laborer	Bamberg County, South Carolina Conf Pensioner App # 1266
Robinson, Green		Listed on the 1926 S. C. Comptroller General's List to the General Assembly		Union County, South Carolina Conf Pensioner
Robinson, Lewis		Listed on the 1926 S. C. Comptroller General's List to the General Assembly	Private	Florence County, South Carolina Conf Pensioner
Robinson, Solomon		Listed on the 1926 S. C. Comptroller General's List to the General Assembly	Private	Aiken County, South Carolina Conf Pensioner
Roche, Aaron	A	20th Regiment, South Carolina Infantry Served As An Attendant To Capt. John M. Partlow	Attendant	Abbeville County, South Carolina Conf Pensioner App # 166
Rosboro, Phillip	E	5th Infantry Regiment South Carolina Served As A Servant To Capt. John Rosboro (Rosborough)	Servant	Cleveland County, North Carolina Conf Pensioner
Rose, William (Willie)		1st Regiment South Carolina Volunteer Infantry (Gregg's) (McGowen's Brigade) Served as a Musician and Servant to Gen. Maxcy Gregg	Musician Servant	Slave, also served as a servant to Col. Butler of the Palmetto Regiment during the Mexican American War.
Ross, Henry		Listed on the 1926 S. C. Comptroller General's List to the General Assembly	Private	Chester County, South Carolina Conf Pensioner

Name		Unit	Role	Location / Notes
Ruff, Sancho	C	2nd Regiment South Carolina Cavalry Served as a servant to Lt. D. W. Ruff	Servant	Richland County, South Carolina Conf Pensioner App # 10185
Russell, James	C	24th South Carolina Volunteer Infantry	Cook	FMC, KIA At Missionary Ridge
Sampson, John	D	4th Regiment South Carolina Infantry Served Under Capt. Shavers And Capt. Cason.	Cook	Lee County, South Carolina Conf Pensioner App # 7517
Sanders, Alpheus	G, K	3rd Battalion South Carolina Light Artillery (Palmetto Battalion) 2nd Lt. Samuel M. Richardson	Body Servant	Sumter County, South Carolina Conf Pensioner App #11276B. Application was submitted by Probate Judge Thomas E. Richardson
Sanders, Jeff		Unknown South Carolina Unit Served Under Col. Ace Evans		FMC, Union County, North Carolina Conf Pensioner
Sanders, John Milton	A	13th Regiment South Carolina Infantry Served Under 1st Sgt William A. Stone	Cook	Newberry County, South Carolina Conf Pensioner App # 8656
Sanders, Sallei		Listed on the 1926 S. C. Comptroller General's List to the General Assembly		Florence County, South Carolina Conf Pensioner
Sanders, Sam	E	5th Regiment South Carolina Infantry Served as a cook to Sgt. James Sanders under Capt. R. L. Bowen	Cook	York County, South Carolina Conf Pensioner
Sartor, Alex		Listed on the 1926 S. C. Comptroller General's List to the General Assembly		Union County, South Carolina Conf Pensioner
Satterwhite, Unknown		Served as a servant to his master John Satterwhite.	Servant	Slave of John Satterwhite of Newberry, S.C. According to his sister Mrs. Maria Cleland, in South Carolina Slave Narratives
Saunders, William		Black's Regiment South Carolina (Capt. Johnson's Company) Served Under Thomas Jones	Cook	Calhoun County, South Carolina Conf Pensioner App # 1715
Sawyer, Luke		Listed on the 1926 S. C. Comptroller General's List to the General Assembly		Fairfield County, South Carolina Conf Pensioner
Scott, Caesar	K	3rd Regiment South Carolina Served Under John Oswald and Capt. William Peeples	Servant	Beaufort County, South Carolina Conf Pensioner App #1544
Scott, John	K	17th South Carolina		Arkansas, St. Francis County Conf Pensioner, application #25003. His widow Sallie received his pension in 1921.
Sease, Louis	C	1st Regiment South Carolina Infantry (Hagood's) Served As A Laborer Under Pvt. Wesley E. Sease and Capt. Isaac S. Bamberg	Laborer	Bamberg County, South Carolina Conf Pensioner App # 1272
Shaw, Joe		Listed on the 1926 S. C. Comptroller General's List to the General Assembly		Williamsburg County, South Carolina Conf Pensioner
Simmons, Joe		Listed on the 1926 S. C. Comptroller General's List to the General Assembly		Dorchester County, South Carolina Conf Pensioner

Directory of African American Confederates in the U.S. Civil War

Simmons, Ransom		Served as a body guard to General Wade Hampton	Body Guard	Slave, South Carolina Conf Pensioner
Simmons, Wylie	G	17th Regiment South Carolina Infantry Served under Capt. Josiah Dickinson	Cook	Allendale County, South Carolina Conf Pensioner App # 623
Sims, Alford		Listed on the 1926 S. C. Comptroller General's List to the General Assembly	Private	Florence County, South Carolina Con? Pensioner
Singetary, Evander		Listed on the 1926 S. C. Comptroller General's List to the General Assembly	Private	Florence County, South Carolina Conf Pensioner
Singleton, Benjamin	E	1st Regiment, South Carolina Infantry (Hagood's) Served Under his master Capt. John H. Thompson. Beaufort Volunteer Artillery Served under Sgt. William Thompson	Servant	Slave of Capt. John H. Thompson of Beaufort, S.C. Beaufort County, South Carolina Conf Pensioner App # 1547
Singleton, James	F	6th Regiment, South Carolina Cavalry (Aiken's Partisan Rangers) (1st Partisan Rangers), Hampton's Brigade Served as a servant to 1stSgt B.M. Schipman, under Capt. M.B. Humphrey	Servant Cook	Slave of F. N. (B.M.) Schipman, Berkeley County, South Carolina Conf Pensioner App # 1653
Small, Elisha		Waccamaw Light Artillery, South Carolina Light Artillery, (Capt. Josh Ward's Company)	Cook	Harry County, South Carolina Conf Pensioner App # 6428
Small, George		Listed on the 1926 S. C. Comptroller General's List to the General Assembly	Private	Florence County, South Carolina Conf Pensioner
Smith, Alvin Bratton	D	3rd Battalion South Carolina Reserves	Private	Slave Of D. J. Smith, York County, South Carolina Conf Pensioner
Smith, Enoch		Listed on the 1926 S. C. Comptroller General's List to the General Assembly	Private	Darlington County, South Carolina Conf Pensioner
Smith, Frank	B	1st Regiment South Carolina Infantry (Hagood's) (Capt. Samelton) Served under David Jimerson	Servant	Bamberg County, South Carolina Conf Pensioner App # 1274
Smith, Harry		Listed on the 1926 S. C. Comptroller General's List to the General Assembly	Private	Aiken County, South Carolina Conf Pensioner
Smith, Jeff		Listed on the 1926 S. C. Comptroller General's List to the General Assembly	Private	Saluda County, South Carolina Conf Pensioner
Smith, John R.	B	14th Regiment, South Carolina (Rutledge Mounted Rifles) (Capt. Claudius E. Earle's Company) Served as a cook and attendant to William And Jesse Smith	Cook Attendant	Oconee County, South Carolina Conf Pensioner App # 9105
Smith, Madison		Listed on the 1926 S. C. Comptroller General's List to the General Assembly	Private	Georgetown County, South Carolina Conf Pensioner

Sparks, Simon		Listed on the 1926 S. C. Comptroller General's List to the General Assembly		Florence County, South Carolina Conf Pensioner
Speed, Luke		Capt. Whites' Company	Servant	Abbeville County, South Carolina Conf Pensioner App # 182
Spencer, George		Unknown South Carolina Unit Served As A Cook To Mr. Ben Harvely	Cook	Abbeville County, South Carolina Conf Pensioner App # 184
Spratt, Solomon		Slave Who Stayed Home And Defended The Home And Family. Fort Mill, South Carolina Monument.		Slave
Springs, Nathan		Slave Who Stayed Home And Defended The Home And Family. Fort Mill, South Carolina Monument.		Slave
Steed, John		Listed on the 1926 S. C. Comptroller General's List to the General Assembly		Charleston County, South Carolina Conf Pensioner
Steeter, Shadrack		4th South Carolina Regiment State Troops	Laborer	North Carolina Conf Pensioner
Stenhouse, Washington	E	Hampton Legion Infantry Regiment South Carolina Served as a body servant to 2nd Lt John Taylor Stenhouse	Body Servant	Slave of Adam Stenhouse. Greenville County, South Carolina Conf Pensioner App # 5663
Stephenson, Olive		Listed on the 1926 S. C. Comptroller General's List to the General Assembly		Florence County, South Carolina Conf Pensioner
Stewart, Dock		Listed on the 1926 S. C. Comptroller General's List to the General Assembly		Barnwell County, South Carolina Conf Pensioner
Stoker, Bill		Partisan Rangers, South Carolina (Capt. Kirk's Company) Served as a cook under Pvt. F. C. Ayer	Cook	Bamberg County, South Carolina Conf Pensioner App # 1289
Stuart, Dock	A	1st Regiment South Carolina Volunteers Served Under Sullivan Weathersbee	Cook	Barnwell County, South Carolina Conf Pensioner App # 1472
Stubbs, Jack	D A	6th South Carolina Cavalry 1st Local Troops, Georgia Infantry Served as a body servant to 1st Sgt. Robert C. Easterling at Sullivan's Island, S.C.	Body Servant	Slave of Henry Easterling, Scotland County, North Carolina Conf Pensioner
Stuckey, Costolo		1st South Carolina Lt Artillery		Yazoo County, MS Conf Pensioner
Sullivan, Milton	B	1st Regiment, South Carolina Rifles (Orr's) Served as a servant to Charles Moseley, under Capt. James M. Perrin	Servant	Greenwood County, South Carolina Conf Pensioner App # 6031
Sumter, Stepney		Beaufort Artillery, South Carolina Artillery Served as a servant to Sgt. Thomas Spann, under Capt. Spann, under Capt. Spann	Servant	Hampton County, South Carolina Conf Pensioner App # 6193
Sweet, Tom		Listed on the 1926 S. C. Comptroller General's List to the General Assembly		Florence County, South Carolina Conf Pensioner
Swinton, Paul		Parker's Company, South Carolina Light Artillery (Marion Artillery) Served as a body servant to his master Pvt. H. M. Palmer	Body Servant	Slave of Pvt. H. M. Parker. Orangeburg County, South Carolina Conf Pensioner App # 9501

Taylor, John	F&S	3rd Regiment South Carolina Reserves (90 Days 1862-63)	Musician	
Taylor, Sippio		7th South Carolina Infantry Battalion	Private	Tallahatchie County, MS Conf Pensioner
Thames, John		Listed on the 1926 S. C. Comptroller General's List to the General Assembly		Florence County, South Carolina Conf Pensioner
Thomas, Benjamin	I A	2nd Regiment South Carolina Cavalry (Capt. M. C. Butler's Company) Cavalry Battalion, Hampton Legion, South Carolina Served as a cook to his master Pvt. Mitchell a Glover	Cook	Slave of Pvt. Mitchell O. Glover. Aiken County, South Carolina Conf Pensioner App # 494
Thomas, Charles	A G	1st Regiment South Carolina Infantry (Hagood's) 25th Regiment South Carolina Infantry (Eutaw Regiment) Served Under Capt. (Judge) James F. Izlar	Servant	Orangeburg County, South Carolina Conf Pensioner App # 9503
Thomas, J. T.		Listed on the 1926 S. C. Comptroller General's List to the General Assembly	Private	Florence County, South Carolina Conf Pensioner
Thompson, Lavina (Female)	A	1st Regiment South Carolina Reserves Served as a cook to Sam Webb, under Capt. Hutto	Cook	Aiken County, South Carolina Conf Pensioner App # 496
Tilley, James Irvin		Served as a Laborer on fortifications at James and Johns Island's under William Gaffner and Capt. Humbert	Servant Laborer	Calhoun County, South Carolina Conf Pensioner App # 1721
Tillman, Ruben	I	2nd Regiment South Carolina Cavalry (Capt. M.C. Butler's Company) Served as a cook and servant to 1st Sgt 3. Monroe Wise	Cook Servant	Edgefield County, South Carolina Conf Pensioner App # 3625
Timmons, Harry		Listed on the 1926 S. C. Comptroller General's List to the General Assembly	Private	Darlington County, South Carolina Conf Pensioner
Tobe, Thomas	G K	Holcombe Legion, Cavalry Battalion South Carolina 5th South Carolina Cavalry	Private	Newberry County, South Carolina Conf Pensioner
Tompkins, Mat	B	Hampton Legion South Carolina Infantry Regiment Served as a servant to Capt. Robert W. Tompkins And Capt. Gus Tompkins	Servant	McCormick County, South Carolina Conf Pensioner App # 8229
Townsend, Doctor	G	8th Regiment South Carolina Served as a cook to his master Capt. Charles Pinckney Townsend	Cook	Slave of Capt. C. P. Townsend. Marlboro County, South Carolina Conf Pensioner App # 8397
Tucker, Sam	I	14th Regiment South Carolina Infantry (Capt. William White's Company) Served as a cook to T. A. Calir	Cook	Abbeville County, South Carolina Conf Pensioner App # 197
Van Lieu, Cap		1st South Carolina Cavalry	Private	Panola County, MS Conf Pensioner, battle injury.

Vance, Nelson	E	7th Regiment South Carolina Cavalry Served as a servant to Pvt. John C. Davis	Servant	
Vause, Elvin	I	7th Regiment South Carolina (Capt. William Prescott's Company) Served Under Lt. Ben Roper	Cook	Abbeville County, South Carolina Conf Pensioner App # 212
Vereen, Wesley	F	7th South Carolina Cavalry (Capt. McDaniel's Company) Served Under J. Bellune	Servant	Georgetown County, South Carolina Conf Pensioner App # 4108
Walker, Jerry	D	2nd Regiment South Carolina Artillery (Capt. R. M. Willis' Company)	Servant	Barnwell County, South Carolina Conf Pensioner App # 1487
Walker, Peter	B	25th Regiment South Carolina Infantry (Eutaw Regiment) (Capt. James F. Izlar's Company) Served as a servant to his master Pvt. Tom P. Oliver	Servant	Slave of Pvt. Tom P. Oliver. Orangeburg County, South Carolina Conf Pensioner App # 9511
Walker, Thomas		Listed on the 1926 S. C. Comptroller General's List to the General Assembly		Greenville County, South Carolina Conf Pensioner
Wallace, Joseph	F&S	3rd Regiment South Carolina Reserves (90 Days 1862-63)	Musician	
Wallace, Marshall	C	Holcombe Legion, Cavalry Battalion South Carolina Served (Capt. Robert Spearman's Company) Served under Samuel W. Spearman	Servant	Newberry County, South Carolina Conf Pensioner App # 8703
Washington, Daniel	A	Harts Battery, Washington Artillery Battalion, Hampton Legion, South Carolina (Capt. Tyler's Company) Served as a servant to Pvt. Patrick J. Jennings	Servant	Orangeburg County, South Carolina Conf Pensioner App # 9516
Washington, Jacob	B	2nd Regiment South Carolina Cavalry (Capt. Thomas E. Screven's Company) Served as a cook and servant to his master Peter Craddock	Cook Servant	Slave of Peter Craddock, Hampton County, South Carolina Conf Pensioner App # 6205
Washington, Ned		Listed on the 1926 S. C. Comptroller General's List to the General Assembly		Williamsburg County, South Carolina Conf Pensioner
Washington, Nias		20th Regiment South Carolina Volunteers (Capt. E. S. Keitt) Served Under Wesley Chappell	Cook	Newberry County, South Carolina Conf Pensioner App # 8707
Washington, Sam		Served working as a Laborer on fortifications on the Sea Coast, Served under D. R. Jones	Laborer	Laurens County, South Carolina Conf Pensioner App # 7346
Washington, William	B	Gen. Garys Brigade South Carolina Served Under Dr. George Robinson	Servant	Greenwood County, South Carolina Conf Pensioner App # 6240
Watson, Erwin	B	5th Regiment South Carolina Volunteers		York County, South Carolina Conf Pensioner App #
Watts, Anthony		Served Under Capt. Zack Pullene And Col. Ball	Cook Laundryman	Laurens County, South Carolina Conf Pensioner App # 7350
Weatherspoon, Robert	K	26th Regiment South Carolina Infantry Served As A Servant To Capt. W.S. Brand	Servant	Clarendon County, South Carolina Conf Pensioner App # 2768

Wheeler, Joseph	H	25th Infantry Regiment South Carolina Served As A Servant To Capt. R. E. Wheeler	Servant	Clarendon County, South Carolina Conf Pensioner App # 2769
White, Anthony		Slave Who Stayed Home And Defended The Home And Family. Fort Mill, South Carolina Monument.	Private	Slave
White, George		Listed on the 1926 S. C. Comptroller General's List to the General Assembly	Private	Cherokee County, South Carolina Conf Pensioner
White, Handy		Slave Who Stayed Home And Defended The Home And Family. Fort Mill, South Carolina Monument.	Private	Slave
White, Henry	K H	5th Regiment South Carolina Infantry 1st Regiment South Carolina Calvary Slave Of Lt. J. W. White	Cook	York County, South Carolina Conf Pensioner App #
White, Henry		Slave Who Stayed Home And Defended The Home And Family. Fort Mill, South Carolina Monument	Private	Slave
White, Jim		Slave Who Stayed Home And Defended The Home And Family. Fort Mill, South Carolina Monument	Private	Slave
White, Nelson		Slave Who Stayed Home And Defended The Home And Family. Fort Mill, South Carolina Monument	Private	Slave
White, Sandy		Slave Who Stayed Home And Defended The Home And Family. Fort Mill, South Carolina Monument	Private	Slave
White, Silas		Slave Who Stayed Home And Defended The Home And Family. Fort Mill, South Carolina Monument	Private	Slave
White, Warren		Slave Who Stayed Home And Defended The Home And Family. Fort Mill, South Carolina Monument	Private	Slave
Whitware, Henry (Whitemore, Whitemire)	E	7th Regiment South Carolina Volunteers (Capt. Stoker's Company) Served Under William Cooner	Cook	Bamberg County, South Carolina Conf Pensioner App # 1297
Wigfall, Sank		, Served Under G. A. Adams In Gen. Freyer's Command, Capt. H. W. Shaw	Cook	Aiken County, South Carolina Conf Pensioner App # 516
Wiggins, Cary		Served Building Fortifications In Charleston, South Carolina	Laborer	Marion County, South Carolina Conf Pensioner App # 8104
Wiggins, Harrison	A	Lucas Battalion South Carolina Servea Under Ranson Calhoun And Capt. Teddy Calhoun	Servant	Oconee County, South Carolina Conf Pensioner App # 9138
Wilkins, Pinkney	G F	7th Regiment South Carolina 5th South Carolina State Troops. (6 Months, 1863-4.) Served Under Capt. Sam Snoddy	Cook	Spartanburg County, South Carolina Conf Pensioner App # 11088
Willard, Henry		Listed on the 1926 S. C. Comptroller General's List to the General Assembly	Private	Abbeville County, South Carolina Conf Pensioner
William, Colden	B, G	1st (Charleston) Battalion South Carolina Infantry	Cook	

Williams, Alex	C	1st Regiment South Carolina Cavalry (Capt. John D. Twiggs and Brown) Served Under Pvt. J. Foreman And Pvt. B. Foreman	Servant	Aiken County, South Carolina Conf Pensioner App # 517
Williams, Alex (Alexander)	L	7th Regiment South Carolina Infantry Served Under Dr. Henry Klugh Capt. W. C. White	Cook	Abbeville County, South Carolina Conf Pensioner App # 206
Williams, Ambrose	A	1st Regiment South Carolina Cavalry (Capt. M. T. Owen's Company) Served as a Servant to Sgt Richard L. Chalmers	Servant	Newberry County, South Carolina Conf Pensioner App # 8728
Williams, Braw (Bram)	F	3rd Regiment South Carolina Cavalry (Capt. H. C. Stuart's Company)	Cook	Allendale County, South Carolina Conf Pensioner App # 634
Williams, Charles		Listed on the 1925 S. C. Comptroller General's List to the General Assembly		Richland County, South Carolina Conf Pensioner
Williams, Green	I	1st Regiment, South Carolina Infantry (McCreary's) (1st Provisional Army) Served under Capt. Alexander Haskell	Laborer	Richland County, South Carolina Conf Pensioner App # 10261
Williams, Harry		Listed on the 1926 S. C. Comptroller General's List to the General Assembly	Private	Abbeville County, South Carolina Conf Pensioner
Williams, Henry		Served making Salt at Charleston For The Confederate Army, worked under Maj. William Hoy	Laborer	Slave of Major William Hoy. Greenville County, South Carolina Conf Pensioner App # 5762
Williams, J.	F&S	1st Regiment South Carolina Infantry (Hagood's)	Musician	
Williams, James		Listed on the 1926 S. C. Comptroller General's List to the General Assembly		Chester County, South Carolina Conf Pensioner
Williamson, James	F	1st Regiment South Carolina Volunteer Infantry (Gregg's)	Musician	
Willson, James	A	16th Regiment, South Carolina Infantry (Greenville Regiment) Served Under Capt. Langston	Cook	Oconee County, South Carolina Conf Pensioner App # 9143
Wilson, Hammett	O	3rd Battalion, South Carolina Infantry (Lauren's) (James') (Capt. George M. Gunnels and Capt. John Harris) Served Under John P. May	Servant	Spartanburg County, South Carolina Conf Pensioner App # 11101
Wilson, Mart	B	1st Regiment South Carolina Cavalry (Capt. Niles Nesbitt's Company) Served Under J. H. Copeland	Servant Cook	Laurens County, South Carolina Conf Pensioner App # 7365
Wilson, Martin	B	1st Regiment South Carolina Cavalry (Capt. Niles Nesbitt's Company) Served Under J. H. Copeland And Joseph Little	Servant Cook	Laurens County, South Carolina Conf Pensioner App # 7366
Wilson, Martin		7th Regiment South Carolina Cavalry Served as a servant to Wash Miller	Servant	

Wilson, Robert	I	7th Regiment South Carolina Cavalry Served Under Capt. B.F. Wilson, served Entire War	Servant	Sumter County,South Carolina Conf Pensioner App # 11270b
Wilson, Simon		Listed on the 1926 S. C. Comptroller General's List to the General Assembly		Florence County, South Carolina Conf Pensioner
Wilson, Squire	A	3rd Regiment South Carolina Infantry (Capt. B. C. Washington Served Under A. W. Teague	Cook Attendant	Laurens County, South Carolina Conf Pensioner App # 7368
Wingate, George Washington	C	8th Regiment South Carolina Served Under Capt. T. E. Powe	Cook	Chesterfield County, South Carolina Conf Pensioner App # 2613
Winn, George		Youngblood's Company, South Carolina Served as a cook under Capt. Youngblood	Cook	Abbeville County, South Carolina Conf Pensioner App # 211
Wise, Ben	A	3rd Regiment South Carolina (Kershaws Brigade) Served Under Capt. George Swygert	Cook	Richland County, South Carolina Conf Pensioner App # 10271
Wise, Lewis	A	3rd Regiment South Carolina Cavalry (Capt. G. H. Kirkland's Company) Served under Pvt. S. S. Wise	Cook	Barnwell County, South Carolina Conf Pensioner App # 1497
Witherspoon, Dan	A	12th South Carolina Volunteers (Palmer Guards)		York County, South Carolina Conf Pensioner
Woodson, Caleb		Served as a Laborer, James M. Gee provided an affidavit, no other information.	Laborer	Richland County, South Carolina Conf Pensioner App # 10272
Wright, Johnson	K	Palmetto Sharpshooters Served Under Capt.	Cook	Oconee County, South Carolina Conf Pensioner
Wright, Solomon		Gen. Martin W. Gary's Cavalry Brigade, Quartermaster Department	Body Servant Teamster	Surrendered at Appomatox Courthouse
Youmans, John	C	3rd Regiment South Carolina Cavalry (Capt. John H. Howard's Company) Served under Pvt. M. Swift Hubbard	Cook	Hampton County, South Carolina Conf Pensioner App # 6211
Young, Isaac	B	4th South Carolina Cavalry (Rutledge's Regiment.), (Capt. Osborne Barber's Company) Served as a cock under Pvt. John L. Young	Cook	Fairfield County, South Carolina Conf Pensioner App # 3808
Young, J. M.		Served under J. W. Thomas	Cook	Abbeville County, South Carolina Conf Pensioner App
Young, Limus C.	C	20th Regiment, South Carolina Infantry Served as a cook and Servant under William Bull, Capt's Elias yenning and Fred Schultz	Cook Servant Teamster	Orangeburg County, South Carolina Conf Pensioner App # 9543
Young, Ross		Served As A Laborer On Sea Islands Fortifications under Mr. Hydrick the overseer	Laborer	Laurens County, South Carolina Conf Pensioner App # 7378

TENNESSEE

Toney Chapman, James Gooch, Charles Murray, Robert B. Patton, Tillman Price Payne, Hardin Starnes, and Marshall Thompson were among the African American combat men that served in the offensive formations of the 4th Tennessee Cavalry. However, it was not just the African American body slaves who fought in the 4th Tennessee Cavalry's non-integrated company (very definitely as these whites wished and maybe as the African Americans themselves, who were proud of serving as an unified band of brothers-in-arms).

As a "Free Person of Color," Private Wiley Stewart of Company "H," 4th Tennessee Cavalry, rode forth. This list directory has revealed not only the identities of an entire organized group of African American Confederates who distinguished themselves in forgotten battlefield roles, but also their exact fighting duties.

Most notably, the 4th Tennessee Cavalry's contributions as armed soldiers were not the only example of a well-organized group of well-armed African American who formed their own combat company and rushed the Yankees on the battlefield while mounted. The personal body slaves of the hard-riding troops under hard-hitting General John Hunt Morgan had formed another "African American company of armed combat men." Morgan rose to prominence as one of the most talented cavalry commanders in the western theater, a counterpoint to Lee's premier cavalryman, General James Ewell Brown Stuart, in the eastern theater.

A number of armed African American, notably Morgan's servant "Old Box," who was well-known for loathing Yankees, went forth on the biggest raid of the Civil War, fulfilling combat duties, especially in crisis circumstances when fighting men were required to A face a severe danger.

During the historic Ohio Raid in June-July 1863, they were part of Morgan's over 1,000-mile journey into the Ohio Valley. Morgan led one of the most effective cavalry raids of the Civil War, ripping across a vast section of not just Indiana but also Ohio, against instructions from General Braxton Bragg not to cross the Ohio River and press farther into Yankee territory.

Indeed, these stealthy Rebel raiders, both black and white, attacked the large metropolis of Cincinnati, spreading fear and terror across the Midwest, extending as far west as Illinois. Morgan got the tragic news of Lee's harsh loss among the hills and fields of Gettysburg while raiding far north of the Ohio River, but this did not prevent this strong cavalryman's boldness while penetrating deep in Union territory that had never tasted war before.

Simply said, Confederate leaders like as the great "John Hunt Morgan" acted as they wished. They handed rifles to an able-bodied African American man, free or slave, who desired to fight for the South." Wesley Hunt, a slave born in 1840, was a African American Confederate raider with intimate links to the Morgan family.

Similarly, during the main cavalry conflicts of the eastern theater, African American Confederates galloped into the fray alongside the best cavalry units. Mounted African American Confederates also played a role in the Civil War's largest cavalry fight, which raged with unfettered ferocity back and forth over the wide fields at Brandy Station, Virginia, on June 9, 1863, at the start of the Gettysburg Campaign. The 12th Virginia's African cooks and slaves organized their own cavalry unit to enter the war at its peak. One Union officer said, "when the army marched into battle, their slaves went too."

Two body servants from Captain George Baylor's 12th Virginia Cavalry, Stuart's Cavalry Corps, Army of Northern Virginia, were among the assailants, and they were caught up in the fierce close-quarter action. At Brandy Station, in the epic cavalry fight. Overton and Tom had seized a number of weapons that had been abandoned by dead and injured Federal troops, and they had charged into the conflict with zeal. The two African Americans "joined in the company charges" after being armed with Yankee guns.

NAME	CO.	UNIT	RANK	SLAVE / FREE MISC
Alfred	A,F	19th Regiment Tennessee Cavalry (Biffle's)	Cook	Slave of Col. J.B. Biffle
Augustus	F	20th Regiment Tennessee Infantry	Private	P.O.W. Captured at Fairfield, Tenn. June 27, 1863
Braxton		Unknown Tennessee Unit Served as a body servant to his master Col. Joseph G. Braxton	Body Servant	Slave of Col. Joseph G. Braxton, Maunry County, TN

We Trust Forrest

General Nathan Bedford Forrest emancipated his slaves before Abraham Lincoln's 1861 Emancipation Proclamation.

Forrest persuaded his African-American slaves to volunteer and serve as his soldiers without coercion in the Civil War, and seven of them were assigned to be his personal "Escort Bodyguards."

After the war, many of Forrest's liberated soldiers and former slaves returned to work as sharecroppers with him.
The most ironic example of leadership was Forrest's decision to send 45 or more slaves to battle, transform them to soldiers, and return them all alive at the end of the war.
The majority of liberated people chose to remain in the Deep South where their relatives and loved ones had worked as slaves for centuries.

They yearned to own and farm their own property rather than being forced to work on the land of white plantation owners. Former slaves in the Sea Islands off the coast of South Carolina had hoped to possess the land they had labored on for decades after General Sherman ordered that freed persons be given ownership of 40-acre tracts and a mule.

The Freedmen's Bureau added to these hopes by directing that former slaves be given leases and rights to land in the South. These efforts, however, were thwarted by President Andrew Johnson who succeeded Lincoln.

In 1865, Johnson ordered the restoration of land to white proprietors, a setback for the newly liberated who had begun to develop the land as their own such as those on the South Carolina Sea Islands. In the end, there was no land redistribution in the South.

The end of slavery signaled the beginning of the transition to wage work. Former slaves, on the other hand, did not experience a new period of economic independence as a result of their conversion.

While they were no longer subjected to the lash, emancipated people were left with little money and required farm implements, food, and other basics to begin their new lives. The crop-lien system allowed store owners to provide credit to farmers in exchange for a percentage of their future harvest as payment.

Creditors, on the other hand, demanded exorbitant interest rates, making it even more difficult for emancipated people to achieve economic independence.

Dan		Unknown Tennessee Unit Served as a cook.	Cook	Slave of Bill Thomas of Brownsville, TN. Served as a Cook, only had one eye and left the service before he could be mustered out. According to his daughter Minerva Davis made a statement in Arkansas Slave Narratives.
Dick	L	14th Tennessee Infantry Served as a Servant of Capt. E. Hewett, P.O.W. at Johnson's Island	Servant	
Edmond	A	7th Regiment Tennessee Cavalry (Duckworth's) Served as a servant to Sgt. W.H. Rollins	Servant	Slave
Eke	B	53rd Tennessee Infantry	Private	P.O.W.
George	2B	154th Senior Regiment, Tennessee Infantry (1st Tennessee Volunteers)	Servant	
George	F	41st Regiment, Tennessee Infantry	Cook	
George	G	6th Regiment Tennessee Infantry		Slave of J. B. Long
Jerry	F	41st Regiment, Tennessee Infantry	Cook	
Jesse	2B	154th Senior Regiment, Tennessee Infantry (1st Tennessee Volunteers)	Servant	
John	K	1st Tennessee Heavy Artillery (Jackson's Regiment)	Private	
Malcomb	F	41st Regiment, Tennessee Infantry	Cook	
Peter	D	37th Tennessee Infantry. (7th Tennessee Regiment Provisional Army 1st East Tennessee Rifle Regiment	Private	
Phelix	F	41" Regiment, Tennessee Infantry	Cook	
Reese	E	16th Regiment Tennessee Infantry Servant of Capt. J. J. Womack	Servant	Died on 10/23/61
Samuel		19th Regiment Tennessee Cavalry (Biffle's)	Private	Slave of Sgt. W. B. Embrey
Tom	K	1st Tennessee Heavy Artillery (Jackson's Regiment)	Private	
William		19th Regiment Tennessee Infantry	Private	
Abernathy, Ruff		3rd Tennessee Infantry	Private	Giles County, TN Conf Pension App. Buried at Aspen Hill Cemetery
Akins, John		9th Regiment Tennessee Cavalry	Private	Davidson County, TN Conf Pension App # C221
Allison, March	E	7th Regiment Tennessee Calvary	Private	
Allison, Sam	L	7th Regiment Tennessee Calvary	Private	Haywood County, TN Conf Pension App # C170, application rejected.
Amy, Pete		Supply Train, (Hoke's Division)	Private	Knox County, TN Conf Pensioner App # C143
Anderson, David	F	29th Regiment Tennessee Infantry	Private	
Anderson, George	C	9th Regiment Tennessee Cavalry		Hickman County, TN Conf Pensioner App # C216
Anthony, Benjamin	E	7th Regiment Tennessee Calvary	Private	

Directory of African American Confederates in the U.S. Civil War

Name		Unit	Rank	Notes
Arnold, Polk		Gen N. B. Forrest (Escort), Tennessee Cavalry	Private	Bedford County, TN Conf Pensioner App # C5
Avant, Alfred Scott		Unknown Tennessee Unit	Private	Rutherford County, TN Conf Pension App # C275, application rejected.
Averitt, Albert	C	18th Tennessee Infantry	Private	Rutherford County, TN Conf Pensioner App # C45
Baker, Jim		Unassigned (Laborer)	Private	Fayette County, TN Conf Pension App # C239, application rejected.
Banks, Porter		2nd Tennessee Infantry	Private	Davidson County, TN Conf Pensioner App # C50
Barber, Henry	E	7th Regiment Tennessee Calvary	Private	
Barksdale, Henderson		12th Tennessee Infantry	Private	Gibson County, TN Conf Pension App # C102, application rejected.
Bates, Henry		Unknown Tennessee Unit Servant of Tom Bates	Private	Monroe County, TN Conf Pension App # C188, application rejected.
Baugh, Willis		Unknown Tennessee Unit	Private	Rutherford County, TN Conf Pension App Missing
Bayly, James	J	37th Tennessee Infantry. (7th Tennessee Regiment Provisional Army 1st East Tennessee Rifle Regiment	Servant	
Beaumont, Ben		10th Tennessee Cavalry		Stewart County, TN Conf Pension App # C109, application rejected.
Bell, Charles (Charley)	K	11th Tennessee Infantry		Dickson, County, TN Conf Pensioner App # C68
Bell, Harrison	D	29th Regiment Tennessee Infantry	Private	
Bell, William Carroll		30th Tennessee Infantry	Private	Robertson County, TN Conf Pension App # C139
Biles, Jerry		Unknown Tennessee Unit	Private	
Biles, William Houston		Unknown Tennessee Unit	Private	
Birch, James A.	F	2nd Tennessee Voluntary Cavalry "Tulloss Rangers"	Servant	
Bird, Terry	F	2nd Tennessee Voluntary Cavalry "Tulloss Rangers"	Servant	
Black, Jack	D	50th Regiment Tennessee Infantry	Cook	
Black, John	D	50th Regiment Tennessee Infantry	Cook	
Black, Joseph	D	50th Regiment Tennessee Infantry	Cook	
Black, William	D	50th Regiment Tennessee Infantry	Cook	
Blackwell, Abe		Regiment not given Served as a Servant to Dave Tubberville		Fayette County, TN Conf Pensioner App #C187
Blackwell, Harden		15th Tennessee Cavalry	Servant	
Bledsoe, William Anthony		6th Tennessee Infantry	Private	Madison County, TN Conf Pensioner App # C127
Bobbitt, Carter		14th Tennessee Cavalry	Private	Madison County, TN Conf Pensioner App #
Boeu, Martin		7th Tennessee Cavalry	Private	Quitman County, MS Conf Pensioner, non-battle injury
Bond, Warrick	E	7th Regiment Tennessee Calvary	Private	
Brantley, David		9th Tennessee Cavalry Battalion	Servant	Copiah County, MS Conf Pensioner
Briggs, John		4th Tennessee Cavalry	Private	

Directory of African American Confederates in the U.S. Civil War

Brown, Alfred		Unknown Tennessee Unit Served as a Servant to Dr. George Brown	Servant	Bradley County, TN Conf Pension App # C233
Brown, Anderson		Unassigned (Horse Shoer)		Madison County, TN Conf Pension App # C209, application rejected.
Brown, John L.	C	20th Tennessee Infantry	Private	Hamilton County, TN Conf Pensioner App # C186
Brown, Tom		Gen. John C. Brown's staff	Private	Buried at the Maplewood Cemetery in Pulaski, TN. Giles County, TN Conf Pensioner
Bryant, Henry		(Recruit Office) Morgan Bryant		Meigs County, TN Conf Pensioner App # C169
Bryant, John	E	14th Regiment Tennessee Infantry	Cook	
Buchanan, Henry		12th Tennessee Infantry	Private	Rutherford County, TN Conf Pension App # C114
Buckner, Wash		Unknown Tennessee Unit	Private	
Buford, William		9th Regiment Tennessee Infantry	Private	Williamson County, TN Conf Pensioner App # C18
Burns, Dave		8th Regiment Tennessee Cavalry	Private	Wayne County, TN Conf Pension App # C123. P.O.W.
Byers, Bill	L	7th Regiment Tennessee Calvary	Private	
Caldwell, John		1st Tennessee Cavalry		Davidson County, TN Conf Pension App # C83, application rejected.
Cannon, Charles	2B	154th Senior Regiment, Tennessee Infantry (1st Tennessee Volunteers)	Servant	Shelby County, TN Conf Pensioner App # C217
Cansler, Hugh Lawson		43rd Tennessee Infantry	Private	Knox County, TN Conf Pension App # C125, application rejected.
Caruthers, John		48th Tennessee Infantry	Private	Wilson County, TN Conf Pension App # C241
Cason, Frazier		31st Tennessee Infantry	Private	Chester County, TN Conf Pension App # C173
Catlett, Torn		Unknown Tennessee Unit Served as a Servant to Bill Catlett	Private	Monroe County, TN Conf Pension App # C189
Chambers, Silvester		38th Tennessee Infantry	Private	Yazoo County, MS Conf Pensioner
Chapman, Toney	A	4th Tennessee Cavalry 8th Tennessee Cavalry	Private	Slave, Davidson County, TN Conf Pensioner App # C15, Attended Confederate Reunion of 1892 at Farmington, TN.
Church, Henry		48th Tennessee Infantry	Private	Williamson County, TN Conf Pensioner App # C19
Churchill, John		Gen. Thomas Churchill's HQ	Servant	Slave, Hardeman County, TN Conf Pension App # C212
Clack, Fed		Col. Calvin J. Clack's staff	Private	Buried at the Maplewood Cemetery in Pulaski, TN. Giles County, TN Conf Pensioner
Clairborne, Henry	L	7th Tennessee Calvary	Private	
Clark, A.		Memphis Appeal Tennessee Artillery	Private	Lafayette County, MS Conf Pensioner, battle injury.
Clayton, Sam		46th Tennessee Infantry	Private	Davidson County, TN Conf Pension App # C234
Cleveland, Maurice Adams		Gen. John Adam's Stfaff	Private	Giles County, TN Conf Pension App # C200. Buried at Maplewood Cemetery
Clickley, Torn		Unknown Tennessee Unit	Private	

As one might expect, African American Confederates mostly served as privates, however at least one ebony soldier advanced to the rank of non-commissioned officer. In an 1862 letter to his brother in Herkimer County, New York, Private Frank Bailey of the 34th New York Volunteer Infantry, also known as the Herkimer Regiment, described an undeniable reality that existed in the Army of Northern Virginia, demonstrating the myth that all African American in the Confederate Army were nothing more than lowly servants, domestics, and only served in logistical support roles far behind the front lines: "... there is according to Private Frank Bailey of the 34th New York infantry."

A long-forgotten African American Confederate named Coffee wore the antique coat of a Confederate brigadier general's uniform when he served with this commander of the Army of Tennessee.

This so-called "sable general" earned a reputation among the Force of Tennessee's fighting men, the main Southern force in the western theater. Coffee was a slave who had been raised in the general's home as a young man, and the two men had remained close throughout their lives. Notably, the excess general's uniform coat was worn by the "sable general" not just in camp and on "gala days," but also throughout the war.

During one battle, Coffee dressed himself as a brigadier general and "rode on the General's spare horse, and mad with joy (then) would charge up and down the field, beyond the reach of the shells and bullets." According to one Confederate, he was also seen at the battlefield's front while "the enemy was in full flight and our troops were pushing... up came the sable General as he careened at breakneck speed over the plain of the battlefield."

Name		Unit	Role	Pension/Notes
Close, George	F	2nd Tennessee Voluntary Cavalry "Tulloss Rangers"	Servant	
Cole, Nat		Captain Ross's Tennessee Cavalry		Gibson County, TN Conf Pensioner App # C181
Coleman, Nelson		Unknown Tennessee Unit		
Collier, Sam	F	6th Tennessee Infantry 51st		Madison County, TN Conf Pensioner App # C211 & C257
Callum, Sam	F	8th Tennessee Infantry	Private	TN Conf Pensioner
Coltart, Ed	L	7th Regiment Tennessee Calvary		
Conn, George Adams		Quartermaster (Maj. Hawes Brigade)		Bedford County, TN Conf Pension App # C198
Cotton, Alonzo		Unknown Tennessee Unit Maj. Edmonson		Davidson County, TN Conf Pension App # C283, application rejected.
Crittenden, John		2nd Tennessee Infantry		Bolivar County, MS Conf Pensioner
Crudup, Henry Davis (Crudy)		7th Regiment Tennessee Infantry		Wilson County, TN Conf Pensioner App # C8
Crutcher, Jack	D	20th Tennessee Infantry		Williamson County, TN Conf Pensioner App # C26
Cullom, Sam W.	F	8th Regiment Tennessee Infantry		Overton County, TN Conf Pensioner App # C58 Robertson County, TN Conf Pension App # C232
Cunningham, Osborne	D	1st Tennessee Cavalry		Williamson County, TN Conf Pensioner App # C87
Curry, Jim	L	7th Regiment Tennessee Calvary		
Dabney, Mack		13th Tennessee Infantry		Maury County, TN Conf Pensioner App # C90. Buried at Brick Church Cemetery
Dance, George		8th Tennessee Infantry Served as a servant to Dr. S.E.H. Dance	Servant	Slave, Moore County, TN Conf Pensioner App = C46
Davis, Archie		2nd Tennessee Calvary		
Davis, Ben		Gen. N. B. Forrest's Headquarters, 3rd Tennessee		Shelby County, TN Conf Pensioner App # C39
Davis, John (I D.)		7th Tennessee Cavalry	Servant	Panola County, MS Conf Pensioner
Degraffenreid, Nathan	B	154th Senior Regiment, Tennessee Infantry		Fayette County, TN Conf PensionerApp#C16
Demoss, Clairborne	E	7th Regiment Tennessee Calvary		
Dickson, Robert		3rd Tennessee Infantry		Monroe County, MS Conf Pensioner
Dillon, Jim		47th Tennessee Infantry		Davidson County, TN Conf Pensioner App # C89
Dismukes, Abraham		Unassigned (Shoemaker)		Madison County, TN Conf Pension App # C67
Donelson, Frank		23rd Tennessee Infantry Battalion	Servant	Holmes County, 'AS Conf Pensioner
Donnell, William. M.		Commissary Department		Bedford County TN Conf Pensioner App # C51
Doris, Prince	E	7th Regiment Tennessee Calvary		
Douglass, Levi		Unknown Tennessee Unit Worked on Breastworks		Haywood County, TN Conf Pensioner App # C99, application rejected.

Drake, G. W.		16th Tennessee Infantry	Servant	Davidson County, TN Conf Pensioner App # C93
Duke, Alfred		3rd (Forrest's) Tennessee Cavalry	Private	Shelby County, TN Conf Pension App # C190, application rejected.
Duncan, James		1st Tennessee Infantry	Private	Hardin County, TN Conf Pension App # C271
Duncan, Ton (Black Satin)	K	20th Tennessee Infantry Served as a servant to three Duncan brothers.	Servant	Sumner County, TN. Paroled at Greensboro, N.C. May 1, 1865
Dunn, James		7th Regiment Tennessee Calvary		Trousdale County, TN Conf Pension App # C121, application rejected.
Dupree, Warner	E	7th Regiment Tennessee Calvary		
Durley, Willis		Unknown Tennessee Unit		
Dyer, Matt (Col.)	H	6th Tennessee Infantry	Chief Cook	Slave of Judge Milton Brown, he was also a Veteran of the War of 1812.
Earns, Joe		4th Tennessee Cavalry		
Earle, Turner		3rd Tennessee Cavalry	Private	Fayette County, TN Conf Pension App # C73
Easley, Edom	I	10th Tennessee Cavalry	Private	Hickman County, TN Conf Pensioner App # C237
Easley, William M.		24th Tennessee Infantry	Private	Hickman County, TN Conf Pensioner App # C10
Eatherly, William		Unknown Tennessee Unit	Private	Davidson County, TN Conf Pension App
Elder, Hal		Unknown Tennessee Unit	Private	Gibson County, TN Conf Pension App # C273
Farley, James	E	25th Regiment, Tennessee infantry	Private	
Ferrell, Kit		7th Tennessee Cavalry		Lafayette County, MS Conf Pensioner
Field, Whitlock		Col. Hume R. Field	Private	Giles County, TN Conf Pensioner Buried at the Maplewood Cemetery in Pulaski, TN.
Fields, Napoleon		Gen N. B. Forrest (Escort), Tennessee Cavalry	Servant	Lee County, MS Conf Pensioner, injured during the war.
Fitzgerald, John Martin	A	48th Tennessee Infantry	Private	Maury County, TN Conf Pensioner App # C74
Floyd, Wash		Unknown Tennessee Unit		
Forrest, Aaron		Gen N. B. Forrest (Escort), Tennessee Cavalry	Servant	Grenada County, MS Conf Pensioner
Forrest, Thornton		Gen. N. B. Forrest's Headquarters, 3rd Tennessee Cavalry He Served as General Forrest's Steward.	Steward	Slave of General Forrest, Shelby County, TN Conf Pensioner App # C48
Foster, Joe		9th Regiment Tennessee Cavalry	Private	Hickman County, TN Conf Pensioner App # C277
Francis, Edward		Hospital Service	Hospital Steward	Franklin County, TN Conf Pension App # C213
Frasier (Frazier), Jack		51st Tennessee Infantry	Private	Yazoo County, MS Conf Pensioner
Freeman, Joseph	E	7th Regiment Tennessee Calvary	Private	
Gallimore, Samuel	F	2nd Tennessee Voluntary Cavalry "Tulloss Rangers"	Servant	

Gantt, Jake	B	4th Regiment Tennessee (Capt. Robertson's Company) Served as a laborer under 1st Sgt Robert J. Estus	Laborer	Aiken County, South Carolina Conf Pensioner App # 329
Garner, George		1st Tennessee Infantry	Private	Franklin County, TN Conf Pensioner App # C29 & C246
Garrett, Noah		Unknown Tennessee Unit	Private	Grainger County, TN Conf Pension App
Gentry, James		17th Tennessee Infantry	Private	Marshall County, TN Conf Pensioner App #
Gibson, John		Unknown Tennessee Unit	Private	Hickman County, TN Conf Pension App # C274
Gibson, Robert		Unknown Tennessee Unit	Private	
Gilliam, Robert		Ballentine's Regiment Tennessee Cavalry	Private	Shelby County, TN Conf Pensioner App # C185
Glasscock, William	I	29th Tennessee Infantry	Servant	
Gober, Silas		3rd Tennessee Cavalry	Private	Fayette County, TN Conf Pensioner App # C140
Goins, George W.	D C	26th Tennessee Infantry Served under Capt. William McConnal and Col. Leland 12th Tennessee Infantry	Teamster	FMC, Grainger County, TN. He submitted for a Conf Pension #8686 but it was not approved because he did not stay in service to the end of the war, even though he became sick during the war.
Gooch, James	I D	45th Tennessee Infantry 4th (McLemore's) Tennessee Cavalry Starnes Cavalry 9th Tennessee Infantry Served as a cook to Capt. William Sykes and Capt. Henry C. Irby	Cook, Private	Davidson County, TN Conf Pensioner App # C240 & C259
Goodrich, Jake		Served as a body servant to his master Hartford Weathers	Body Servant	Slave of Hartford (Hatford) Weathers of Madison County, TN. According to his statement in Arkansas Slave Narratives.
Gordon, Nathan		11th Tennessee Cavalry		Maury County, TN Conf Pensioner App # C253. Buried at Waco Cemetery
Gore, Henry		8th Regiment Tennessee Cavalry Served as a Servant to Col. Gore	Servant	Davidson County, TN Conf Pensioner App # C132
Graham, Levin	G	2nd Tennessee Infantry Served as a Fifer and Attendant to Capt. J. Welby Armstrong	Attendant Fifer	FMC, According to Capt. Armstrong, Levin "Refused to stay in camp, obtaining a musket and cartridges, went across the river with us. He fought manfully, and it is known that he killed four of the Yankees."
Gray, Albert	H	24th Tennessee Infantry	Private	Hickman County, TN Conf Pensioner App # C224
Gray, Dock	S	48th Infantry Tennessee Regiment Served as a Servant to Maj. John Gray Jr.	Scout	Hickman County, TN Conf Pensioner App #C218
Green, Solomon		Was impressed and served as a laborer working on breastworks	Laborer	Slave of Gen. Hayes and Jack Hayes of Memphis, TN. According to his daughter Diana Rankins 'In Arkansas Slave Narratives.

Name		Unit	Role	Notes
Greer, Jones		Gen. N.B. Forrest's Escort 3rd Tennessee Calvary Served as a Servant to Lt. G. Cowan	Body Servant	
Gregory, Ned	C	1st (Turney's) Tennessee Infantry	Private	Franklin County, TN Conf Pensioner App # C3
Grigsby, Thomas A.		16th Tennessee Cavalry 15th Calvary		Shelby County, TN Conf Pension App # C30, application rejected.
Grimes, Daniel W.		11th Tennessee Infantry	Private	Robertson County, TN Conf Pensioner App # C228 & C231
Halley, Albert	F	44th Tennessee Infantry		Davidson County, TN Conf Pension App # C56, application rejected.
Hairston, John		Unknown Tennessee Unit		Lincoln County, TN Denied Conf Pension, App # C183, application rejected.
Hale, Reuben Grissim	C	4th Tennessee Infantry (Qtrmaster Department)	Private	Wilson County, TN Conf Pensioner App # C6
Haliburton, Anthony	E	7th Regiment Tennessee Calvary	Private	
Hanna, George		Gen. N.B. Forrest's Escort, 3rd Tennessee Calvary	Private	Hickman County, TN Conf Pensioner App # C252
Hannah, Jerry		18th Tennessee Infantry 9th Battalion Tennessee Cavalry	Private	Maury County, TN Conf Pensioner App # C254
Harding, James		9th Regiment Tennessee Cavalry		Davidson County, TN Conf Pension App # C25, application rejected.
Harris, Charley		11th Tennessee Infantry	Private	Dickson County, TN Conf Pension App # C
Harris, Wash. (Washington)		Cheatham's Division		Giles County, TN Conf Pension App # C163, application rejected. Buried at Maplewood Cemetery
Harthown		Unknown Tennessee Unit	Private	Brownsville, TN Attended the UCV Reunion in Arkansas 1928
Hastings, Alex	A	17th Tennessee Infantry	Private	Bedford County, TN Conf Pensioner App # C141
Hawthorne, E. D.	L	7th Regiment, Tennessee Calvary	Private	Lauderdale County, TN Conf Pensioner App # C105
Hayes, Caesar		154th Senior Regiment, Tennessee Infantry	Private	Shelby County, TN Conf Pensioner App # C34
Haynes, Washington		5th Tennessee Infantry	Private	Henry County, TN Conf Pension App # C64
Hays, Luke		Unknown Tennessee Unit		Slave of Newt Nunn, Crockett County, TN Conf Pension App # C279, application rejected.
Henderson, Henry C.		45th Infantry Tennessee Regiment Served as a servant of Col. William F. Henderson, a medical doctor	Cook Servant	White County, TN Conf Pensioner App # C88 he received one check before he died. Buried at the Old Union Cemetery in southern White County, TN.
Henry, West (Wes)		2" Tennessee Infantry 21st Tennessee Cavalry Served as a cook for Mark Henry	Cook	Trousdale County, TN Conf Pensioner App # C78
Hensley, Lee		4th Tennessee Infantry	Private	Slave, Caswell County, NC Conf Pensioner

Nickerson, Clay	K	24th Tennessee Infantry	Private	Coffee County, TN Conf Pension App # C79
Hill, Charles		Gen N. B. Forrest (Escort), Tennessee Cavalry	Errand Boy	Panola County, MS Conf Pensioner
Hord, Frederick Richard	E	2nd Tennessee Cavalry (Ashby's) Served with his Master John Ellis	Servant	Hawkins County, TN Conf Pension App # C62, Slave. Buried at the Lyons Chapel Church Cemetery near Church Hill, TN.
Hornbeak, Rash		9th Battalion Tennessee Cavalry Servant of Capt. Eli Hornbeak	Servant	Hickman County, TN Conf Pension App # C260
House, Charles		4th Tennessee Cavalry	Private	
Houston, Trace	A	37th Tennessee Infantry	Servant	
Howard, Roach		3rd Tennessee Cavalry	Private	
Humphreys, Dan	G	7th Regiment Tennessee Calvary He was a cook and aide to the Humphreys brothers in Co. G, 7th TN Cavalry	Cook	He attended the Confederate Convention in Dallas, Texas in 1902 with men who served from Henry County, TN
Hunter, Booker		Gen. Preston Smith's Staff	Private	Williamson County, TN Conf Pension App # C92
Hyde, Henry		Unknown Tennessee Unit	Private	
Inman, Ezekiel		5th Tennessee Cavalry	Private	Perry County, TN Conf Pension App # C43
Irby, James		3rd Tennessee Cavalry		Panola County, MS Conf Pensioner
Irwin, Albert (Maj. Mud)	E	7th Regiment Tennessee Calvary	Private	
Ivie, Wiley Sutton		Quartermasters	Private	Bedford County, TN Conf Pension App # C52
Jackson, Henry		Gen. N. B. Forrest's Tennessee Cavalry 3rd Tennesse Cavalry	Private	Shelby County, TN Conf Pensioner App # C149
Jarnigan, David		16th Tennessee Cavalry	Private	Knox County, TN Conf Pensioner App #C31
Jarrett, Thompson	E	7th Regiment Tennessee Calvary	Private	
Jennings, Joseph		12th Tennessee Cavalry		Hamblen County, TN Conf Pensioner App # C116
Johnson, Chapman	E	7th Regiment Tennessee Calvary	Private	
Johnson, George Floyd		Wilcox Brigade	Private	Knox County, TN Conf Pensioner App # C201
Johnson, Marshall	I	29th Regiment Tennessee Infantry	Servant	
Johnson, Peter	L	24th Infantry Regiment Tennessee Capt. Lycurgus Bennet		Hickman County, TN Conf Pensioner App # C191
Johnson, Richard	I	14th Mississippi Infantry	Private	Shelby County, TN Conf Pensioner # C4C
Johnson, Tom		50th Regiment Tennessee Infantry	Private	Williamson County, TN Conf Pensioner App # C75
Johnson, Tom		10th Tennessee Cavalry		Oktibbeha County, MS Conf Pensioner, application rejected.
Johnson, William		Capt. White's Battery		Williamson County, TN Conf Pensioner App # C27
Jones, Benjamin 3.		3rd Tennessee Infantry		Knox County, TN Conf Pensioner App # C
Jones, Leroy		4th Tennessee Infantry		Tipton County, TN Conf Pension App #C120

Jones, Monroe	A	1st Mississippi Light Artillery	Private	Shelby County, TN Conf Pensioner # C41
Jones, Zack (Jack)		24th Tennessee Infantry	Private	Hickman County, TN Conf Pensioner App # C117
Jordan, Wes	B	50th Regiment Tennessee Infantry	Servant	
Joyner, William		12th Tennessee Cavalry	Servant	Marshall County, MS Conf Pensioner
Kendael, Hiram		5th Regiment Tennessee	Cook	
Kindley, James (Kennedy)	C	46th Tennessee Infantry		Henry County, TN Conf Pension App # C253, application rejected.
King, Bill	E	20th Tennessee Regiment (Battle's) Served as a servant to Pvt. Jack King	Servant	Slave of Pvt. Jack King of Nolensville, TN.
Kinnard, Taylor (Kinnon)	K	54th Tennessee Infantry	Private	Haywood County, TN Conf Pensioner App # C227, first application rejected, second application approved.
Kirk, Sam		Hospital Service	Private	Rutherford County, TN Conf Pensioner App #
Kittrell, Bill		Unknown Tennessee Unit	Private	Maury County, TN Conf Pension App # C266
Knight, Lewis		17th Tennessee Infantry	Private	Franklin County, TN Conf Pensioner App # C124
Knox, George		Served as a Servant to his master, he later deserted and served the Federal Forces.	Servant	Wilson County, TN
Lacy, George		14th Tennessee Cavalry	Private	Madison County, TN Conf Pension App # C223
Lankford, Archie Davis		2nd Tennessee Cavalry	Private	Tipton County, TN Conf Pension App #C208
Lawrence, Drucy		Unknown Tennessee Unit	Private	
Ledbetter, Ralph		1st Tennessee Infantry	Private	Davidson County, TN Conf Pension App # C54
Lester, Richard	G	3rd Tennessee Infantry	Private	Giles County, TN Conf Pensioner App # C4. Buried at Maplewood Cemetery
Lester, Robert	K	8th Tennessee Infantry	Private	Davidson County, TN Conf Pensioner App # C126. Buried at Maplewood Cemetery in Giles County.
Liggett, R. M.	E	2nd Tennessee Cavalry	Private	Roane County, TN Conf Pension App # C160
Ligon, Henry	H	14th Tennessee Infantry	Private	Obion County, TN Conf Pensioner App # C
Lipscomb, Tricmas		9th Battalion Tennessee Cavalry	Private	Obion County, TN Conf Pension App # C
Littrell, Charley(Luttrell)	A	14th Tennessee Cavalry	Private	Hardeman County, TN Conf Pensioner App # C168
Livingston, Essex	E	7th Regiment Tennessee Calvary	Private	
Locke, Alfred	D	1st Tennessee Cavalry	Private	Rhea County, TN Conf
Love, Henry		5th Regiment Tennessee	Cook	
Lynch, Samuel		44th (Consolidated) Tennessee Infantry	Cook	

MacLin, James	B	7th Regiment Tennessee Calvary	Private	Lauderdale County, TN Conf Pensioner App # C192
Mainord, John	E	28th Regiment Tennessee Infantry (2nd Tennessee Mountain Volunteers)	Servant	
Maney, James	I	1st (Feild's) Tennessee Infantry Gen. Maney's Headquarters Served as a Body Servant to Lt. James Keeble Capt. Jackson's Company, Tennessee Cavalry Served as a Body Servant to Capt. Richard Keeble	Body Servant	Slave, Rutherford County, TN Conf Pensioner App # C164
Mann, Frank	E	7th Regiment Tennessee Calvary	Private	
Mann, Thomas	E	7th Regiment Tennessee Calvary	Private	
Mason, Charles	D	29th Regiment Tennessee Infantry	Cook	
Mason, Plunk		Unassigned, Wagon Train	Private	Hickman County, TN Conf Pensioner App # C182
Mathis, Dall (McFarland)		Gen. Cheatham's Headquarters Served as a Servant to Tom McFarland	Private	Haywood County, TN Conf Pensioner App # C159
Maxwell, Sam			Private	Giles County, TN Conf pensioner Buried at the Maplewood Cemetery in Pulaski, TN.
May, Nick		Served with his master Dr. May. He was then drafted by the Federal Army.	Private	
Mayberry, Jim		24th Tennessee Infantry	Private	Hickman County, TN Conf Pension App # C204
Mayes, Harrison		1st Tennessee Cavalry	Private	Maury County, TN Conf Pension App # C44
McCarter, William		62nd Tennessee Infantry	Private	Blount County, TN Conf Pension App # C171
McClarson, Bob		Unknown Tennessee Unit	Private	
McClasen, Bob		13th Tennessee Cavalry 14th Tennessee Cavalry		Shelby County, TN Conf Pension App # C180
McCullough, Ned		17th Tennessee Infantry		Rutherford County, TN Conf Pensioner App # C137
McDowell, Andrew		5th Battalion Tennessee Cavalry		Putnam County, TN Conf Pension App # C230
McEwan, A. A.		Gen. N.B. Forrest's Escort V Tennessee Calvary	Body Servant	
McEwen, George W.	H	1st Tennessee Infantry	Private	Davidson County, TN Conf Pensioner App # C95
McLemore, Daniel		4th Regiment Tennessee Cavalry (McLemor's) Served as Servant to Col. McLemore	Servant	
McMillian, William		37th Tennessee Cavalry		Knox County, TN Conf Pensioner App # C210, application rejected.
McNeal, Sam Simpson	E	7th Regiment Tennessee Infantry	Private	Shelby County, TN Conf Pensioner Apo #C146
McNeeley, Sam		14th Tennessee Cavalry	Private	Shelby County, TN Conf Pension

Directory of African American Confederates in the U.S. Civil War

McNeely, Rush	A	27th Tennessee Infantry	Private	Madison County, TN Conf Pension App # C172
McNeil, Ausburn		Unassigned	Team	Fayette County, TN Conf Pension App # C115
McRae, Henry		44th (Consolidated) Tennessee Infantry	Cook	
Mickles, Stephey		9th Regiment Mississippi Infantry	Private	Shelby County, TN Conf Pensioner # C174
Miller, Wash		Served as a cook for the Miller	Cook	Sumner County, TN
Miller, William		11th Tennessee Cavalry	Private	Rutherford County, TN Conf Pension App # C162, application rejected.
Minor, Ned		10th Tennessee Cavalry	Private	Stewart County, TN Cool Pensioner App # C110
Mitchell, Neal			Private	Giles County, TN Conf Pensioner Buried at the Maplewood Cemetery in Pulaski, TN.
Mitchell, Shem		27th Tennessee Infantry		Madison County, TN Conf Pension App
Mitchell, Zeal	D	29th Regiment Tennessee Infantry	Private	
Moon, Lewis		2nd Tennessee Cavalry		Lee County, MS Conf Pensioner
Moore, Benjamin		Unknown Tennessee Unit Served with Gen. Longstreet & Gen. P. T. Bauregard	Private	Bradley County, TN Conf Pensioner App # C250
Moore, Giles		9th Regiment Tennessee Cavalry 9th Alabama (Malone's Cav)	Private	Giles County, TN Conf Pensioner App # C22. Buried at Maplewood Cemetery in Pulaski, TN.
Moore, Joe	L	7th Regiment Tennessee Calvary	Private	
Moore, John		10th Tennessee Cavalry	Private	Hickman County, TN Conf Pension App # C263
Moore, Lewis		2nd Tennessee Cavalry	Private	Lee County, MS Conf Pensioner
Morris, Paden		Unknown Tennessee Unit	Private	Haywood County, TN Conf Pensioner App # C256
Morrison, Wyatt		Unknown Tennessee Unit	Private	Rutherford County, TN Conf Pension App # C247
Morton, Bob		Morton's Company, Tennessee Light Artillery, Served under Capt John W.	Cook	
Moses, John		7th Regiment Tennessee Calvary	Private	Madison County, TN Conf Pensioner App # C69
Moss, Henry		Unknown Tennessee Unit	Private	Slave, From a Plantation in Virginia. Ran away and joined the Confederate Army in Tennessee. According to his son Moses Moss in Arkansas Slave Narratives. Later became a Justice of the Peace in Yell County, Arkansas
Murray, Branch (Maury)	K	17th Mississippi Infantry	Private	Fayette County, TN Conf Pension App # C128, application rejected.
Murray, Charles		4th Regiment (Murray's) Tennessee Cavalry	Private	Shelby County, TN Conf Pension App # C226, application rejected.
Musgrove, Billie Webster	A	18th Mississippi Cavalry Battalion	Servant	Shelby County, TN Conf Pension App # C215, application rejected.
Muzzall, Lewis	E	20th Tennessee Cavalry	Private	Henry County, TN Conf Pensioner App # C65

Name		Unit	Role	Notes
Name not known	D	12th Regiment Tennessee Infantry 20th Regiment Tennessee Infantry Served as a Servant to Lt. John Russell Dance	Servant	Slave of 1st Lt. John Russell Dance Gibson County, TN
Name not known	I	16th Regiment Tennessee Infantry Served as a cook and servant to 3rd Lt Seitz, A.T.	Cook S e	According to 3rd Lt Seitz his servant sickened and died while in the Cheat Mt. Campaign 8/9/61
Neal, Henry		Unknown Mississippi Regiment Served his two young masters who were killed at the battle of	Body Servant	Madison County, TN Conf Pensioner # C130
Ned, James	F	2nd Tennessee Voluntary Cavalry "Tulloss Rangers"	Servant	
Nelson, Henry		19th & 20th Tennessee Cavalry		Gibson County, TN Conf Pension App # C23
Nelson, James Henry		3rd Regiment Tennessee Infantry (Clack's) Served as a Hostler to his master Henry M. Stanley	Hostler	Slave of Henry M. Stanley. States he was only seven years old when he went with his master to tend to his horses. captured and at a Mill by a Union soldier on a white horse and was taken to Pulaski, Tennessee and then he was in the Yankee army, he was then captured (rescued) by Gen. Forrest and his army. According to his statement in Arkansas Slave Narratives.
Nelson, Joe	L	7th Regiment Tennessee Calvary	Private	
Nelson, Louis Napoleon	M	7th Regiment Tennessee Calvary	Bodyguard, Chaplain, Cook, Forager	Lauderdale County, TN Conf Pensioner App # C32 Attended the UCV Reunion in Arkansas 1928, Attended 39 Confederate Veteran Reunions.
Newsom, Sam		Tennessee Cavalry Served as a Servant to Lt. Will Newsom who was killed in Chickamauga, he then took his masters body home.	Body Servant	Slave, Davidson County, TN Conf Pensioner App # C270. WIA, wounded in the Battle of Sullivan's Creek
Newsom, Silas		20th Tennessee Infantry	Private	Davidson County, TN Conf Pensioner App # C80
Nicholson, Isaac A.		Commissary Department, Polk's Corps		Davidson County, TN Conf Pensioner App # C60
Nolen, Alex	B	14th Tennessee Infantry		Montgomery County, TN Conf Pensioner App # C66
Northcross, Henry	E	7th Regiment Tennessee Calvary	Private	
Nowell, Smith	L	7th Regiment Tennessee Calvary		Lauderdale County, TN Conf Pensioner App # C156
O'Dell, Stephen	L	7th Regiment Tennessee Calvary	Private	
O'Neal, William		12th Mississippi Calvary		Madison County, TN Conf Pensioner # C157
Officer, Abe		Unknown Tennessee Unit		
Otey, Ephriam		Quartermaster Department	Private	Williamson County, TN Conf Pension App # C20
Oxendine, Levi		Camp Myers, Tennessee	Private	FMC, Mustered in July 30th 1861 by A.B. Hardcastle
Paragin, Lee		9th (Consolidated) Tennessee Cavalry	Private	Putnam County, TN Conf Pension App #

Parrish, John	F	2nd Tennessee Cavalry		Williamson County, TN Conf Pension App # C166, application rejected.
Patterson, Ed		Morton's Company, Tennessee Light Artillery, Served under Capt John W. Morton Jr.	Hostler	
Patton, Robert Bruce	F	4th Regiment Tennessee Cavalry (McLemore's)	Private	FMC, Davidson County, TN Conf Pension App # C24, application rejected.
Payne, Tillman Price		4th Tennessee Cavalry	Private	Trousdale County, TN Conf Pension App # C81
Payne, Tink		Unknown Tennessee Unit		Obion County, TN Conf Pension App # C284, application rejected.
Pearce, George		8th Regiment Tennessee Cavalry	Private	Gibson County, TN Conf Pension App # C135
Pearce, Green		Unknown Tennessee Unit	Laborer	
Pearson, J. B.		Gen. N.B. Forrest's Escort 3rd Tennessee Calvary	Body Servant	Marshall County, TN Conf Pensioner App # C61. Buried at Grove Cedar Cemetary, near Belfast, TN.
Perkins, Chanie		Unknown Tennessee Unit	Private	
Perkins, Jerry		31st Tennessee	Cook Servant	Slave of Charles Perkins who was KIA on 22 July 1864. Jerry Perkins was a member of the Hiram S. Bradford Bivouac and attended all the veterans reunions.
Perkins, John	E	7th Regiment Tennessee Calvary	Private	
Phillips, Asa		1st Tennessee Infantry		Franklin County, TN Conf Pension App # C220, application rejected.
Polk, Arnold		3rd Tennessee Calvary Gen. N.B. Forrest's Escort	Private	
Porter, Alex	F	20th Tennessee Cavalry		Henry County, TN Conf Pensioner App # C38
Prince, William		154th Tennessee Infantry	Servant	Holmes County, MS Conf Pensioner, injured during the war.
Pugh, Dawson	L	7th Regiment Tennessee Cavalry (Duckworth's)	Pvt	Slave, Haywood County, TN Conf Pensioner App # C197
Pugh, Jeff	L	7th Regiment Tennessee Calvary	Private	
Quarles, Harvey		8th Tennessee Infantry	Private	Davidson County, TN Conf Pensioner App # C214
Ransom, Alexander	A	24th Tennessee Infantry	Private	Bedford County, TN Conf Pensioner App #
Read, Henry	M	7th Regiment Tennessee Calvary	Private	Lauderdale County, TN Conf Pensioner App # C272
Ready, Albert		23rd Tennessee Infantry	Private	Rutherford County, TN Cone Pensioner App # C97
Reed, Alexander	E	7th Regiment Tennessee Calvary	Private	
Reeves, James	F	7th Regiment Tennessee Infantry	Private	Wilson County, TN Conf Pension App # C33, application rejected.
Reid, Nathan	K	6th Tennessee Infantry	Private	Obion County, TN Conf Pensioner App # C
Rennolcls, Fielding	D	5th Regiment Tennessee	Cook	

Reynolds, Joseph			Private	Buried at the Maplewood Cemetery in Pulaski, TN. Giles County, TN Conf Pensioner
Rice, Richard		29th Tennessee Infantry Regiment		Knox County, TN Conf Pension App # C138, application rejected.
Rivers, Argile		Served with his master Col. Rivers hauling food and other provisions for soldiers	Teamster	Slave of Col. Rivers of Somerville, TN. According to his daughter Mary Williams, in Arkansas Slave Narratives.
Rivers, Matt	F	11th Tennessee Cavalry		Giles County, TN Conf Pension App # C153, application rejected. Buried at the County Farm Cemetery
Roberts, Preston		3rd Tennessee Calvary Gen. N.B. Forrest's Escort Quartermaster	Cook Private	
Robertson, William		Dunk Cooper's Company		Maury County, TN Conf Pension App # C142, application rejected.
Robinson, James		Capt. Manley's Battery, Tennessee Artillery	Private	Davidson County, TN Conf Pensioner App # C35
Robinson, John Oscar		Col. Duncan's Cavalry		Carroll County, TN Conf Pensioner App # C199
Robinson, Mose	E	7th Regiment Tennessee Calvary	Private	
Rodgers, William		31st Tennessee Infantry	Private	Lake County, TN Conf Pensioner App # C115
Rucker, William		2nd Tennessee Infantry	Private	Rutherford County, TN Conf Pensioner App # C111
Russell, Frank		3rd Tennessee Calvary Gen. N.B. Forrest's Escort	Pvt	Williamson County, TN Conf Pensioner App# C17
Russell, Peter		Col. Napier's Regiment		Lewis County, TN Conf Pensioner App# C265
Sanford, Peter		Looney's Regiment		Tipton County, TN Conf Pensioner App # C144
Schoolfield, Henry Mathis	F	24th Tennessee Cavalry		Roane County, TN Conf Pension App # C112
Scott, Drew	B	50th Regiment Tennessee Infantry	Servant	
Seay, Frank M.	C	24th Tennessee Infantry		Williamson County, TN Conf Pensioner App # C145
Seward, Tode		28th Tennessee Infantry	Private	
Shad, Stephen		10th Tennessee Cavalry	Private	Gibson County, TN Conf Pensioner App# CS2
Shayse, Cal (Sharpe)		3rd Tennessee Calvary Gen. N. B. Forrest's Escort	Private	Hickman County, TN Conf Pension App# 2248
Shelby, Wallace (Shelly)		Hospital Service (Unassigned)		Davidson County, TN Conf Pension App # C219, application rejected.

Smith, Boney		14th Tennessee	Private	During Pickett's Charge at Gettysburg the Color Corporal was struck down Boney Smith took the colors carring them forward... The colors of the 14th Tennessee got within fifty feet of the east wall before Boney Smith hit the dirt ---wounded. Jabbing the flagstaff in the ground, he momentarily urged the regiment forward until the intense pressure forced the men to lie down to save their lives."
Smith, Coleman Davis		1st Tennessee Volunteers Infantry (Rutherford Rifles), (Coleman's Scouts) Served as a Body steward of Captain Sam Davis	Body Servant	Slave and childhood friend of Capt. Sam Davis. Shelby County, TN Conf Pensioner App Missing, After being captured Capt. Davis was hanged as a spy as Coleman watched
Smith, J. Wess		17th Tennessee Infantry	Private	Moore County, TN Conf Pension App # C47
Smith, Lewis		16th Tennessee Cavalry	Private	Davidson County, TN Conf Pensioner App # C108
Smith, Presley (Press)		6th Tennessee Infantry	Private	Madison County, TN Conf Pension App # C70
Starnes, Hardin	F	4th Regiment Tennessee Cavalry (McLemore's) Worked For Col. J.W. Starnes(Dr)	Private	Davidson County, TN Conf Pensioner App # C238
Stegall, Robert		Quartermaster Department	Private	Lincoln County, TN Conf Pension App # C76
Stephenson, Monroe		9th Battalion Tennessee Cavalry	Private	Maury County, TN Conf Pensioner App # C11
Stewart, Wiley	H	4th Tennessee Cavalry (Murray's) Capt. Q. C. Sanders Company)	Private	FMC
Stone, Fee		Worked on Island Number 10	Laborer	Gibson County, TN Conf Pension App # C158, application rejected.
Stover, Robert		Unknown Tennessee Unit Served with Samuel M. Stover	Private	Carter County, TN Conf Pensioner App # C91
Swift, Aaron	A	12th Tennessee Infantry	Private	Crockett County, TN Conf Pension App # C57, application rejected.
Taliaferro, Dobyns	L	7th Regiment Tennessee Calvary	Private	
Tansie, Ed (Tansii)		31st Tennessee Infantry	Private	Weakley County, TN Conf Pensioner App # C7
Taylor, Aaron	E	7th Regiment Tennessee Calvary	Private	
Taylor, Cornelius	E	7th Regiment Tennessee Calvary	Private	
Taylor, DECK	L	7th Regiment Tennessee Calvary	Private	
Taylor, George	L	7th Regiment Tennessee Calvary	Private	
Taylor, Hark	L	7th Regiment Tennessee Calvary	Private	
Taylor, James	F	2nd Tennessee Voluntary Cavalry "Tulloss Rangers"	Servant	
Taylor, Newton	E	28th Regiment Tennessee Infantry (2nd Tennessee Mountain Volunteers)	Servant	
Terrill, John	D	6th Regiment Tennessee Cavalry (Wheeler's Served as a Body Servant to Pvt. J.B. White	Servant	

Name		Unit	Role	Notes
Terry, John	F	2nd Tennessee Cavalry		Hamilton County, TN Conf Pensioner App # C255
Thomas, Add		General And Staff Officers, Enlisted Men, Staff Department Served with BGen. W. B. Bates	Servant	Maury County, TN Conf Pensioner App # C267
Thomas, Jackson	E	5th Tennessee Cavalry (McKenzie's)		Captured at Big Creek 1862. KIA May 1863
Thompson, Joe		Gen N. B. Forrest (Escort), Tennessee Cavalry	Servant	Newton County, MS Conf Pensioner since 1905
Thompson, Marshall		11th' Tennessee Cavalry 4th Regiment, Tennessee Cavalry (McLennoreTs) Worked For Col. J.W. Starnes (Dr)	Porter	Davidson County, TN Conf Pensioner App # C229
Thornton, Edward		Unassigned, Tennessee Unit	Team	Tipton County, TN Conf Pension App # 0177, application rejected.
Tidwell, Marshall		24th Tennessee Infantry		Hickman County, TN Conf Pension App # 0268
Townsend, Jack		17th Tennessee Cavalry Battalion	Servant	Clay County, MS Conf Pensioner
Travis, Jack	1	27th Tennessee Infantry		Carroll County, TN Conf Pension App # C42, application rejected.
Tucker, Ed	E	7th Regiment Tennessee Calvary		
Tuggle, Richard		18th Tennessee Infantry		Shelby County, TN Conf Pensioner App # C176
Tulloss, George	F	2nd Tennessee Voluntary Cavalry "Tulloss Rangers"	Servant	
Tullus, Blunt		4th Tennessee Cavalry		
Turner, Peter		30E- Tennessee Infantry		Robe7tson. County, 7-N Conf Pensioner App # C103
Tuttle, Americus (Female)		Unknown Tennessee Unit Followed the Unit of Col. James M. Tuttle supporting the Confederate soldiers.	Servant	Slave of Col. James Middleton Tuttle of Richland of Fayetteville, TN. According to Seabe Tuttle in Arkansas Slave Narratives.
Tuttle, Barbary (Female)		Unknown Tennessee Unit Followed the Unit of Col. James M. Tuttle supporting the Confederate soldiers.	Servant	Slave of Col. James Middleton Tuttle of Richland of Fayetteville, TN. According to Seabe Tuttle in Arkansas Slave Narratives.
Tuttle, Mark		Unknown Tennessee Unit Followed the Unit of Col. James M. Tuttle supporting the Confederate soldiers.	Servant	Slave of Col. James Middleton Tuttle of Richland of Fayetteville, TN. According to Seabe Tuttle in Arkansas Slave Narratives.
Tuttle, Unknown		Unknown Tennessee Unit Followed the Unit of Col. James M. Tuttle supporting the Confederate soldiers.	Servant	Stave of Col. James Middleton Tuttle of Richland of Fayetteville, TN. According to his son Seabe Tuttle in Arkansas Slave Narratives.
Walker, Bailey		13th Tennessee Infantry		Dyer County, TN Conf Pensioner App # C18
Walker, Dick	E	7th Regiment Tennessee Calvary		
Walker, Isaac L.		Unknown Tennessee Unit		Slave of Warrarh Easley, Hickman Court., TN Conf Pensioner App #c258
Walls, Henry		15th Tennessee Infantry Served as a servant to Dr. John Walls	Servant	Kemper County, MS Conf Pensioner, battle injury.

Name		Unit	Role	Location / Pension
Ward, Mose	C	24th Tennessee Infantry	Private	Hickman County, TN Conf Pensioner App # C262
Ware, Charles		16th Tennessee Infantry	Servant	Warren County, TN Conf Pensioner App # C205
Warren, Joe		5th Regiment Tennessee	Cook	
Watkins, Wade		48th Tennessee Infantry Served as a Servant to a Surgeon	Servant	Lauderdale County, TN Conf Pensioner App # C269
Webb, Charlie		13th Tennessee Infantry	Private	Fayette County, TN Conf Pensioner App #
Wharton, Alex (Big Alex)		154th Senior Regiment, Tennessee Infantry	Private	Madison County, TN Conf Pensioner App # C71
Wharton, Alex (Little Alex)		21st Tennessee Cavalry	Private	Madison County, TN Conf Pensioner App #
Wharton, Frank		14th Tennessee Cavalry	Private	Haywood County, TN Conf Pensioner App # C167
Whitaker, Ike		Unknown Tennessee Unit Served as a Blacksmith	Blacksmith	Slave of George and Bill Whitaker of Murray County, Tennessee. According to his son Joe Whitaker in Arkansas Slave Narratives.
White, Dick		6th Tennessee Infantry	Private	Haywood County, TN Conf Pensioner App # C134
Whitelow, Wright (Whitelaw)		7th & 3rd (Forrest) Tennessee Cavalry 16th Tennessee Cavalry		Haywood County, TN Conf Pension App # C206 & C236, application rejected.
Whiteside, Charlie		48th Tennessee Infantry	Private	Hickman County, TN Conf Pensioner App #
Wilkerson, Charles	I	1st Tennessee Cavalry	Private	Haywood County, TN Conf Pensioner App # C59
Wilkes, Nim		Gen. N.B. Forrest's Escort, 3rd Tennessee Calvary Served as a Personal Servant to Gen. Forrest	Team	Maury County, TN Conf Pensioner App # C1
Williams, George Henry	I	18th Tennessee infantry	Private	Rutherford County, TN Conf Pensioner App # C98
Williams, Unknown		Unknown Tennessee Unit	Private	Slave of John and Lizzie Williams of Davidson County, Tennessee. According to his sister Lizzie McCloud he was KIA in Arkansas Slave Narratives.
Williams, UnKnown		Unknown Tennessee Unit Served as a Blacksmith	Blacksmith	Slave of John and Mary Williams According to his daughter Sarah Williams Wells, in Arkansas Slave Narratives.
Wilson, John	E	7th Regiment Tennessee Calvary	Private	
Wilson, Noah		9th Tennessee Cavalry Battalion	Servant	Lafayette County, MS Conf Pensioner
Windrow, Wyatt		Unknown Tennessee Unit Confederate Army	Servant	Rutherford County, TN Conf Pensioner App # C257
Winfield, Henry		Served as a Bodyguard to Jeff Davis	Bodyguard	Shelby County, TN Conf Pensioner App # C282
Winston, Maniel	E	9th Regiment Tennessee Infantry	Private	Shelby County, TN Conf Pensioner App # C155
Withers, James W.	F	3rd Mississippi Calvary	Private	Shelby County, TN Conf Pensioner #C133

Wood, M. E.		Morgan's Cavalry	Private	Hamilton County, TN Conf Pension App # C222, application rejected.
Woods, John		Col. Napier's Regiment	Private	Lewis County, TN Conf Pensioner App # C264
Woods, Smith	G	20th Tennessee Cavalry	Private	Dyer County, TN Conf Pension App # C77
Word, George		20th Tennessee Cavalry	Private	Gibson County, TN Conf Pensioner App # C28
Wright, Austin	6	7th Regiment Tennessee Calvary	Private	Tipton County, TN Conf Pension App # C280, application rejected.
Wright, Simeon		3rd Mississippi Infantry	Private	Quitman County, MS Conf Pensioner
Youree, Henry		2nd Tennessee Cavalry Served as a servant to Patrick Youree	Servant	Sumner County, TN Conf Pensioner App # C12

Texas

Native American Stand Watie, a difficult Cherokee chieftain who signed away his ancestral lands and fought for the South in the Civil War, terrifying many of his own people, was the last Confederate general to surrender. How did a high-ranking Indian in the Deep South sign away his ancestral lands and become a Confederate commander during the Civil War? And why did he attack other Native people so vehemently during the conflict?

Stand Watie lived at a tumultuous period for his people—and for the fledgling American nation. Indians were increasingly uprooted from their homelands and, in some cases, massacred throughout the nineteenth century. Internal strife arose over complex problems such as slavery—some Indians were slaveowners themselves—and whether or not to sign treaties that forced them to choose between their ways of life and their own survival. Indians were compelled to take sides in the white man's war once the South seceded from the Union.

Cherokee Stand Watie picked the South.

Slaves were owned by his family. Stand Watie was born in 1806 in Oothcaloga, Cherokee Nation (near present-day Rome, Georgia) to a Cherokee father and a mixed-race (half-Cherokee, half-European) mother. His Cherokee name was Degataga, which meant "stand strong."

His father, Oo-wa-tie, changed his son's name to Isaac S. Uwtie after he was baptized into the Moravian Church as David Uwatie. As an adult, though, Isaac merged his Cherokee and Christian names (omitting the "U") to create Stand Watie. In 1889, Texas began paying destitute Confederate veterans and their widows annuities. Texas, like most other southern states, limited its Confederate service pension payments to disabled or impoverished soldiers or their widows who have lived in Texas since 1880. Between 1899 and 1975, the Office of the Comptroller of Public Accounts received

Stand Watie Confederate commander

54,634 applications. Between 1934 and 1980, these Confederate Pension Applications were handed to the Texas State Library and Archives Commission. In 1899, Texas established the Confederate Pension Law. According to the statute, a Confederate soldier or sailor was eligible if he or she was a native Texan or a resident of Texas prior to 1880, over sixty, and disabled as a result of service during the Civil War.

In addition to soldiers and sailors, widows who had never remarried and had lived in Texas since 1880 were entitled for a stipend. Many of these limits were ultimately removed from the pension law, especially for widows.

Texas State Library and Archives Commission
1201 Brazos St, Austin, TX 78701
Phone: (512) 463-5455
Web Site: www.tsl.texas.gov/

.

Mandingo Overseer

Absentee plantation ownership management was increasing as the war proceeded and these owners had to select slaves with the most leadership, organizational and social skills to manage the plantation.

Southern plantation owners departing for the war needed to make sure their most highly qualified male slaves were in place to take over responsibilities and maintain day-to-day operations which supplied the confederacy army with vital goods .

Encouraged to be a loyal warrior on the home front, a slave might enjoy more autonomy than ever before, including the freedom to identify more strongly and openly with African roots. This image instance was instigated by the slave owner to create an atmosphere of his superiority.

The South learned during the shortage of manpower in the Civil War that slaves were useful not only in agriculture but also that they worked well in manufacturing and other similar industries.

Toward the very end of the war, the South flirted with the idea of exchanging freedom for slaves' services in the Confederate Army. Since white manpower was at a premium in the South, black manpower became all the more important.

By 1862, the South relied on a draft for its Army manpower. One of the most controversial exemptions from military service was for white men who owned 20 slaves.

This exemption reflected the South's age-old fear of slave revolts. The law also exempted some overseers for it was believed that only a tough male overseer could keep numbers of slaves under control.

Most men in the Southern armies were not slave owners. The Twenty-Slave Law exemption for slave owners led some to mutter that it was "a rich man's war and a poor man's fight" and any incentives were used to find the right choices. One particular slave was told about his ancestral origins and was inspired to be a plantation work production leader, as recounted in the historical part fiction graphic novel Uncle T and the Uppity Spy.

Directory of African American Confederates in the U.S. Civil War

NAME	CO.	UNIT	RANK	SLAVE I FREE MISC NOTES
Alex		8th Regiment, Texas Cavalry (Terry's) (1st Rangers) (8th Rangers) Served as a Body Servant to Pvt. Isaac Dunbar Affleck	Body Servant	
Alexander	B	24th Texas Cavalry (Wilkes' Regiment. 2nd Texas Lancers. 2nd Regiment, Carter's Brig.)	Cook	
Austin	D	23rd Texas Cavalry (Gould's Regiment. 27th Texas Cavalry.)	Cook	
Ben	D	23rd Texas Cavalry (Gould's Regiment. 27th Texas Cavalry.)	Cook	
Ben	G	24th Texas Cavalry (Wilkes' Regiment. 2-d Texas Lancers. 2-' Regiment, Carter's Brig.)	Cook	
Bill	K	Morgan's Regiment Texas Cavalry	Private	
Bob	K	Morgan's Regiment Texas Cavalry	Private	
Bob		Hogg's Brigade General and Staff Officers, Non- Regimental Enlisted Men, CSA Served as a body servant to his master BGen. (Dr.) Joseph Lewis Hogg	Body Servant	BGen Hogg of Cherokee County, Texas caught a disease and died in Corinth, MS.
Caesar	C	26th Texas Cavalry	Cook	
Cornelius	H	4th Regiment Cavalry, Texas State Troops	Private	
Dorsey	H	23rd Texas Cavalry (Gould's Regiment. 27th Texas Cavalry.)	Private	
Frank	D	23'd Texas Cavalry (Gould's Cook Regiment. 27th Texas Cavalry.)		
George	H, I	4th Regiment Cavalry, Texas State Troops	Private	
George	F	1st Texas Heavy Artillery	Private	
George	G	Mann's Regiment Texas Cavalry	Private	
Green	B	24th Texas Cavalry (Wilkes' Regiment. rd Texas Lancers. 2nd Regiment, Carter's Brig.)		
Hall	D	23ld Texas Cavalry	Cook	
Henry	F	Mann's Regiment Texas Cavalry (Bradford's Regiment)	Private	
Henry		Served as a servant to Henry Wigfall the son of Senator and Gen. Louis T. Wigfall	Body Servant	Slave
Isaac	K	Morgan's Regiment Texas Cavalry	Private	
Isaac	B	1- Texas Infantry	Private	
Isham	I	3ourland's Regiment Texas Cavalry	Private	
Jim		±.:.- (Spaight's) Battalion Texas Volunteers	Chief Cook	
Job		23-: Texas Cavalry	Laundryman	
John	F	24:- Texas Cavalry	Private	
Lucy (Female)		24:- Texas Cavalry (Wilkes' Regiment. 2nd Texas Lancers. 2rd Regiment, Carter's rig.)	Slave	Slave

Lud	A	11th (Spaight's) Battalion Texas Vols.	Cook	
Maple		Unknown Unit		Sulpher Springs, TX Attended the UCV Reunion in Arkansas 1928
Marlborough	B	7thTexas Infantry Regiment Served as a servant to Maj. Raleigh S. Camp. Also served the State of Georgia	Servant	
Moses	C	26th Texas Cavalry	Cook	
Nathan	C,I	11th Texas Infantry	Cook	
Nathan		8th Texas Cavalry (Terry's Texas Rangers)		
Nathan	H	7th Regiment, Texas Infantry Gregg's)	Slave	Slave
,Nelson	B	24th Texas Cavalry (Wilkes' Regiment. 2nd Texas Lancers. 2nd Regiment, Carter's Brig.)		
Pate	A	23rd Texas Cavalry	Laundress	
Sam	D,E	23rd Texas Cavalry (Gould's Regiment. 27t" Texas Cavalry.)	Private	
Will	K	Morgan's Regiment Texas Cavalry	Private	
Auster, J.	D	23rd Texas Cavalry (Gould's Regiment. 27th Texas Cavalry.)	Cook	
Avant, Jake		3rd Texas Cavalry		Panola County, MS Conf Pensioner
Bell, Robin		15th Texas Infantry		Hinds County, MS Conf Pensioner
Blain, Nick	G	7th Regiment Texas Infantry Served as a servant to George Blain	Servant	
Boyd, Richard Henry (Dick Gray)		Served as a Body Servant to Mr. Gray	Body Servant	Slave
Braxton, Abraham		3rd Texas Cavalry		Bolivar County, MS Conf Pensioner
Braxton, Cato		3rd Texas Cavalry		Yazoo County, MS Conf Pensioner
Braxton, Jerry		3rd Texas Cavalry		Yazoo County, MS Conf Pensioner
Brown, Ike		Texas Unit Served in shops supporting the Confederacy in Texas.	Blacksmith	Arkansas, Lincoln County Conf Pensioner. Application #29202. 1923 petition by U.C.V. pension for Ike Brown(ex-slave)
Calvin, Winters		6th Texas Infantry	Cook	Warren County, MS Conf Pensioner
Cape, James		Served as a soldier in an unknown Texas Unit	Private	Slave of Bob Houston of Southeast Texas. According to his own statement in Texas Slave Narratives he was a Substitute for a Dr. Garroll.
Cartwright, Osey C.	D	4th Texas Infantry Served under Capt. D. M. Short As a servant to Americus Peyroux Cartwright	Servant	Conf Pension denied
Clark, Robert		6th Texas Cavalry		Yazoo County, MS Conf Pensioner
Collier, Holt	I	9th Texas Regiment (Capt. Perry Evans Cavalry Company)	Private	Freed Slave, Washington County, MS Conf Pensioner
Crump, Cornelius		Cobb's Co Texas Cavalry (Scouts)	Servant	Hinds County, MS Conf Pensioner

Directory of African American Confederates in the U.S. Civil War

Daily, Calvin P.	G	10th Texas Infantry	Servant	
Dandridge, Unknown		Served as a laborer and Supervisor in Tyler, Texas supervising approximately 50 others making bullets for the Confederate Army.	Laborer	Slave of James Railey and Matilda Railey. According to statements made by his son Lyttleton Dandrige in Arkansas Slave Narratives.
Davis, (Hill) Crockett		8th Texas Cavalry	Servant	Served as a Servant to Five Hill Brothers in the Unit.
Davis, G. W.		13th Texas Infantry (Bates)		Arkansas, Miller County Conf Pensioner, application #7402. His application was rejected in 1905.
Diggs, Green (Greenwood)		3rd Texas Cavalry	Private	Yazoo County, MS Conf Pensioner
East, George Washington	H	4th Texas Calvary	Private	Davidson County, TN Conf Pensioner #C13, application rejected.
Esclavon, Jacques	A	Ragsdale's Battalion Texas Cavalry	Cook Teamst	Free Mulatto of Calcasieu Parish, LA.
Fletcher, Thomas	E	29th Regiment Texas Cavalry (DeMorse's)	1st Lt	
Hampton, George H.	C	4th Texas Cavalry	Private	Texas Conf Pensioner #39149
Hood, Bill			Private	Houston, TX. Attended the UCV Reunion in Arkansas 1928
Howard, Henderson		Hood's Texas Brigade	Private	
Johnson, Ike	K	Col. James Duff's 33rd Texas Cavalry, Partisan Rangers	Servant	Grenada County, MS Conf Pensioner
Johnson, Joshua		6th Texas Cavalry	Servant	Madison County, MS Conf Pensioner
King, Fred	K	17th Regiment, Texas Cavalry (Moore's)	Cook	
Lemons, C. C.			Private	Calvert, TX, Attended the UCV Reunion in Arkansas 1928
Mabry, Jeff	G	3rd Texas Cavalry Servant of Col. Hinche Parham Mabry He was known as the "Head Chicken Thief of the 3= Texas Cavalry"	Body Servant	Slave, Member of the Ashcroft Camp #170, U.C.V. in Sulpher Springs, Texas.
McConnell, Lewis		Served as a Servant to Capt. W. H. McConnell	Servant	Slave
Miller, Levi	C	5th Texas Infantry Served with Captain J. E. Anderson,	Private	Slave, VA Conf Pensioner According to Capt. Armstrong "Levi Miller stood by my side-- and man never fought harder and better than he did-- and when the enemy tried to cross our little breastworks and we clubbed and bayoneted them off, no one used his bayonet with more skill, and effect, than Levi Miller."
Moore, Henry		32nd Texas Cavalry	Private	Madison County, MS Conf Pensioner
Murphy, Isaac		5th Texas Regiment Cavalry Partisans	Servant	Jefferson County, MS Conf Pensioner
Murray, Branch	K	17th Texas Infantry	Private	Denied TN Conf Pension
Pohalski, Hamilton		11th Regiment, Texas	Servant	

Price, John	B	4th Texas Infantry (The Torn Green Rifles) Served as a servant to John T. Price	Body Servant	Slave
Shaw, Jessie		7th Texas Infantry		Yazoo County, MS Conf Pensioner, battle injury.
Shropshire, Robert	A	5th Texas Cavalry Served Under of Maj. John Shropshire	Teamster	Slave
Smith, Edward		3rd Texas Infantry		Yazoo County, MS Conf Pensioner
Smith, Solomon	A	10th Regiment Texas Infantry (Nelson's)	Private	
Stewart, Jerry		5th Texas Infantry	Regt Teamster	Hinds County, MS Conf Pensioner, non battle injury.
Stoker, George	G	10th Texas infantry	Servant	
Stokes, Nathan	I	8th Regiment Texas Cavalry (Terry's Texas Rangers) Served as a Body Servant to Maj. George Washington Littlefield	Servant	Slave
Vesey, Randolph (Uncle Ran)		Served as a body servant to General William Lewis Cabel	Body Servant	Georgia Slave
Walton, Scott		27th Texas Cavalry		Madison County, MS Conf Pensioner
Williams, Henson		Unknown Texas Unit	Private	Brazos County
Williams, L.	B	24th Texas Cavalry (Wilkes' Regiment. 2nd Texas Lancers. 2nd Regiment, Carter's Brig.)		
Winston, Dan	E	5th Texas Infantry (Dixie Blues) Served as a body servant to Cap:.Tom Baber	Body Servant Cook	Washington County, TX. He was a member of Hood's Texas Brigade Association. He attended the 1904 Assocation meeting in Ennis, TX.
Woodward, Dennis		1st Texas Infantry	Wash And Cook	Calhoun County, MS Conf Pensioner

Virginia

A Confederate Sharpshooter's Union's account. The marksmanship of African American Confederate skirmishers and sharpshooters is documented in a number of Union sources. Captain C. A. Stevens recounted the following event in April 1862 during the siege of Yorktown, Virginia, in Berdan's. United States Sharpshooters in the Army of the Potomac, 1861-1865. (Reprint: The Press of Morningside Bookshop, Dayton, Ohio, 1972)

During the siege, the enemy had a African American rifle shooter in front of them who kept up a close fire on our soldiers, and despite the enormous distance, he caused more or less aggravation by his relentless firing. While on a detail at the forward positions, the writer and his squad got the opportunity to see this determined darky's ability with his well-aimed gun. With sandbags stacked up for cover at a hole on the edge of a wood in front of the treeless expanse of ground around the opposing works, this rebellious black made his appearance at the side of an officer during the forenoon and began firing at us under his orders. This accidental shooting was kept up for a long time, the black standing out in plain sight and calmly drawing bead, but it failed to provoke any re-

sponse, despite our orders to remain silent and not be observed. So the Negro had the pit to himself, and his pop, pop, against the sand bags on the pit's edge was common, while other near shots amid the trees demonstrated that he was a strong long-range shooter.

Before he died, he had earned quite a reputation for shooting among the scouts and pickets and had developed quite a reputation for marksmanship. A plan worked, and his doom was sealed. One morning in camp, "a scouting team having cornered the nigger on a chimney top a quarter of a mile distance, where he had been disguised, eventually dragged him down," and thus ended his pastime with his life. Sergt.

Andrews of Company (Subsequently, the captain) spotted the person in the second story of the ancient chimney,—a standing monument of ruin, of which there were many along this Peninsula route,—and found him firing through a hole in the rear of the fireplace with the assistance of his magnificent telescope.In 1888, 1900, and 1902, the Virginia General Assembly passed Confederate pension legislation, as well as a series of additional acts between 1903 and 1934.

Union Civil War Coffee Wagon

In early 1863 a young pharmacist in Philadelphia, Pennsylvania, by the name of Jacob Dunton saw the need for a machine that could brew large amounts of coffee, very quickly to meet the demand of the soldiers in the Union Army. His answer was a horse drawn "coffee wagon." It is constructed somewhat like a battery caisson, so that the parts can he unlimbered and separated from each other.

The 'limber,' or forward part, bears a large chest which is divided into compartments to contain coffee, tea, sugar, and cornstarch, with a place, also, for two gridirons and an axe. From the rear portion rise three tall smoke-pipes above three large boilers, under which there is a place for the fire, and under the fire a box for the fuel.

Each boiler will hold twelve gallons, and it is estimated that in each one, on the march, ten gallons of tea, or coffee, This coffee wagon was present at Appomattox April 9th, 1865 which was the end of the American Civil War for General Robert E. Lee and the Confederate Army of Northern Virginia.

It was surrendered to Lt. General Ulysses S. Grant and black and white confederate soldiers departed for home.
The Re-enactor's Missions for Jesus Christ (RMJC) refurbish

and hauled a replica of this Civil War era coffee wagon to the re-enactment, which marked the anniversary of the battles to end the American Civil war. The replica coffee wagon was made in 1970. The patent for such a wagon was originally issued in 1863. Hot beverages were served to Union and Confederate soldiers alike throughout the war.

"They did not see blue or gray. They saw human beings in need," said Chaplain Alan Farley, of RMJC

The USCC was also one of the few organizations that actively recruited women, who were wanted for their cooking skills, Harker said. Wounded soldiers were fed the same food as fighting men, but a woman named Annie Wittenmyer knew sick men couldn't return to health on a poor diet, so the USCC sought out wives and mothers, who made special meals with treats such as eggs and butter.

"Thousands of black and white soldiers went home at the end of the war because of these ladies The confederate soldiers of the Civil War were often hungry. They mostly ate hard crackers made from flour, water, and salt called hardtack. Sometimes they would get salt pork or corn meal to eat. To supplement their meals, soldiers would forage from the land around them. They would hunt game and collect fruits, berries, and nuts whenever they could. By the end of the war, many soldiers in the Confederate army were on the verge of starvation. Food shortages and military privation contributed in part to the Confederate mystique.

Virginia

The act of 1888 established annuities for disabled Confederate soldiers, sailors, and marines, as well as widows of those slain in combat. Following legislation, all veterans, their widows, and their unmarried or widowed daughters were covered.

The acts stipulated that candidates must be Virginia residents. Veterans or their survivors who lived in the District of Columbia were later covered in later legislation.

This collection contains pension applications and amendments filed by Confederate veterans and widows living in Virginia. The applications include declarations regarding the applicants' service records, as well as medical examinations, information about the veterans' or widows' income and property, and, in the case of widows, the date and site of marriages. The collection also includes claims from over 500 African Americans who served in the Confederate army as cooks, herders, laborers, Servants, or teamsters.

The database of pension applications can be searched by applicant name and status The database of pension applications can be searched by the applicant's name, the applicant's status (for example, veteran, widow, or Servant), the date of the pension act, and the applicant's current address (county or city). Each article also includes links to digitized photographs of the actual applications as well as supporting documentation. This database is a fully searchable version of the applicants' Electronic Card Index.

Note: The name "Servant" refers to those who served in the Confederate army as chefs, herders, Servants, laborers, or teamsters.

Library of Virginia
Archives Division
800 East Broad Street
Richmond, VA 23219
Telephone: 804-692-3888
web Site: www.lva.virginia.gov/
Phone: 804-692-3500

NAME	CO.	UNIT	RANK	SLAVE / FREE MISC NOTES
Abram		Served as a Body Servant to CSA Signal Corps, Ger. Edward Porter Alexander of the Staff of General James Longstreet, 1st Corps, Army of Northern Virginia	Body Servant	
Adam		Capt. Daniel Shanks' Company Virginia Horse Artillery	Private	
Adam	E	32nd Regiment Virginia Infantry	Cook	Slave
Albert	A	25th Battalion Virginia Infantry (Richmond Battalion Virginia Infantry. City Battalion Virginia Infantry,)	Cook	
Alex		7th Virginia Cavalry	Teamster	
Alexander	K	32th Virginia Infantry	Cook	
Andrew	G	25th Battalion Virginia Infantry (Richmond Battalion Virginia Infantry. City Battalion Virginia Infantry.)	Cook	
Armisted		7th Regiment Virginia Cavalry	Teamster	
Ben		16th Virginia Infantry		
Ben		48th Regiment Virginia Infantry Mahone's Brigade) Served under Capt. Francis Smith Robertson	Camp Boy	FMC
Ben		7th Sediment Virginia Cavalry	Teamster	
Berry		Confederate Quartermaster's Stable, under Capt. McCormack Died while in Confederate Service, buried in the Confederate Cemetery in the Negro Section. Lynchburg, VA.	Hospital Attendant	Slave of Capt. Barksdale

Directory of African American Confederates in the U.S. Civil War

Bill		Liggon Hospital, Richmond, VA	Servant	Slave of W. OTHO HILL, Asst. Surgeon C. S. A., Battery
Bill (Bill Doins)		Served as a regimental cook, and was known for his ingenious ways of cooking food under difficult circumstances.	Cook	Freed Slave
Blake		Camp Winder General Hospital, Division 2, Richmond, Virginia	Cook	
Bob		48th Regiment Virginia Infantry (Mahone's Brigade) Served under Capt. Francis Smith Robertson	Camp Boy Servan	Slave,Served at Sailors Creek
Bob		Capt. B. H. Smith's Company, Artillery (Third Company, Richmond Howitzers) Virginia Artillery	Cook Teamster	
Bob		3rd Regiment Virginia Cavalry (Stuart's Brigade) Served as a servant to Gen. J.E.B. Stuart	Musician Servant	Also served as a Musician,
Bob		Hospital No. 10, Richmond, Va.	Nurse	
Bob		Virginia State Rangers	Servant	
Bob	D	7th Virginia Infantry Regiment Served as a Servant to Samuel B. Shannon and Joseph C. Shannon	Cook	
Brown		7th Regiment Virginia Cavalry	Teamster	
Burns		36th Virginia Infantry Regiment Served as a Body Servant to General "Tiger" John McCausland	Body Servant	FMC
Cambridge		Served working at the Tredegar Iron Works, VA	Laborer	Slave
Catherine		Jackson Hospital Richmond, Virginia		Slave of Mrs. J. N. Cooper
Chapman		Charlottesville Artillery	Servant	
Charles		5th Virginia Cavalry	Private	
Charles		Goucester Company Guards	Cook	
Charles	A	25th Battalion Virginia Infantry	Cook	
Charles	F&S	13th Regiment Virginia Infantry Served as a Servant to Gen. Ambrose Powell Hill "Light Division"	Servant	
Cosar (Caesar)		Served as a Hospital Attendant and died while in Confederate Service, buried in the Confederate Cemetery in the Negro Section. Lynchburg, VA.	Hospital Attendant	Slave of Mrs. Raney
Cyrus		7th Virginia Cavalry	Teamster	
David		Goochland Light Artillery, Virginia	Cook	
Dudley		2nd Division, Winder Hospital	Slave	Slave of Mr. Allsop of Pittsylvania County, VA.
Edmund		2nd Virginia Cavalry	Slave	Participated in Charge and killed enemy leader Averhart; mentioned in dispatches by Gen. J.E.B. Stuart.
Edmund		Served working at the Tredegar Iron Works, VA	Blacksmith	Slave of William Robinson of Danville, Va.
Ephraim	1st	Capt. R. M. Anderson's Company, Light Artillery (First Company, Richmond Howitzers),Virginia Artillery		

Ezekiel	F	32nd Virginia Infantry	Cook	
Fleming		Served working at the Tredegar Iron Works, VA	Laborer	Slave
Francis	D D	7th Virginia Cavalry (McDonald's Company) 11th Virginia Cavalry Regiment 17th Virginia Cavalry Regiment	Private	Hardy County, West Virginia
Frank		Goochland Light Artillery, Virginia	Cook	
Frank	K	11th Virginia Cavalry	Private	
Frederick		Goochland Light Artillery, Virginia	Cook	
Gabriel		Camp Winder General Hospital, Division 2, Richmond, Virginia	Nurse	
George	A,G	25th Battalion Virginia Infantry	Chief Cook	
George	C	11th Regiment Virginia Served as a cook for Cpl. Robert Cooke	Cook	
George	F	32nd Virginia Infantry	Cook	
George	G	24th Virginia Infantry	Cook	
Grace (Female)		Camp Winder General Hospital, Division 2, Richmond, Virginia	Laundress	
Gustin	F	32nd Virginia Infantry	Cook	
Hampton		Served as a Hospital Attendant and died while in Confederate Service, buried in the Confederate Cemetery in the Negro Section. Lynchburg, VA.	Hospital Attendant	Slave of J. W. Woodson of Appomattox County, Virginia
Hannah (Female)	B	25th Battalion Virginia Infantry	Cook	
Henry		Chimborazo Hospital, Richmond VA	Servant	
Henry		7th Virginia Cavalry	Teamster	
, Henry		Served as a body servant to Capt. G. W. Alexander, Assistant Provost Marshal	Body Servant	Killed when a pistol accidently when off striking him.
Henry	G	25th Battalion, Virginia Infantry (Richmond Battalion) (City Battalion)	COOK	
Henry	H	6th Virginia Cavalry	Private	
Hiram		7thVirginia Cavalry	Teamster	
Hiram			Private	Slave of Capt. J. Sheppard
Horace		7th Virginia Cavalry	Teamster	
Howard		Served as a Hospital Stewart and Servant to J. H. Slater in service to Dr. John H. Clairborne (Surgeon)	Hospital Stewart	Surrendered at Appomattox
Hudson		Chimborazo Hospital, Richmond VA	Servant	Slave
f Jack	G	25thBattalion Virginia Infantry	Chief Cook	
James	A	25th Battalion Virginia Infantry	Cook	
James	F	62nd Virginia Infantry	Cook	From Carr, VA
Jane (Female)		Served as a Hospital Attendant and died while in Confederate Service.	Hospital Attendant	Slave of Col. W. H. Brown. Buried at the Old City Cemetary in Lynchburg, VA. She was the only female buried in the Confederate section, she died in 1864.
Jim		7th Virginia Cavalry	Teamster	
Jim		Charlottesville Artillery	Servant	

Name		Unit	Role	Notes
, Jim		Served as a Servant to Gen. Thomas J. (Stonewall)	Servant	
, Jim		Slave of 1st Lt. T. M. Detrick of 24th Regiment, Virginia Cavalry	Unknown	Surrendered at Appomattox
, Jim		Served as a servant to his master President Jefferson Davis	Servant	Slave
, Jim (Twin)		Served with Col. J. H. Averill, Trainmaster, Richmond & Danville Railroad	Private	Age 14 twin brother of Tom
Joe	H	13th Virginia Cavalry	Teamster	
John		5th Regiment Virginia Cavalry (12 months, 1861-62) (Mullins')	Bugler	
, John		Chimborazo Hospital, Camp Winder, Virginia	Slave	Slave of Dr. McCraw
, John	B	12th Virginia Cavalry (Baylor Light Horse) Served as a Servant to Capt. George Baylor	Servant	Slave
, John		Army of Northern Virginia Served as a Servant to Maj. Henry E. Payton	Servant	Slave of Maj. Henry E. Payton
, John "Black Hawk"		7th Regiment Virginia Cavalry Served as a Cook and Servant to Dr. James Battle Averitt.	Servant Cook	Dr. Averitt was one of the first Chaplains of the Army of Northern Virginia
, John G.		2nd Division, Winder Hospital, Commissary	Private	From Prince Edward, VA.
Joseph	A	49th Regiment Virginia Infantry	Cook	
, Joseph	F	62nd Virginia Infantry	Cook	From Lawrence, VA
, Julius		Jackson Hospital, 3rd Division, Richmond, Virginia	Nurse	Slave of Samuel Bailey
, Levi		Served as a Hospital Attendant and died while in Confederate Service, buried in the Confederate Cemetery in the Negro Section. Lynchburg, VA.	Hospital Attendant	Slave of Dr. Wise
, Lewis		7th Virginia Cavalry	Teamster	
, Lewis		Reid's Factory Hospital Served as a Hospital Attendant and died while in Confederate Service, buried in the Confederate Cemetery in the Negro Section. Lynchburg, VA.	Hospital Attendant	Slave of Richard Smiley
Luke	H	6th Virginia Infantry	Private	
, Marshall		2nd Division, Winder Hospital	Slave	Slave of C. S. Franklin
, Mike		Chimborazo Hospital, Richmond	Servant	
, Morgan	F&S	8th Regiment Virginia Infantry Served as a Servant to Gen. Eppa Hunton of Virginia	Servant	Served a: Sailor's Creek
, Mortiner		Goochland Light Artillery, Virginia	Cook	
Moses	F	5th Regiment Virginia Cavalry (Prince George Cavalry) Served as a Body Servant to his master Pvt. Robert (Bob) Bland	Servant	Prince George County, VA
, Murry		12th North Carolina Infantry Served as a Servant to Col. Henry Eaton Coleman	Servant	Slave owned by Mr. Logan of the Oakville Plantation, Virginia

Nat		2nd Division, Winder Hospital	Slave	Slave of N. Welsh of Richmond, VA.
Ned		John Powell Academy Servant to Thomas Watkins Leigh at Battle of Staunton River Bridge	Servant	
Nottingham	K	32nd Regiment Virginia Infantry	Servant	
Oliver		Bellevue Hospital Served as a servant	Servant	
Oliver		7th Virginia Cavalry	Driver	
Oscar	E	53rd Regiment Virginia Infantry Served under Capt. Benjamin Farinholt	Servant	Slave
Ottaway	A	25th Battalion, Virginia Infantry (Richmond Battalion) (City Battalion)	Cook	
Overton	B	12th Virginia Cavalry (Baylor Light Horse) Served as a body servant and cook to seven Timberlake siblings of company B., Serving under Capt. George Baylor, he and another servant named Tom Langford took a Federal officers servant prisoner	Body Servant Cook	Slave of Timberlake's, Was known to have armed himself and actively joined in company charges against the enemy at Brandy Station.
Pad	D	40th Regiment Virginia Infantry	Servant	
, Patrick		He did not serve in a unit but captured three Yankee soldiers who had escaped from Hancock's Corps, near Goode's Crossing, using a sythe blade he demanded their unconditional surrender, they complied.	Slave	Slave of T. B. Joppling of Bedford, County, Virginia
Peter	K	32th Virginia Infantry	Cook	
, Pry		Richmond and Danville Railroad Company Served as a Laborer for the railroad which was working for the Confederate Army	Laborer	Slave of Walker Washington, of Caroline county
, Reuben		Richmond and Danville Railroad Company Served as a Laborer for the railroad which was working for the Confederate Army	Laborer	Slave of Alexander Hutcheson, of Richmond, VA.
, Richard		3rd Regiment Virginia Infantry (Kemper's Brigade, Picket's Division) First master Thomas G. Pollack was KIA, then served as a servant to Lt. K. Nelson, then to Col. Joseph Mayo	Servant	Slave of Thomas G. Pollack of Warrenton, Virginia
, Robert		48th Virginia Infantry Regiment	Private	Washington County, VA.
, Robert		Chimborazo Hospital Served under J. B. McCaw Surgeon in Chief	Private	Slave of Mrs. Harwood
, Robert	G	25th Battalion, Virginia Infantry (Richmond Battalion) (City Battalion)	Cook	
, Robin		Gen. Thomas (Stonewall) Jackson's Brigade	Private	

Name	Co.	Unit / Service	Role	Notes
, Sam		48th Virginia Infantry (Mahone's Brigade) Served under Capt. Francis Smith Robertson	Camp Boy	FMC
, Sam	K	32nd Virginia Infantry	Cook	
, Samuel		Goochland Light Artillery,	Cook	
, Samuel	H	6th Virginia Cavalry	Private	
, Samuel	K	55th Virginia Infantry Side	Private	
, Scott	A	25th Battalion, Virginia Infantry (Richmond Battalion) (City Battalion)	Cook	
, Taylor		7th Virginia Cavalry	Driver Teamst	
, Taylor		Served as a Hospital Attendant and died while in Confederate Service, buried in the Confederate Cemetery in the Negro Section. Lynchburg, VA.	Hospital Attenda nt	Slave of Col. Withers or Capt. Getty
, Texas	I	32od Virginia Infantry	Cook	
, Thomas	F	32nd Regiment Virginia Infantry	Cook	Slave
, Thomas	G	25th Battalion, Virginia Infantry (Richmond Battalion) (City Battalion)	Cook	
, Thornton	F	25th Battalion, Virginia Infantry (Richmond Battalion) (City Battalion)	Cook	
, Tim		Served working at the Tredegar Iron Works, VA	Laborer	Slave of Mr. Jas. Duvall, of Caroline County, Va
Tom		7th Virginia Cavalry	Servant Boy	
Tom		7th Virginia Cavalry	Teamster	
Tom	2nd	Capt. L. F. Jones' Company, Artillery (Second Company, Richmond Howitzers), Virginia Artillery	Servant	Capt. L. F. Jones' Company, Artillery (Second Company, Richmond Howitzers), Virginia Artillery
, Tom	B	12th Virginia Cavalry (Baylor Light Horse)	Body Servant	Was known to have armed himself and actively joined in company charges against the enemy
, Tom	G	25th Battalion Virginia Infantry	Cook	
, Tom (Twin)		Served with Col. J. H. Averill, Trainmaster, Richmond & Danville Railroad		Age 14, twin brother of Jim
, William		Unknown Virginia Infantry	Private	
, William	F	25th Battalion, Virginia Infantry (Richmond Battalion) (City Battalion)	Cook	Slave
, Willis		Liggon Hospital, Richmond, VA	Servant	Slave of W. OTHO HILL, Asst. Surgeon C. S. A., Battery No. 7.
Abbitt, Archer		Evergreen Virginia Infantry Served building breastworks at Dinwiddie, Virginia	Infantry Laborer	Slave of George Abbitt. Appomattox County, VA Conf Pensioner
Adams, Lewis		Capt. R.M. Anderson's Company, Virginia Light Artillery (1st Company, Richmond Howitzers)	Cook	

Directory of African American Confederates in the U.S. Civil War

Name		Unit / Service	Role	Notes
Adams, Powhatan	D	Crenshaw Light Artillery Regiment Virginia Hauled provision for the CSA supplying the soldiers, Served under Capt. John Gary	Teamster	Slave of D. Henry Holloman. Goochland County, VA Conf Pensioner
Alexander, Allen		Served as Laborer working on Breastworks near Richmond	Laborer	Slave of Mark Alexander. Mecklenburg County, VA Conf Pensioner
Allen, James		Served as Laborer working on Breastworks on Drewry's Bluff	Laborer	Slave of Miss Mary Perkinson. Richmond County, VA Conf Pensioner
Allen, Jim		Jackson Hospital Division 2, Richmond, Virginia	Cook	Slave of G. Mears
Allen, Samuel	F	1st Virginia Reserves Served as a Servant to Capt. William H. Burton	Servant	Slave of Capt. William H. Burton, Hanover County, VA Conf Pensioner
Allison, William		Virginia Light Artillery		
Anderson, Albert		Douthat's Company, Virginia Light Artillery (Botetourt	Servant	VDCMR
Anderson, Charles H.		Served picket duty in San Diego, Texas	Private	Slave of J. L. Woodson of Richmond, VA. According to his statement in the Ohio Slave Narratives.
Anderson, Davis Lewis	G	4th Virginia Cavalry Served under Pvt. Charles H. Day	Hostler	Slave of William O. Day, Hanover County, VA Conf Pensioner
Anderson, Isaac		Unknown Virginia Unit		County, VA Conf Pensioner
Anderson, John		Capt. R.M. Anderson's Company, Virginia Light Artillery (1st	Cook	
Anderson, John		Snead's Company, Virginia Light Artillery (Fluvanna Artillery) Cavalry and Breastworks	Teamster	Slave of William P. Snead, Fluvanna County, VA Conf Pensioner
Anderson, John G.	H	22nd Battalion Virginia Infantry (Hill's Division, Jackson's Corps) Served under Capt. John Carter		Fluvanna County, VA Conf Pensioner
Anderson, John Thomas		Took care of Horses, served under Capt. Rook	Teamster Holster	Amherst County, VA Conf Pensioner
Anderson, Peter W.		Served as a Servant to Gen. Joseph E. Johnston, also worked for Amelia County Sheriff Aaron Haskins	Waltman	FMC, Amelia County, VA Conf Pensioner
Anderson, Robert		Served in the CSA building breastworks at Yorktown and other places, under Gen. John B. Magruder	Laborer	Slave of Truly Vaughan, Amelia County, VA Conf Pensioner
Andrew J. Andrews	D / A	1st Virginia Artillery (2nd Virginia Artillery) 26th Virginia Infantry Capt. B. H. Smith's Company Virginia Artillery	Private	Slave, of Cpl. George Mordecai of Co. K, 1st Virginia Artillery. Wake County, NC Conf Pensioner Attended Zeb Vance Camp, UCV Conference May 1930
Andrews, Andrew	K	1st Virginia Artillery, (Captain L. F. Jones Company) Served under George Mordecai	Servant	Slave, NC Conf Pensioner Zeb Vance Camp, UCV Conference May 1930
Archer, George W.		Served at a Confederate Shop at Gordonville, Serving under Capt. Jim Smith.	Blacksmith	Greene County, VA Conf Pensioner

Name		Service	Role	Notes
Armstead, Moses		Served as a Laborer working on breastworks	Laborer	Slave of William Clarke. Cumberland County, VA Conf Pensioner
Armstead, William	H	22nd Virginia Infantry Regiment	Chief Cook	
Arnold, Henry		Served as a Laborer on breastworks at Chickahominy	Laborer	Slave of Wyatt Arnold. Roanoke County, VA Conf
Arrington, Angus	F	7th Regiment Virginia Infantry Served as a Body Servant to Gen. James L. Kemper	Body Servant	FMC, Madison County, VA Conf Pensioner
Ashton, John	H B	32nd Regiment Virginia Infantry 1st Regiment Virginia Artillery Served under Capt. Lucian W. Richardson	Cook	FMC, Westmoreland County, VA Conf Pensioner
Austin, Edward		Served caring for and feeding horses, later dug pitts for artillery and ammunition. Served under Mr. Burton	Laborer Stableman	Slave of Abraham Austin Bedford County, VA Conf Pensioner
Ball, Penny		Served as a body servant and teamster under Lt Col. Barlow and Col. Boyd	Body Servant Teamster	Slave of Miss alive Faris. Fairfax County, VA Conf Pensioner
Banks, Jasper		Served under Gen. Charles Jones as a cook and in	Cook	Buckingham County, VA Conf Pensioner
Banks, Sr., John L.		Served as a Laborer working at the Iron Furnace in Louisa, and making supplies for the Confederate Army,	Laborer	Slave of William Stout Jr. Culpeper County, VA Conf Pensioner
Barnhart, Richard		Served under Col. Kenton Housifer	Body Guard Holster	Staunton County, VA Conf Pensioner
Bartlett, James (John) Archer	C	42nd Regiment Virginia Infantry Served under Capt. Robert M. Garrett	Teamster	Slave of I. Bowden. York County, VA Conf Pensioner
Baskerville, Reuben		Mahone's Brigade Served as a Teamster driving an ammunition wagon	Teamster	Slave of B. K. Baskerville. Mecklenburg County, VA Conf Pensioner
Beeden, John	D	2nd Regiment Virginia Infantry, Local Defense Served as a Teamster and a laborer in the munitions factory under Capt. John Tanner	Laborer Teamster	Slave of John Stinson., Warren County, VA Conf Pensioner
Bell, Benjamin		Served as a Laborer working on breastworks and as a Teamster serving under Maj. Fields.	Laborer	Slave of William Cowherd. Pulaski County, VA Conf Pensioner
Bell, John H.		Surry Light Artillery, Virginia Artillery	Bugler	
Bell, William		Served as a Laborer working on breastworks under Capt. Carter	Laborer	Slave of Tom Treadway. Prince Edward County, VA Conf
Bell, Wyatt	D	19th Virginia Infantry Served as a Body Servant and cook to his master Benjamin Morris	Body Servant Cook	Slave of Benjamin Morris. Chesterfield County, VA Conf Pensioner
Berry, James		5th Regiment Virginia Cavalry (Prince George Cavalry) Served as a Body Servant to his master Henry Harrison,	Body Servant	Prince George County, VA Conf Pensioner, P.O.W. at Fredericksburg and sent to Ft. Monroe and re eased.
Berry, John		Served as a Teamster under Richard Knight	Teamster	Slave of Richard Shelton. Amherst County, VA Conf Pensioner
Blackford, Charles		Served working at the Tredegar Iron Works, VA	Laborer	Slave of Mrs. F. G. Skinner, Culpeper County, VA.

Name		Service	Role	Notes
Blair, Davy		Served in the Infantry under his master Jimmy Davis as a Teamster and as a servant to Maj. J. W. Gilmor.	Teamster	Slave of Jimmy Davis. Rockbridge County, VA Conf Pensioner
Blakey, Abe		Served building breastworks around Richmond, Chickahominy Swamp and Petersburg under Mr. Smith.	Laborer	Slave of P. Elliott. Rockingham County, VA Conf Pensioner
Blanmire, George	A	3rd Regiment Virginia Infantry	Musician	VDCMR
Bolanz, G. M.		Served as a Mechanic's helper in a shop owned by his father which was under the use of the Confederacy	Mechanic's Helper	FMC, Pittsylvania County, VA Conf Pensioner
Bolden, Clem Read	A	4th Regiment, Virginia Reserves Served as a Teamster driving a mule team at Dutch Gap under Sgt. William L. Barnett.		Slave of David Read. Roanoke County, VA Conf Pensioner
Booker, Branch		Helped Nurse Wounded Soldiers at the Lockett House which was used as a Hospital		Slave, Lockett House, Slaves of Mrs. Lelia Lockett
Booker, Cornelius	D B	3rd Regiment Virginia Light Artillery 25th Battalion Virginia Infantry Served building breastworks and digging trenches worked under Capt. John W. Fisher in Hanover Junction	Laborer	Slave of Joshua Davis. Buckingham County, VA Conf Pensioner
Booker, Henry		Helped Nurse Wounded Soldiers at the Lockett House which was used as a Hospital		Slave, Lockett House, Slaves of Mrs. Lelia Lockett
Booker, Henry		Served working on breastworks	Laborer	Amelia County, VA Conf Pensioner
Booker, J. Churchill	H	Averett's Battalion, Virginia Reserves Served as a Servant to 2nd Lt. E.P. Davis	Orderly Servant	Slave of Henry Wood. Amelia County, VA Conf Pensioner
Boone, Anthony		Worked on trenches throwing up breastworks at Portsmouth, Point Suffolk, and Richmond Served under Capt. William Jones, and Capt. Callaghan	Laborer	FMC, Nansemond VA Conf Pensioner
Boone, Jason	K	41st Virginia Infantry Served building breastworks under Robert Jones.	Laborer	FMC, Nansemond VA Conf Pensioner
Booth, Robert	I	3rd Virginia Cavalry Regiment 13th Virginia Cavalry Regiment Served as a Servant and Nurse to his Master 2nd Lt. Hadrian Neaves	Nurse Servant	Slave, Sussex County, VA Conf Pensioner
Borzotra, William (Borzotra)		Served as a Teamster driving wagons in the Quartermaster Department.	Teamster	Slave of Col. Charles Dunmore. Roanoke County, VA Conf Pensioner
Bowman, Henderson	F F	5th Regiment Virginia Cavalry 13th Regiment Virginia Cavalry Served as a Servant	Servant	Slave of Pvt. Henry Teller Cocks. Prince George County, VA Conf Pensioner
Boxwell, Aaron M.	F	31st Virginia Militia Served under Capt Bayou Lovett and Lt. Thomas Carter	Teamster	Winchester County, VA Conf Pensioner. His widow Susann
Boyd, Isaac		Served hauling supplies in Buchanan, Russell and Tazwell Counties for the Confederates Army	Teamster	Buchanan County, VA Conf Pensioner

Boyd, Jim		Served as Laborer on Artillery Breastworks at Drewry's Bluff.	Laborer	Slave of Mr. Boyd. Mecklenburg County, VA Conf Pensioner
Boyd, William		Served as a Cook to Capt. W. G. Boyd and his messmates in the Virginia Cavalry	Cook	Slave of Alfred Boyd. Mecklenburg County, VA Conf Pensioner
Boyd, William Henry		2nd Engineer Regiment Engineer Department. Served under Robert A. Boyd.	Cook	Slave of Richard Boyd. Danville County, VA Conf Pensioner
Bradley, Edmund		Served working as a laborer on breastworks	Laborer	Charles City County, VA Conf Pensioner
Branch, Jim		Served as a Laborer on breastworks.	Laborer	Slave of William Watts. Roanoke County, VA Conf
Branch, Willis		Served as a Hostler under A. T. Price.	Hostler	Slave of A.B. West. Prince Edward County, VA Conf
Braxton, Henry	A	21st Virginia Militia Served as a Laborer working on breastworks at Drewry's Bluff.	Laborer	Slave of Capt. Joseph A. Dobson. Powhatan County, VA Conf Pensioner
Brice, Samuel		Lynchburg Home Guard	Servant	Slave
Brightwell, Frank P.	H	58th Regiment Virginia Infantry Served after he was conscripted by R. V. Davis to collect rations for soldiers, also issued rations to soldiers' families every Friday, served under Maj. George Booker in the Quarter Master Department	Teamster	Prince Edward County, VA Conf Pensioner
Broady, William H.	H	27th Virginia Infantry Served under Maj Paxton at Lynchburg Served under Maj. Kirker and Capt. Hopkins.	Courier Holster	Slave of C. B. Claiborne. Amherst County, VA Conf Pensioner
Brogden, George		Served as a Laborer working fortifications at Staunton River near Randolph in Halifax County and at High Bridge.	Laborer	FMC, Charlotte County, VA Conf Pensioner
Broock, H. L.	C	21st Regiment Virginia Infantry Served as a cook to Capt. Johnny Oliver	Cook	Mecklenburg County, VA Conf Pensioner
Brooks, William	A	7th Virginia Infantry (Holcombe Guards) Served under his Master Capt. John J. Winn	Cook Servant	Slave, Albermarle County, VA Conf Pensioner
Brown, Benjamin F.		Unknown Virginia Unit	Servant	P.O.W. at Camp Morton, Indiana Died there and now buried at Greenfield Park,
Brown, Booker		Unknown Virginia Unit	Body Servant	Slave of John Crowder of Prince Edward County, VA.
Brown, Daniel		3rd Division, Camp Jackson Hospital, Richmond, Virginia	Cook	
Brown, Dick		Served as a servant in the Cavalry to Maj. Coloaco Vaiden	Servant	James City, VA Conf Pensioner
Brown, Douglas	D F	3rd Regiment Virginia Cavalry 2nd Regiment Virginia Cavalry Served as a servant to Dr. Junius Roane (Surgeon)	Servant	Richmond County, VA Conf Pensioner
Brown, Gabriel		Served as a Laborer working on breastworks at Drewry's Bluff	Laborer	Slave a of Isaac Carrington. Charlotte County, VA Conf Pensioner

Brown, Gus		Served as a body servant to his master William Brown	Bodyguard	Slave of William Brown of Virginia
Brown, John		Served as a Cook and Servant to Capt. Jonathan Farrar who served in the infantry	Cook Servant	Mecklenburg County, VA Conf Pensioner
Brown, Kit		Virginia Cavalry Served as a body servant and cook to Capt. Walker Robertson. The Captain was wounded and Kit Brown took him home until he could recover	Body Servant Cook	Slave of Dr. D. W. Robertson. Chesterfield County, VA Conf Pensioner
Brown, Randol		Served as a Laborer working on breastworks	Laborer	Slave of James Shell. Cumberland County, VA Conf Pensioner
Brown, Robert Lewis		Served as a Cook for Lt. Charles Merriwether Christensen	Cook Body Servant	Hanover County, VA Conf Pensioner
Brown, S. T.	K	53rd Regiment Virginia Infantry (Charles City Southern Guards) Served as a Body Servant to Maj. George Waddell	Body Servant Cook Holster	FMC, Charles City County, VA Conf Pensioner
Brown, Sam	I	2nd Virginia Cavalry Served working building trenches under the supervision of his Master Pvt. John R. Brown (Dick)	Laborer	Slave of John R. (Dick) Brown. Campbell County, VA Conf Pensioner
Brown, Thornton S.	E	Capt. Carrington' Company, (Charlottesville Artillery) Virginia Light Artillery 7th Regiment Virginia Infantry	Servant	
Brown, William		Served as a Laborer working on breastworks for Artillery under Maj. Dense	Laborer	Slave of Judy Flournoy. Powhatan County, VA Conf Pensioner
Brown, William		Libby C.S. Military Prison Served as servant to Dr. E. G. Higginbotham, Surgeon of the Post.	Servant	FMC
Brown, William B.		Jeffress' Company, Virginia Light Artillery (Nottoway Light	Corporal	Powhatan County, VA Conf Pensioner
Brugh, R. M.		Served in the Commissary Department in Buchanan and Salem. (Possible slave of Lt. Edward Brugh)	Teamster	Botetourt County, VA Conf Pensioner
Bundy, Nat		9th Virginia Cavalry Served under Capt. Coffin	Cook	Slave of Ham Kay. Caroline County, VA Conf Pensioner
Bundy, Ryburn L. (Bundle, Rybune L.)	F	47th Regiment Virginia Infantry Commissary Department Served under Maj. Robinson and Capt. Samuel P. Gresham	Teamster	FMC, Essex County, VA Denied Conf Pension
Burke, Henry		Served as a Laborer working on breastworks in Prince George	Laborer	Slave of Albert Borum. Prince Edward County, VA Conf Pensioner
Burks, Pharaoh		Served as a cook and working on breastworks for the Lynchburg Home Guard. Also worked under the supervisor of his Master on a burial detail.	Cook	Slave of George A. Burks Campbell County, VA Conf Pensioner
Burnett, Joe		Served driving ration wagons, worked under Ed.	Teamster	Slave of Mrs. R. Redd. Henry County, VA Conf Pensioner
Burrell, Carter	H	32nd Regiment Virginia Infantry	Chief Cook	Slave

Directory of African American Confederates in the U.S. Civil War

Burton, Aaron		Col. Mosby's Regiment Virginia Cavalry Served as a body servant to his master's son Col. John S. Mosby	Body Servant	Slave of A. A. Mosby
Butts, Irwin	A	5th Battalion Virginia Infantry (Brunswick Guards)	Cook	Slave of Tom Heartwell. Brunswick County, VA Conf Pensioner
Byrd, James Henry		26th Regiment Virginia Infantry Served as a cook to his master Sgt. William Dulton	Cook	Slave of William Dulton. Gloucester County, VA Conf Pensioner
Cabe", William		Served hauling supplies from Richmond to Drewry's Bluff under Maj. Giske	Teamster	Slave of Mrs. Nancy Scruggs. Buckingham County, VA Conf Pensioner
Cain, Charles		Served as a cook at Appomattox	Cook	Northumberland County, VA Conf Pensioner
Canaday, Wilmore		Served as a Servant to Capt. Faust	Body Servant	James City, VA Denied Conf Pension
Canedy, Simeon (Kennedy, Simon)	B	10th Cavalry Regiment Virginia (Also served state of North Carolina)	Servant	
Carey, Ephraim		Was drafted and served as a Laborer building C.S. Army breastworks near Richmond under Capt. Crawford.	Laborer	Slave of Samuel Burks. Roanoke County, VA Conf Pensioner. Brother of Tom Carey.
Carey, Tom		Was drafted and served as a Laborer building C.S. Army breastworks. Listed in Ephraim Carey's Pension Application.	Laborer	Slave of Samuel Burks. Older brother of Ephraim Carey a Roanoke County Pensioner
Carrington, Henry	C	3rd Regiment Virginia Cavalry (Capt. William H. Easley's Company)	Teamster	Slave of William J. Howerton. Halifax County, VA Conf Pensioner
Carrington, Linous	H	1st Regiment Virginia Artillery Served as a Body Servant and Cook to his master Cushing Sawyer Irwin, who was killed at Brandy Station. 1st (Strawbridge's) Louisiana Infantry Then he hired himself to Capt. William Quirk (Provost Marshall General)	Cook	Richmond County, VA Conf Pensioner
Carter, Bob		Worked on Breastworks in Virginia	Laborer	Fayette County, TN Corf Pensioner App# C101
Carter, Gabriel		Richmond Howitzers Served under Capt. Brown, Capt. Segar and his Master Col. Hayes.	Cook	Gloucestor County, VA Conf Pensioner
Carter, Henry		Quarter Master Department Also served	Teamster	Slave of W. H. Rose. Amherst County, VA Conf Pensioner
Carter, Lewis		Worked on Confederate Breastworks at Petersburg, VA	Laborer	Slave of Nat Jones. Prince Edward County, VA Conf Pensioner
Carter, Richard W.		Capt. Moore's Company Virginia Light Artillery	Cook Privat	
Carter, Sr., Anderson		Served working on breastworks, fortifying Richmond, Petersburg and Lynchburg.	Laborer	Amherst County, VA Conf Pensioner

Carter, William	C	25th Battalion, Virginia Infantry (Richmond Battalion) (City Battalion)	Cook	
Cary, Tom		Served working on breastworks for Confederate forces.	Laborer	Buckingham County, VA Conf Pensioner
Chandler, George		Served as a cook under his master Billie Mansfield	Cook	Slave of Billie Mansfield. Franklin County, VA Conf
Chapman, Peter		Unknown Virginia Unit		Richmond, VA.
Chappell, Henry	C	3rd Regiment Virginia Cavalry	Cook Servant	
Cheatham, Albert		Served as a Laborer on breastworks near Richmond	Laborer	Slave of Tom Cheatham. Lunenburg County, VA Conf Pensioner
Gheeley, Lewis		Served as a Laborer and Teamster working on breastworks	Laborer	Slave of Asa Dickinson. Prince Edward County, VA Conf Pensioner
Cherry, Ralph	A	3rd Regiment Virginia Infantry	Musician	VDCMR
Chiles, Edward (Chives	B	9th Regiment Virginia Cavalry Served as a Servant to Maj. Charles Waite	Servant Hostler	Fairfax County, VA Conf Pensioner
Chisman, Oliver	I	32nd Regiment Virginia Infantry	Cook	
Chivis, Jabe		Served in the Quartermaster Department under Capt. Poindexter and Maj. Richards in Gordonsville, VA.	Teamster	Slave of Johnston Roberts. Culpeper County, VA Conf Pensioner
Christian, William	F	25th Battalion, Virginia Infantry (Richmond Battalion) (City Battalion)	Cook	
Clark, Adam		Served as a laborer working on breastworks under his Master Bowling Clark and Mr. Duncan	Laborer	Campbell County, VA Conf Pensioner
Clark, Charlie		Stonewall Jackson's Company, South Carolina	Bodyguard	
Clark, Jipp		Stonewall Jackson's Company, South Carolina	Bodyguard	
Clark, John	A	4th Regiment Virginia Cavalry Served as a Body Servant to his Master Mai. William W. Thornton	Body Servant	Caroline County, VA Conf Pensioner
Clay, Henry	D	2nd Infantry Regiment Virginia Served as a Servant to his master Pvt. George Pannill Sr., he later served as a Nurse in a Confederate Hospital.	Nurse Servant	Slave of Pvt. George Pannill. Orange County, VA Conf Pensioner
Cleapor, Charles		Commodore Tucker's Brigade, Lee's Division,	Sailor	VDCMR
Clore, Champ	C	82nd Militia Infantry Regiment Virginia Served as a Laborer working on breastworks, also worked under his Master Pvt. Aaron Clore in the Quarter Master Department.	Laborer	Slave of Pvt. Aaron Clore. Culpeper County, VA Conf Pensioner
Cole, Elijah		Unknown Virginia Unit	Private	Fairfax County, VA
Cole, John		Served as a Teamster driving a government wagon, under Capt. Gcodwyn.	Teamster	Slave of John Dodson. Dinwiddie County, VA Conf Pensioner
Cole, William		3rd Regiment Virginia Cavalry	Blacksmith	FMC

Coleman, James		Served as a Laborer on breastworks near New London, worked under his master Capt. Lindsay Coleman.	Laborer	Slave of Capt. Lindsay Coleman. Lynchburg County, VA Conf Pensioner
Coleman, John		1st Regiment Virginia Infantry, Commissary Served as a Servant to Capt. T. W. Talley	Servant	Richmond County, VA Conf Pensioner
Coleman, Jordan	C	15th Regiment Virginia Infantry (Patrick Henry Rifles) Served under Capt. C. W. Dabney building breastworks. Then served under Mr. Joseph Leadbetter while working at Mechanicsville, then under Mr. John Brice working at Drewry's Bluff	Teamster	Slave of Nathaniel Cresnshaw, Hanover County, VA Conf Pensioner
Coles, Peyton		Company Band, 18th Regiment Virginia Infantry Served as a Servant to his master Pvt. Samuel L. Crute, carrying his baggage.	Servant	Slave of Pvt. (Musician) Samuel L. Crute. Prince Edward County, VA Conf Pensioner
Corner, Henry	I	2nd Regiment Virginia Cavalry		
Corner, James J.		Served as an Armorer making grapeshot, cannon balls, and iron bar for the Confederate Army in Shenandoah, Virginia in the No. 2 Furnace under his master Henry Farrer. Also under the supervision of Major Wheat's Battalion and Capt. Joseph Monger.	Armorer	Slave of Henry Farrer. Page County, VA Conf Pensioner
Comfort, Wilson		13th Regiment Virginia Infantry	Cook	FMC, Orange County, VA Conf Pensioner
Conaway, Hyram	F& S B B,E	15th Regiment Virginia Cavalry 15th Battalion Virginia Cavalry (Critcher's) (Northern Neck Rangers) 40th Regiment Virginia Infantry Served as a bodyguard and cook to Maj. Cyrus Harding Jr.	Bodyguard Cook Servant	Lancaster County, VA Conf Pensioner. P.O.W. near Winchester VA.
Connally, Green		Served as a Laborer working on breastworks at Manassas Junction	Laborer	Slave of Franklin Connally. Pittsylvania County, VA Conf Pensioner
Conway, Harry		Served as a servant to Maj. E. S. Ruggles, looking after his horse and cooking for him.	Servant	Slave of L. V. Wing. King George County, VA Conf Pensioner
Cook, George Edmond		24th Regiment Virginia Cavalry Served as a Servant to Dr. William Henry	Servant	Slave of Frank Taylor. Fredrick County, VA Conf Pensioner
Corbin, Daniel		Served as a servant to his master James Frazer.	Servant	Slave of James Frazer from Spotsylvania, VA. He later settled in Georgia
Cores, John		Curtis' Company, Virginia Artillery (Fredericksburg Artillery) Served as a Laborer on breastworks under his Master Pvt. Walter C. Shelton	Laborer	Slave of Walter C. Shelton, Hanover County, VA Conf Pensioner
Cox, George		Jackson Hospital Richmond,	Nurse	FMC
Coy, William		No other information given	Cook	FMC, York County, VA Conf Pensioner

Directory of African American Confederates in the U.S. Civil War

Crawley, Silas		Served as a Mail Carrier in Charlotte County.	Mail Carrier	Slave of Tom Garrett. Charlotte County, VA Conf Pensioner
Creasy, Wyatt		Drafted and served as a laborer on breastworks at Drewry's Bluff, under the supervision of Sheridan Lagade, Mr. Duncan and Mr. Vaughan.	Laborer	FMC, Campbell County, VA Conf Pensioner
Cress, Richard (Cross)		Served as a servant and orderly to Capt. Griffin of the Dinwiddie Artillery	Orderly Servant	Dinwiddie County, VA Conf Pensioner
Crowley, Charlie (Charley)		Served as a Body Servant to CSA Signal Corps, Gen. Edward Porter Alexander of the Staff of General James Longstreet, 1st Corps, Army of Northern Virginia	Body Servant	Served at Sailors Creek
Crump, George	B	15th Regiment Virginia Infantry Served as a cook and laborer, waited on officers by the names of Meredith, Dickerson, and Haskins	Cook Laborer	FMC, Cumberland County, VA Conf Pensioner
Cubbage, David F.	H	10th Regiment Virginia (Capt Rippoto's Company) 33rd Regiment Virginia Infantry (Capt. William D. Rippetoe)	Private	Culpepper County, VA Denied Conf Pension
Cypress, Eldridge		Served as a Laborer building breastworks at Chesterfield County and in the defenses of Richmond	Laborer	Slave of S. V. Burgess. Chesterfield County, VA Conf Pensioner
Cypress, James		Surrey Cavalry Served as a Body Servant to Richard Holloway and as a laborer when necessary	Body Servant	Slave of Dr. Jesse Holloway. Southhampton County, VA Conf Pensioner, Died before he could receive his pension.
Dabney, William	H	9th Regiment Virginia Cavalry (Johnson's) Served as a servant to Capt. Thomas Haynes	Servant	Slave of Dr. Elliott Hawes Richmond County, VA Conf Pensioner
Daniel Corbin	C	35th Battalion Virginia Cavalry Served with his Master James Frazer	Private	Slave
Davenport, Alexander D.	E	53rd Regiment Virginia Infantry Served digging trenches, cooking and washing clothes, under Col. Benjamin Farinholt	Laborer	FMC, Gloucestor County, VA Conf Pensioner
Davidson, Nathan		Served making salt peter and carrying water. The Pension Board stated the mentioned duties performed did not fit the prerequisites for a pension even though the duties performed were in support of the Confederacy.	Laborer	FMC, Scott County, VA Conf Pension Denied
Davis, Davie		Served working on breastworks at Dewry's Bluff, Chesterfield County.	Laborer	Brunswick County, VA Conf Pensioner
Davis, George W.		Served as a Servant to Capt H. Davis Tuyrion	Body Guard	Slave of Davis Tuyrion. Madison County, VA Denied Conf Pension
Davis, James	C	38th Virginia Infantry	Cook	VDCMR
Davis, John		Served under Dr. John H. Clairborne (Surgeon)	Hospital Stewart	Surrendered at Appomattox
Davis, Reuben	E	20th Battalion, Virginia Heavy Artillery Served as a cook for his Master Sgt. William D. Crump	Cook	Slave, New Kent County, VA Conf Pensioner

Name		Unit / Service	Role	Notes
Day, John		1st Regiment Virginia Artillery Served as a Teamster driving teams, cooking and looking after horses for officers in the company under Capt. Hupp	Teamster	FMC, Roanoke County, VA Conf Pensioner
Dean, Ben		Served as a Hostler and carried Confederate mail, when Col. Harrison was killed he and Ephraim Turner carried his body off of the field.	Hostler Mailman	Slave of Nelson Page. Prince Edward County, VA Conf Pensioner
Deaton, Caleb		Served as a Teamster after he was pressed into service by the government. Served near Christianburg.	Teamster	Slave of Billy Davis. Montgomery County, VA Conf Pensioner
Delaney, McDowel	A	14th Regiment Virginia Infantry Served as a servant to Capt. Alpheus M. Chappell.	Cook	FMC, Cumberland County, VA Conf Pensioner
Deskins, James	M	Ferguson's (Guyandotte) Battalion, Virginia Cavalry	Sgt	
Detrick, Jim	B	24th Virginia Cavalry Surrendered at Appomatox Courthouse	Team	Slave of Lt.T. M. Detrick
Dickenson, Willis		Served working at the Tredegar Iron Works, VA	Laborer	Slave
Dickerson, George W.	B	50th Regiment Virginia Infantry Served as a Laborer working on breastworks at Richmond	Laborer	Slave of Pvt. John D. Garrett. Rockbridge County, VA Conf Pensioner
Dickerson, Giles		Served as a Teamster in the Commissary Department hauling salt peter under the supervision of David Graves.	Teamster	Slave of Crispin Dickerson. Pittsylvania County, VA Conf Pensioner
Dix, Austin	F&S	18th Regiment Virginia Infantry	Drummer	Freed Slave
Dixon, Jim		22nd Virginia Cavalry	Servant	Lee County, MS Conf Pensioner, non-battle
Dixon, Right		Served as a waiter at the end of the war. According to Luke D. Dixon his son in Slave Narratives.	Waiter	Slave of Jim. Dixon of Elmo County, Virginia. Son of Sam and Phyllis Abraham
Dixon, Unknown		Served as a waiter at the end of the war. According to Luke D. Dixon his nephew in Slave Narratives. He was the brother of Right Dixon.	Waiter	Slave of Jim Dixon of Elmo County, Virginia. Son of Sam and Phyllis Abraham
Dobyns, Griffin	B B	10th Batt'n. Virginia Heavy Artillery 14th Virginia Infantry	Body Servant	
Donovan, Stephen	G	11th Regiment Virginia Cavalry	Laborer	
Douglas, Randall	C	40th Virginia Infantry	Private	Northumberland County, VA Conf Pensioner
Dovel, Peter S.		Served as a Blacksmith's helper making harness irons under his master George Short Jr. who was the shop foreman at Stony Furnace.	Black smith	Slave of George Short Jr. Page County, VA Conf Pensioner
Drew, Cornelia (Female)		Served as a cook at Petersburg, Virginia	Cook	Surry County
Drew, Edmund		Charlottesville Light Artillery Regiment Virginia	Barber	
Drew, Tyler		19" Regiment Virginia Infantry Served as a Body Servant to Col. Phillip St. George Cocke and as a Laborer on breastworks.	Body Servant Laborer	Slave of Col. Phillip St. George Cocke. Powhatan County, VA Conf Pensioner

Duncan, W. R.	E	54th Virginia Infantry (Trigg's Regiment) Served under Capt. J. J. Wade	Private	Montgomery County, VA Conf Pensioner
Early, Ferdinand	K	50th Regiment Virginia Infantry Served as a Laborer on breastworks below Richmond under Booker Law.	Laborer	Slave of William Childress. Roanoke County, VA Con? Pensioner
Edmonds, Frank	G	3rd Regiment Virginia Cavalry Served as a Body Servant to Col. Robert Hubard.	Body Servant	Slave, Buckingham County, VA Conf Pensioner
Edmondson, Isaac	A	53rd Regiment Virginia Infantry Served as a Servant to Maj. Henry A. Edmondson	Servant	Buckingham County, VA Conf Pensioner
Eggleston, John		Served hauling ammunition in Suffolk.	Teamster	Slave of James Eggleston. Montgomery County, VA Conf Pensioner
Ellis, Charles		Served building the breastworks on Williamsburg Road and Mechanicsville.	Laborer	Amherst County, VA Conf Pensioner
Ellis, Wilson D.		Camp Winder Virginia Served as a water Servant at a Camp Winder Hospital	Hospital Servant	Slave of Lawrence G. Taylor. Buckingham County, VA Conf Pensioner
Epes, David	E	3rd Virginia Cavalry Served as a Body Servant to Dr. D. H. Hardaway	Body Servant Hostler	Nottoway County, VA Conf Pensioner
Epps, Daniel	C	3rd Virginia Cavalry	Cook Servant	
Epps, George		Served driving a wagon for Maj. Allen of Tennessee, and Gen. McCaub of Maryland.	Teamster	Slave of Col. William C. Knight. Henrico County, VA Conf Pensioner
Epps, Milton M.		Served working on breastworks	Laborer	Slave of Mrs. Lucy Bradshaw of Prince Edward. Amelia County, VA Conf Pensioner
Estes, Callie Hill	K	38th Regiment Virginia Infantry (Armistead's Brigade) Served as a Servant and cook to his Master, Capt. Benjamin Estes	Cook Servant	Slave of Capt. Benjamin Estes. Pittsylvania County, VA Conf Pensioner
Evans, Aaron		Served building breastworks and burying the dead, also served at Staunton River Bridge	Laborer	Slave of Capt. Charles Bruce. Halifax County, VA Conf Pensioner. U.S. Senator William Cabell submitted a letter of support for his pension.
Evans, Marshall	D	4th Virginia Cavalry (Little Fork Rangers) Volunteered and served under Capt. William A. Hill	Cook Holster	Culpeper County, VA Conf Pensioner
Farabee, Thomas	B	10th Virginia Cavalry Served with his Master Pvt. Joseph C. Farabee	Servant	Slave, Davidson County, NC Conf Pensioner
Farrar, Plummer	D	19th Regiment Virginia Infantry Served as a laborer working on breastworks at Chaffin's Farm under his master Samuel Farrar	Laborer	Slave Samuel Farrar. Mecklenburg County, VA Conf Pensioner
Fauntleroy, Lewis W.		9th Regiment Virginia Cavalry	Servant Teamster	Lancaster County, VA Conf Pensioner
Fauntleroy, Thomas	F	47th Regiment Virginia Infantry Served as a cook and servant to Co. Robert Mayo.	Cook Servant	Slave of Henry Hathaway. Lancaster County, VA Conf Pensioner

Fentress, George	C	15th Virginia Cavalry	Private Cook	
Ferguson, Tom		Served as a Servant to former U.S. Vice President and then Confederate Secretary of War Brackenridge		
Ferguson, Walker	H	4th Virginia Cavalry Served as a Servant to his Master's son Thomas Harris	Servant	Slave of Henry Harris. Goochland County, VA Conf Pensioner
Fields, James Emmett		Served as a Laborer in the Navy Yards and Hospital in Petersburg	Laborer	Slave of John Dobson. Richmond County, VA Conf Pensioner
Figgett, Ferdinand	E	55th Regiment Virginia Infantry	Fifer	FMC
Finney, William		Served as a servant to Jackson Finney helped in making salt peter.	Laborer Servant	Pittsylvania County, VA Conf Pensioner
Fleming, George	E	4th Regiment Virginia Cavalry Served as a Laborer working on breastworks in Richmond under Capt. John Lay,	Laborer	FMC, Powhatan County, VA Conf Pensioner
Fleming, Isaac		Served cooking, washing and cleaning guns for young Master Phillip Campbell	Holster Servant	Slave of Phillip and James Campbell, Hanover County, VA Conf Pensioner
Ford, Carter	C,F	Col. Mosby's Regiment Virginia Cavalry Served as a cook and servant to Col. William H. Chapman	Cook Servant	Slave of James R. Jones. Fairfax County, VA Conf Pensioner
Ford, Fred		Served as a Teamster near Richmond	Teamster	Slave of Charles Oliver. Nottoway County, VA Conf Pensioner
Ford, Lindsay		Unknown Virginia Unit		Fairfax County, VA
Foster, Jack		36th Virginia Infantry Regiment		Slave
Fowlkes, Howson C.		Capt. Jeffress' Company, Virginia Light Artillery (Nottoway Light Artillery)	Orderly	
Fowlkes, John S.	E	3rd Regiment Virginia Cavalry	Servant	
Fowlkes, Patrick H.	D C	Montague's Battalion, Virginia Infantry 53rd Regiment Virginia Infantry	Drummer	
Fralin, Jim		57th Regiment Virginia Infantry Served driving a team and hauling iron.	Teamster	Slave of Pvt. Robert (Bob) Fralin. Franklin County, VA Conf Pensioner
Freeman, John	E	25th Battalion Virginia Infantry (Richmond Battalion) (City Battalion)	Cook	
Freman, Andrew		Was drafted and served as a laborer working on reastworks	Laborer	FMC, Campbell County, VA Conf Pensioner
Fry, Albert	A	7th Virginia Infantry	Cook	Slave of Mr. Long. Fairfax County, VA Conf Pensioner
Fund, Doctor	M	Capt. Dance's Company (Powhatan Artillery) Virginia Artillery Served as a Cook and orderly to Lt. John M. Cunningham	Cook	Slave of Buck Meadow. Richmond County, VA Conf Pensioner
Gaines, Lucian	A	7th Regiment Virginia Cavalry	Teamster	VDCMR
Gallahan, Joe M.	E	30th Regiment Virginia Infantry Served under Capt. Allen	Cook	FMC, Spotsylvania County, VA Conf Pensioner

Gaskins, Beverly		Served as a Servant to Maj. Andrews	Cook Holster Servant	Lancaster County, VA Conf Pensioner
Gates, Thomas		Served under Sgt. Bruce as a stableman.	Stableman	Slave of Thomas Threat. Richmond County, VA Conf Pensioner
Gentry, William H.		Served by assisting in strengthening batteries	Laborer	FMC
George, Duke		Served as a driver to his master Edward Tyson, then he was sold to Judge Edmund L. Taylor who then sent him to a Confederate Hospital in Lynchburg where he worked.	Servant Teamster	Slave of Edward Tyson, and Judge Edmund L. Taylor. Culpeper County, VA Conf Pensioner
Gilbert, Jackson		Served as a Hostler for D. Freeman.	Hostler	Slave of George Gilbert. Pittsylvania County, VA Conf Pensioner
Giles, Freeman		Served as a Laborer working on breastworks under Michael Carter	Laborer	Slave of Kit Crute. Prince Edward County, VA Conf Pensioner
Glascoe, George T.		Served as a Teamster after President Jefferson Davis requested slaves to assist the Army as Teamsters. His Master sent him.	Teamster	Slave of William Lewis. Culpeper County, VA Conf Pensioner
Godfrey, J. W.	A	49th Regiment Virginia Infantry Served as a servant and helped nursing wounded soldiers and burying those who died. Stated his father and five uncles also served in the same regiment.	Servant	FMC, Fairfax County, VA Conf Pensioner
Goff, James		Served at Jordan's Furnace, cutting wood for the furnace to melt iron	Laborer	Bedford County, VA Denied Conf Pension
Gofney, Robert M.		Unknown Virginia Unit		Fairfax County, VA
Goode, Patrick H.		Served at Petersburg, building breastworks worked under his supervisor and Master Samuel Hobson	Laborer	Slave, Bedford County, VA Conf Pensioner
Goodwyn, Thomas		Served as a Body Guard and Hostler to Capt. McGoodwyn.	Body Guard Hostler	Slave of M.C. Goodwyn. Petersburg County, VA Conf Pensioner
Goolsby, John	S	24th Virginia Infantry Regiment General and Staff Regiment CSA Served as a body servant to Maj. Peter W. Hairston	Body Servant	Slave
Gordon, Jack	K	3rd Regiment Virginia Infantry Served as a Servant to Nat Wilson	Body Servant	Amelia County, VA Denied Conf Pension
Graham, ɔonr		Nelson Light Artillery Regiment VA. Amherst Light Artillery Regiment VA. Served as a Servant to John Lewis Berkley. Served under Capt. William Wilson.	Servant	Slave of Landon C. Berkley, Hanover County, VA Conf Pensioner
Graham, Richard R.		Served as a Laborer on breastworks at Fulton near Richmond and at Camp Winder under Spencer Hancock	Laborer	Richmond County, VA Conf Pensioner
Grant, Thornton		7th Virginia Cavalry	Servant	
Grayson, William		30th Virginia Infantry	Cook	Slave of Mary Covington. Fairfax County, VA Conf Pensioner

Directory of African American Confederates in the U.S. Civil War

Green, Claiborne		Served in the Quarter Master Department hauling provisions, worked under James Bane	Teamster	Slave of Robert Morton. Bland County, VA Conf Pensioner
Green, Frank	I	2nd Regiment Virginia Cavalry Served as a Teamster	Infantry Teamster	Slave of William D. Hix. Appomattox County, VA Conf Pensioner
Green, Joseph		Servant to Gen. Thomas "Stonewall" Jackson.	Body Servant	
Green, Louis		Served, waiting on wounded soldiers at a Confederate Hospital in Lynchburg under Dr. Spencer , he also worked as a Holster at the Fair grounds and at a camp outside of Lynchburg under Maj. Praxton.	Nurse Orderly Waiter	Slave of Dr. Reuben Long. Culpeper County, VA Conf Pensioner
Green, Silas	D	28th Regiment Virginia Infantry Capt. Henry J. Franklin	Private	Slave of Mark Cardeu.Lynchburg County, VA Conf Pensioner According to the Pension Board and, with respect to his service it was discussed that Silas Green Served as a Confederate Soldier and not as a servant it was then recommended, he receive a soldiers pension instead of a servants pension.
Grimes, George	H	47th Regiment Virginia Infantry	Private	
Grimes, Stafford	H	47th Regiment Virginia Infantry	Private	
Groves, Jacob		Unknown Virginia Unit	Servant	P.O.W. at Camp Morton, Indiana Died there and now buried at Greenfield Park,
Hackley, Joseph	A	2ndBattalion Virginia Infantry, Local Defense Served under Lt Col. D. E. Scruggs	Teamster	Fairfax County, VA Conf Pensioner
Hackney, Joseph	B	31st Regiment Virginia Infantry Served as a Servant to John W. Chewning	Body Servant	Slave of Robert Chewning, Albermarie County, VA Denied Conf Pension
Hailstack, John		30th Virginia Regiment	Drummer	FMC, From Fredricksburg, VA. He also served as a Drummer in the Mexican-American War.
Haines, Ned	C,D	1st Virginia Infantry Regiment (Williams Rifles) Served as a body Servant to Capt. John Dooley	Body Servant	
Hairston, D. W.		Served in Danville as a Railroad Construction Carpenter, also aided in building stables to care for horses and mules.	Laborer	Slave of Marshall Hairston. Henry County, VA Conf Pensioner
Hairston, James	H	Served the Confederacy as a horse attendant after he was sent to serve by his Master.	Attendant	Slave of Sam Hairston, Tazewell County, West VA Conf Pensioner
Hall, Austin		Served building breastworks near Richmond under Madison	Laborer	Slave of W. P. Farrell Bedford County, VA Conf Pensioner
Hall, Leroy		Commissary Department Served under Maj.William S.		Slave of Mr. Buckner, Caroline County, VA Conf Pensioner
Hambrick, J. C.		Served as a Holster, Teamster and Armorer's Assistant repairing swords under Capt. Creed Taylor.	Holster Teamster	Montgomery County, VA Conf Pensioner

Hardy, Jim	J	34th Virginia Infantry Served building breastworks near Richmond. Served under Capt. David M. Newsome	Laborer	Slave of Capt. Him Hardy Bedford County, VA Conf Pensioner
Hardy, William		Served building breastworks around Jamestown. Then drove a wagon for the Confederate Army	Laborer Teamster	Slave of John Weldon, Surry County, VA Conf Pensioner
Harris, Edward	F	160th Regiment Virginia Militia Served as a Teamster and waiting on soldiers, under Col. Jonathan Crawford	Servant Teamster	FMC, Louisa County, VA Conf Pensioner
Harris, John W.	H	1st Virginia Reserves (Amelia Reserves) Served as a Servant to his Master Capt. Richard (Dick) M. Scott at High Bridge and Battery near Chula	Servant	Amelia County, VA Conf Pensioner
Harris, William	A	44th Battalion Virginia Infantry	Ambulance Driver	FMC, Mecklenburg County, VA Conf Pensioner
Harrison, George F.		Col. Mosby's Regiment Virginia Cavalry Served taking care of horses in the mountains away from federal raiders for Col. John S. Mosby	Holster	Fairfax County, VA Conf Pensioner
Harrison, William		Capt. R.M. Anderson's Company, Virginia Light Artillery (1st Company, Richmond Howitzers)	Cook Servant	
Harrison, William H.		Served as a Servant to Gummel L. Harrison.	Body Servant	Slave of Anderson Harrison of Richmond, VA. Brother of Sam Hodge who also served. Was captured at Bulls Gap and forced to join the Union Army, mustered out at Chattanooga, TN. According to his statements in Arkansas Slave Narratives.
Haskins, Miles	A	34th Regiment Virginia Militia Served working on breastworks under Thomas Dearing	Laborer	Slave of William Worsham. Amelia County, VA Conf Pensioner
Haskins, Sib	H	3rd Regiment Virginia Cavalry Served Capt. Clement Carrington	Cook	Slave of Dr. W. H. Carrington. Halifax County, VA Conf Pensioner
Hawthorne, Rufus		Served as a Laborer on breastworks, began his service at Appomattox River worked under his master H.C. Hawthorne.	Cook Laborer	Slave of H.C. Hawthorne. Lunenburg County, VA Conf Pensioner
Hays, William	F	9th Regiment, Virginia Cavalry (Johnson's) Served as a cook and taking care of horses, worked under Robert L. Ware	Cook	Essex County, VA Conf Pensioner
Heck, J.		Commodore Tucker's Brigade, Lee's Division, Naval Brigade	Sailor	VDCMR
Henderson, Archie		Served under Mr. Sinclair	Teamster	Albermarle County, VA Conf Pensioner
Henderson, Caesar		Served as a Hostler, taking care of horses and waiting on his master Conscript Officer Perrin Graves.	Hostler	Slave of Perrin Graves. Orange County, VA Conf Pensioner

Name		Service	Role	Notes
Henderson, Jesse		Served in the Engineering Department building brides and cooking, served under Lt. Herbert Harris	Cook Laborer	Slave of Henry Harris. Orange County, VA Conf Pensioner
Henderson, Thomas		Captain J. W. Drewry's Company Virginia Artillery Served as a Servant to his Master Capt. James B. Jones at Drewry's Bluff	Servant	Slave, Bedford County, VA Conf Pensioner
Henderson, William		Served building breastworks in Richmond	Laborer	Slave of Frank Henderson Bedford County, VA Conf
Henry, Major	G	56th Virginia Infantry	Servant Private	
Henson, James	C	60th Regiment North Carolina Infantry Served under Capt. Thomas W. Patton in the Commissary Department driving wagons between Rutherfordton, N.C. And Spartanburg, S.C.	Teamster	Slave of Phillip Henson Sr. Richmond County, VA Conf Pensioner. WIA in right arm, waist and thigh.
Hill, Stephen	D	6th Regiment Virginia Cavalry Served as a cook and Holster attending horses in Lynchburg. Served under his master Pvt. James D. Hill.	Cook Holster	Slave of James D. Hill. Cumberland County, VA Conf Pensioner
Hill, William		Served as cook and teamster under John Clayton	Cook Teamster	FMC, Surry County, VA Conf Pensioner
Hobson, Isaac		Served as a Laborer working on breastworks in Richmond	Laborer	Slave of David Bradley. Cumberland County, VA Conf Pensioner
Hodge, Sam		Served as a Servant to Gummel L. Harrison.		Slave, Served in the same unit as his brother William H.
Hodnett, Dave		Served as a Teamster driving a wagon to Lynchburg, Chatham and other places from C.S.A. Stables at Col. Joab Watson's Plantation.	Teamster	Slave of Asa Hodnett. Pittsylvania County, VA Conf Pensioner
Holland, Claiborne		Served as a Laborer working on breastworks	Laborer	Slave of Johnson Holland. Franklin County, VA Conf Pensioner
Holland, Cornelius		Served under Gen. Jubal Anderson Early as a cook and Teamster	Cook Teamster	Slave of Tommy J. Holland. Franklin County, VA Conf Pensioner
Holland, Creed		Served as a Teamster for the Infantry and hauling supplies under Capt. Chandle	Teamster	Slave of Bill Holland, Franklin County, VA Conf Pensioner
Holley, Austin	G	1s' Battalion, Virginia Reserves Served in the Artillery building breastworks in Richmond, discharged by Capt. Abe Lewis Stiff	Laborer	Bedford County, VA Conf Pensioner
Hollins, Archie		Served building breastworks 1863- 1865	Laborer	Slave of George Ambler. Amherst County, VA Conf
Holman, Harrison		Served working on breastworks at Richmond and Manchester.	Laborer	Slave of W. Walker. County, VA Conf
Holmes, John	H	54th Virginia Infantry Served as a Servant to Capt. Charles Otey working at Dublin, Lynchburg and Staunton.	Cook	Bedford County, VA Conf Pensioner

Holmes, Lewis W.		Served as a Teamster and Mill worker in a C.S.A. Tanning yard and Mill.	Teamster Laborer	Slave of C. A. Chrisaman. Pulaski County, VA Conf Pensioner
Howard, David		29th Regiment Virginia Infantry Served as a Teamster under Col. A. C. Moore.	Teamster	Wythe County, VA Conf Pensioner
Howard, George		Served as a Laborer on Breastworks at Walker's	Laborer	Slave of Melvin Moore. Wythe County, VA Conf Pensioner
Howell, Richard		Served in as a Cook in the Infantry at Harding's Bluff.	Cook	FMC, Charlotte County, VA Conf Pensioner
Hubbard, Robert		Served as a Laborer and Teamster on working on breastworks	Laborer Teamster	Slave of Allen Hubbard. Pittsylvania County, VA Conf Pensioner
Huff, William Henry	H	4th Regiment Virginia Reserves Served as a Cook and Hostler for Capt. J. B. Haden and other officers.	Cook Hostler	Slave of Bird Huff. Roanoke County, VA Conf Pensioner
Hughes, Richard		Served as a Laborer working on breastworks and fortifications	Laborer	Slave of Robert H. Vest. Fluvanna County, VA Conf Pensioner
Humbles, James	C	1st Virginia Cavalry	Bugler	
Hundley, William		Served as a laborer working on breastworks in Henrico	Laborer	Slave of Thompson Herrick. Amelia County, VA Conf Pensioner
Hundley, William Robert		Served as a laborer working in a sword factory in a CSA armory at Snowville, Virginia	Laborer	Radford County, VA Conf Pensioner
Hunt, Gabe		Served caring for horses for artillery and infantry soldiers. Served under Capt. Richards and Lt. Jones.	Holster	Slave of Sam Pannill of N.C. Campbell County, VA Conf Pensioner
Hunter, Phillip		Served as a Laborer on breastworks first at Manassas Gap, then at Cnickahominy Swamp.	Laborer	Slave of Mrs. Eliza Evans. Lynchburg County, VA Conf Pensioner
Hurt, James		Served as a Laborer on breastworks at Drewry's Bluff	Laborer	Slave of William Watts. Roanoke County, VA Conf Pensioner
Hutcheson, Henry	E A	14th Regiment Virginia Infantry 3rd Regiment Virginia Cavalry Served as a Laborer building breastworks and as a cook to Sgt. Peter A. Gayle and his mess mates.	Cook Laborer	Slave of Joseph C. Hutcheson. Mecklenburg County, VA Conf Pensioner
Ingram, Anderson		3rd Regiment Virginia Cavalry	Cook Servant	Slave of Dr. Tom Ingram. Lunenburg County, VA Conf Pensioner
Ivy, Lewis Henry		Served as a Laborer on working on breastworks	Laborer	Slave of Judge George Gilmer. Pittsylvania County, VA Conf Pensioner
Jackson, George		7th Virginia Cavalry	Servant	
Jackson, Henry	F & S	13th Regiment Virginia Infantry Served as a Servant to Gen. Ambrose Powell Hill "Light Division", then Gen. lames Walker.	Servant	Culpeper County, VA Conf Pensioner
Jackson, Lewis	D	9th Regiment Virginia Cavalry , Capt. James K. Ball, Col. Merriwether Lewis) Served as a Body Servant to Pvt. Sam Williams	Body Servant Teamster	Lancaster County, VA Conf Pensioner
Jackson, Minor	A	7th Regiment Virginia Infantry Served in the Quartermaster Department driving teams.	Blacksmith Teamster	Sieve of 2nd Lt. George N. Thrift. Madison County, VA Conf Pensioner

Jackson, Nelson		Served as a Laborer working on breastworks	Laborer	
Jackson, Robert	F	61st Virginia Infantry	Cook	
Jackson, Taylor		Served as a Nurse and Attendant at a Confederate Hospital under his master Dr. T. H. Carrington	Attendant Nurse	Slave of Dr. T. H. Carrington. Culpeper County, VA Conf Pensioner
Jackson, Thomas		4th Regiment Virginia Cavalry Served as a Body Servant to Allan and Norvelle Nuckols	Body Servant	Slave of Hardin Nuckols, Hanover County, VA Conf Pensioner
James, Charles		Served as Cook and Holster no unit information	Cook Holst	Slave of Bruce Jones. Franklin County, VA Conf Pensioner
James, John	G	13th Virginia Cavalry Served under Capt. B. C. Drew	Cook	FMC, Surry County, VA Conf Pensioner
Jamison, William		Jackson Hospital Richmond, Virginia	Nurse	FMC
Jasper, Carry		Served working on breastworks and trenches under George Thranes	Laborer	Slave of William R. Barksdale. Amelia County, VA Conf Pensioner
Jefferson, Henry		Virginia State Troops	Private	Bolivar County, MS Conf Pensioner
Jenkins, 3. E.	C	53rd Virginia Regiment Pickett's Division (Old Dominion Riflemen) Stated he served in this unit as a Servant to his father (above)	Servant	Prince Edward County, Denied VA Conf Pension
Jennings, Joseph		38th Regiment Virginia Infantry Served as a servant and cook for several officers in the unit.	Body Servant	Slave of John Fox. Fairfax County, VA Conf Pensioner
Johns, Preston		Unknown Tennessee Unit	Teamster	Amherst County, VA Conf Pensioner
Johnson, Andrew	D	1st Battalion, Virginia Infantry, Local Defense (Ordnance Battalion) (Armory Battalion) Served as a laborer working on breastworks also served as a cook under his master Maj. Henry Fitzgerald Jr.	Cook Laborer	Slave of Maj. Fitzgerald. Dinwiddie County, VA Conf Pensioner
Johnson, Burroughs Whitfield		Served as a laborer on breastworks under Capt. Moody	Laborer	Slave of Capt. Silas Banner.
Johnson, Edmund		2nd Virginia Cavalry (Munford's) Served building breastworks	Laborer	FMC, Bedford County, VA Conf Pensioner
Johnson, Henry	G	1st Battalion Virginia Reserves Served at Chaffin's Bluff with the Artillery building breastworks and placing cannon. Served under Capt. Abraham Lewis Stiff	Laborer	Slave of William Johnson Bedford County, VA Conf Pensioner
Johnson, Jacob		Served as a Laborer on breastworks around Richmond under supervision of W. S. Cook.	Laborer	Slave of Ket Valentine, Louisa County, VA Conf Pensioner
Johnson, Jacob	K	6th Virginia Cavalry Served as a Servant to Capt. William (Bill) Meade and Sgt. Charlie Ball	Cook Servant	Slave of Joe Meade father of Capt. Meade, Augusta County, VA Conf Pensioner
Johnson, Joseph		Commodore Tucker's Brigade, Lee's Division, Naval Brigade	Sailor	
Johnson, Melvin		Served working on breastworks between Chula and Mattoax, Virginia under Mr. Singleton.	Laborer	Slave of William Ware. County, VA Conf Pensioner

Johnson, Nathan	D	4th Regiment Virginia Cavalry Served as a Teamster under his master 12Lt. Oswald (Oz) M. Corbin	Teamster	Slave of Joseph Armstrong. Culpeper County, VA Conf Pensioner
Johnson, Stillman	F&S	18th Regiment Virginia Infantry Served as a servant to Dr. Thomas L. Shield and Dr. Richard P. Walton (Surgeon).	Servant	Cumberland County, VA Conf Pensioner
Johnson, Watt		Served as a Laborer working on breastworks	Laborer	Slave of Spencer Osborne. Cumberland County, VA Conf Pensioner
Jones, Albert		Served working at government saw mills in Belmont making lumber for Chickahominy Swamp and Manasas Gap to be used on breastworks.	Laborer	Slave of Tom Robertson. Buckingham County, VA Conf Pensioner
Jones, Ben		Field's Division, Quarter Master Served as a Teamster hauling ammunition to the battlefield for the Confederate Army, under Capt. Norton.	Teamster	Slave of Dr. Isaac Rich. Richmond County, VA Conf Pensioner
Jones, Emmanuel		5th Regiment Virginia Cavalry (Prince George Cavalry) Served as a Body Servant to Willie Wilcox	Body Servant	Prince George County, VA Conf Pensioner
Jones, George R.	2E	10th Virginia Cavalry Served as a Body Servant to Capt. W. E. Hinton	Body Servant	Amelia County, VA Conf Pensioner
Jones, Henry		Served working on breastworks, worked on Mulberry Island under Maj. Robert Cousins	Laborer	Slave of Daniel W. Burton. Amelia County, VA Conf Pensioner
Jones, Isaac		Served as a stable boss and driving wagons serving under his master Col. W. A. Forbes.	Holster Teamster	Slave of Col. W. A. Forbes. B Buckingham County, VA Conf Pensioner
Jones, James A.		Served as a Servant and coachman to Confederate President Jefferson Davis	Coachman Servant	He later lived in Raleigh, North Carolina
Jones, James A.	D	46th Regiment Virginia Infantry	Private	VA Dept of Conf Mil Rcds, VDCMR
Jones, Louis		Served as a Teamster and building breastworks	Teamster Laborer	Amherst County, VA Conf Pensioner
Jones, Moses		Served building breastworks and driving a wagon. Began service Chickahominy, Virginia.	Laborer Teamster	Slave of Edward Glover. Buckingham County, VA Conf Pensioner
Jones, Sam A.		Served as Laborer in the Infantry working on Breastworks around Richmond under J. Hardy.	Laborer	Slave of Mrs. Mary Jones. Mecklenburg County, VA Conf Pensioner
Jones, Sidney		Served hauling ammunition in the Supply Branch under Maj. Crockram	Teamster	Slave of Newton Harper. Dinwiddie County, VA Conf Pensioner
Jones, Simon	F A	20th Regiment Virginia Infantry 57th Regiment Virginia Infantry Served as a body servant to Maj. Garland B. Hanes	Body Servant	Buckingham County, VA Conf Pensioner
Jones, Tom	B	25th Battalion, Virginia Infantry (Richmond Battalion) (City Battalion)	Chief Cook	

Jones, Watt		Hounshell's Battalion, Virginia Cavalry (Partisan Rangers) Served as a Laborer working on breastworks at Petersburg, Richmond and Chaffin's Bluff under his master Pvt. Benjamin Tinsley.	Laborer	Slave of Pvt. Benjamin Tinsley. Roanoke County, VA Conf Pensioner
Jones, Wiley		Served as a Teamster in the Commissary Department, drove wagons in Clarksville. Worked under J. Snead.	Teamster	Slave of William Jones. Mecklenburg County, VA Conf Pensioner
Jones, William		Army of Northern Virginia Served as a Messenger/Courier to Gen. Robert E. Lee	Courier	
Jones, William	H	32 Virginia Infantry Served as a messenger to Gen. Robert E. Lee.	Cook	Slave of Dr. Willis Robertson. Richmond County, VA Conf Pensioner
Jordan, Charles	A	47th Virginia Infantry Served his Master Col. Charles Green and was hired out to the CSA cutting wood	Body Servant Laborer	Amherst County, VA Conf ,Pensioner
Jordan, Richard		Served as a Laborer working on breastworks near Petersburg under Lt. Bolling	Laborer	Slave of William 3. Powers. Powhatan County, VA Conf Pensioner
Kasey, Stephen		Served as a Laborer on breastworks around Richmond.	Laborer	Slave of Gen. Tom Kasey. Franklin County, VA Conf Pensioner
Kean, Aleck	2nd	Capt. L. F. Jones' Company, Artillery (Second Company, Richmond Howitzers), Virginia Artillery Served as a Body Servant to Pvt. John Henry Vest, served at Sailor's Creek	Body Servant	Slave
Kelly, John W.	C	2nd Virginia Infantry Regiment Served under Lt. Edward Brugh hauling supplies from stations at Amsterdam, Buchanon, Fincastle Barracks	Teamster	Botetourt County, VA Conf Pensioner
King, Bill		20th Tennessee Regiment	Servant	
Knight, James Reuben		Served as a camp errand boy, performing general camp duties.	Servant	Slave of Dr. Reuben De Jarnette Prince Edward County, VA Conf Pensioner
Kyger, John S.		Unknown Virginia Unit	Servant	P.O.W. at Camp Morton, Indiana Died there and now buried at Greenfield Park, Indianapolis
Kyle, Calvin		Served as a Laborer working on breastworks in Richmond, and as a sapper miner. He worked for White Mine being in charge of men from Montgomery County.	Laborer Miner	Slave of J. H. Otey. Montgomery Pensioner
Lacy, Horace		Served as a Body Servant and attending to horses for his master.	Body Servant	Charlotte County, VA Conf Pensioner
Lamb, George C.	D	17th Virginia Infantry Served as a Body Servant of Capt. William H. Dulany	Body Servant	FMC, Fairfax County VA Conf Pensioner

Langford, Tom	B	12th Virginia Cavalry (Baylor Light Horse) Served as a servant to Capt. George Baylor, he also took up arms and along with another servant named Overton, took a Federal officers servant prisoner at Brandy Station.	Hostler	
Lanier, Heartwell		No unit information provided	Body Servant	Slave of Leroy Bowden. Dinwiddie County, VA Conf
Lansdown, Charles		Served as a Hostler, Servant and Teamster in the Virginia Infantry	Hostler Servant Teamster	Slave of Cassius Foley. Prince William County, VA Conf
Law, Jack		Served as a Laborer working on breastworks at Chickahominy Swamp, Richmond, Charles City and the Nine Mile Road area.	Laborer Teamster	Slave of Thomas Law. Franklin County, VA Conf Pensioner
Lawson, Abner	C	3rd Regiment Virginia Cavalry Served under Capt. William H. Easley	Cook Servant	Slave of David Lawson. Danville County, VA Conf Pensioner
Lawson, Joseph	B	30th Virginia Infantry Served as a Servant to Capt. James Knox, and Lt. Robert Knox	Servant Cook	From Spotsylvania, VA.
Lee, A.		Unknown Virginia Unit	Servant	P.O.W. at Camp Morton, Indiana Died there and now buried at Greenfield Park,
Lee, Frank	F	9th Regiment Virginia Cavalry Served as a servant to his master Lt. Waring Lewis	Servant	Slave of Lt. Waring Lewis. Essex County, VA Conf Pensioner
Lee, George		Served building breastworks and toting water under James Jennings	Laborer	Slave of Thomas Lee. Amherst County, VA Conf
Lee, Thomas (Snoddy, Tom)		Served as a Laborer building breastworks at Chaffin's Bluff and worked on trenches at Brook Turnpike.	Laborer	Slave of John J. Snoddy, Buckingham County, VA Conf Pensioner
Lee, Tom	I	3rd Virginia Reserves Served waiting on Capt Godsey, and building breastworks	Servant Laborer	Appomattox County, VA Conf Pensioner
Lee, William		Unknown Virginia Unit		Fairfax County, VA
Lee, William Mack (Rev)	G	29th Virginia Infantry Served as a Body Servant to Gen. Robert E. Lee During the entire war.	Cook Body Servant	Freed Slave, Norfolk County, VA Conf Pensioner
Leigh, Samuel		Served as a Teamster for the Artillery between Richmond and Petersburg, Virginia. Worked under Holly Anderson.	Teamster	Slave of Judge William Leigh. Halifax County, VA Conf Pensioner
Lemons, John		22nd Regiment Virginia Infantry (1st Kanawha Regiment) Served as a laborer working on breastworks and as a servant to his master Pvt. George L. Lemons.	Laborer Servant	Slave of Pvt. George L. Lemons. Franklin County, VA Conf Pensioner
Lewis, James	B	25th Battalion Virginia Infantry Served as a Body Servant to Pvt. Alexander Pendleton He was also a Servant to Gen. Thomas Jonathan "Stonewall" Jackson. He Led "Little Sorrel", Jackson's Horse during the funeral Procession.	Body Servant	FMC

Name		Service Description	Role	Status
Lewis, Stephen		Drafted and served as a Laborer working on breastworks near Richmond.	Laborer	Slave of W. H. Barrow. Nottoway County, VA Conf Pensioner
Lightfoot, Addison		Confederate Hospital Charlottesville, North Carolina. Served as a Hospital Worker in caring for sick and wounded soldiers and dressing wounds.	Attendant Nurse	Slave of Oliver Pinkard. Culpeper County, VA Conf Pensioner
Lightfoot, Henry Clay	G	61st Virginia Infantry Served as a Servant to William Halcomb	Body Servant	FMC, VA Conf Pensioner
Lightfoot, Jim		Served working at the Tredegar Iron Works, VA	Laborer	Slave
Linthicum, Carter		Served hauling supplies for the Amy, under Capt. Watson.	Teamster	Slave of William Linthicum. Campbell County, VA Conf Pensioner
Lipscomb, William E.		Served as a laborer working on breastworks and made salt petre	Laborer	FMC, Cumberland County, VA Conf Pensioner
Loey, William (Illegible,		Virginia Infantry	Illegible	FMC, Cumberland County, VA Conf Pensioner
Logan, Candace		Jackson Hospital Richmond, Virginia	Cook	FMC
Lovelace, Sam		Served as a Teamster in the Commissary Department in Pittsylvania County collecting provision for the C.S. Army.	Teamster	Slave of Miss Polly Wooding. Pittsylvania County, VA Conf Pensioner
Lucas, Cornelius S.	A	47th Virginia Infantry Capt. Pollock's Co., Light Artillery (Fredericksburg Artillery) Served as a Servant to Capt. William G. Pollock	Body Servant	Fredericksburg County, VA Conf Pensioner
Lumpkins, Ned	C	1st Battalion, Virginia Infantry, Local Defense (Ordnance Battalion) (Armory Battalion) Served as a Teamster working under his master Pvt. Abner Anthony.	Teamster	Slave of Pvt. Abner Anthony. Franklin County, VA Conf Pensioner
Lyle, Sam		Served as a Laborer working on breastworks in Richmond	Laborer	Slave of Jesse Michaux. Prince Edward County, VA Conf Pensioner
Mabrey, Frank		Served as a servant for his master James Guthridge, also treated his wounds when he was wounded.	Servant	Slave of James Guthridge. Richmond County, VA Conf Pensioner
Madison, Charles H.		Paris' Company, Virginia Artillery (Staunton Hill Artillery) Served as a Servant to Maj. Richard V. Gaines	Servant	Charlotte County, VA Conf Pension Denied. Ref. from Charles Slaughter (Colored)
Majors, Tillman		6th Virginia Cavalry	Cook	Slave of S. G. Majors. Halifax County, VA Conf
Majors, William	3rd	Capt. B. H. Smith's Co., Artillery (Third Co., Richmond Howitzers), Virginia Artillery Served as a Body Servant to his Master Pvt. Samuel Majors	Body Servant	Slave, Person County, NC Conf Pensioner
Mallory, Littleton		Served as a Teamster for Engineers until sent home by his master.	Teamster	Slave of B. F. T. Conway. Madison County, VA Conf Pensioner
Manns, George		Served as a Cook for Lt. D. W. Spencer in Danville.	Cook	Slave of Mr. J. Wilson. Henry County, VA Conf Pensioner

Mansfield, George		Served as a Cook for Capt. Cemuis? Other application information is illegible.	Cook	Louisa County, VA Conf Pensioner
Marks, Robert		Served as a gunsmith and working on breastworks	Laborer	Albermarle County, VA Conf Pensioner
Marshall, Daniel	G	54th Regiment Virginia Infantry Served under Capt. Jeremiah (Jerry) Spence	Teamster	
Marshall, James Leonard	G	54th Regiment Virginia Infantry Served under Capt. George Turman and Capt. Jerry Spence	Teamster	Carroll County, VA Conf Pension Denied
Marshall, Levi S.		Hillsville Army Hospital, Virginia Served under Thomas N. Marshall whom he nursed and cared for	Servant Nurse	Carroll County, VA Conf Pension Denied
Marshall, Thomas	H	3rd Regiment Virginia Cavalry	Private	VDCMR
Martin, Joe		Served as a Laborer working on breastworks near Richmond	Laborer	Slave of B. T. Tinsley. Roanoke County, VA Conf
Martin, John Wesley		34th Regiment Virginia Infantry Served under Capt. Tom Peters	Wagoner	Slave of Mrs. Sophia Martin, Bedford County, VA Conf Pensioner
Martin, Scott	D	18th Battalion Virginia Heavy Artillery Served as a laborer on breastworks under Mr. Bacon.	Laborer	Slave of Pvt. Dabney Martin. Campbell County, VA Conf Pensioner
Martin, Silas		Served building breastworks	Laborer	FMC, Amherst County, VA Conf Pensioner
Martin, Thomas S.	D	18th Regiment, Virginia Infantry		Prince Edward County, VA Conf Pensioner
Matthews, Brice		Snead's Company, Virginia Light Artillery (Fluvanna Artillery) Served as a cook to his master Pvt. William P. Jennings	Cook	Slave of Pvt. William P. Jennings. Fluvanna County, VA Conf Pensioner
Mayo, Edward		Capt. Weisiger's Company Virginia Light Artillery. (Manchester Light Artillery.) Served as a Cook for Capt. William R. Weiseger (Surgeon) and his officers.	Cook	FMC, Richmond County, VA Conf Pensioner
Mayo, Henry	G	56th Regiment Virginia Infantry	Private	Slave, P.O.W. at Camp Morton, Indiana Died there and now buried at Greenfield Park, Indianapolis. VDCMR
Mayo, Joe		Parker Light Artillery Regiment Virginia	Servant	
Mayo, Robert	I	16th Regiment Virginia Infantry	Cook	
Mayo, William		Douthat's Company, Virginia Light Artillery (Botetourt	Servant	VDCMR
McKinney, James	B	34th Regiment Virginia Infantry	Musician	
McKinney, Pink	A	44th Regiment Virginia Infantry Served as a Servant to Capt. Samuel Overton	Cook	Appomattox County, VA Conf Pensioner
McKnight, Henry Clay		Served after he was sent by his Master to help build breastworks in Virginia	Laborer	Slave of Alexander McKnight, Franklin County, NC Conf Pensioner

McMannaway, John A.		Served as a Laborer working on breastworks and as a Teamster hauling supplies for the confederate army between Lexington and Staunton, Virginia.	Laborer Teamster	FMC, Rockbridge County, VA Conf Pensioner
McMillan, William		77th Virginia Cavalry		Knox County, TN Conf Pensioner App # C210
Meade, John		Wright's Company, Virginia Heavy Artillery (Halifax Artillery) Served helping to build battery, ammunition magazines, under Confederate Engineers.	Laborer	Brunswick County, VA Conf Pensioner
Menefee, J. H.		Served as a Laborer working on breastworks in Prince Edward County	Laborer	Franklin County, VA Conf Pensioner
Michens, Roderick		Served as a Teamster	Teamster	Slave of Garland Waddy. Louisa County, VA Conf Pensioner
Miles, Mitchel		Served as a Laborer on Breastworks at Drewery's Bluff.	Laborer	Slave of D. L. Morrow. Charlotte County, VA Conf Pensioner
Miller, Alex		Served under Capt. Clay Harvey and Lt. Davis caring for Cavalry and Artillery horses, served at Chalk Level.	Hostler	Slave of George Miller. Pittsylvania County, VA Conf Pensioner
Miller, Andrew	C	25th Battalion Virginia Infantry Served as a Teamster under his master Pvt. Washington Snoddy.	Teamster	Slave of Pvt. Washington Snoddy. Buckingham County, VA Conf Pensioner
Miller, Carter C.	B,D ,S	1st Battalion Infantry Regiment Virginia Served as a Body Servant to 1st Lt. Robert Dickenson	Body Servant	Slave of Judge Asa Dickenson. Nottoway County, VA Conf Pensioner
Miller, James		Served as a Laborer working on breast works around Richmond serving under Capt. Davis and Capt. Cole.	Laborer	Slave of Henry D. Sayers. Pulaski County, VA Conf Pensioner
Miller, Sam		Served under Capt. Clay Harvey and Lt. Davis caring for Cavalry and Artillery horses, served at Chalk Level.	Hostler	Slave of George Miller. Pittsylvania County, VA Conf Pensioner
Miller, Thomas S.	D	1st Regiment Virginia Infantry Served as a Servant to Capt. Robert Martin and as a Teamster transporting supplies and delivering rations to needy families of Confederate Soldiers.	Private Teamster	Slave of Capt. Robert Martin. Prince Edward County, VA Conf Pensioner
Mitchell, George		Served as a Teamster in the Quartermaster Department, and worked on breastworks at Blandford.	Teamster	Slave of Green Mitchell Dinwiddie County, VA Conf Pensioner
Mitchell, Jackson (Mitchell, Tap)		Served as a Laborer on breastworks.	Laborer	Henry County, VA Conf Pensioner
Mitchell, Unknown		Served as a Teamster in the Quartermaster Department	Teamster	Slave of Green Mitchell. From Dinwiddie County, VA. Brother of George Mitchell.
Mitchell, W. J.		Served building breastworks and in the Hospital Division	Laborer	Nelson County, VA Conf Pensioner
Montague, Porter	D	8th Regiment Virginia Cavalry Served as a cook and Servant for Pvt. Matthew M. Walker	Cook Servant	Slave of M. M. Walker., Westmoreland County, VA Conf Pensioner

Directory of African American Confederates in the U.S. Civil War

Moody, Peter	A	5th Regiment Virginia Cavalry	Team	Gloucestor County, VA Conf Pensioner
Moody, Phillip	A	5th Regiment Virginia Cavalry	Body Guard Cook	Gloucestor County, VA Conf Pensioner
Moore, Henderson D.		Served in the Engineer Department under Dinkun and Capt. Chambers. Captured by Union soldiers.	Servant Private	Slave of S. T. Moore. Brunswick County, VA Conf Pensioner
Moore, Henry C.		Served on the railroad train with his master George Abbot in the service of the Confederacy.	Servant	Slave of George Abbott. Charlotte County, VA Conf Pensioner
Moore, Jesse		Served as a Body Servant to A. P. Kelly	Body Servant	Slave of William Moore Culpeper County, VA Conf
Moore, John	A	20th Battalion Virginia Heavy Artillery (Capt. Samuel H. Overton) Served as a body Servant to his Master Tharp Nause	Body Servant	Slave of Tharp Nause. Campbell County, VA Conf Pensioner
Moore, Richard	F	30th Battalion Virginia Sharp Shooters Served under Maj. Thomas F. Roche	Blacksmith	Albermarle County, VA Goff Pensioner
Morgan, Sam		Virginia Cavalry, unit information not provided.	Cook	Slave of Thomas Jackson. Dinwiddie County, VA Conf Pensioner
Morgan, Walker		Served as a Laborer in breastworks with the Engineers.	Laborer	Slave of Dick Morgan, Campbell County, VA Conf Pensioner
Mosby, James		Floyd's Brigade	Body Servant	FMC
Mosby, Wash	D G	13thRegiment Virginia Infantry Served under Capt. Dayton. Cokemer 23rd Virginia Infantry Served under 2nd Capt's Robert M. Trice and. Richard A. Trice	Ambulance Driver Cook	Slave of Jonathan Hancock. Louisa County, VA Conf Pensioner
Moseley, Ben		Served as Laborer working on Breastworks near Richmond	Laborer	Slave of A. G. Jeffreys. Mecklenburg County, VA Conf Pensioner
Moseley, Cambridge	F	25th Battalion Virginia Infantry (Richmond Battalion Virginia Infantry City Battalion Virginia Infantry) Served building breastworks for the Confederate Artillery	Laborer	Slave of Col. Thomas L. Bondurant (Surgeon). Buckingham County, VA Conf Pensioner
Moss, Tobe		Served in the Quarter Master Branch, as a Cook, Holster, Minor of Salt Peter and Teamster. He served under Capt. Valentine Rush.	Cook Holster Teamster	Freed Slave, Washington County, VA Conf Pensioner
Murray, Dallas		4th Regiment Virginia Cavalry	Blacksmith	Slave of F. Holmes, Prince William County, VA Conf
Name not known		Army of Northern Virginia Served as a servant to J.F. J. Caldwell.	Servant	FMC, Mr. Caldwell later wrote an article requesting that all Confederate states issue pensions to Negros who served the Confederacy and told of how his servant who had hired himself out to him had saved his life in the battle field
Name not known		Confederate States Arsenal, Richmond, VA.	Laborer	Slave of Mr. James H. Grant

Name not Known		Served as a Servant to General Beverly Robertson, when General Robertson was WIA, and left on the battlefield left for dead by his men, his servant searched and found him alive, removing him from the battlefield and took him home to Virginia.		Slave of General Beverly Robertson.
Name not known	E	1st Battalion Virginia Infantry Served as a servant to his master Maj. Charles A. Davidson	Servant	Slave of Major Charles A. Davidson
Name not known		Servant of Dr. John H. Clairborne (Surgeon) (16 year old slave)	Hospital Stewart	Slave
Name not known		Servant of Gen. Henry Wise at Sailor's Creek	Servant	Slave
Name not known (Female)		Servant of Dr. John H. Clairborne (Surgeon) (mother of 16 year old slave)	Hospital Stewart	Slave
Name not known	B	1st Virginia Cavalry Served as a Body Servant to Lt. William T. Noll	Body Servant	
Name not known	D	Virginia, Buried in the Confederate Cemetery in Chatanooga TN	Private	
Nelson, Hattie		Served as a cook at the wagon yards in Danville, Virginia	Cook	Surry County
Nelson, John	G	Hospital No. 6, Danville, Virginia Served under Capt. Tucker and Bill Fretful!	Cook Hospital Mess Boy	Slave of William R. Wilson. Surry County, VA Conf Pensioner
Nelson, W. B.	C	32nd Regiment Virginia Infantry	Cook	
Newby, John	G	Served under Capt. Connolly	Cook Teamster	Nansemond County, VA Conf Pensioner
Nicholas, Cass Lewis	B H	13th Regiment Virginia Infantry 24th Regiment Virginia Infantry Served as a Teamster and working in a Blacksmith shop.	Teamster	Slave of Lt. William S. Redd. Rockbridge County, VA Conf Pensioner
Oliver, Kitt		Served as Laborer working on Breastworks at Drewry's Bluff.	Laborer	Slave of Harrison Oliver. Halifax County, VA Conf Pensioner
Oulds, Henry	C	1st Regiment Virginia Cavalry	Teamster	Slave of Thomas Oulds. Campbell County, VA Conf
Overby, Ned		Served as a Laborer working on breastworks	Laborer	Slave of H. G. Bagley. Lunenburg County, VA Conf
Paell, Armstead	H	22nd Regiment Virginia Infantry (1st Kanawha Regiment)	Cook	
Page, Charles W.	E	32nd Regiment Virginia Infantry	Cock	
Page, Jacob		Served hauling the wounded from Seven Pines to Richmond.	Ambulance Driver Teamster	Slave of Alexander Dudley. Richmond County, VA Conf Pensioner
Page, Samuel	A	20th Battalion Virginia Heavy Artillery Served under Lt. McKinney	Body Servant Laborer	FMC_ Appomattox County, VA Conf Pensioner
Palmer, Thaddeus		Served as a body servant and cook to his master Capt. Robert T. Mitchell	Body Servant	Slave of Robert T. Mitchell. Floyd County, VA Conf Pensioner

Parker, John		He was serving as a Laborer working on fortifications when he was pressed into battle as an Artilleryman at the Battle of 1st Manassas.	Laborer Private	Kings and Queens County, VA
Parker, Robert		Unknown Virginia Unit	Body Servant	
Parrish, Edmon		Served driving a provision wagon serving under S. Hillary. Also served building breastworks at Mulberry Island.	Teamster	Slave of Thomas Hames. Goochland County, VA Conf Pensioner
Pegram, Arthur		Served working on breastworks and the Railroad served under his Master Capt. Hinton	Laborer	Slave, Amelia County, VA Conf Pensioner
Pegram, Paul		He was put in the Army by him master then served as a Teamster hauling rations from Dinwiddie Count to Blackstone Virginia.	Teamster	Slave of Madison Gill. Dinwiddie County, VA Conf Pensioner
Perry, Manson		Served in Virginia		Unknown Status of TN Conf Pension
Peters, Paul		Served working at Salt works in Washington and Smyth Counties	Labore Holster Wagoner	FMC, Amherst County, VA Conf Pensioner
Peters, Samuel		Served in the Artillery as a Holster under Capt. Dane.	Holster	FMC, Richmond County, VA Conf Pensioner
Peters, Tom		Served as a Teamster at Sailors Creek, Virginia	Teamster	
Petty, B. S.		Served as Laborer working on Breastworks on Chapin	Laborer	Slave of Doris Petty. Halifax County, VA Conf
Pitts, Robert		55th Regiment Virginia Infantry Served under Lt. P.C. Waring	Servant	Essex County, VA Conf Pensioner
Pleasants, Ross		Hugenot Springs Hospital, Powhatan Virginia Served as a Nurse and Servant under Dr. Thomas McKenzie	Nurse Servant	Slave of Richard McKenzie. Powhatan County, VA Conf Pensioner
Pollard, Emanuel	C	9th Regiment Virginia Cavalry (Col. W. T. Robinson) Served waiting on officers and moved their horses to the rear during battles.	Hostler Servant	Gloucestor County, VA Conf Pensioner
Pool, Berd	H P	3rd Virginia Cavalry Capt. Gregory's Company, Virginia Infantry Served his master Sgt. Amos G. Pool	Servant	Granville County, North Carolina Conf Pensioner
Pool, Simeon		Medical Corps Served under Gen. W. E. Jones at Abingdon, He was then assigned to Capt. Watkins on a detail working on Salt Petre works. Mr. Pool was again transferred to the Hospital at Emory and Henry College doing work for the Assistant Quarter Master.	Teamster	Washington County, VA Conf Pensioner

Poplar, Richard (Dick)	H	13th Regiment Virginia Cavalry, (Sussex Light Dragons) P.O.W. at Fort Delaware and Point Lookout, MD, for nineteen months. He was asked several times to take the oath of allegiance to the U.S. for his freedom, but refused.	Private	He died in 1886, his pallbearers were: Colonel Everard Meade Field, Commander, 12th VA Infantry Captain Edward A. Goodwyn, Company E, 13th VA Cavalry Captain John R. Patterson, Provost Guard, 12th VA Infantry Captain Stith Bolling, Company G, 13th VA Cavalry Private Jesse Miller Newcomb, Company F, 13th VA Cavalry Private Rufus M. Dobie, Company H, 13th VA Cavalry
Porter, Albert	F	13th Regiment Virginia Infantry Served as a cook and Holster for his master Capt. William Parras	Cook Holster	Slave of Charles Graves. Madison County, VA Conf Pensioner
Preston, Alexander		Served as a Laborer on breastworks at Petersburg.	Laborer Servant	Slave of Stephen Preston. Roanoke County, VA Conf Pensioner
Preston, Isaac Lewis		Field Hospital, Lynchburg Virginia Served under Dr. Jones, and Capt. Norris	Hospital Attendant	Slave of Thomas Preston. Lynchburg County, VA Conf Pensioner
Price, Alexander	E	1st Regiment Virginia State Reserves (2nd Class Militia) Served as a Holster and Servant to Major Benjamin W. Richardson	Holster Servant	Hanover County, VA Conf Pensioner
Price, George		Served as a carpenter building stables and breastworks at Petersburg.	Laborer	Slave of Piler Saunders. Franklin County, VA Conf Pensioner
Price, George	F&S	18th Regiment Virginia Infantry	Drummer	FMC
Price, James		Quartermaster Department Served as a Teamster in the QM Dept. in Hanover Junction	Teamster	Madison County, VA Conf Pensioner
Price, Jordan		Served working on breastworks at Mattoax, Virginia and batteries under his Master Lt. Southall.	Laborer	Slave of Lt. Southall. Amelia County, VA Conf Pensioner
Prichard, John		Served working on breastworks at Drewry's Bluff under Capt. Mason,	Laborer	Slave of Tom Prichard. Franklin County, VA Conf Pensioner
Pullen, Thomas	A	8th Battalion Virginia Reserves (1st Battalion, Valley Reserves)	Teamster	Slave of Samuel Updike Jr., Bedford County, VA, Denied Conf Pension
Ramsey, Nat		Served as a Laborer working on Breastworks	Laborer	Pittsylvania County, VA Conf Pensioner
Randolph, Alfred Thompson		Served as a Laborer working on breastworks	Laborer	Slave, Cumberland County, VA Conf Pensioner
Randolph, Samuel		Served as a teamster hauling supplies from Cartersville to Richmond.	Teamster	Slave of S. Booker. Cumberland County, VA Conf Pensioner
Redd, Silas		Served as a Laborer working on breastworks and rifle pits around Richmond worked under Col. Carter	Laborer	Slave of Charley Redd. Prince Edward County, VA Conf Pensioner
Reed, Henry Clay		Served taking care of horses under Capt. Wicker	Hostler	Tazewell County, West VA Conf Pensioner
Reed, John (Also Known as John Spencer)	D,F	12th Battalion Virginia Infantry Served as a Laborer working on Breastworks.	Laborer	Slave of Capt. Thomas S. Spencer. Campbell County, VA Conf Pensioner. P.O.W. at Harts Island

Directory of African American Confederates in the U.S. Civil War

Reeves, Armstead	A	37th Battalion, Virginia Cavalry (Dunn's Battalion, Partisan Rangers) Served under Pvt. Jacob J. Dent	Cook	Slave of Josiah Reeves. Franklin County, VA Conf Pensioner
Richeson, James D.		Served guarding a road at Blue Ridge Mountain and caring for horses	Guard	Slave of James Rickeson Amherst County, VA Conf Pensioner
Richeson, Joseph S.		Served at Allwood, Virginia as a Nurse waiting on sick soldiers under Ruben Rhodes.	Nurse Servant	Slave of Joe Lane, Rockbridge County, VA Conf Pensioner
Rivers, Freeman	A	5th Battalion Virginia Infantry Served working on breastworks and ammunition magazines under Sheriff Charles Turnbull	Laborer	FMC, Former slave of William Samford, Brunswick County, VA Conf Pensioner
Roane, General		Served under his master Capt. Latane as a Holster and Servant.	Holster Servant	Slave of Capt. Latante. Hanover County, VA Conf Pensioner
Roberts, Cope	G	13th Regiment Virginia Cavalry Served as a Servant to Capt. Benjamin Drew. Also worked on breastworks	Servant	FMC, Surry County, VA Conf Pensioner
Roberts, Press "Uncle"		Served as a Body Servant for Col. Edward Bourne	Servant	
Robertson, Richard		Served as a Teamster hauling supplies near Petersburg.	Teamster	Slave of James Robertson. Franklin County, VA Conf Pensioner
Robertson, Warner (Robinson), Warner	G	4th Regiment Virginia Cavalry Served as a Cook under Sgt. Garland N. Thompson (Gallie)	Cook	Hanover County, VA Conf Pensioner
Robinson, Carter	B	12th Regiment Virginia Cavalry (Baylor Light Horse)	Mess Cook	
Robinson, George		Served In the Infantry as a Laborer	Laborer	Warren County, VA Conf Pensioner
Robinson, George Washington.	C	11th Regiment Virginia Infantry (Clifton Grays) Served under Col. Samuel Garland and Cols. J. R. Hutter	Laborer	Slave of Maj. Robert Saunders. Campbell County, VA Conf Pensioner
Robinson, James Henry		Served as a Holster and as a miner, mining salt.	Laborer	Slave of John Robinson. Cumberland County, VA Conf Pensioner
Robinson, Lindsay		Unknown Virginia Unit	Ambulance Driver	
Robinson, Parker		Served as a Laborer digging ditches and building batteries at the James River in Richmond and Bragg's Mill.	Laborer	Slave of Garland Berkley. Charlotte County, VA Conf Pensioner
Robinson, Solon	J	35th Battalion Virginia Cavalry Served as a Body Servant and cook to his Master Pvt. Franklin B. Davis	Cook Servant	Slave of Pvt. Franklin B. Davis. Orange County, VA Conf Pensioner
Roe, Ben		Served shoeing horses for the Confederacy in Richmond, on orders of his master.	Blacksmith	Slave of Col James W. Ferguson. Madison County, VA Conf Pensioner. Brother of Ben Roe.
Roe, Montello		Served shoeing horses for the Confederacy in Richmond.	Blacksmith	Slave of I. S. Ferguson. Madison County, VA Conf Pensioner. Brother of Ben Roe.
Roe, Robert	C	3rd Regiment Virginia Cavalry	Cook Servant	
Rogers, James (Price, James)	G	3rd Regiment Virginia Cavalry Served as a servant to his master Pvt. William D. Price Jr. and of Capt. William Price Sr.	Body Servant Teamster	Slave of Pvt. William D. Price Jr. Charlotte County, VA Conf Pensioner

Rose, Given		Served building breastworks for the Confederate Government near Richmond	Laborer	Amherst County, VA Conf Pensioner
Rowe, Daniel		7th Regiment Virginia Infantry Served in the Quartermaster Department driving teams by request of Gen. James L. Kemper.	Teamster	Slave of Hiram Rogers. Madison County, VA Conf Pensioner
Rown, C. C.		2nd Division, Winder Hospital, Commissary		From Prince Edward, VA.
Russell, Unknown		Served carrying messages and other duties	Courier Servant	Slave of John Jones of Prembroke, VA.Elizabeth City County, VA Conf Pensioner
Russell, William		Served as a servant an courier carrying messages and other duties.	Courier Servant	Slave of John Jones of Pembroke. Elizabeth City County, VA Conf Pensioner
Rutherford, Neal		Served as a Teamster for General Lee's Army under Capt. Coker.	Teamster	Montgomery County, VA Conf Pensioner
Sadler, Henry	A	17th Regiment Virginia Infantry Served as a cook and body servant to Capt. Raymond Fairfax	Cook Body Servant	Buckingham County, VA Conf Pensioner
Sanderson, Carter		Served as a wagon driver at Petersburg, Virginia.	Teamster	Slave of Willis Sanderson. Cumberland County, VA Conf Pensioner
Saunders, James (Rev) (Stone, Sam)		Served as a Hostler driving cattle and as a railroad laborer, also collected supplies for the Army Commissary Department at Danville under Mr. Jim Lovelace.	Hostler Laborer	Slave of Miss Lizzie Stone. Pittsylvania County, VA Conf Pensioner
Saunders, Radford		61st Regiment Virginia Infantry Served as a Servant to Rev. Hillery Hatcher (Chaplain)	Servant	Slave of Rev. Hillery Hatcher. Roanoke County, VA Conf Pensioner
Scott, James		Served as a Laborer working on breastworks around Richmond worked under Col. Carter	Laborer	Slave of Tom Treadway. Prince Edward County, VA Conf Pensioner
Scott, John		2nd Virginia Cavalry Major Turner's Battalion Served as a servant to Charles Minor Blackford	Body Servant	FMC, John Scott also served as a Servant to Capt. Gardener in the Mexican American War.
Scott, Morris		Served as a Laborer working on breastworks and as a cook at Brown's Church until he was wounded in 1865.	Laborer	Slave of Lee Scott. Cumberland County, VA Conf Pensioner
Scott, Robert		Served as a Hostler and Teamster attending horses and cattle for the C.S. Army under A. T. Price.	Hostler Teamster	Slave of Robert West. Prince Edward County, VA Conf Pensioner
Scott, Wise		Unknown Virginia Unit	Private	Slave of Isaac Stanfield. Lynchburg County, VA Conf Pensioner
Scott, Zebedee		Served as a Teamster driving an Ambulance wagon, taking wounded soldiers to the Hosptials at Dutch Gap, Petersburg, Drewry's Bluff and Chaffin's Bluff, under Capt. William B. Simes.	Ambulance Driver	Slave of Capt. William B. Simes. Richmond County, VA Conf Pensioner
Scruggs, Unknown		Confederate Cavalry Headquarters Served under Capt. Smith	Cook	FMC, Brother of William T. Scruggs

Scruggs, William T.		Confederate Cavalry Headquarters Served under Capt. Smith at Luray Valley	Cook	FMC, Amelia County, VA Conf Pensioner
Sears, Tom		Served working on breastworks and building roads for John Dunkum	Laborer	Slave of Dr. Pratt. Buckingham County, VA Conf Pensioner
Seay, William		Served as a servant to Capt. William Allen in the Quarter Master Department. Also helped in the kitchen as a cook and attending to the horses.	Cook Servant	Fluvanna County, VA Conf Pensioner
Sergerant, Horace	1st	Capt. R. M. Anderson's Company, Light Artillery (First Company, Richmond Howitzers), Virginia Artillery	Driver	
Sheffield, George W.	A, C	18th Battalion Virginia Heavy Artillery Served as a- Teamster ender his supervisor and master William A. Sheffield and Capt. Massey in Company A.	Teamster	Slave of Pvt. William A. Sheffield. Henry County, VA Conf Pensioner
Shields, Jefferson (Jeff) (John)	H	27th Virginia Infantry, Stonewall Brigade (Rockbridge Rifles)	Body Servant Cook	Slave, He also claimed to be a Servant to Gen. Thomas J. "Stonewall" Jackson.
Shields, Tom		Virginia Cavalry Served as a cook and body servant to Thomas Cook.	Cook Body Servant	Buckingham County, VA Conf Pensioner
Shields, Wash	B	18th Regiment Virginia Infantry Served as a Laborer working on breastworks near Richmond, served under Capt. Richard McCulloch	Laborer	Slave of Mrs. Nancy Glasgow. Rockbridge County, VA Conf Pensioner
Short, Isaac N.		Served as a Blacksmith's helper making bridle pits, and harnesses at Columbia Mills, under M.A. McAlister his master and shop supervisor.	Blacksmith Servant	Slave of M. A. McAlister. Page County, VA Conf Pensioner
Short, John		Served as a Blacksmith's helper making bridle bits, and iron hauls for artillery for army use at Columbia Mills, under M.A. McAlister the shop supervisor.	Blacksmith Servant	Slave of M. A. McAlister. Page County, VA Conf Pensioner
Simms, Lewis		Served as a Laborer working on breastworks under his master Capt. S. M. Payne	Laborer Teamster	Slave of Capt. S. M. Payne. Culpeper County, VA Conf Pensioner
Sinclair, Archie	C	49th Regiment Virginia Infantry	Cook	VDCMR
Skaggs, Henry		Served as a guard to defend his masters family from bush raiders while his master served in the Army.	Holster Servant	Slave of John Skaggs. Lee County, VA Conf Pensioner
Skipwith, Ben Fuller		Served as a Teamster hauling provisions	Teamster	Slave of Fuller Skip with. Charlotte County, VA Conf Pensioner
Slate, Dick (Old Dick)	F & S	18th Regiment Virginia Infantry	Drummer	
Slater, George		1st Virginia Infantry		Yazoo County, MS Conf Pensioner
Slaughter, Charles	A	21st Regiment Virginia Infantry Served under Cpl. Benjamin Sublett (Colored) Transporting soldiers to Pamplin and High Bridge, Virginia	Servant Teamster	Slave of Charles H. Slaughter., Charlotte County, VA Denied Conf Pension

Slaughter, William H.		Served as a body servant and requested to go into battle.	Body Servant	Culpeper County, VA Conf Pensioner Attended the Confederate Veterans Reunion in 1928
Smith, Abram	2nd K	Capt. L.F. Jones' Company, Virginia Artillery (2nd Company, Richmond Howitzers) 1st Regiment Virginia Artillery Served a cook for J.R.B. Winston	Cook	Slave of Pvt. William C. Winston. Hanover County, VA Con? Pensioner
Smith, Billy	H	12th Regiment Virginia Cavalry	Private	VDCMR
Smith, Charles		3rd Regiment Virginia Cavalry	Blacksmith	FMC, Richmond, VA.
Smith, Charles	I	32nd Regiment Virginia Infantry	Cook	
Smith, Daniel	B	3rd Regiment Virginia Light Artillery (Local Defense) Served as a Laborer on breastworks near Richmond under Capt. J. R. Featherstone.	Laborer	Franklin County, VA Conf Pensioner
Smith, G. W.	C	32nd Regiment Virginia Infantry	Cook	
Smith, Harrison (Chaffin, Harrison)	G	28th Regiment Virginia Infantry Served as a Laborer working on breastworks in Richmond serving with his master Pvt. William H. Chaffin.	Laborer	Slave of Pvt. William H. Chaffin. Richmond County, VA Conf Pensioner
Smith, John	I	44th Regiment Virginia Infantry (Mossingford Rifles) Served as a cook for his master 1st Lt. Edward A. Roberts and served at Ft. Monroe and Manassas Gap under Capt. Robert H. Gilliam	Servant	Slave of Lt. Edward A. Roberts. Charlotte County, VA Conf Pensioner
Smith, Matt	I	28th Regiment Virginia Infantry Served as a Body Servant of Alex Smith	Body Servant	Slave of Alex McDonald Smith. Roanoke County, VA Conf Pensioner
Smith, Noah	H	12th Regiment Virginia Cavalry	Private	**VDCMR**
Smith, Samuel	B	3rd Regiment Virginia Light Artillery (Local Defense) Served as a Laborer on breastworks near Richmond under Capt. J. R. Featherstone.	Laborer	Slave of Samuel Walker. Franklin County, VA Conf Pensioner
Smith, Unknown	D	Col. Mosby's Regiment Virginia Cavalry Served as a Servant to Col. Richard P. Montjoy	Body Servant	K.I.A.
Smith, William		Served as a Laborer working on breastworks	Laborer	Slave of Theo Webb. Franklin County, VA Conf Pensioner
Sorrell, John	B	12th Regiment Virginia Cavalry (Baylor Light Horse)	Teamster	
Spinner, Henry	F&S	22nd Battalion Virginia Infantry Served under his Master Capt. John Turpin hauling supplies	Teamster	Slave of Capt. John Turpin, Bedford County, VA Conf Pensioner
Spratley, Sandy	H	13th Regiment Virginia Cavalry Served as a Servant to Lewis Hargrove	Cook Servant	Sussex County, VA Conf Pensioner
Sprigg, Lewis		Served as a servant to his master and as a Teamster distributing supplies to the wives of soldiers	Servant Teamster	Slave of H. G. Hartwell. Petersburg County, VA Conf Pensioner

Stewart, Osborne	E	5th Regiment Virginia Cavalry (Capt. Edward C. Fox's Company) Served as a Holster and horse boy to his master Sgt. Andrew Willis Eastwood	Holster Servant	Slave of Sgt. Andrew Willis Eastwood. King William County, VA Conf Pensioner	
Stewart, Richard	C	30th Regiment Virginia Infantry	Cook Waitman	FMC, Dinwiddie County, VA Conf Pensioner	
Stith, Cupid		Served as a Teamster for the Confederate Army	Teamster	Slave of John T. Jamerson. Prince George County, VA Conf Pensioner	
Strother, Joseph	I	7th Regiment Virginia Cavalry (Ashby's)	Teamster		
Stuart, Mary (Female)		Confederate Hospital Served as a Hospital Nurse, Servant and as a cook.	Cook Nurse Servant	Culpeper County, VA Conf Pensioner	
Sublett, Ben		Transported soldiers to Pamplin and High Bridge, Virginia	Servant Teamste	Slave of Charles H. Slaughter	
Talbert, W. H.		Provided rides to soldiers on his wagon	Teamster	Carroll County, VA Denied Conf Pension	
Tarpley, Stephen	B	21st Regiment Virginia Cavalry Served as a Blacksmith at Swansonville making instruments used for war under John and Jackson Hall.	Blacksmith	Slave of Robert Tarpley. Pittsylvania County, VA Conf Pensioner	
Tatem, Samuel	D	61st Regiment Virginia Infantry	Cook		
Taylor, Charles		He served as a cook and also served the Union (U.S.C.T. Veteran)	Cook	Slave of Jefro and Charley Jenkins The words of Charles Taylor, aged 52 in 1898, when he applied for his pension as a **Veteran of the Union Army.-** "I first served about 3 months as a cook in the Confederate Army during the summer of 1863.	
Taylor, Davy		Served as a labor working on breastworks around Richmond worked under Capt. Mason at Drewry's Bluff.	Laborer	Nelson County, VA Cortf Pensioner	
Taylor, John		3rd Division, CSA Served as a Nurse at Chimborazo Hospital caring for wounded soldiers	Nurse	Slave of Dr. Edward Harrie Smith (Chief Surgeon). Dinwiddie County, VA Conf Pensioner	
Taylor, Leelia (Female)		Jackson Hospital, 3rd Division, Richmond, Virginia	Laundress	Slave of E. S. Maynard	
Taylor, Richard		Served as Laborer working on Breastworks and fortifications under his master Jonathan Taylor at Drewry's Bluff and Clifton Farm.	Laborer	Slave of Jonathan Taylor. Mecklenburg County, VA Conf Pensioner	
Taylor, Samuel		Served hauling provisions	Teamster	Roanoke County, VA Conf Pensioner	
Taylor, Thornton		Served in the Quartermaster Department as a Teamster and doing wagon repair.	Teamster	Slave of Mr. Hunter, Essex County, VA Conf Pensioner	
Taylor, Washington		Served as Laborer working on Breastworks and helped move the dead.	Laborer	Slave of Dr. C. D. Whittle. Mecklenburg County, VA Conf Pensioner	
Taylor, Willie		Served as a Teamster and Servant to his master Capt. John Taylor who was killed in the war.	Servant Teamster	Slave of Capt. John Taylor. Mecklenburg County, VA Conf Pensioner	

Name		Unit / Service	Role	Notes
Terry, C. P.		Commodore Tucker's Brigade, Lee's Division	Sailor	P.O.W. at Lookout Point, MD. VDCMR
Terry, James		Served as a cook and bodyguard to his master John Terry who served under Gen. P. G. T. Beauregard	Bodyguard Cook	Slave of John Terry. Campbell County, VA Conf Pensioner
Thomas, George Lee		Served as a Laborer working on breastworks and building rifle pits.	Laborer	Slave of Mrs. May Gardiner. Hanover County, VA Conf Pensioner
Thompson, Charles		Battery B, 10th Battalion Virginia Artillery Served as a Servant and Cook to 1st Sgt Samuel Thompson, he also assisted in rounding up deserters and runaway slaves with the Home Guard, Samuel Thompson was a Captain in the Home Guard.	Cook Servant	Slave of Capt. Samuel Thompson, Pittsylvania County, VA Conf Pensioner
Thompson, Jerry		Served as a Servant to his master Dr. William Pendleton in Isle County, North Carolina	Servant	Slave of Dr. William Pendleton. Louisa County, VA Conf Pensioner
Thompson, John R.	H	8th Regiment Virginia Cavalry Served as a Body Servant, Cook, and Hostler, served under Capt. Henry Bowen.	Body Servant Cook	Slave of Gen. Rees T. Bowen., Tazewell County, West VA Conf Pensioner
Thornhill, William	E	2nd Regiment Virginia Artillery Served as Drewry's Bluff, Richmond, Petersburg and Gettysburg digging trenches and waited on his master Sgt. James Henry Harding	Body Servant Laborer	Charlotte County, VA Conf Pensioner
Thornton, Joe May		Unknown Tennessee Unit	Private	Louisa County, VA Conf Denied Pension
Thrash, Mark Anthony		Served as a Body Servant to Dr. Christopher Thrash	Body Servant	Slave
Thurston, Joe May		18th Regiment Virginia Cavalry Served as a cook and servant, cooking and washing clothes for Mr. Porter	Cook Servant	Slave of Levi Baker. Denied Pension, Luisa County, VA Denied Conf Pensioner
Tinsley, Clem		Served as a Laborer working on fortifications at Drewry's Bluff	Laborer	Montgomery County, VA Conf Pensioner
Tinsley, Flem		Served hauling provisions to Lynchburg, working under Samuel Fishburne	Teamster	Slave of Hillis Tinsley. Roanoke County, VA Conf Pensioner
Tinsley, Joseph		Drafted and first served repairing telegraph lines, then as a Teamster	Teamster	FMC, Drafted, Hanover County, VA.
Tompson, Robert W.		Served as a Laborer building bridges under Capt. Breneman	Laborer	Slave of Robert Burrus. Rockingham County, VA Conf Pensioner
Topp, Jack		Served as a Laborer working on breastworks around Richmond worked under Jim Michael Carter	Laborer	Slave or Branch Worsham. Prince Edward County, VA Conf Pensioner
Trent, Carter		19th Regiment Virginia Infantry Served as a Servant to Col. Phillip St. George Cocke and as a Laborer on breastworks	Servant	Slave of Col. Phillip St. George Cocke. Powhatan County, VA Conf Pensioner
Tucker, Lewis		Served working as a blacksmith and Holster, and cared for horses for Confederate Soldiers	Blacksmith Holster	Slave of Samuel R. Wortham. Amherst County VA Conf Pensioner

Name	Co.	Regiment / Service	Role	Notes
Tucker, Pompey	F&S	41st Regiment Virginia Infantry Served Under Capt. Nash and Everett Dreary	Cook	Slave of Dr. Jonathan Tucker, Dinwiddie County, VA Conf Pensioner
Tucker, William	I	3rd Regiment Virginia Cavalry Served under Col. William Davis Served working for the Commissary as a Teamster collecting provisions and hauling supplies for the Conf. Army	Cook Servant Teamster	Slave of Cal. Hart Tucker. Dinwiddie County, VA Conf Pensioner
Turner, Arthur		Served as a Laborer working on breastworks in Richmond under Giles Clingenpeel	Laborer	Slave of George C. Turner. Franklin County, VA Conf Pensioner
Turner, Charles		Served working on breastworks at Richmond	Laborer	Floyd County, VA Conf Pensioner
Turner, Ephraim		When Col. Harrison was killed he and Ben Dean carried his body off of the field		
Turner, Henry	A	13th Regiment Virginia Cavalry Served as a Body Servant to Pvt. Theophilus G. Little	Body Servant	Southampton County, VA Conf Pensioner
Turner, Phil		Served as a Blacksmith and Railroad track worker under Buck Gills his supervisor	Blacksmith Laborer	Slave of Archer Gills. Prince Edward County, VA Conf Pensioner
Turpin, Henry		Served as a Laborer on breastworks around Richmond and Petersburg, worked under Mr. Wilson	Laborer	Slave of Roland Turpin. Lynchburg County, VA Conf Pensioner
Tweedy, Sam		Served working on Breastworks and hauling supplies	Laborer Teamster	Slave of Capt. Ben Tweedy. Campbell County, VA Conf Pensioner
Tyree, Sr., Henry D.	K	3rd Regiment Virginia Cavalry (Prince Edward Dragoons) Served as a cook for W.C. Shackleford	Cook Private	Albermarle County, VA Conf Pensioner
Valentine, Jim (Valentine, James)		Served as a Cook and Servant in the Infantry to Capt. Haskins	Cook Servant	FMC, Mecklenburg County, VA Conf Pensioner
Waddell, Thomas	F	26— Regiment Virginia Cavalry Served working as a Servant in a Hospital near Sailor's Creek under his Master Capt. Jim A. Hillsman	Servant	Slave of Capt. J.A. Hillsman. Amelia County, VA Conf Pensioner
Walker, Chilse	I	32nd Regiment Virginia Infantry	Chief Cook	
Walker, Frank	I	46th Regiment Virginia Infantry	Private	Fredericksburg County, VA Conf Pensioner. VDCMR
Walker, Samuel		Served working on breastworks, seared under Gen. Samuel McGowan	Laborer Teamster	Slave of Nat Walker, Franklin County VA Conf Pensioner
Walker, William	F&S	1st Regiment Virginia Cavalry (Fitzhugh Lee's Cavalry, Col. William Davis)	Cook	Slave of Robert Neblett. Dinwiddie County, VA Conf Pensioner
Wallace, Henry		Served as a cook to John Hull	Cook	Slave of Harles (Charles)? Smith. Culpeper County, VA Conf Pensioner
Waller, Ferdnand		Served as a Laborer working on breastworks, serving two tours in Richmond and one tour in Danville	Laborer	Slave of Hampton Waller Pittsylvania County, VA Conf Pensioner

Waller, Lewis Henry	K	1st Regiment Virginia Cavalry Served as a waterboy and drum carrier, was only 12 years old, served with his master Pvt. William (Willie) Harnsberger	Drum Carrier Waterboy	Pittsylvania County, VA Conf Pensioner
Waller, Richard		Served in the Virginia Cavalry as a Holster and Servant	Holster Servant	Slave of William Hanaberger. Roanoke County, VA Conf
Warner, William		Served taking care of horses for Capt. Cowen	Body Servant	Slave of Col. Charles Given of Rappahannock. Amherst County, VA Conf Pensioner
Washington, George		Served working at the Tredegar Iron Works, VA	Laborer	Slave
Washington, Lewis		Served as a Servant to Capt. P. Rice cooking and washing	Servant	Slave of Preacher Rice. Essex County, VA Conf Pensioner
Washington, Richard	E	55th Regiment Virginia Infantry Served as a Servant to Col. William Baker	Body Servant	Slave of Archibald (Archer) Alexander. Rockbridge County, VA Denied Conf
Watkins, Frank	C	11th Regiment Virginia Infantry Served as a Body Servant to his master Pvt. James M. Terrell who was later killed in action.	Body Servant	Slave of Pvt. James M. Terrell. Mecklenburg County, VA Conf Pensioner
Watkins, William		Staunton Hill Artillery Served as a cook under Capt. Andrew B. Price.	Cook	Charlotte County, VA Conf Pensioner
Watson, John		Served as a Teamster hauling weapons to Danville and Lynchburg.	Teamster	Slave of Jacob Watson. Pittsylvania County, VA Conf Pensioner
Weaver, Frank		Served as a Laborer on breastworks near Richmond	Laborer	Slave of Peter Close. Madison County, VA Conf
Webb, William	K	53rd Regiment Virginia Infantry (Charles City Southern Guards) Served working on breastworks on Mulberry Island, and served as a cook to Gen. MaGruder, Phil Buffin, John Ragland	Laborer Servant	Slave of Ned Phillips. Charles City County, VA Conf Pensioner
Webster, Daniel	H	44th Regiment Infantry Virginia Served as a Servant to his Master Capt. Fernando	Body Servant	Amelia County, VA Conf Pensioner
Webster, Robert	A,D	58th Regiment Virginia Infantry Served under Capt. DeWitt C. Booth		Slave of Anthony Simmons. Roanoke County, VA Denied Conf Pension
Wells, James		Served as a labor working on breastworks at Drewry's Bluff under Maj. Smith Stark.	Laborer	Slave of W. W. Harris. Nelson County, VA Conf Pensioner
West, Richard	A	32nd Regiment Virginia Infantry	Cook	
Wester, Robert	D	58th Regiment Virginia Infantry Served as a cook for Capt. Dewitt C. Booth	Cook	Slave of Anthony Simmons. Roanoke County, VA Conf
Whitaker, Daniel		Served the Confederacy by preparing the body's and burying dead Confederate Soldiers.	Undertaker	Appomattox County, VA
Whitaker, R. D.		Served the Confederacy by driving a wagon and helping his father Daniel Whitaker burying dead Confederate Soldiers.	Wagon Driver	Appomattox County, VA Conf Pensioner

White, Henry	F	5th Battalion Virginia Reserves.' Served as a Body-Servant to Col. Patrick M.	Body Servant	Franklin County, VA Conf Pensioner
White, Richard		Served as Laborer working on Breastworks and building rifle_pitts, served under his Master Capt. William White.	Laborer	Slave of Capt. William White. Halifax County, VA Conf Pensioner
Whittle, Walter	B	4tH Virgnia Cavalry Regiment	Private	Mulatto
Wilkerson, James		Served as Laborer working on Breastworks under Mark A. Wilkerson	Laborer	Halifax County, VA Conf Pensioner
Wilkins, Sam	F	51st Virginia Infantry Served as a cook for John Savage and Dr. H. H. Hunter (Assistant Surgeon)	Cook	Gates County, North Carolina Con? Pensioner
Williams, Charles	E	Regiment Virginia Infantry Served as a Laborer working on breastworks building fortifications and deepening the James River under Capt. James Ryan	Laborer	Montgomery County, VA Conf Pensioner
Williams, Edgar	1st	Capt. R. M. Anderson's Company, Light Artillery (First Compnay, Richmond Howitze7s),Virginia Artillery	Cook	
Williams, Flemming		Served as a Cook in the Virginia Cavalry under Cant. Henry Williams	Cook	Slave of Nathaniel Williams. Pulaski County, VA Conf
Williams, Isam	F&S	7Regiment Virginia Infantry Served and drove a commissary wagon under his master Capt. John Lightfoot.	Teamster	Slave of Capt. John Lightfoot. Culpeper County, VA Conf Pensioner
Williams, James		Served as a Laborer on breastworks below Richmond under Capt. Burks	Laborer	Slave of George P. Tayloe. Roanoke County, VA Conf Pensioner
Williams, Joe Thomas		Served hauling confederate soldiers to be operated on by his master Dr. Hemming Dodson	Ambulance Driver	Slave of Dr. Hemming Dodson, Southampton County, VA Conf Pensioner
Williams, John		Served as a cook and Servant to his master Humphrey (illegible)	Cook Servant	Slave of Humphrey . Essex County, VA Conf Pensioner
Williams, Phil	B	12th Regiment Virginia Cavalry (Baylor Light	Hostler	
Williams, Rowland		Served as a Servant to his master William Graham.	Servant	Slave of William Graham. Montgomery County, VA Conf Pensioner
Williams, Simon		Served as a Nurse in the Hospital Service at Richmond and Lynchburg under Mr. Ferguson and Mr. Campbell.	Nurse	Slave of William Morgan. Fairfax County, VA Conf Pensioner
Williams, Steptoe	B	25th Regiment Virginia Cavalry Served as a cook for Maj. George S. Lawson	Cook	Slave of George Cox. Lancaster County, VA Conf Pensioner
Willis, Charles	B	9th Regiment Virginia Cavalry Served as a Teamster in a wagon train for Gen. Robert E. Lee	Teamster	Goochland County, VA Conf Pensioner
Willis, James	G	40th Regiment Virginia Infantry Served as a Servant to his Master Capt. Walter	Servant	Slave of Capt. Walter Bourne. Fredericksburg County, VA Conf Pensioner

Willis, John		Served as a Body Servant to Dr. J. B. Keaton, (Kenton)? number of regiment is illegible	Body Servant	Slave of W. Keaton. (Kenton) Westmoreland County, VA Conf Pensioner
Wilson, Robert (Uncle Bob)	H	16th Regiment Virginia Infantry	Private	Elgin (Illinois) Daily Courier-News, Monday, April 12, 1948 - "Robert **(Uncle Bob) Wilson,** Negro veteran of the Confederate army who observed his 112th birthday last January 13, died early yesterday morning in the veterans' hospital at the Elgin State hospital...He enlisted as a private in Company H of the 16th regiment of Virginia Infantry on Oct. 9, 1862 and discharged May 31, 1863.
Wilson, William Anthony		Served as a Laborer working on breastworks, forts and stables at Greenfield.	Laborer	Slave of Dr. John Wilson. Pittsylvania County, VA Conf Pensioner
Wimbish, Henry (Wimbush)		Served as Laborer building Breastworks and battery emplacements near Petersburg, Virginia	Body Servant	Slave of "Dock" Anderson, Halifax County, VA Conf Pensioner
Winfield, Isham	I	3rd Regiment Virginia Cavalry (Stuart's Brigade) Served as a cook, servant arc building breastworks.	Cook	Slave of 2nd Lt. Berryman J. Hill. Dinwiddie County, VA Conf Pensioner
Winfree, Alpheus	G	1st Regiment Virginia Cavalry Served under Capt. C. R. Irving	Cook	Slave of R. H . Marshall Amelia County, VA Conf Pensioner
Winfree, Augustus		Served with the Cavalry. Other Information is not legible.	Servant	Slave of Capt. Miller. Cumberland County, VA Conf Pensioner
Winslow, Edmond		Commissary Department Served as a teamster hauling lumber for the camp under his master Capt. John Lewis	Teamster	Slave of Capt. John Lewis Culpeper County, VA Conf Pensioner
Winston, Daniel		Served as a Servant under Capt. Samuel Richardson, also carried mail and helped to barricade roads.	Body Servant	Slave of Capt. Samuel Richardson. Rockbridge County, VA Conf Pensioner
Withers, John B.	F	Col. Mosby's Regiment Virginia Cavalry Served as a cook and servant to Col. John S. Mosby who was a great friend of his master.	Cook Servant	Slave of William Bussey. Culpeper County, VA Conf Pensioner
Wood, Charles H.		Served as a cook in the Quartermaster Department under Capt. Freeman	Cook	Slave of Miss Lucy Blair. Cumberland County, VA Conf Pensioner
Wooden, Lewis		Capt. Donkin's Company Served under QuarterMaster James Mundy	Teamster	Slave of William H. Garrett, Botetourt County, VA Conf Pensioner
Woodford, Edward		4th Regiment Virginia Cavalry	Cook Servant	
Woodson, George		Served as a laborer working on breastworks	Laborer	Slave of James Woodson of Buckingham County. Cumberland County, VA Conf Pensioner
Woody, Peter		Served as a Laborer working on breastworks	Laborer	Franklin County, VA Conf Pensioner
Wooldridge, William		Served as a laborer working on breastworks and as a cook	Cook Labore	Slave of B. Brooks. Cumberland County, VA Conf Pensioner

Worshman, Lewis (Stump)		Chimborazo Hospital, Camp Winder, Virginia	Slave	Slave of Samuel Hargrove
Wright, Morris	F&S	Mosby's Regiment Virginia Cavalry (Partisan Rangers) 43rd Battalion Virginia Cavalry Served under Adjutant William Mosby	Body Servant Laborer	Slave of Alfred D. Mosby., Washington D.C., Conf Pensioner
Wyatt, George		Served as a servant and cook at Drewry's Bluff and Yorktown.	Cook	Slave of Horace Mitchell. Dinwiddie County, VA Conf Pensioner
Wyatt, Johnson	B	13th Regiment Virginia Cavalry Served his master's step-brother Lt. John Kerr	Servant	Slave of Dr. Robert Walker. Richmond County, VA Conf Pensioner
Wynne, Ben		Camp Jackson Hospital, Richmond VA Served waiting on and attending to wounded soldiers, under Dr. Scott, Dr. Jenkins, and Dr. Heath	Servant	Slave of Thomas Starke. King William County, VA Conf Pensioner
Yerbey, Joe	K	9th Regiment Virginia Cavalry	Cook	
York, Jefferson		Cutshaw s Battalion Confederate Artillery.	Sgt	
York, Wesley		Served building breastworks at Drewry's Bluff worked under Mr. Jim Flannagan	Laborer	Slave of Thomas Garland. Rockingham County, VA Conf Pensioner
Young, Humphrey		General & Staff Officers, Corps, Division & Brigade Staffs, Non-corn. Staffs & Bands, Enlisted Men, Staff Departments, C. General John George Walker's staff	Body Servant	Servant for Capt. W. Augustine Smith
Yowell, John L.	L	10th Regiment Virginia Infantry	Teamster	Culpeper County, VA Conf Pensioner. Son of Stuart Yowell whom he succeeded.
Yowell, Stuart	L	10th Regiment Virginia Infantry	Teamster	
Zink, W. H.		Served as a Teamster in the Quarter Master and Commissary Departments under Capt. Hancock, hauling supplies to a Hospital in Bedford.	Teamster	Montgomery County, VA Conf Pensioner

Unknown Confederate State units and soldiers

NAME	CO.	UNIT	RANK	SLAVE / FREE MISC NOTES
, Ben		Unknown Confederate Unit		P.O.W. at Camp Chase, Ohio.
, Bob		Unknown Confederate Unit	Teamster	Slave of David Bridges. Surrendered at Appomatox Courthouse
Dr. Carver		Unknown Confederate Unit	Servant	P.O.W.
Dulaney		Unknown Confederate Unit		P.O.W. at Camp Chase, Ohio.
George		Unknown Confederate Unit		P.O.W. at Johnston's Island. Refused to take an oath of allegiance to the U.S. Government

Gus ("Uncle")	Served as a Body Guard, Teamster and Soldier	Bodyguard Teamster	
	Col. Donovan's Cavalry Regiment Served as a Servant to Capt. Johnson	Servant	(Dunovant)
	Served as a Servant of Capt. J. R. Wilson	Servant	P.O.W. at Johnson's Island
Reuben		Private	P.O.W.
Applegate, L.	General and Staff Officers, NonRegimental Enlisted Men, CSA	Colored Orderly	
Barnes, William A.	Unknown Confederate Unit		Attended the Joint 1938 Grand Army of the Republic and the United Confederate Veterans Veterans Reunion at Gettysburg, Pennsylvania at the time he was living in California and was 112 yrs old.
Blanton, Alexander	Unknown Confederate Unit	Servant	P.O.W. at Camp Morton, Indiana Died there and now buried at Greenfield Park, Indianapolis
Bones, Tom	Served feeding soldiers, he fished for shad in the James River	Forager	Slave
Bradfield, Nannie	Served as a servant taking food to her master's son William Chambers and other soldiers.	Servant	Slave of James and Rebecca Chambers. According to her statements in the Alabama Slave Narratives,
Brophy, Tom	Unknown Confederate Unit		In an action on 7 th April the 108M New York Infantry captured him and made him servant of the New Yorkers, He later lived in New York until his death in 1888.
Brown, John	Unknown Confederate Unit Served as a Servant to Capt. Brown	Servant	P.O.W.
Brown, Peter	Unknown Confederate Unit		Mustered oct at Memphis Tennessee. Later lived in Arkansas
Butler, John	Unknown Confederate Unit		P.O.W. Captured near Centerville, VA.
Calloway, Peter	Served in the war with his overseer Gus Taylor		Possibly from Texas or Arkansas?
Carver Dr.	Unknown Confederate Unit		P.O.W., possibly a doctor's servant?
Doyld, William	Served as a Servant to Jack Hoskins	Waiter	Slave of Jim Doyld , According to Willie Doyld his son in Arkansas Slave Narratives.
Frazier, George	Unknown Confederate Unit		P.O.W. at Camp Morton, Indiana Died there and now buried at Greenfield Park, Indianapolis
Hall, Moses	Unknown Confederate Unit		P.O.W at Point Lookout, MD.
Harden, Sitas	Unknown Confederate Unit	Laborer	Captured at Washington, DC
Hardy, G.W.	Unknown Confederate Unit	Servant	P.O.W at camp Morton, Indiana died there and now buried at Greenfield Park. Indianapolis
Harris, John J.	Unknown Confederate Unit	Laborer	P.O.W Captured at Cedar Point, VA

Directory of African American Confederates in the U.S. Civil War

Henderson, Henry		Unknown Confederate Unit	Body Servant	According to his statement in the Oklahoma Slave Narratives.
Jackson, Henry		Unknown Confederate Unit	Body Servant	
Kendall, Hermann		Unknown Confederate Unit		
Levell, Samuel		Served as an Officers Servant	Servant	P.O.W. Alton, Illinois
Longstreet, Hudson		Served as a Surgeons assistant was wounded at Corinth, MS.	Surgeon's Assistant	
Mack, Richard		Served as a servant to Capt. Cherry in the Confederate Cavalry	Body Servant	
May, Jerry W.		Unknown Confederate Unit		
McConnell, Lewis		Unknown Confederate Unit		Resident of College Hill, Arkansas Attended the UCV Reunion in Arkansas 1928
Mitchell, J.C.		Unknown Confederate Unit	Servant	P.O.W. at Camp Morton, Indiana Died there and now buried at Greenfield Park, Indianapolis
Name not known		Unknown Confederate Unit		According to Henry Bohannon's statements in the Alabama Slave Narratives his father went with is master to fight in the war, no further information provided.
Name not known		Served as a servant to his master Dick Hewett who became a POW.	Servant	Slave of Dick Hewett. His servant followed him into captivity then later cried over his master's coffin when he died.
Name not known		Served as a servant to his master Frank Adams.	Servant	Slave of Frank Adams, possibly from Alabama?
Name not known		Served as a servant to his master Edward Burruss.	Servant	Slave of Edward Burruss
Name not known		Served as a servant to nis master	Servant	Slave, KIA according to his daughter Judy Parker.
Parnell, Unknown		Served as a laborer working on breastworks	Laborer	Slave, According to his son Samuel S. Parnell's statement
Phelps, Thomas A.		Unknown Confederate Unit	Private	Slave
Pope, Harrison (Shep)		Unknown Confederate Unit Served as a laborer working on docks (Stevedore)	Stevedore	He died in the Confederate army near Little Rock. He violated a military law, he was punished, he then contracted pneumonia and died.
Porter, William		POW at Point Lookout, MD.		
Robinson, Ephraim		Unknown Confederate Unit Served as a Body Servant to Capt. Allen Morrison	Body Servant	Slave
Scales, Richmond		Served as a Body Servant to his Master's son John Durham	Body Servant	Slave of Jimmie Scales
Scott, John		General and Staff Officers, Enlisted Men, Staff Departments C. S. A. Major Thomas P. Turner's Battalion	Private	FMC
Williams, George		Gen. Price of the Conf Army	Striker	Slave
Woolsey, John		Unknown Confederate Unit	Servant	P.O.W. at Camp Morton, Indiana Died there and now buried at Greenfield Park, Indianapolis
Yerby, Joe		Unknown Confederate Unit	Cook	Died as POW at Point Lookout, MD

Bibliography

Tennessee Confederate Soldiers and Widows Pension Applications, Tennessee State Library and Archives. TSLA microfilm, 173 reels Pension applications were granted and refused by soldiers (113 reels), widows (60 reels), and "colored troops" (2 reels). Listed in order of application number. Personal background as well as supporting documents attesting to the veteran's character and military experience are included. See also the Index of Confederate Pension Applications in Tennessee. 1964, Tennessee State Library and Archives (E 548.T2) (E 548.T2) (E 548.T2)

Confederate Indigent Families Lists (1863-1865), Texas State Library and Archives Commission, Indigent Families are identified by Counties. Some of the following components may be found in information: soldier's name; currently serving; injured or killed in action; unit; acting household head Manuscripts and Archives TSLC is a database that may be accessed online.

Adjutant General's Office of the United States of America Official Army Register of the United States Army Volunteer Force, 1861-1965. 1965, Washington, D.C.

M275, Official Records of the Union and Confederate Navies, 1861-1865, United States National Archives and Records Administration

The United States of America Pension Index, National Archives. T288 Microfilm Series

The United States of America National Archives and Records Administration. In 1860, the United States conducted its eighth census. T825. Microfilm Series

The United States of America National Archives and Records Administration. Enumerating Union Veterans and Widows of Union Veterans of the Civil War in the Eleventh Census of the United States, 1890. 123 Microfilm Series

Compiled Service Records of Volunteer Union Soldiers from Kentucky, United States National Archives. There are 515 reels in all. M397 at the National Archives. In general, service records include the date and location of mustering in and enrollment, as well as the muster roll data and the muster out date. The information is organized by unit and kind.

The soldiers' names are listed alphabetically. Personal papers, such as enrollment records and casualty sheets, can be found on reels 498-515. The solder's name is listed alphabetically.

The United States of America National Archives and Records Administration. "Official Records of the Union and Confederate Navies in the War of the Rebellion," according to the ORN. There are 31 volumes in all. The United States Government Printing Office published this book in 1914.

The United States of America Index to Compiled Service Records of Volunteer Union Soldiers Who Served with US Colored Troops, National Archives. There are 98 reels in all. TSLA MF. #1454. National Archives M589. The soldiers' surnames are listed alphabetically in the index. Unit, company, and rank are also included.

The United States of America Consolidated Index to Confederate Soldiers' Compiled Service Records, National Archives. There are 535 reels in all. M253 at the National Archives. All states where Confederate forces were constituted are included in the index. The soldiers' surnames are listed alphabetically. Company, unit, and rank are also included.

The United States of America Compiled Service Records of Confederate Soldiers Who Served in Organizations from Tennessee, National Archives. There are 359 reels in all. National Archives and Records Administration. In general, service records include the date and location of mustering in and enrollment, as well as the muster roll data and the muster out date. The soldiers' surnames are alphabetized and organized by unit.

The United States of America Compiled Service Records of Volunteer Union Soldiers of Tennessee, National Archives. There are 220 reels in all. M395. National Archives. In general, service records include the date and location of mustering in and enrollment, as well as the muster roll data and the muster out date. The information is organized by unit and kind.

The soldiers' surnames are listed alphabetically.

The United States of America Compiled Service Records of Confederate Soldiers Who Served in Organizations from the State of Texas, National Archives. National Archives M323, 445 reels In general, service records include the date and location of mustering in and enrollment, as well as the muster roll data and the muster out date. The soldiers' surnames are alphabetized and organized by unit. 1961.

Tennessee State Library and Archives, Confederate Soldiers and Widows Pension Applications. 173 reels of TSLA microfilm Soldiers (113 reels), widows (60 reels), and "colored troops" all submitted pension applications (2 reels). The applications are listed in order of application number. The veteran's personal history, as well as supporting documentation attesting to his or her character and military service, are provided. Also check Tennessee's Index of Confederate Pension Applications. Tennessee State Library and Archives, 1964. (E 548.T2) (E 548.T2) (E 548.T2) (E 548.T2) (E 548.T2) (E 548.T2)

Indigent Families are designated by Counties in the Confederate Indigent Families Lists (1863-1865), Texas State Library and Archives Commission. Information may have some of the following elements: name of soldier; unit; acting household head; presently serving; wounded or killed in action Archives and Manuscripts TSLC is a searchable database that may be accessed over the internet.

Official Army Register of the United States Army Volunteer Force, 1861-1965, Adjutant General's Office of the United States of America, Washington, D.C., 1965.

United States National Archives and Records Administration, M275, Official Records of the Union and Confederate Navies, 1861-1865

Pension Index of the United States of America, National Archives, T288 Microfilm Series

The National Archives and Records Administration of the United States of America. The eighth census of the United States was taken in 1860. T825. Microfilm Collection

The National Archives and Records Administration of the United States of America. In the Eleventh Census of the United States, 1890, Union Veterans and Widows of Union Veterans of the Civil War were enumerated. Microfilm Series 123

United States National Archives, Compiled Service Records of Volunteer Union Soldiers from Kentucky. There are a total of 515 reels in this game. The National Archives holds M397. The date and place of mustering in and enrollment, as well as the muster roll data and the muster out date, are all included in service records. The data is categorized by unit and kind.

The names of the servicemen are given alphabetically. On reels 498-515, you'll find personal paperwork like enrollment records and casualty forms. The name of the solder is listed alphabetically.

The National Archives and Records Administration of the United States of America. According to the ORN, "Official Records of the Union and Confederate Navies in the War of the Rebellion." There are a total of 31 volumes. This book was produced in 1914 by the United States Government Printing Office.

National Archives, Index to Compiled Service Records of Volunteer Union Soldiers Who Served with US Colored Troops in the United States of America. There are a total of 98 reels in this game. TSLA MF. #1454 TSLA MF. #1454 TSLA MF. #1 M589. National Archives. In the index, the soldiers' surnames are arranged alphabetically. There's also information on the unit, company, and rank.

National Archives of the United States of America, Consolidated Index to Confederate Soldiers' Compiled Service Records. There are a total of 535 reels in this game. M253 may be found at the National Archives. The index includes all states where Confederate armies were organized. The surnames of the servicemen are presented alphabetically. There's also information on the company, unit, and rank.

The National Archives of the United States of America compiled service records of Confederate soldiers who served in Tennessee organizations. There are a total of 359 reels in this game. The National Archives and Records Administration is in charge of keeping records. The date and place of mustering in and enrollment, as well as the muster roll data and the muster out date, are all included in service records. The surnames of the troops are alphabetized and arranged by unit.

National Archives, The United States of America Compiled Service Records of Volunteer Union Soldiers of Tennessee. There are a total of 220 reels in this game. National Archives, M395. The date and place of mustering in and enrollment, as well as the muster roll data and the muster out date, are all included in service records. The data is categorized by unit and kind.

The surnames of the servicemen are presented alphabetically.

The National Archives of the United States of America compiled Confederate Soldiers Who Served in Organizations from the State of Texas. M323, 445 reels, National Archives The date and place of mustering in and enrollment, as well as the muster roll data and the muster out date, are all included in service records. The surnames of the troops are alphabetized and arranged by unit. 1961.

General Index to Pension Files, 1861-1934, Microfilm Publication T288:, United States National Archives. Between 1861 and 1916, the Army, Navy, and Marine Corps served. The majority of the records are for Civil War duty, however some are for earlier service by Civil War veterans. There are no Federal pension records for Confederate forces service. Each card in the general index contains information on a veteran's name, rank, unit, and period of service, as well as the names of any dependents, the filing date, the application number, the certificate number, and the state in which the claim was submitted. The darker cards all have something to do with naval duty. There are 544 rolls in all.

The United States of America Record Group 109 of the National Archives' War Department Collection Of Confederate Records. On the 74 rolls of microfilm, there are compiled records showing military units' service in Confederate organizations. Reproductions of Publications The compiled records of Confederate military units' histories. The National Archives and Records Administration (NARA) is a government agency that manage Administration of General Services U.S. Office of Naval Records and Library, Washington, 1973. Official Union and Confederate Naval Records from the War of the Rebellion. GPO, Washington, 1894-1922.

The United States of America Department of the Navy Confederate States Navy Officers' Register, 1861-1865. GPO, Washington, 1931.

The United States of America Department of the Quartermaster. Numbers I-VI of the Roll of Honor, Names of Soldiers Who Died in Defense of the American Union and Are Interred in National Cemeteries, 1868. Genealogical Publishing, Baltimore, 1994.

The War Department of the United States of America. Official Records of the American Revolutionary War. GPO, Washington, 1880.

ARTICLES

"Free Men of Color in Grey," Civil War History, Vol. 32, Sep 1986: 247 255. Bergeron, Arthur W. Jr., "Free Men of Color in Grey," Civil War History, Vol. 32, Sep 1986: 247 255.

"Black North Carolina Confederate Pensioners," by Russell Scott Koonts. Journal of the North Carolina Genealogical Society XXI:4 (November 1995).

"Confederate Slave Impressment Legislation, 1861-1865," Journal of Negro History, Vol. 31, No. 4 (October 1946), pp. 392-410. Nelson, Bernard H., "Confederate Slave Impressment Legislation,

1861-1865," Journal of Negro History, Vol. 31, No. 4 (October 1946), pp. 392-410.

"The Unlikely Story of Blacks Who Were Loyal to Dixie," Smithsonian, March 1979: 94-101. Obatala, J.K. "The Unlikely Story of Blacks Who Were Loyal to Dixie," Smithsonian, March 1979: 94-101.

Series 2, Volume 1, National Historical Society, Harrisburg, Pennsylvania, 1987. Official Records of the Union and Confederate Navies in the War of the Rebellion, Series 2, Volume 1, National Historical Society, Harrisburg, Pennsylvania, 1987.

Prologue Magazine, Fall 2001, Vol. 33, No. 3: Black Men in Navy Blue During the Civil War, Joseph P. Reidy, Joseph P. Reidy, Joseph P. Reidy, Joseph P. Reidy, Joseph P. Reidy, Joseph P. Reidy, Joseph P. Reidy, Joseph

The Employment of Negros as Soldiers in the Confederate Army, Journal of Negro History, Vol. 4, #3 (July 1919), pp. 239-253. Wesley, Charles H. The Employment of Negros as Soldiers in the Confederate Army, Journal of Negro History, Vol. 4, #3 (July 1919), pp. 239-253.

BOOKS

Black Confederates In The U.S. Civil War, A Compiled List of African-Americans Who Served the Confederacy. By: Ricardo J. Rodriguez

By Sea and by River: The Naval History of the Civil War, Bern Anderson. 1962, New York.

Anne Bailey. Texas as a member of the Confederate Cavalry. 1995, Colleyville, Texas. -

Civil War Battles and Leaders, Vols. 1-2, New York, 1887-1888.

"Free Men of Color in Grey," Civil War History, vol. 32, no. 2, 1986, pp. 247-255. Bergeron, Arthur. "Free Men of Color in Grey." Civil War History, vol. 32, no. 2, 1986, pp. 247

Confederate Veterans Larry O. Blair and Thomas E. Lyle are buried in the Confederate Cemetery in Marietta, Georgia, Maryville, Tennessee, in 1991.

"Records of Louisiana Confederate Soldiers and Louisiana Confederate Commands," by Andrew B. Booth. 3 Volumes The year is 1920, and the setting is New Orleans, Louisiana.

Blockade Running During the Civil War and the Effect of Land and Water Transportation on the Confederacy, by Francis B. C. Bradlee. Salem, Massachusetts, 1925. (Porcupine Press reprinted it in 1974.)

The Confederate Negro: Virginia's Craftsmen and Military Laborers, 1861-1865, by James H. Brewer. 1969, Duke University Press.

These Honored Dead: The Union Casualties at Gettysburg, by John W. Busey. 1988, Hightstown, New Jersey

Gray uniforms and black soldiers: black pensioners in Lauderdale County & other information on black Confederates. Calhoun, S. W. Gray uniforms and black soldiers: black pensioners in Lauderdale County & other information on black Confederates. 2000

Adjutant General of the State of California. Records of Californians who fought in the American Civil War from 1861 to 1867 J. D. Young, Supt. State Printing, Sacramento, 1890

Stephen Chicoine, Stephen Chicoine, Stephen Chicoine, Stephen Chicoine

Prosperity, Civil War, and Decline for the Confederates of Chappell Hill, Texas

Blockade Runners of the Confederacy, by Hamilton Cochran. The year is 1958, and the location is Indianapolis, Indiana.

Ray Charles Colton, Ray Charles Colton, Ray Charles Colton, Ray Charles Colton Arizona, Colorado, New Mexico, and Utah were all involved in the Civil War in the Western Territories. The year is 1959, and Norman, Oklahoma is the setting.

Robert Franklin Durden, Robert Franklin Durden, Robert Franklin Durden, Robert Franklin Durden, Robert

The Confederate Debate on Emancipation: The Gray and the Black.

Confederate Military History, 18 vols. Extended Edition, edited by Clement A. Evans. Broadfoot, Wilmington, 1987. (this is a reprint of the 1899 edition)

Board of State Institutions of Florida. Florida soldiers in the Seminole Indian-Civil War and the Spanish-American War. Democrat Book and Job Print, Live Oak, 1903.

General Lee's Army: From Victory to Collapse, Joseph T. Glatthaar, Joseph T. Glatthaar, Joseph T. Glatthaar, Joseph T. Glatthaar,

W. W. Goldsbourough, W. W. Goldsbourough, W. W. Goldsbourough,

Alexia J. Helsley, Alexia J. Helsley, Alexia J. Helsley, Alexia J. Helsley, Alexia J. Helsley, Alexi Robert Henry. The Confederacy's History 1911, New York.
Lawrence L. Hewitt and Arthur Bergeron. Louisianians in the Civil War. 2002

Louisiana Native Guards: the Black Military Experience During the Civil War, by James G. Hollandsworth. Louisiana State University Press, Baton Rouge, 1995.

I WAS A SLAVE, True Life Stories Dictated by Former American Slaves in the Civil War, Donna Wyant Howell, Donna Wyant Howell, Donna Wyant Howell, Donna Wyant Howell, Donna Wyant Howell, Donna Wyant Howell, Donna Wyant Howell

Book 2: The Lives of Slave Men, published in 1995, is set in the 1930s.

Wilbert L. Jenkins, Wilbert L. Jenkins, Wilbert L. Jenkins, Wilbert

L. Jenkins, Wilbert L. Jenkins, Wilbert L. Jenkins, Wilbert L. Jenkins, Wilbert L. Jenkins, Wilbert L. Jenkins

Whittington B. Johnson, Whittington B. Johnson, Whittington B. Johnson, Whittington B. Johnson, Whittington B. Johnson, Whittington B. Johnson

Ervin L. Jordan, Ervin L. Jordan, Ervin L. Jordan, Ervin L. Jordan, Ervin L. Jordan, Ervin L. Jordan, Ervin L. Jordan, Ervin L. Jordan, Ervin L. Jordan, Ervin L 1995, University of Virginia.

A History of Lumsden's Battery, by George Little and James Robert Maxwell, C.S.A. 1902.

Claude H. Nolen, Claude H. Nolen, Claude H. Nolen, Claude H. Nolen, Claude H. Nolen, Claude H. Nolen, Claude H. Nolen, Claude H

"The Unlikely Story of Blacks Who Were Loyal to Dixie," Smithsonian, March 1979: 94-101. Obatala, J.K. "The Unlikely Story of Blacks Who Were Loyal to Dixie," Smithsonian, March 1979: 94-101.

"Illinois Men in the Union Navy During the Civil War," Illinois Libraries, XLIV, no. 6 (June 1962), pp. 435-459, Marion D. Pratt, Marion D. Pratt, Marion D. Pratt, Marion D. Pratt, Marion D. Pratt, Marion D. Pratt, Marion D. Pratt, Marion D. Pratt, Marion D. Pratt, Marion D. Prat

"Into The Fight - Pickett's Charge at Gettysburg," by John Michael Priest, published in 1998.

Benjamin Quarles 1989: The Negro in the Civil War

The Jewish Confederates, by Robert N. Rosen, Columbia, South Carolina, 2000.

History Of The Confederate States Navy, From Its Organization To The Surrender Of Its Last Vessel, by J. Thomas Scharf, A.M., LL.D., 1894.

Ralph Semmes, Ralph Semmes, Ralph Semmes, Ralph Semmes During the War Between the States, the Confederate cruisers Sumter and Alabama had a fascinating career afloat. 1887, Baltimore, Maryland

Alicia Simpson is a writer. Commonwealth of Kentucky, Index of Confederate Pension Applications (Frankfort, KY: Division of Archives and Records Management, Department of Library and Archives, 1978).

Texas in the War of 1861-1865, edited by Harold B. Simpson. Hill Junior College Press, Hillsboro, 1965.

George Barrie Publisher, Philadelphia, 1890, "The Army and Navy of the United States 1776-1891."

The Official Records of the Union and Confederate Armies in the War of the Rebellion. Volumes 128. 1880-1901 Washington OFFICIAL RECORDS OF THE UNION AND CONFEDERATE NAVIES IN THE REBELLION WAR, by George Washington, Secretary of the Navy. Printing Office of the United States Government, 1903.

Texas CSA Pension Files Index, Virgil D. White (Waynesboro, TN: National Historical Publishing Co., 1989).

Southern Negroes (1861-1865), by Bell Wiley. 1938, Yale University

George W Williams 18611865, History of the Negro Troops in the Civil War. Originally published in 1888 by the Negro University Press.

A Roster of Military Officers and Soldiers Who Served in New York Regiments in the Civil War as Listed in the Annual Reports of the Adjutant General of the State of New York, Vols. I A-K and Vol. II L-Z. 1999. Wilt, Richard A. NEW YORK SOLDIERS IN THE CIVIL WAR, A Roster of Military Officers and Soldiers Who Served in New York Regiments in the Civil War as Listed in the Annual Reports

Ralph Wooster is a fictional character in the American television series Wooster. In The Civil War, Texas and Texans 1995 in Austin, TX

Slave Narratives: A Folk History of Slavery in the United States Based on Interviews with Former Slaves: Volume II, Arkansas Narratives, Part 2. Work Projects Administration, 2004. (E-Book)

Slave Narratives: A Folk History of Slavery in the United States Based on Interviews with Former Slaves: Volume II, Arkansas Narratives, Part 3. Work Projects Administration, 2006. (E-Book)

Voices from Slavery: 100 Authentic Slave Narratives, Norman R. Yetman, Norman R. Yetman, Norman R. Yetman, Norman R. Yetman, Norman R. Yetman, Norman R. Yetman.

Personnel of the Civil War, Vol. 1: Confederate Armies, Yoseloff, Thomas New York, 1961, edited by William Frayne Amann.

NEWSPAPERS

Brownsville Brownsville, Texas' The Herald The Charleston Mercury is a South Carolina newspaper published in Charleston. The Corpus Christi Caller Times is a newspaper based in the Texas city of Corpus Christi. Meridian Star (Mississippi) is a local newspaper in Meridian The Richmond Enquirer (Richmond, Virginia) is a daily newspaper published in Richmond, Virginia. The San Antonio Express News is a newspaper published in San Antonio, Texas. Grenada, Mississippi: The Daily Sentinel-Star New York City, New York, New York, New Austin's Weekly State Gazette is a weekly newspaper published by the city of Austin, Texas. New Orleans, Louisiana's Texas Daily Delta. New Orleans, Louisiana's Daily Picayune. New Orleans, Louisiana's Daily Crescent

www.ingramcontent.com/pod-product-compliance
Lightning Source LLC
Chambersburg PA
CBHW041134120626
46547CB00019B/2990